Sabina Spielrein

Sabina Spielrein

The Woman and the Myth

Angela M. Sells

SUNY PRESS

Cover Art: Katie Hoffman, *Queen Mab and the Little Death*, Oil on Canvas, 2009.
© Katie Hoffman.

Published by State University of New York Press, Albany

Printed in the United States of America

For information, contact State University of New York Press, Albany, NY
www.sunypress.edu

Production, Eileen Nizer
Marketing, Kate R. Seburyamo

Library of Congress Cataloging-in-Publication Data

Names: Sells, Angela M., 1987– author.
Title: Sabina Spielrein : the woman and the myth / Angela M. Sells.
Description: Albany : State University of New York Press, [2017] | Includes bibliographical references and index.
Identifiers: LCCN 2016034116 (print) | LCCN 2016038874 (ebook) | ISBN 9781438465791 (hardcover : alk. paper) | ISBN 9781438465784 (pbk. : alk. paper) | ISBN 9781438465807 (ebook)
Subjects: LCSH: Spielrein, Sabina. | Women psychoanalysts—Europe—Biography. | Mentally ill women—Europe—Biography. | Psychoanalysis—History.
Classification: LCC RC440.82.S66 S45 2017 (print) | LCC RC440.82.S66 (ebook) | DDC 150.19/5092 [B] —dc23
LC record available at https://lccn.loc.gov/2016034116

10 9 8 7 6 5 4 3 2 1

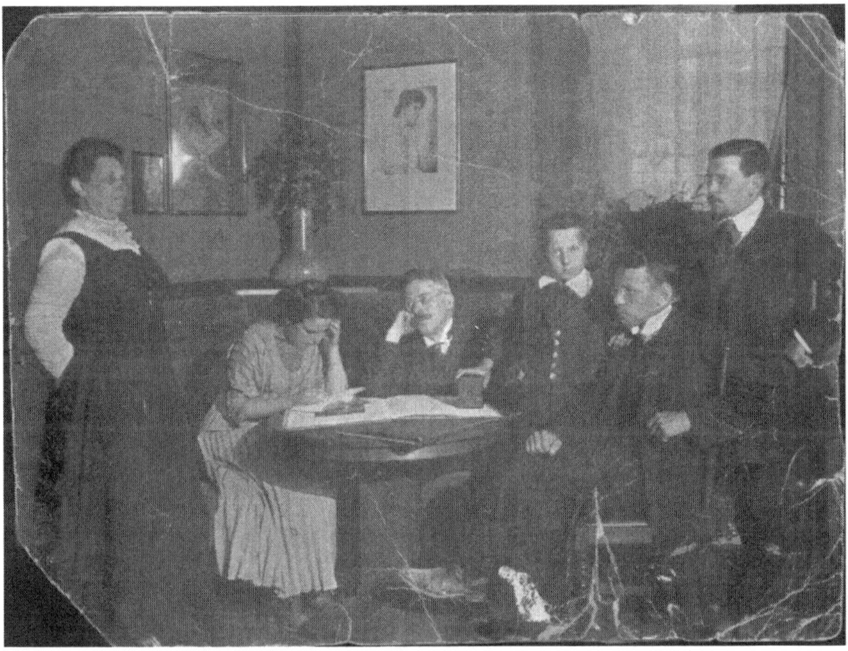

Sabina Spielrein, 1909 Photograph.

To all who encouraged and assisted me
throughout the writing process.
And to Dr. Sabina Spielrein,
whose words inspired me in the first place.

Contents

Images

Introduction

> And what about the noble idea of my youth—to roam the earth surrounded by students like the ancient Greek philosophers, while teaching my students in harmony with nature [and] the great outdoors?
>
> —Sabina Spielrein, 28 August 1909

Who was Sabina Spielrein? Clearly, with the release of the 2011 film, *A Dangerous Method*—based in part on the fictionalized play *The Talking Cure* by Christopher Hampton—the story of Sabina Spielrein is still stirring in collective consciousness, though the scope has been greatly limited. Outside of the current cultural trend of presenting Spielrein solely as C. G. Jung's patient and mistress, relatively little has been written (in English) on her academic contributions to the field of psychology. Additionally, Spielrein's professional and personal writing proves profoundly important not only to psychology, but also to the fields of mythology and literary autobiography, and to the larger psychosocial concerns of gender equity and female suppression.

Accordingly, I explore from the kaleidoscope lens of mythology, psychology, and gender studies the life, early academic publications, and personal diaries and correspondence of Dr. Sabina Spielrein, one of the first female psychoanalysts in history. Spielrein (1885–1942) was institutionalized at the age of nineteen at the Burghölzli Clinic in Zurich, Switzerland, where she became a patient of C. G. Jung from 1904–05, and where, subsequently, the two engaged in an intimate relationship. However, instead of examining Spielrein as a "patient" of, or "mistress" to Jung, I attempt to see beyond this pathologizing and analyze her contributions to the field on their own merit.

Indeed, after healing from a period of trauma, Spielrein enrolled in the University of Zurich, completed her doctorate in psychiatry, and formed her own philosophical and psychological insights about female sexuality, the "death instinct," and child psychology. Her professional career continued for more than thirty years after her split from Jung; in a 1911 diary entry, she felt precious, determined, and confident of her vocation, which diverged from the "traditional" female role: "I resist, because I have something noble and great to accomplish and am not made for the mundane. It is a struggle between life or death."[1] She also helped to establish psychoanalysis in her native Russia, where she practiced as a teacher and analyst until her untimely death during the Holocaust in 1942.

Yet what has been written about her has predominately been from a clinical perspective and myopically focuses on her affair with Jung. Contrary to this, I argue that the affair was not a "romance," but instead a relationship built upon unequal power dynamics as well as a breach of professional trust. History has also stigmatized Spielrein as mentally ill, maligning her with labels such as "schizo," "seductress," "Jewess," and "hysteric." However, leading cultural critic Elaine Showalter agrees: "Hysteria is no longer a question of the wandering womb; it is a question of the wandering story, and of whether that story belongs to the hysteric, the doctor, the historian, or the critic. The stories of race and gender in hysteria still remain to be told."[2] Paramount to any discussion about Spielrein is her constructed narrative (or existing *mythos*) as maintained in recent scholarship, which has often used her "hysteria" as a weapon to discredit and devalue her academic work.

While I will examine Spielrein's significant relationship with Jung as maintained in the scholarship surrounding them both, I will also examine her own perspective on the affair as it appears in her diaries and letters. I explore her words from mythopoetic and feminist perspectives, instead of solely on clinical or diagnostic terms; in other words, I underscore the literary, symbolic (mythic), and psychosocial aspects of her writing. Undoubtedly, by reducing Spielrein to the intrigue of pathology, a wellspring of emotionally charged philosophical inquiry and personal insight by a prominent female scholar in the history of depth psychology is denied a wide audience. What this means is: Spielrein's diaries (and work) are less about Jung and more about *her*.

Her diaries and letters reveal her own transformational narrative as related to her personal and professional lives. She confronts such diverse topics as sexual desire, indigenous iconography, animal symbolism, death, and love. Therefore, her writing is interpreted both in relation to the history of depth psychology, as well as significant to the study of autobiography and female expression. Through these interpretations, I hope to link Spielrein's writing to the literary line of such profound women writers and confessional poets as H.D., Anaïs Nin, and Sylvia Plath. Apropos, the notion of "madness," and specifically female madness, will be examined in relation to Spielrein's history.

What did Sabina Spielrein offer to psychoanalysis in the early stages of its development, and are these insights relevant or even correct today? A number of questions follow from this initial query: What was her experience in the early years of psychoanalysis? What consequences did her personal life have on her professional reputation? What contributed to the suppression of her voice? I will contend with these questions in light of Spielrein's diaries, letters, and her early academic works, including "Destruction as the Cause of Coming into Being" and "Contributions to the Knowledge of a Child's Soul," the latter of which I have translated from the original German.[3] Spielrein's role in depth psychology will be further analyzed in relation to the concept of the *anima* (or the "female element" of the psyche respectively, according to Jungian theory), which I interpret as an enacted psychosocial reality concerning the issue of gender (in)equality.[4]

Hermeneutically speaking, the suppression of female expression as well as the denial of the "feminine" find representation in the mythological narrative of Ovid's "Echo and Narcissus" within translations of the *Metamorphoses*. I will interpret this story through the Aristotelian definition of myth, meaning simply "plot," to illustrate that myths provide, as the late analyst James Hillman would say, a "dynamic coherence and meaning to the dispersed narrative of our lives."[5] Echo is unable to authentically express her own opinions and she is also physically denied by Narcissus and excluded from a male-dominated reflection. Hence, I interpret Echo's longing for Narcissus as a desire for inclusion and equity.

Narcissus's denial of Echo will be examined in chapter 2 in relation to objectification, demonization of the "Other," and the sacrifice of female expression, as mirrored by Luce Irigaray's sentiment in *This Sex Which Is Not One*: "If you/I hesitate to speak, isn't it because we are afraid of not speaking well? . . . What hierarchy, what subordination lurks there, waiting to break our resistance?"[6] In particular, I will question how the systematic suppression of Echo that subsequently leads to her disembodiment may be translated as the exclusion of women's perspectives from the status quo, and will explore Sabina Spielrein as the primary figure for this discussion.

Sabina Spielrein and Current Controversy

In August 2012, in Rostov-on-Don, Russia (Spielrein's hometown), a controversial protest took place critiquing a plaque that memorialized the 27,000 citizens who were systematically killed by the Nazis during World War II and "buried" in a ravine (I say "buried" because there was nothing gentle nor ceremonial about it). Sabina Spielrein and her two daughters were murdered during the two-day slaughter in August 1942, and lie in this mass grave. Ironically, Russian officials had the original plaque, which honored the mostly Jewish individuals in the grave (ravine), replaced with a new plaque omitting any reference to Jewish ancestry, as it was viewed as a symbol of potential ethnic tension.[7]

During the protest, which was held on the seventieth anniversary of the genocide at the Zmiyovskaya Balka (Snake Ravine), Dr. Shimon Samuels, Israel Emeritus Chief Rabbi, termed this removal of Jewish heritage a *memoricide*. Stripping the plaque, and by extension its occupants, of Jewish roots, seems a deliberate attempt to suppress the historical horror that occurred at the site in order to avoid the discomfort of others. To Rostov's Jewish population, this revisionist tactic actually and historically denies the experience of those murdered. Directly relating to Spielrein, the contemporary controversy mirrors the attempts made in academia to systematically diminish her particular perspective in history. Incidentally, due to the protest, a Russian court agreed to revise the plaque again, though in a polarizing compromise the new text commemorates its "Soviet citizens" rather than its specifically "Jewish citizens."[8]

Rostov's memoricide is reminiscent of Elie Wiesel's comment in *Night*, an autobiographical account of a young boy in a concentration camp, which states: "To forget the dead would be akin to killing them a second time."[9] While many of the individuals buried in the mass grave remain unknown, Sabina Spielrein is known. The choice to then further revision Spielrein out of history, or to transfigure her into merely the "mistress" or the "patient" appears to mimic, as Wiesel intimates, another form of murder. Therefore, it is my objective to underscore Spielrein's less examined perspective in history.

My Own Sabina Spielrein Story

I heard the name "Sabina Spielrein" for the first time in 2011, during a course on Jungian psychology. She was mentioned only in passing, but for an unknown reason, her name had taken hold of me, as had the fire of curiosity. I became interested in her life, her diaries, and her work. I was intrigued by her tainted reputation and by her intense personal writing, which I saw as ancestral to the line of other female writers engaged in the poetic dance between destruction and creation.

In early 2011, the film *A Dangerous Method* had not yet been released, and it was much more difficult to find information about her. Luckily, I came across Aldo Carotenuto's *A Secret Symmetry*, and began a relationship with Spielrein's diaries, shortly thereafter immersing myself in the German language. As a student in the Mythological Studies program with an emphasis in depth psychology at Pacifica Graduate Institute, I began interpreting her life and work mythopoetically for my doctoral dissertation, and *not,* as I kept reading, as a schizophrenic stigma. In 2012, I traveled to Zurich, Switzerland, to visit the university and what used to be the Burghölzli Clinic. The clinical information I read about Spielrein did not match the profundity I found in her academic work. Neither did I fully believe in the legend of her as the seductress, as she was characterized in René Major's influential article "Love for Transference and Passion for Signifiers: Between Sabina S. and Anna G" and in multiple scholars' work since.[10] To me, Spielrein trail-blazed in the "man's" world of psychology in the early 1900s.

Hers has been a voice calling to me from the distance, the face in need of reflection. I was then encouraged and reassured by Wiesel as he states in *Night*: "It is not always the events that have touched us personally that affect us the most."[11] Her creative and intellectual inspiration led to a career, a life, and a legacy that is only now being fully discovered in academia. As follows, in my critique of Spielrein's life and work, it must also be admitted with transparency that a bias is clearly present in the attempt to contribute to the discourse.

Brief Definition of Terms

There is always a risk of essentializing when using gendered terms such as *masculine* and *feminine.* Marc Manganaro, author of *Myth, Rhetoric, and the Voice of Authority* (1992), critiques the essentializing that has occurred in much of mythological studies, exposing the problem of equating "Other:Same."[12] William Doty, acclaimed mythographer, further explains: "Essentializing has been the enemy of historicism . . . typically dichotomizing in order to reinterpret from a transcendental point of view."[13] While I observe Doty's critique and am informed by scholars of the "feminine" like philosopher Luce Irigaray, stereotypes of gender remain under scrutiny, specifically in relation to the exclusion of female figures in history (Spielrein). For all intents and purposes, "feminine" will be contextualized and deconstructed in order to bring clarity to the term's usage during a particular period in Western[14] history and is analyzed in regard to the interpretation of gender. As emphasized by gender theorist Celeste Schenck, I write of Spielrein with "concern with constituting a female subject—a precarious operation . . . assuming a subjectivity long denied, *and* maintaining the vigilant, disruptive stance that speaking from the postmodern margin provides [without assuming] the autobiographical genre may be paradigmatic of all women's writing."[15]

Similarly, while I primarily examine a cisgendered figure, the terms *female* and *woman* are used in direct reference to a self-identified and suppressed woman in history. Also, it is worth noting that her character has been largely demeaned due to such gendered terms as *hysterical* and *mistress*. However, my aim is to demonstrate how Spielrein in fact challenged such stereotypes assigned to women at the time, while at the same time her personal and professional work continues to provide insight into sexuality and identity distinctly from a woman's perspective. While I acknowledge the problematic and often political nature arising around the topics of gender and identity, I do not strive to enter into a debate about gender per se, but to question the characterizations often assigned to women, and to Spielrein in particular, based on preconceived and socially constructed notions of "femininity."

"Femininity" to Spielrein did indeed have a gendered and biological connotation, but it was also used in line with Jungian theory, namely, the "feminine" aspect of the psyche (or the *anima,* as noted earlier) as removed from sex. Though this, too, remains riddled with contradiction and conflation, which will be further examined in subsequent chapters. I will challenge the conflation of the "feminine" with gender (*woman*), as I believe Spielrein did, as well as explore the biased characteristics often assigned to the principle of the feminine, specifically in relation to female expression and speech.

I will also situate the archetypal (meaning prototypical) *anima* in context as it relates to gender, aligning with Marina Warner's statement in *From the Beast to the Blonde: On Fairy Tales and Their Tellers*:

> The theory of archetypes, which is essentially ahistorical, helps to confirm gender inevitability and to imprison male and female in stock definitions. . . . When history falls away from a subject, we are left with Otherness. . . . An archetype is a hollow thing, but a dangerous one, a figure or image which through usage has been uncoupled from the circumstances which brought it into being and goes on spreading false consciousness.[16]

Through Spielrein's story, we will be able to explore some of the historical trappings that the "feminine" archetype as conflated with gender carried—and still carries—today, in hopes of reanimating the term. Similar complications in semantics arise with many psychological terms, such as the "masculine" principle of the psyche (or the *animus* in Jungian terminology), as well as with female epithets such as "seductress" and "hysteric"; it is in my exact interest to question, but not to answer, the effects of these terms when enacted onto culture. Regardless, the primary purpose of this book is to analyze the life and work of Sabina Spielrein, her lost voice, and her consequent historical suppression; as such, semantic examination is largely confined to language used in direct reference to her.

Chapter Overview

Chapter 1 deepens the historical biography of Sabina Spielrein with reference to both her institutionalization and her affair with Jung. This chapter focuses primarily on exploring the narrative of Spielrein as constructed in existing scholarship, giving specific attention to the language used in reference to her professional standing, to her mental state, and to her gender (e.g. "seductress"). The existing "story" of Spielrein—as a mentally ill mistress—is challenged. An analysis of Spielrein's background, beyond her involvement with Jung, is also intended to give a deeper understanding to the letters, diaries, and work that are examined in subsequent chapters.

Chapter 2 extends Spielrein's experience in relation to Jung and to academia beyond subjectivity and into the mythological metanarrative of "Echo and Narcissus," where Echo's prohibitive ability to speak is explored as is her denial from reflection, here interpreted as female exclusion from a patriarchal culture; this is then related to Spielrein's exclusion and stigmatization. Lines from Echo's narrative are not compared directly to Spielrein's work, but rather the interpretation of Echo as a suppressed female voice serves as the lens through which to view Spielrein's personal and professional history.

Chapter 3 addresses Spielrein's treatment and the relationship between her and Jung (transference) from a mythic and feminist perspective, with the aid of Spielrein's early letters to and from Sigmund Freud. I emphasize the denial of Spielrein's perspective from history and question the subsequent categorization of her affair with Jung by scholars as a "love cure."

Chapter 4 examines Spielrein's diaries to reveal an authentic process of self-discovery. In these passages, Spielrein confronts her dreams, her career, her relationship to Jung, her "death instinct," and her Self. Since her diaries are interpreted through the lens of mythopoiesis and autobiography, I will draw from an array of literary sources, including Teresa of Ávila, H.D., Anaïs Nin, and Simone Weil.

Chapter 5 analyzes the suppressed intellectual theories of Spielrein in regard to her seminal academic publication and asserts its current mythic relevance. The principle article to be examined is "Destruction as the Cause of Coming into Being" (1912) which originated the "death instinct" as referenced in Freud's *Beyond the Pleasure Principle* (1920). In her article, she contemplates sexuality's mythic relationship to eroticized death imagery and personal transformation.

Chapter 6 more deeply examines the letters of Sabina Spielrein to and from Jung (and to a lesser extent, Freud) as well as the former's contribution to the archetype of the *anima*. Further questioned in light of these letters is the dynamic between the conceptual "feminine" (*anima*) and its gendered reality, as demonstrated by Spielrein in her challenge to stock stereotypes of the time.

Also explored in this chapter are the pathologizing, or Otherizing, epithets "Jewess" and "hysteric" as well as the infantilizing title of "girl," which have all been casually and derogatorily used in reference to Spielrein.

Chapter 7 concludes this book by providing political and historical context to Spielrein's life in relation to her presentation to the Vienna Psychoanalytic Society on female eroticism and the emerging "New Woman" of Russia. Her two articles on the development of child psychology are then given attention: "Contributions to the Knowledge of a Child's Soul" (1912) and "The Origin of the Child's Words 'Papa' and 'Mama' " (1922). The social upheaval confronted in her adult life is emphasized here in order to counter the common notion that her importance to the field relies on her relationship with Jung.

In the Afterword, I briefly summarize Spielrein's life and work, and its relationship to the myth of "Echo and Narcissus," and explore why it remains relevant today in light of female suppression, mythopoetics, and representation. What is her legacy and how is it important to the field? How does this revisioning affect the current "Spielrein narrative"? What happens when Spielrein's perspective is added to the reflection?

i am accused of tending to the past [sic]

i am accused of tending to the past
as if I made it,
as if I sculpted it
with my own hands, I did not.
this past was waiting for me
when I came,
a monstrous unnamed baby,
and I with my mother's itch
took it to breast
and named it
History.
she is more human now,
learning languages everyday,
remembering faces, names and dates.
when she is strong enough to travel
on her own, beware, she will.

—Lucille Clifton, "i am accused of tending to the past." Reprinted with permission

1

Sabina Spielrein

A Life and Legacy Explored

There is no death in remembrance.

—Kathleen Kent, *The Heretic's Daughter*

Sabina Spielrein (often transliterated as Shpilrein or Spilrein) was born on November 7, 1885, in Rostov-on-Don, Russia, into a Jewish family of seven: one sister, Emily; three brothers, Jan, Isaac, and Emil; and a businessman father, Nikolai Spielrein, and his wife, Eva. Spielrein was highly encouraged in her education and, unlike many young girls at the time, was afforded lessons in Warsaw, though her youth is often characterized as a troubled one, a time when her mother was emotionally unavailable and her father exerted immense authority over the household.[1] However, Spielrein was a bright and intelligent child, and as a budding scientist, she kept liquids in jars expecting "the big creation" to take place in her near future.[2] Remembering her early desire to create life, Spielrein once noted: "I was an alchemist."[3]

Sadly, the death of Emily, who died at six years old, sent Spielrein into a dizzying confrontation with mortality at the tender age of fifteen. This loss, coupled with confusing abuse at the hands of her father—discussed in the next chapter—spun her into a period of turmoil for which she was institutionalized. In August 1904, at age nineteen, she was sent to the Burghölzli Clinic in Zurich, Switzerland, where she became a patient of a then twenty-nine-year-old and married Dr. Carl Jung. She was to be one of his first patients, subsequently diagnosed with "hysteria" and exhibiting symptoms of extreme emotional duress, such as screaming, repetitively sticking out her tongue, and shaking.[4] She was a guinea pig for a new "talking cure," based on free association, dream interpretation, and talk therapy, as innovated by Dr. Sigmund Freud in Vienna, Austria.

Russian historian Victor Ovcharenko (see "Love, Psychoanalysis, and Destruction," 1999) believed that an affair soon began between Spielrein and Jung and was in full swing by the completion of her in-treatment in June 1905. Without ambiguity, it is known that Spielrein was deemed cured by Jung and by Dr. Eugen Bleuler, the director of the clinic, before she began her own studies at the University of Zurich that same year. Her relationship with Jung then lasted with varying intensity for approximately four years while Spielrein was an outpatient. While many scholars have defined Spielrein's affair with Jung as a "romance," I do not, and I will continue to question this categorization throughout the book.

Spielrein eventually earned her doctorate in psychiatry in 1911 from the University of Zurich to become a pioneering figure in the field of psychoanalysis: one of the first female psychoanalysts as well as one of the first—if not the first—child psychologists. When she became a mother in 1913, she focused her academic interest primarily on child psychology and went on to teach, publish, and practice psychoanalysis in Geneva, Switzerland, for almost a decade. She then helped to buttress the psychology program at the (State) Moscow Institute of Psychoanalysis upon her return to Russia in the early 1920s.

During the communist purges under Stalin, Spielrein receded into the background, as her three brothers were all taken to and executed in gulags in the 1930s. Though she managed to survive the deaths of both of her parents (of natural causes) and her husband, Spielrein and her two daughters were murdered in Rostov during its second Nazi occupation in August 1942.[5] She then faded into the annals of history until her diaries and letters were discovered and published by Aldo Carotenuto in 1977. Today, her personal and professional works remain and continue to exhibit tremendous insight into identity, death, heartbreak, and transformation during an era of cultural and social upheaval.

In the words of Viktor Frankl, *these are the dry facts*.[6] While details of all aforementioned facts will be examined in depth, this chapter is devoted to challenging the existing narrative constructed around Spielrein's life, given that much of modern scholarship consistently reduces her existence to the roles of "hysteric" and "mistress."[7] This only degrades and demeans her academic and personal writing as mere symptoms of a stigmatized mental illness or a gendered objectification.

Sabina Spielrein in Scholarship and the Construction of a Narrative

John Kerr, in his extensive and groundbreaking biographical research on Spielrein in *A Most Dangerous Method: The Story of Jung, Freud, and Sabina Spielrein*, examines her life from a clinical perspective and notes her academic work in relation to Jung and to the other grandfather of psychoanalysis, Sigmund Freud. He presents her as a figure worth attention in the so-called feminist age, due to her being a woman "insisting on her point of view."[8] Aside from this somewhat condescending implication, Kerr states:

> She [Spielrein] had a crucial contribution of her own to make, one that was potentially central to the overall structure of psychoanalytic theory. Yet that contribution, like her earlier protests as a patient and as a lover, was ignored and then deliberately obscured. The silence that for so long attended her story is emblematic of a more insidious silence that gradually overtook psychoanalysis during this time.[9]

While Kerr asserts that Spielrein's work contributed to the development of the field, he continually refers to her solely as "lover" or "patient" and maintains that his study is primarily about Freud and Jung's early partnership. However, Kerr emphasizes that suppression of women's voices in the field began at the literal beginning of analytical psychology, with Jung's very first "hysterical" patient: Sabina Spielrein. It would follow then, that the subsequent dismissal of Spielrein's work in contemporary academia contributes to the "insidious" silencing of her voice in an attempt to selectively reorganize the history of psychology, as we will see.

Kerr goes on to say that his book "is not a love story . . . it is an unusually gruesome ghost story."[10] Ironically, he recounts nearly the entirety of Spielrein's life in relation to the "love affair" that Jung and Spielrein maintained while she was his patient at the clinic, which not only suffocates her own narrative; it definitively turns the book into a love story. Such a "love story" denies the breach of trust between client and therapist that resulted in an affair in favor of providing a romantic characterization of their relationship. Also, by asserting that Spielrein's story is "gruesome," though granted her death may be deemed a tragedy, he diminishes the extraordinary insight inherent in her personal and professional work, and devalues the events of her life during the thirty years she stood on her own as a scholar and as a woman. Beyond her tie to Jung is a narrative with autonomous and interdisciplinary value that requires reassembling so to give a full account of her as an analyst and original thinker in her own right.

The late Freudian psychoanalyst Johannes Cremerius characterized Spielrein as the "guilty party . . . who must be sacrificed" by Freud in order to save his own place as head of the psychoanalytic movement, as if this justifies Freud's subsequent complicity in suppressing her contributions at the time.[11] In his response to the publication of Spielrein's diaries, Cremerius also revealed the probable reason she has been suppressed in history: her sexuality. Demeaning and gendered labels such as "hysteric" and "mistress," the epithets continually attached to Spielrein, are largely responsible for her historical marginalization.

Yet, as stated by Dr. Bleuler (director of the clinic) upon Spielrein's discharge in 1905: "Miss Sabina Spielrein from Rostov/Don, resident at this institution and planning to matriculate at the medical faculty in the summer term, *is not mentally ill.* She was here for treatment for a nervous complaint with hysterical symptoms. We must therefore recommend her for matriculation" [emphasis mine].[12] Of course, it could be argued that being "mentally ill" or not; Spielrein's contributions need not be discredited or devalued. But a continual weapon of attack in scholarship is that Spielrein remained "ill," and her work and personal diaries have thus been regarded as symptomatic of a condition that was thought cured. Therefore, all of Spielrein's writing after 1905 may be understood not as the ranting of a "hysterical" patient, but as the expression of a talented and complex woman during her professional career.

The Loss of Spielrein's Beloved Sister

Though Spielrein's treatment at the clinic and her childhood trauma will be revealed in the next chapter, it is worth noting the mental and emotional state she was in after her sister Emily passed. During her time as an in-patient (1904), Spielrein wrote a last will:

> After my death I will permit only my head to be dissected, if it is not too dreadful to look at. No young person is to be present at the dissection. Only the very keenest students may observe. I bequeath my skull to our school. It is to be placed in a glass container, decorated with everlasting flowers. The following is to be inscribed on the container in Russian: "And let young life play at the entrance of the tomb and let indifferent nature shine with external splendor." My brain I give to you [unknown]. Just place it, as it is, in a beautiful vessel, also decorated, with the same words on it. My body is to be cremated. . . . Divide the ashes into three parts. . . . Scatter the second part on the ground over the biggest field. Plant there an oak tree and write on it: "I too was once a human being. My name was Sabina Spielrein."[13]

While this has been previously interpreted as suicidal ideation, Spielrein also demonstrates an existential sensibility often overlooked. While some have understood the above statement to be a symptom of "mental illness," I interpret the will as a rather poetic confrontation with the trauma of grief, loss, and death.[14] Her words reveal a kind of mythic romanticism in the portrayal of unified opposites: youth dancing at a tomb amid the ephemeral "splendor" of nature. While exhibiting a devastated teenager's attempt to cope with mortality, the quote actually emphasizes a profound sense of life affirmation and continuation for those who will live on in her absence. She also provides lucid instructions for her body and ashes, which highlights a pragmatic aspect to her personality retained in her adult years. She may have believed that she, like her sister, could similarly fall ill at a young age; surely she is not alone in her attempt to control what happens to her body postmortem.

The fact that Spielrein did not want young children present acts as a protective shield for the innocence of youth, and perhaps a defense against what she herself felt too young to have witnessed upon the death of her sister, which clearly had a shattering effect on her. That she planned to donate her brain to scientific study also foreshadows her devotion and interest in the fields of psychology and biology, which manifested throughout her academic career, and suggests that she felt she belonged in the academic arena. Spielrein's desire for dissection signifies her belief that her brain was one worth understanding and one worthy of scientific discovery.

Her wish to have her skull visible through a glass container is twofold: she confronts the metaphorical fear of "staring" death in the face and desires for others to be present with the idea of mortality, but is insightful enough to insist on a literal container for it. In her request to decorate the container of her skull with flowers, Spielrein reaffirms the beauty she obviously felt inherent to life and again integrates seemingly opposing realities: life and death. This imagery is reminiscent of the Hispanic Día de los Muertos ("Day of the Dead") tradition, wherein each November 1 and 2 deceased ancestors are honored with rituals and, among other things, decorated sugar skulls and flowers, and children and adults are painted in skeleton makeup, in celebration of the tension and interconnectivity between life and death.

In addition to Spielrein's mythic imagery, her words find resonance with William Wordsworth's sonnet, "Intimations of Immortality:"

> What though the radiance which was once so bright
> Be now for ever taken from my sight,
> Though nothing can bring back the hour
> Of splendor in the grass, of glory in the flower;
> We will grieve not, rather find

Strength in what remains behind;
In the primal sympathy
Which having been must ever be;
In the soothing thoughts that spring
Out of human suffering;
In the faith that looks through death,
In years that bring the philosophic mind.[15]

Spielrein's last will may be read as just such a meditation, and one that perhaps helped to alleviate her own grief. There is also an air of nostalgia in Spielrein's words that mimic Wordsworth's aging sentimentalism, in her desire to find beauty in childhood, as both authors conjure images of an innocence (or naïveté) that precludes the onset of age and experience. Spielrein, in her philosophic mind, looks through and past death to imagine a life that continues, plants that grow, and children at play. Her tone, like Wordsworth's, muses on the cyclical aspect of nature, reminding whomever she imagined to be the reader of the will that she was once a human being in the middle of a certain splendor, desiring to be remembered beyond her own suffering.

Her need to be remembered as a human being is her most affecting statement as Spielrein calls herself by name, asserting personal agency, history, and presence. She gives herself as much to nature as to science, which describes her life and work possibly more than any analysis could, as she demonstrates integrated scientific and mythopoetic insights from an early age. Similarly, she would continue to express ideas of physical and mystical union throughout her life and career.

Spielrein's Will also recalls Honoré de Balzac's *The Fatal Skin*, wherein Balzac describes the depth of grief: "Ordinary people suffer a fall without serious hurt, like children who tumble such a short distance that they get up unharmed. When a great soul is smashed to pieces, however, he must have fallen from a great height, or from the skies where he had glimpsed a paradise beyond his reach."[16] It is possible that Spielrein, in her "great soul" and deep grief, was for a time unable to process the effects of death in a manner acceptable to those around her. Perhaps she expressed her emotion in writing as a way of transforming her feelings as they manifested after the death of her "favorite" and "beloved" sister, resulting in a period of psychological overwhelm rather than a sustained case of hysteria.[17]

The concept of death, and not, it should be noted, of suicide, in Spielrein's will is related in paradisiacal imagery, lending us an alternative interpretation of her mental state, outside of the clinical model; Balzac again relates of his protagonist: "As in the yellowish circles around the eyes and the hectic flush of the cheeks, a doctor might have attributed these to some heart or lung ailment; but a poet would have seen in these symptoms the ravages of study, shadows left by . . . a passion."[18] As Balzac underscores that there are more than a few ways to interpret a person's self-expression and behavior, so too are there multiple interpretations to the less examined "passions" of Spielrein's writing. As it were, she was effectively "cured" and released from the clinic to begin her studies at the University of Zurich in 1905.

Sabina Spielrein's Unfortunate Reintroduction to the Academy

Aldo Carotenuto, the author responsible both for rediscovering Spielrein and infusing the academic world with her diaries and letters, is also responsible for the retroactive labeling of Spielrein as a schizophrenic victim poised at the center of a love triangle—and little more.[19] While Carotenuto brought her personal writing to light, he also constructed her narrative as the lovesick mistress with a mental illness, examined only in relation to the interpersonal tension that later arose between Freud and Jung. She is repeatedly staged "in between" the two men rather than beside them, immediately introducing and enforcing a hierarchy of talent, and subliminally blamed as a woman who disrupted the friendship of men. Even her later attempt to reconcile the two theorists is described by him, for an unknown reason, as "pathetic."[20]

On June 11, 1909, Spielrein wrote a letter to Freud in attempt to clear her name from Jung's accusation that she was the instigator of their affair: "4 ½ years ago, Dr. Jung was my doctor, then my friend, and finally my 'poet,' i.e. my Beloved. He came to me and it went how it usually does with 'poetry.' He preached polygamy, that his wife was supposedly agreeable to it, etc., etc."[21] Her letter is said by Carotenuto to be sexually motivated in an attempt to cause tension between Freud and Jung. She is thus transfigured into the image of, in his words, a "sick young girl" caught between two powerful men, though she was at that time a doctoral student and an adult woman in her twenties who had been discharged from the clinic for more than four years.[22]

The problem that arises in blaming Spielrein for the tension between Freud and Jung is that it implies she is responsible for the actions of men in her life whether it is Jung's professional transgressions or Freud's subsequent unease with them. To be sure, Freud would feel his "personal relationship with your [Spielrein's] Germanic hero [Jung] has definitely fallen apart. His behavior was too bad. My judgment about him has greatly changed since I received that first letter from you."[23] Freud's opinion of Jung changed in the years following his knowledge of the affair, though a split was not cemented between the two until years after Spielrein's initial 1909 letter, as his above response was not written until 1913. It is also common knowledge that Freud and Jung split largely due to diverging theoretical methodologies. There is also no evidence whatsoever to support the theory that Spielrein and Freud were anything more than friends and colleagues, which they later became upon her reception into Freud's Psychoanalytic Society, so Carotenuto maligns her reputation with clinical labels and sexual motives that were simply not there. It seems that Spielrein wrote to Freud in the letter above in order to speak to her experience of the affair rather than have her narrative defined for her by Jung.

Immediately suspicious of her motivations even in her later attempts to reconcile the theories of the two men, Carotenuto laid the groundwork for the next thirty years of Spielrein being considered primarily in relation to his own retroactive diagnosis of her as a so-called schizoid, as he further asserts: "We ought to ask ourselves what could have been the motivation that drove her to a unified vision of the two theories . . . any attempt at synthesis can be taken as a difficulty in accepting conflict."[24] Spielrein's initial and factual diagnosis of "hysteria" is here transformed into schizophrenia, which is then used by Carotenuto as the guiding lens through which to interpret her diaries, letters, scholarship, and life—all of which were written and/or experienced in the years after her discharge from the clinic. Her life is reorganized around this wrongfully applied stigma, which simultaneously serves to discredit her work.

Carotenuto, a professor of history and Jungian clinician in his own right, continued to find fault with Spielrein's personality: "It is hard to imagine how a person can be incapable of tolerating conflict," as if to suggest that Spielrein was an anomaly in her discomfort with conflict, or to imply that any individual uncomfortable with conflict is therefore schizophrenic.[25] It could also be argued that, while living under Nazi occupation and Stalinist communism upon her return to Russia in later life, Spielrein was extremely adept at living under conflict. Strangely, Carotenuto constructs the image of Spielrein in his commentary as a schizoid incapable of conflict after he has already stated that Spielrein was a pathetic hysteric driven to create said conflict, meaning he *creates* a case of dual personality disorder out of his own schizophrenic semantics. Sadly, he is not alone in assigning retroactive diagnoses to Spielrein, as many scholars who came after Carotenuto would rely on his flimsy labels; discussed shortly. Yet it *is* possible to view her as a stable and autonomous scholar as a third option to such characterizations.

By describing Spielrein as "the schizophrenic patient" even after her discharge from the clinic, Carotenuto rubber stamps Spielrein's history with an illness that was never hers.[26] To reiterate, Spielrein's letters, diaries, and, of course, the remainder of her life, occurred after her institutionalization. By using mental illness as a weapon, Spielrein is stigmatized in her achievements and the fact that she was able to heal and was in fact "cured," is undermined. She becomes not a woman or a scholar, or a mother, or a person, but *The Ever-Patient.* Amusingly, Carotenuto himself lamented on the dangers of "rubber-stamping" labels onto patients, though by doing so to Spielrein, he successfully created an academic atmosphere that continues to discredit and suppress her intellectual merit on account of an imagined illness.[27]

Sabina Spielrein as "Seductress"

It was the noted analyst René Major, in her article "Love for Transference and Passion for Signifiers: Between Sabina S. and Anna G." (1984), who introduced Spielrein as the seductress, or the *agent provocateur* in regard to her relationship with Jung.[28] An "agent provocateur," by definition, is something or someone that "entices another to commit an act," and the term is merely used here as a tactic of slut-shaming.[29] Major assumes the "act" in question is the affair between Spielrein and Jung; whether the act committed was brought about by suggestion, by desire, or by overt seduction is unclear, but seems to imply that Spielrein, when she was an in-patient of Jung's, was in a position of acting power. Actually, it was Jung who, as an authority of the clinic, was both psychologically (as her therapist) and professionally responsible for her care. The inherent power imbalance present at the time of her treatment is dismissed by Major in favor of presenting the affair as a transference seduction, or as a "love," which is a popular narrative frequently associated with Spielrein.[30] However, reducing her to the role of the seductress—patient-as-victimizer—not only strips her of her later academic accomplishments, it also undermines the emotional confusion expressed by Spielrein in her diaries and letters at the time of her alleged enticing—topics explored further in the following chapters.

Also problematic when maintaining Spielrein and Jung's relationship as a "romance" is that it can be used to justify further abuses of power within therapist-client (patient) relationships in general, and reinforces the image of Spielrein-as-mistress. In fact, it is suggested by Major that the alternatives for acting on desire in therapy vacillate between, essentially, *don't give in* and *do give in*. She relies on the philosophically inclined though dubious "psychoanalytic ethics" of Jacques Lacan, which are rooted in the belief that there are separate ethics for those in the psychoanalytic profession than there are for everyone else.[31] This implies that those in the psychoanalytic profession hold a large amount of power that *could* be, if one so chose, exerted over a patient as a means of manipulation and control, due to the emotional and psychological vulnerability of a client within the room of his or her therapist. Clearly, these "separate" ethics, when taken to their logical extreme, could be used to erase professional ethics entirely, dismissing the fact that such ethics are in place for the emotional and psychological protection of both client *and* therapist.

Spielrein's narrative is constructed so that Jung appears to be the conquest of a seductress. In her article, Major quotes an early letter to Freud wherein

Jung claims his strict professional relationship to Spielrein as her (married) doctor, though admittedly under the thrall of her targeted seduction. In this letter, Jung does not admit to wanting to have an affair with Spielrein, but states that he has been compelled by her "sexual wiles," using language similar to entrapment.[32] Spielrein's perspective is not included, which makes the implication clear: Jung could not help himself because Spielrein tempted him, and demanded it even, with her supposed sexual "wiles." She is thus cast as a sexual predator and defined by the role of seductress, regardless of the fact that it was not just any man and woman engaged in an affair, but a woman and her therapist. If we were talking about a similar situation today, we would not categorize such a relationship as a romance, but as a felony.

Henry Zvi Lothane, a Jungian analyst and scholar (an exception among those who blame Spielrein for her own death), states in his article "In Defense of Sabina Spielrein" (1996) that while Jung was Spielrein's outpatient therapist, he accepted no payment, and was therefore exempt from ethical boundaries.[33] However, this statement, if applied to analysis today, suggests that for pro bono work even when done under the guise of therapy, an analyst is under no ethical bounds to refrain from sexual relations with a client. That we are speaking of a case from the early 1900s in no way detracts from this horror; just because an action was normalized does not mean it was justified. Regardless, Spielrein's family indeed believed Jung to be accountable for acting as a professional toward their daughter. In fact, Jung received a letter to this effect from Spielrein's mother (which does not survive) and wrote back to her in 1909: "In order to set boundaries on my position as a doctor, which you are hoping that I retain, I suggest you set aside a fee for me as appropriate compensation for my efforts. You can be sure in doing this that I will respect my duty as a doctor under all circumstances."[34] Lothane refers to this letter as justification for an analyst's behavior, which begs the question: At what price can a patient assume the therapist's "respect"? Would a sliding scale then be perverted into a hierarchy of ethics?

The late psychoanalyst Bruno Bettelheim, in his response to the affair, asserts that while Jung may not have accepted payment per se, it was common to accept gifts in place of payment, as was actually customary and often expected.[35] The idea that Jung's intimate relationship with Spielrein is excusable solely based on the fact that he was not accepting payment is, then, challenged. Spielrein also explicitly stated, in a letter to Freud in 1909: "She [her mother] had given him gifts instead of money to express her friendly disposition. Of course it all became complicated (because he no longer figured as a doctor to me anymore)," though we know that in Jung's letter to Freud (noted earlier), he had already admitted to still assuming the role of her doctor.[36] Bettelheim also noted that under the clinic's policy, many doctors treated patients gratis, and it was actually a call for immediate dismissal should a doctor become sexually involved with his patient, again suggesting less of a "romance" and more of a breach of professional regulations *very much intact* during Jung's employment.[37] Spielrein's intermittent outpatient treatment with Jung ceased shortly after the above letter was written and their so-called affair ended approximately one year thereafter.

The "irony" in the sound the name "Sabina Spielrein" makes out loud has also been cited as a point of maligning, Major having stated its relation to the German *spielen* and *sauber*, meaning to "play cleanly."[38] While this is an interesting linguistic coincidence, the implication remains unclear as to the meaning of this coincidence: Is Spielrein's name ironic because she was in fact *not* clean, because she was a "mistress"? Or is it ironic because, during therapy, her "seduction" is seen as synonymous with playing a game? If nothing else, Major's comment does highlight the dichotomy of "clean" and "dirty" enforced upon female sexuality at the time of Spielrein's affair, as well as the perpetuation of the Virgin/Whore bipolarity in contemporary culture, as reinforced by such pointed sentiments as these.

Not for nothing, "spiel" is also related to "extravagant speech," a fitting description considering the intellectual power later displayed by Spielrein. The verb *spielen* in German is also frequently used in regard to "perform," as in a piece of music, which would also be appropriate given that Spielrein was a gifted pianist and for a time wanted to devote herself to a career in music. Pamela White Hadas, a poet made famous for revisioning mythological stories as well as recreating narratives of unknown women, speaks to this musical understanding of the name *Spielrein* in her poem "Jung and Easily Freudened': Sabina Spielrein's Analysis":

> At last, I understand. *Spielrein*:
> plays clean, sublime; plays. All masters flow
> from my fingers, white keys, black keys. Music
> expands all my life contracted.[39]

Hadas reinforces the notion that many interpretations of Spielrein's name exist, as many interpretations of her work exist, and she is not confined or limited merely by one.

In her article, and further complicating the details of the "romance," Major deems it part of a larger "Freudian fiction" rather than as part of actual history.[40] This should not invalidate Spielrein's experience nor translate her own account of the affair in her diaries and letters into a "fiction." But let us first delve into what exactly one means by "Freudian Fiction" by employing James Hillman, who in *Healing Fiction* defines the term as relating to stories told within the therapeutic process, meaning "tales . . . and primal scenes that had not occurred in the literal historical past."[41] While Spielrein's work is subject to interpretation, the actual and substantiated existence of the relationship between her and Jung as viewed through years of correspondence, diaries, and records—the majority of which occurred outside of the therapeutic process—may be understood as "historical" facts.

Still, Major does note with suspicion the erasure of Spielrein from history and implies that forces were devoted to "hiding all traces of [her], as well as of her role in Jung's life and work, [and] her name in the history of psychoanalysis."[42] However, she, too, continued to undermine the validity of Spielrein's entire existence: "Sabina's history seems so strange that one has the impression that what is considered reality is a matter of pure fiction."[43] Again, Spielrein's personal experience is called into question as an attempt to revision her out of her historical narrative. By transforming her into a figure of fiction, or as an *agent provocateur*, doubt is cast upon Spielrein's perspective, and once this is done, her credibility as a serious scholar is jeopardized. This may be a good time to note that the reason I refer to her by her last name is to purposefully give her the respect that her male peers are regularly afforded, as with Freud or Jung.

Unfortunately, the issue of credibility brings up questions of truth and fiction in cases where inequalities of gender and power are used to invalidate the character of an individual coming forward with his or her own perspective on the "truth." For example, in the recent controversy surrounding Woody Allen, in a place of fame and power, and his adopted daughter Dylan Farrow, it was *her* credibility that was instantly degraded so that her truth became a work of fiction, while her mental health was questioned and her story mined for fault. Similarly, Bill Cosby's multiple accusers were, at first, subjected to the same kind of scrutiny, disbelief, and character assassination in order to keep an untainted image of Cosby intact. These stories parallel Spielrein's, since her history includes a personal account of a relationship with a man of power and stature being turned into a personal delusion, or worse, used to discredit her entire body of work.

Sabina Spielrein as a Scholar

In 1911, upon graduation, Dr. Spielrein joined the Vienna Psychoanalytic Society (VPS), finding acceptance within Freud's circle and resonating with his methodology, due to Freud's emphasis on sexuality. It was his associative method, after all, though administered by Jung, which had helped her to heal. Be that as it may, she would always retain her sense of metaphysical and mythological insight, directly influenced by Jung. In Rosemary Balsam's article, "Women of the Wednesday Society: The Presentations of Drs. Hilferding, Spielrein, and Hug-Hellmuth" (2003), information is gathered and presented from the minutes of the weekly Wednesday meetings of the VPS; she introduces three pioneering women psychoanalysts of the day and argues: "Some of the ideas that were devalued at the time can now be seen to have foreshadowed the most promising directions in recent analytic thinking."[44]

At the same time, Balsam immediately devalues Spielrein by stating that she is "ultimately less impressive" than the other two, even though she is the only one who is mentioned—by Freud, no less—as anticipating aspects of his own research.[45] Also, Spielrein was the youngest woman, at twenty-six, and only the second woman to join as a member of the society. She also presented to the all-male VPS in 1911 and 1912 on the topics of the "death instinct," death to her necessitating rebirth, particularly in relation to artistic renderings of sexuality, and on female masturbation respectively, and she regularly contributed in conversation during the meetings with such notables as Otto Rank, Sigmund Freud, Hanns Sachs, and Wilhelm Stekel. Under the gender constrictions of the time, given that female sexuality was considered a symptom of "hysteria," when it was even considered, it may be viewed as distinctly progressive of Spielrein to present on the female perspective of sexuality at all.

The notes taken in 1912 on Spielrein's latter presentation refer to "female masturbation—hand rubbing . . . 'psychic masturbation' stimulated by reading novels or seeing pictures. She [Spielrein] accepts that women are 'generally more erotic' than men and that virtually anything can arouse the desire to masturbate [like] listening to music."[46] Though a closer look at her presentation may be found in chapter 7, Spielrein's ideas can be interpreted as anticipating twentieth-century feminist philosophy while challenging the ever-present assumption that women are less sexual or sensual beings than men. Spielrein, in renegade fashion, also presented on a subject that was considered a symptom of the diagnosis she herself had been given years earlier.

A short reflection on European social behavior is in order, to contextualize the climate in which Spielrein was presenting. Dan Agin, a cultural historian and philosopher, states in "An Evil Age: An Essay on Marriage and Sex in the Victorian Era":

> The two great engines of despair during this era were the oppression of women by men and the repression of sexuality by the state and the Church. The consequence could only be the production of misery on a large scale . . . by placing the Victorian woman on a purity pedestal, by making her untouchable and with a distaste for sex . . . boys and girls who sexually transgressed were burdened by guilt.[47]

In addition, the reigning authority on human sexuality in the late 1800s and early 1900s was William Acton's book, *The Functions and Disorders of the Reproductive Organs*, wherein he states: "I should say that the majority of women (happily for them) are not very much troubled with sexual feeling of any kind."[48] Acton, a prominent medical doctor and gynecologist of the time, believed that women "submitted" to sex for the pleasure of their husbands only, and that the sexual impulse in women was a symptom of nymphomania, which was in itself a sign of hysteria.[49] This is the era into which Spielrein was born and the era in which she experienced "hysteria." This climate, in regard to women's sexuality, lends a deeper understanding into the radical nature of Spielrein's presentation on female eroticism and masturbation in Vienna to a room full of men.

In 1910, just one year before Spielrein joined the VPS, women were not even allowed admittance into the society. Freud, to his credit, later encouraged inclusivity while at the same time expressing: "It is true that women gain nothing by studying."[50] Fellow member of the VPS Fritz Wittels seemed to agree with Freud on the topic: "The average half-way normal student regards his female colleague as nothing but a prostitute," while others agreed that a woman's position was best as a "mother" or a "nurse," and that a woman's behavior was geared only toward attracting other men.[51] By her immersion in such a hostile environment regarding the nature and status of women, for whom sexuality was equated with hysteria, motherhood, or prostitution, Spielrein may be considered at least a little "impressive." It seems as though Balsam diminishes the importance of Spielrein's presentation in order to elevate the contributions of her other two subjects.

Ironically, though she decidedly states that Spielrein is "less impressive" than the other two, her article's text is devoted mostly to the former's role in the society as well as to her involvement with Freud and Jung. Balsam insinuates that to Freud, Spielrein "could no doubt be cultivated as an attractive spy or courier" due to her relationship with Jung.[52] However, if this assumption is correct, and the only appealing interest Freud saw in Spielrein was the fact he could turn her into a spy, it does not mean he succeeded. Spielrein had clear ambitions of her own and opinions running at times counter to Freud's (e.g., female sexuality), which suggests she was not a malleable puppet.

Such accusations contribute to the construction of Spielrein's narrative identity as being a woman *between* two men, Freud and Jung, instead of a woman *beside* these two men. The placement of Spielrein between these men actually situates her beneath them, tied to them only as a physical object, as a "spy" or a "mistress," and forever cloaks her in the tattered garment of inferiority. Furthermore, even if Freud initially saw an opportunity, or what he perceived to be an opportunity, to spy on Jung, he and Spielrein soon became friends and fellow colleagues, keeping up a correspondence for the next decade.

Blame is further placed on Spielrein's so-called borderline personality in this article for the tension that subsequently arose between Freud and Jung: "A fracture had been in the making for some time between the two men. However, the potential of borderline patients to turn two people with whom they are involved against each other is a common experience in hospital-ward dynamics."[53] Simply put, Spielrein was not a patient (and far from a hospital ward) at the time of Freud and Jung's fracture, but a grown woman and an academic in her own right. Balsam's diagnosis of Spielrein as a "borderline" is retroactive and based primarily on the presumption that she was attempting to do anything other than find her own voice and further her career.

Further invoked is the notion that Spielrein was the reason that Freud and Jung "broke up," or as she states, "helped to drive the wedge between them."[54] Spielrein is reduced to the status of a malignant and destructive force, and relegated once again to a woman between men and not beside them. Balsam goes so far as to say that Spielrein "may have been more pivotal for psychoanalytic politics than her intellectual work *per se*."[55] Her role as a femme fatale is posited as more notable than her actual life, diaries, or scholarship, the latter of which is seen by Balsam as only derivative of Jung. The notion that Spielrein was pivotal to Jung's early theoretical formations is not considered, nor is the idea that being influenced by a scholar need not be synonymous with being derivative.

Oddly, Spielrein's attempt to reconcile the two men has been so well documented that it has been used as both "proof" of schizophrenia as well as evidence of her role as a nurturing mediator.[56] Was Spielrein a schizophrenic unable to effectively cope with tension? Was she a hysteric? Was she a borderline who sought chaos? Was she a mediator attempting to unite opposing forces? Or was she simply a female scholar trying to survive in a field dominated by men? I offer this last interpretation as being closest to the truth, with the addition that it was perhaps to her own benefit, should she attempt to bridge the tension between Freud and Jung, that a healed relationship between the two would offer greater academic acceptance to her own interdisciplinary work.

To force Spielrein into the role of a nemesis, or a vengeful mistress, is to disregard her actual independent scholarship and personal life apart from Freud and Jung, including her roles as teacher, psychologist, and mother. Ignoring her contributions by favoring the narrative identity of a femme fatale transfigures her into *The Ever-Patient* with motives linked to pathology instead of to intellect. Point of fact: Spielrein had not been institutionalized for seven years when she presented to the VPS in 1912 and had been effectively cured, a point frequently dismissed.

Balsam cites a footnote written by the editor of the VPS's *Minutes* that states: "Spielrein was my colleague at medical school . . . she suffered a psychotic episode," interpreted as a "warning to the reader."[57] It is unclear whether or not this warning refers to the episode in Spielrein's past, though the point is rather moot considering that this information is only used to discredit and suppress her scholarship. In the construction of Spielrein as an inferior scholar, Balsam also asserts: "At this stage of her career, when she was writing extremely ambitious theoretical papers, Spielrein had had no clinical experience other than her own."[58] This statement is markedly untrue, as she had worked tirelessly with a schizophrenic patient in preparation for her dissertation (on the mythic structure of schizophrenia) and had clinical experience with female patients prior to her presentation to the VPS. Spielrein's competence and authority need not have been demeaned in order for Freud and Jung to maintain theirs.

This inferiorizing of Spielrein continues when Balsam goes on to say that: "[Spielrein's] intellectual life seems to have been dominated by whatever male [e.g., Jung, Freud, and later, child psychologist Jean Piaget] was her champion."[59] Jung, who helped her to heal from adolescent trauma, also engaged in an affair with her at the time, and in doing so may be titled something other than a "champion." Freud, too, while having a profound influence on Spielrein's theoretical methodology, can be considered an "influence" rather than a dominating power. Like her male colleagues, Spielrein was extremely affected by Freud, though she is the only one to be considered "dominated."

The implicit objective of identifying Spielrein as "dominated" is to suggest she is submissive, or subject to male power with no autonomous merit. It is to also bring the sludge of gender politics into academia, where Spielrein, as a woman, is viewed as being dominated rather than purely influenced. The very fact that she presented on topics such as female sexuality to a society that previously did not accept women as members is a testament of her own thinking, her own agenda, and her own ambition as a scholar. Had her ideas been well received, instead of merely tolerated by her peers, as is intimated, perhaps her work would be more widely known and appreciated.

Historian Mireille Cifali iterates that the famed child psychologist Jean Piaget was briefly Spielrein's patient in the 1920s during her time in Geneva: "She is praised for her moral qualities, her serene stoicism and her intellectual qualities . . . her name appears with Piaget's, who mentions her in his work . . . but she resists confining herself to a solely Piagetian orientation," instead insisting that " 'his construction of reality in the infant,' is . . . too one-sided."[60] Cifali, in her thoughtful piece, regards Spielrein as *with* Piaget, rather than beneath him or "dominated" by him. In this recounting, Spielrein forms and maintains her own opinions even if they diverge from an esteemed male peer. Further, Piaget could hardly be viewed as Spielrein's "champion," since he regarded her with some suspicion after negatively associating her with his own mother; though, to be fair, he also granted her scholarship its originality.[61] Her influence on Piaget has yet to be fully explored.

Strangely, Spielrein's other notable presentation to the society has been similarly regarded as symptomatic of mental illness. In this presentation in November 1911, primarily dedicated to the "death instinct," or the mystical idea that lovers want to dissolve into each other, Spielrein also set forth an idea of an archaic (archetypal) mother image that exists in the psyche unbounded by time, citing "The Mothers" in *Faust* as an example; she also expanded on the theory that experiences in childhood affect an adult's older life. Nonetheless, her line of thinking was linked by Balsam to Spielrein's "borderline personality." To her, Spielrein's "imaginative and globally ranging style of mind" is used as evidence of such psychological "vagueness," rather than being an example of an *imaginative and globally ranging mind.*[62] In this narrative construction, Spielrein is not an interdisciplinary scholar, but is again transformed into *The Ever-Patient*, both demeaned and dismissed. It is also of note that Balsam's other two female subjects were, like Spielrein, killed during the Holocaust, though neither is accused, as is Spielrein, of having been suicidal at the time.

Why Spielrein's understanding of mythology and psychology is linked to mental illness instead of innate intelligence seems an attempt to suppress her voice and confine her within the role of a dominated woman. Additionally, her personal and professional work is continuously mined for "proof" of an illness rather than explored for its psychological and philosophical significance. The question arises: Is it possible to view Spielrein's life and work without a diminutive label that seeks to undermine the value of her work?

Spielrein's fascination with the concepts of life and death is further claimed to be "dependent" on Freud and Jung, which dismisses Spielrein's own childhood confrontation with mortality after the death of her sister, following which she wrote her last will, which very clearly demonstrates preexisting mythopoetic and scientific interests.[63] The suggestion that Spielrein's interest was dependent upon men is defamatory and inflammatory. In relation to such a notion, Ovcharenko, like Carotenuto before him, classifies Spielrein as a "schizophrenic" due, it would seem, to the challenges she posed to the men of the VPS, as it is documented that her theories "did not fit" with theirs, presumably because of her emphasis on male *and* female sexuality.[64]

Spielrein's gender is rarely examined in relation to her academic reception, though her experience finds imaginal representation in Sylvia Plath's poem, "Edge:" "Woman" is described as "perfected" and smiling, though her body remains stone "dead" as her inanimate children suckle at her two emptied and dried "pitchers" of milk.[65] In the poem, "Woman" is perfected in gruesome irony, and in reality rendered an idle statue while the milk that was once nourishing is transformed into nothingness. Similarly, when the vitality of Spielrein's work is transfigured into an image of seduction or mental illness, her "children," or her words, are stripped of life. This metaphor of vital female autonomy emptied of its meaning resurfaces when scholars slap Spielrein with the label of schizophrenia.[66]

As if that weren't unsettling enough, Ovcharenko cited her work on the "death instinct" as nothing more than "her own psychological baggage."[67] Academic research is rarely, if ever, considered "baggage" in relation to Spielrein's male counterparts and such a characterization infantilizes and condescends her contributions, both personal and professional, to the field. Instead of being touted as intellectual prowess, her work is consistently viewed as a lingering effect from her relationship with Jung, which fails to recognize the fact that her scholarship continued for thirty years *after* the so-called affair and encompassed much more than her theory of a "death instinct." That her life influenced her work is clear, in the way that a subjective experience may influence a passionate interest in academic research for any scholar, male or female.

In her book, *Jewish Women in Fin de Siècle Vienna*, Alison Rose includes Sabina Spielrein as a woman of Freud's circle and an eminent figure in the history of the field, but maligns her nonetheless as being important due to her having been Jung's patient with "a preoccupation with defecation . . . masochistic fantasies," and a woman that merely embodied Jung's "Jewess" fantasy.[68] While Rose briefly mentions Spielrein's membership in the VPS, she quickly reverts to describing her as the woman who "may have contributed to the growing animosity between Jung and Freud," thus concluding her study of Spielrein.[69] The fact that Spielrein's clinical record, or her behavior as a teenager when under emotional duress, is continuously used against her character and her work further promotes the construction of Spielrein as *The Ever-Patient*. Such a construction also entirely dismisses what is *in* her work.

However, in 2006, Jungian analyst Brian Skea underscored the original "hysterical" diagnosis given to Spielrein, contrary to the later diagnoses of "schizophrenia" (see Carotenuto in 1982) and "borderline personality" (see Hoffer in 2001; Balsam in 2003).[70] He also rightly reminds us that her symptoms remitted after a few months in the clinic. Aiding in the construction of Spielrein's narrative as an autonomous woman in his article, Skea points out that she graduated with honors in psychiatry, finishing her dissertation under Jung's supervision in 1911.

In her doctoral work, she conducted interviews with a schizophrenic patient and linked her patient's "psychoses" to an alternatively patterned way of thinking and speaking as found in mythology, folktales, dreams, and alchemy—at a time when Spielrein herself had been influenced by *Visions of Zosimos*, Zosimos being a mystic of figure of the Gnostic tradition defined by his search for wisdom and enlightenment in the third and fourth centuries CE. Spielrein's own integrative and interdisciplinary research style enabled her to recognize her patient's fantasies as not simply the ranting of an ill patient, but as the language of myth. Spielrein was thus one of the first people in history to write on the presence of myth in an individual's mind.

While Hillman claimed that "Jung was perhaps the first in our time to understand the psychic reality as myth; this he learned from the tales told him by his psychiatric charges at Zurich's Burghölzli asylum," Spielrein was among the first to understand the mythic structure of the psyche and relay her findings.[71] Jung, then, did not learn solely from "psychiatric charges," but also from his young doctoral student's dissertation. Again, her contribution fades from history as her character is fused with the erroneous image of a woman institutionalized.

Spielrein also posited that mythic symbols ordered the patient's chaos, and would later argue, anticipating internationally regarded mythologist Joseph Campbell, that this kind of mythic imagination was not only present in schizophrenics but in each individual's psyche, and that the symbols and complexes "do not belong merely to personal experiences, for we also have inherited a deposit of ancestral experiences," meaning, "the language of the mythological thought process."[72] It appears as though Spielrein gave voice to the meaning of mythology in the modern imagination, as influenced by prototypical, ancestral, and primordial images. In her writing, one is reminded of Jung's later definition of the term *archetype,* or "archaic remnants" that he found to be present in dream images, art, and religious literature.[73] Sounding uncannily similar to Spielrein, Jung would suggest that the symbol-making aspect of the psyche is accessed through "ideas, myths, and rites."[74]

Brian Skea maintained: "Despite immersing herself in Frau M's [Spielrein's patient] psychotic material, Spielrein was able to maintain her objective stance and successfully wrote it up . . . I believe a case can be made for recognizing Spielrein as an important contributor to Jung's emerging theory of the collective unconscious."[75] Spielrein was decidedly objective in her doctoral training, and not schizophrenic or borderline or hysterical. Here, she has finally been presented not as a patient or as Jung's mistress, but as a successful professional distinctly *not* caught up in her patient's psychosis. Spielrein's work may be considered pivotal to fundamental ideas in depth psychology.

These dates are rather important, due to Jung's published work, *Symbols of Transformation*, in 1912, in which Jung defers to Spielrein's work on multiple occasions in reference to her case studies, formulation on archaic symbols, and the "death instinct." In a footnote:

> I wish to refer here to the interesting correlation of mythological and pathological forms disclosed in the analytic investigation of Dr.

> S. Spielrein, and expressly emphasize that she has discovered the symbolisms presented by her in the *Jahrbuch*, through independent experimental work, in no way connected with my work.[76]

This footnote has since been omitted from subsequent editions, though Jung cited Spielrein's research as being conducted in 1912, rather than in 1911. This is a slight error but one in which Spielrein's research can be understood as occurring *before* Jung's; though the article that appeared in the *Jarbuch* was not published until 1912, it developed directly from her dissertation's material, published in 1911. This issue of primacy will be discussed again in chapter 6 through the letters between Jung and Spielrein, where she is very clearly acknowledged by him as having been original in her research.

By Jung admitting that her work was "in no way connected" to his own, one may conclude that Spielrein was capable without being "dominated" by him, as has been previously suggested. Skea asserted, quite contrary to popular opinion: "For this reason, I consider Spielrein to be the first into print with examples of mythological motifs arising out of a case study conducted by the author."[77] Regardless of who was "first," Spielrein publishing in the field of mythology as a woman in 1911 is still quite a feat, though the entirety of her dissertation remains untranslated.[78]

Sabina Spielrein's Marriage

Spielrein married Dr. Pavel (Paul) Scheftel in Summer 1912, of which little is known, and gave birth to their daughter Renata, meaning "rebirth," in 1913. Though he left her in 1915, due to Spielrein's choice to continue her professional career outside of Russia, they would later reconcile and have a second child in 1926, before his health-related death in the 1930s. In a 1996 article, psychoanalyst and author Zvi Lothane judges her marriage as "without love" and as a quick, misguided attempt to forget Jung.[79] In this characterization, Spielrein's own volition is dismissed, as is her ability to love a man other than Jung. The fact that she married quickly does not negate the possibility for love, nor does it mean—granting the assumption that she still harbored feelings for Jung—that she was unable to love more than one man simultaneously, which would undermine the sterile depiction of her marriage. No matter, as any opinion here is pure speculation, since so little is actually known about their relationship.

As a result of her choice not to follow her husband, Spielrein continued her career as a young psychoanalyst: she went on to practice in Berlin, Vienna, Geneva, and Zurich; she studied music composition and was a passionate pianist; she became fluent in three languages (Russian, German, and French, and she would teach in all three); she published more than thirty articles in prominent psychoanalytic journals; and she took, according to record, "an active part in work at meetings, conferences and congresses as teacher, psychologist, psychiatrist and psychoanalyst," all in addition to being a mother in her late twenties and thirties in the early 1900s.[80] Simply because Spielrein's choices in her relationship do not match a certain "traditional" assumption of marriage, they do not diminish the probability that she did, in fact, care for her husband. Because of her nebulous relationship to Paul Scheftel, Spielrein retains her name throughout this book, in line with other scholars, as "Sabina Spielrein," her most widely recognized name, rather than as the hyphenated "Spielrein-Scheftel."

It should also be noted that after revealing her marriage in her diary, she stated: "To be continued."[81] This may seem trivial, but her lack of expounding here, though it appears in the last available diary entry, has been used by Kerr in 1994, Lothane in 2003, and analyst (and film reviewer) Tom Kirsch in 2012 as evidence that she was not in love with her husband. However, she frequently promised to return to a subject throughout her diary, an example of which can be found in an earlier entry where after revealing Jung's love for her, she writes: "More about that later."[82]

Others (see Ovcharenko in "Love, Psychoanalysis, and Destruction") have implied that Spielrein's marriage was based on the loss of her illusions of romance rather than on love, simultaneously disparaging her marriage while implying that her affair with Jung, or the breach of trust between a woman and her therapist that subsequently caused a high degree of suffering and stigmatization in modern academe, should be considered more "romantic" than a marriage based on Spielrein's choice and her desire for children. Confining Spielrein to the role of Jung's mistress is to confine her to the role of youth and to the role of patient.

Sabina Spielrein's Return to a "New World" in Russia

Historian Mireille Cifali provides an alternative interpretation to the life and work of Spielrein in her research on the history of psychoanalysis. In her article "Sabina Spielrein: A Woman Psychoanalyst, Another Picture" (2001), she notes that in 1922 the local Geneva paper, the *Journal de Genève*, read: "Mrs. Spielrein . . . former assistant of Professor Freud of Vienna, is available on Tuesday evenings for free consultation with people desirous of information on educational and scientific psychoanalysis."[83] This presents, as Cifali's title suggests, another picture of Sabina Spielrein as a post-Jung academic—she is even referenced here in relation to Freud—who would produce articles on the subjects of love, death, and human nature. We might also marvel at the fact that Spielrein took such a teaching post in Geneva, not in the least daunted by having to speak and teach in French.

While Cifali relays that Spielrein first became famous by association with Freud and Jung rather than solely on her own merit, she does cite her as the first child psychoanalyst, and underscores Spielrein's awareness of her own upward struggle to prove herself. For example, when reflecting on the ease of acceptance that Freud's daughter was receiving, she mused in October 1910: "She [Anna Freud] has the advantage of a well-known father, which I do not possess. I must rely on my own strengths which is, consequently, much more difficult."[84] She had to rely on her own name and work, which is not to say that Anna Freud was not brilliant in her own right, but simply that Spielrein did not have the same advantage (both at the time and in retrospect). To the contrary, after news spread of Spielrein's affair with Jung, she was at quite the social and professional disadvantage.

However, Cifali also aids in another common construction to Spielrein's narrative: that she committed herself to her work for the love of Jung, instead of for her own passion: "She tries to transfer her passionate love for Jung to work in common. There [was] between them a transfer of ideas, a sharing."[85] To imply that Spielrein's intellectual capability, her published work, and her practice were nothing more than attention-seeking exploits is to discount her agency as an independent thinker. It is to strip her of the very nature of her being, as she states herself in a 1923 reentry paper to Russia, that her work was her "meaning to life."[86] Her initial academic interest was clearly influenced by Jung, but her continued interest and devotion to her work for the thirty years she lived outside of his circle would indicate that her work was her own.

In fact, her devotion to her work even during the affair is noted early on by Spielrein in another 1910 diary entry:

> Would my memory fail me if I wanted to hear about art history and mythology because it contains and indexes so much information already? Would I be lost? Would I be able to work systematically? This is how gloomy I felt when I came home and decided to force myself to sit down and read about pathology. No wonder I had a hard time focusing. . . . I blamed my friend [Jung] because I was able to work very well during the first couple days. I would never be able to prepare for my examination; I would have to stop seeing him.[87]

Spielrein, conflicted between wanting to work and wanting to be with Jung, resigns herself in this moment to work, demonstrating her own ambition and dedication to her other love: education. Actually, it is in this entry that Spielrein writes of an acquaintance, a patient of Jung's, whom she describes as *one of the many* of his romantic interests (see chapter 4), an indication that Spielrein understood her own interchangeability within the dynamics of the relationship.

It was, of course, soon after this entry that Spielrein ended the relationship, finished her degree, and began her career in Vienna. However, by 1923, after her years teaching and practicing psychology in Europe, primarily in Geneva, she was unable to find further advancement. With the loss of her financial backing after her family had been devastated by the Russian revolution of 1917, and her career halted (and perhaps missing her family), Spielrein returned to Russia with her young daughter in tow.

In addition to the effects of World War I and the revolution, Spielrein was likely also called to return to Russia in hopes of participating in the "construction of [Russia's] new world," though her return has been cited by others as attributable to her being dried up, uninspired, or "broken" by her relationship with Jung.[88] Perhaps, like her politically active family, Spielrein was intrigued by revolution and the possibility of her own professional development, given the fact that she became an integral part of Moscow's State International Psychoanalytic Institute upon arriving.

When Spielrein returned to her native land, she had to undergo a rigorous reentry process, which has been preserved by the Moscow city archives:

> I worked in a psychiatric clinic with Professor Bleuler, in a psychoneurological clinic with Professor Bonhoeffer (Berlin), and in psychoanalysis with Doctor Jung in Zurich and Professor Freud in Vienna. In Munich I worked on mythology and the history of art, and as a teaching-doctor in psychology at the Rousseau Institute in Geneva . . . I researched source material for the *Niebelungenlied* [the epic poem that inspired Wagner's opera *The Ring of the Nibelung*], and other folktales . . . I enjoy my work, and feel as if it were made for me, as if I were called to the work, and without it I see no other meaning to my life.[89]

Spielrein does not, upon her reentry, speak of her institutionalization or of her affair with Jung, not only because that would have been absurdly irrelevant, but because she had grown and matured as a person. She speaks here not as a patient, but as a professional and experienced woman, indicating how she wished to be perceived and possibly remembered. She does not include her children or her marriage in this short biography; instead, her work is named as the essential meaning to her life, which is quite profound considering what would have been expected of her gender at the time. She was not bound by what was "supposed" to be the most meaningful part of her life, which is not to imply that her children we unimportant to her, but that she wished to be known for her devotion to work in the attempt to find employment as a psychoanalyst. A self-described teacher and doctor, she also describes her primary interest in analyzing mythic motifs in folktales, which was pioneering and innovative research in the field.

According to historian Martin Miller, the roots of Russian psychoanalysis are documented in detail, but Spielrein is again both acclaimed and demeaned. Miller names her one of "Russia's leading Freudians . . . establishing a reputation for originality within the international analytic community," though he quickly reminds that she "suffered for years from uncontrollable attacks of hysteria. . . . Jung became more deeply involved in the case . . . and then had an affair with her."[90] Clearly, this latter information is superfluous to Spielrein's position at the institute.

In truth, Moscow formed the country's first Institute for Psychoanalysis, and the third such institute in Europe:

> To accomplish this, the Russians needed to gain approval from Freud's Institute. Among the major requirements for a new institute were the presence of training analysts, a curriculum of courses in psychoanalytic theory and practice, and a clinic. The conditions were met . . . Sabina Spielrein, who returned to Russia from Lausanne early in 1923, [was] recognized as . . . capable of directing a clinical program. . . . The course curriculum was arranged by Spielrein, Ermakov, and Wulff [prominent Russian psychoanalysts of the time] . . . Spielrein taught the courses on the psychology of subliminal thought and on the psychoanalysis of children. The latter course, the largest in the new institute, with thirty members attending, became Spielrein's specialization in her practice.[91]

Marked by the promise of academic recognition and stationed as a leader in the Russian psychoanalytic movement, Spielrein worked as professor and director of the clinical program to train analysts in Moscow when she was just thirty-seven years old, a single mother (for all intents and purposes), and the only female practitioner on the board at the time. Given that she designed the curriculum with Ermakov and Wulff, she no doubt aligned with their fields of study as well, with Ermakov's teaching on the psychology of creativity and Wulff's teaching the works of Nikolai Gogol.[92] She, a distinct Freudian, musician, writer, and analyst with a specialization in children, rounded out the interdisciplinary curriculum. In addition, the Institute took on an experimental project devoted to deal "with the crucial problem of finding a link between the collectivist ethos of a society committed to Communist principles on the one hand, and the radical 'bourgeois' individualism in Freud's psychoanalytic principles on the other."[93]

According to Alexander Etkind in *Eros of the Impossible: The History of Psychoanalysis in Russia*, there existed "a walk-in clinic conducted by Spielrein in tandem with her new assistant" in conjunction with "her lectures and seminars on child psychoanalysis, a practicum with elementary pupils."[94] The institute is described as an "elite" group, in which no one was "ever initiated into its ranks," with the notable exception of Spielrein, who also took part in analyzing children at the nearby Orphanage-Laboratory. However, Stalin soon applied pressure to the orphanage so that she "could not observe the children personally, nor put the teachers through analysis," even though Stalin's son, Vasily, had been one of the children whose upbringing was "overseen" by the orphanage.[95] Sadly, psychoanalysis as a whole was soon condemned as part of opposition to the existing political regime.

By the mid-1920s, according to Max Ettington, a psychoanalyst at the time: "[The] analysts in Soviet Russia are, by the way, having a bad time. From somewhere the Bolsheviks have caught the opinion that psychoanalysis is hostile to their system. You know the truth that our science is not able to be put into the service of any party, but that it needs a certain liberal-mindedness in turn for its own development."[96] The Moscow Society slowly ceased to exist by the early 1930s as Joseph Stalin's regime began suspecting intellectuals, and especially psychoanalysts, of treason.

Interestingly, Etkind questions why Spielrein moved to Rostov after only a year in Moscow, though he provides the following information: "At the end of 1924, the Psychoanalytic Institute and the International Solidarity Orphanage-Laboratory were administratively separated after the Institute's budget was cut in half. In addition, all of the teachers working there were fired."[97] Perhaps intuiting that this was the beginning of the end, she decided to move back to her hometown in 1924, where the rest of her family was still located, and where she would reunite with her husband. Also, it is known that Spielrein's colleagues in Moscow treated her with hostility, possibly due to her gender, as they, according to Ovcharenko's study, "knew very well that no one in the Institute could match her professional psychoanalytic qualifications."[98]

Additionally, in the late 1920s and '30s, Stalin's Great Terror effected purges (elimination) of suspected "terrorists," which included the psychoanalytic community of intellectuals, to which Spielrein and her brothers, who were professors at the time, were subjected. Stalin's methodology can be summed up in this early megalomaniacal announcement: "We will mercilessly destroy anyone who, by his deeds or his thoughts—yes, his thoughts!—threatens the unity of the socialist state. To the complete destruction of all enemies, themselves and their kin."[99] Victims of Stalinist purges would later include Spielrein's three brothers, who were captured and executed in forced labor camps.

Nina Scheftel, Pavel's daughter conceived in Spielrein's absence by another woman, states that Spielrein worked as a "pedologist in a school in Rostov-on-Don from the end of the 1920s through the early 1930s," and is remembered as treating patients in a solitary room with blacked-out windows and a single couch.[100] Pedology was considered a Russian science of "transforming human nature during childhood" and eventually as the study of Soviet's "new man of the masses," though it too became a casualty of Stalinist suspicion when it developed an intolerable "deviation" from the Party line.[101]

Spielrein's "end" is described by Etkind as "unhappy and unemployed . . . the best illustration of how the psychoanalytic profession was perceived" which serves to transform her into a tragic figure instead of a symbol of endurance and a woman capable of holding true to her life's passion during the communist persecution and the continual threat of war.[102] Spielrein was not only a psychoanalyst, but also a Jewish woman and mother. Enduring grief does not make Spielrein an example of unhappiness, nor does her death turn her life into an illustration of tragedy.

Sabina Spielrein's Death as "Destiny"

While there are multiple versions of her death, the most widely accepted is that Spielrein died during the second Nazi occupation of Rostov in August 1942, rather than in a synagogue shooting during the '41 occupation. This second occupation led to the massacre of 27,000 mostly Jewish citizens, who were shot over a period of *two days* and piled into the Snake Ravine (Zmeyevsky Balka), which has been substantiated by the Russian historical archives as well as Rostov's own population.[103]

Perhaps the most confounding notion in the construction of Spielrein's narrative is that her murder was somehow desired, and is seen as a "sacrifice," merely because she had previously been interested in the concept of death ("death instinct"). In Coline Covington and Barbara Wharton's 2003 *Sabina Spielrein: Forgotten Pioneer of Psychoanalysis* (a clinical examination of Spielrein's history), she is described as "approaching her final sacrifice" and obsessed with "idealization of self-sacrifice" at the time of her death.[104] Further, her "death instinct" is made synonymous with self-sacrifice and is interpreted as a lifelong obsession with self-destructive masochism, rather than as the philosophical, mythological, and biological concept that it was—as we shall see in chapter 5. This transfigures Spielrein's murder into an act of self-imposed martyrdom and also implies that she had a choice in the matter.

Spielrein's death, characterized as a "sacrifice," not only romanticizes her reality, but presumes that there was an idealized desire to die on her part (that she "wanted it"), with no regard for the safety of her two daughters who were killed at the same time. This language pathologizes Spielrein as an older woman, turning her again into *The Ever-Patient* at fifty-seven years old, as if she were that same teenaged girl writing a last will before "sacrificing" herself to a mass genocide. On the contrary, at this time Spielrein had been a doctor for thirty years, had similarly not written on the "death instinct" for almost that long, and had been discharged from the clinic for almost forty years. There is simply no evidence to suggest that she desired death in her adulthood or that she believed her imminent death to be a romanticized sacrifice. Therefore, labeling Spielrein's murder as such is a dangerous revisioning of her history, which at the time of her death included both Nazi occupation and Stalinist oppression.

The construction of a specific narrative identity is made apparent again when her adult office, which included the aforementioned blacked-out windows, is described by Covington as "[a] wish to provide a womb-like environment within which her patients could regress to experience the loss of ego that she sought herself."[105] Again, this perpetuates the notion that Spielrein, in her later life, was continually searching to lose herself (or to self-destruct), for which there is absolutely no evidence. Additionally, the "womb" of the room, which was enclosed by blackness, may be understood as a precaution against discovery and capture (and execution), given that Stalin had banned psychoanalysis. It may also be seen as a deliberate act of courage, rather than a "regression," to maintain the work she believed in during a time of profound social suppression.

Similarly, Ovcharenko asserts in his text: "Work of this type was practically speaking already a form of particularly dangerous crime against the State," and labels Spielrein's behavior as "life-threatening" and characteristically "suicidal" based yet again on her prior treatment and interest in the "death instinct."[106] This language constructs Spielrein once more as *The Ever-Patient,* instead of recognizing her as a committed analyst (and an adult) willing to risk a certain amount of danger for the work that gave her life meaning. To clarify, Spielrein's "death instinct" was developed by Spielrein with distinctly sexual connotations, relating to the idea of being consumed by a beloved during physical union (see chapter 5). The impulse to be consumed by love, paired with the mythic imagery of transformation and rebirth—she cites Christ as an example—is markedly different than being "suicidal."

Spielrein continued to publish until 1931, and presumably ceased publication in order to maintain a level of anonymity under communist rule, though she would continue to practice psychotherapy from home. By the time her brothers were murdered, her mother and father had also passed away. Her husband then passed away in 1937, though the two had a second child—Eva, named after her mother—in 1926 after successfully reconciling. These facts are given to provide the personal, professional, and social obstacles that Spielrein faced during her decision to continue her psychoanalytic work and to continue to treat clients through the 1930s. Perhaps Spielrein's practice provided not a "sacrifice," but a necessary solace and purpose after surviving the loss of her entire nuclear family.

To further debunk her character, Ovcharenko remarks on the "ironic" nature of Spielrein's murder, musing that she should have been able to anticipate the Nazis' sadism being "the author of the psychoanalytic concept of destruction and of the sadistic aspects of attraction."[107] This is a sentiment, horrifying as it is, that has not been questioned. As has been noted, Spielrein's concept of destruction revolves around the existential aspects of sexuality and *not* mass genocide; this casual victim blaming dismisses the fact that very few people could have predicted the depth of horror known as the Holocaust. Even given Spielrein's philosophical inquiry into the concept of death, nowhere does she ponder the sadistic rape, mutilation, surgical experimentation, forced labor, and extermination that became prevalent in Nazi tactics—not usually associated with "attraction." Plainly speaking, there is nothing "ironic" about the murder of Spielrein and her daughters, as there is nothing ironic about genocide. The use of "irony" does not actually apply here at all, lest Spielrein's work be misinterpreted and literalized out of its mythological, philosophical, biological (sexual), and psychological meaning. Hers was a study of the, at times violent, desire to consume and be consumed by a beloved, and not a study of random or premeditated acts of terror.

In a seeming non sequitur, Ovcharenko also points out how Spielrein was "poorly dressed" and "mortally tired" at the time, though he underscores the fact that Rostov was "subjected to bitter attacks by the Fascist airforce" until the conveyer-belt annihilation began in the summer of 1942.[108] Provided here is another perplexing aspect in the construction of Spielrein's narrative: the attention given to her dress at the time of death. Here, Ovcharenko further maligns Spielrein, and makes light of her murder, when her dress is subjected to sartorial jabs and biased aesthetic critique. His comment also needlessly genderizes war by viewing Spielrein's appearance within patriarchal expectations of how she *should* look, as if being immaculately coiffed and attired at the time of Nazi occupation and mass murder would have been more appropriate.

Similarly, Covington aided in this "spinster" construction of Spielrein's identity when offering the image of "a solitary figure, intense, serious, working long hours and puritanical in her dress."[109] Her older, more serious appearance and demeanor are noted as being due to never having healed from her relationship with Jung, with whom she had been out of contact for decades: "The secret transference love that Spielrein continued to harbor for Jung must have taken its toll."[110] As an adult, she is again presented as a patient, tied to Jung as his heartbroken mistress, incapable of having a life apart from him, even though there is no evidence that Spielrein "harbored" anything for Jung after the cessation of their correspondence. Perhaps what had taken its toll on her was the nearly twenty years she spent enduring a communist regime, the continual threat of Nazi occupation, and the deaths of her husband, parents, and siblings. That Spielrein's intensity, seriousness, and appearance are linked with puritanical spinsterhood and harbored love, instead of with scholarly devotion or personal aesthetic taste, undermines her autonomy and her personal agency as a grown woman.

She fares no better in Brian Skea's depiction of her: "This 57 year-old woman in black clothes, saw clients secretively in her Rostov home in a dark windowless room."[111] While Skea does emphasize Spielrein's work with clients, he does not go on to examine the necessity of such secrecy. Excessive reference *is* made, though, to her black clothing, aiding in the construction of a morose spinster, though the fact that she was a widow at this time (and likely still mourning the death of her family) is not considered. We are reminded again of Sylvia Plath's poem "Edge," in which the woman who has been sucked dry of her vitality, in her perfected dead image, "is used to this sort of thing," her black clothes "crackle and drag."[112]

Since her clothes have been called into question on numerous accounts, it is worth pausing to reflect on the history of Russian fashion in relation to women, from a social, rather than a clinical, interpretation of her wardrobe. According to Christine Ruane in *The Empire's New Clothes: A History of the Russian Fashion Industry 1700–1917*:

> Ever since the nihilist revolt of the 1850s, members of the radical intelligentsia had refused to follow fashion's dictates and so created their own anti-fashion statements. . . . Because so much pressure was placed upon women to follow fashion's dictates, Russian feminists became the most outspoken critics, enlisting other arguments to provide a more sweeping critique of fashion. . . . Feminists also employed moral and philosophical arguments in their appeals to women to reconsider their relationship to their clothing.[113]

Feminist reactions to fashion only intensified after the revolution as women's roles widened, until later Stalinist oppression would call for a return to "traditional" femininity. Even so, Spielrein's clothes become a central figure in her constructed image yet again by Nina Scheftel in *Eros of the Impossible: The History of Psychoanalysis in Russia*: "She [Spielrein] looked like a little old woman, although she wasn't that old. She was bent, wearing some old, black skirt that reached the ground. She wore boots with clasps that people now call 'farewell, youth' boots."[114] She is presented as a "little" figure for amusement (what exactly *are* "farewell, youth" boots?), in the image of an aged eccentric, no longer intriguing as a young "lover" and dismissed as a scholar. Continually, Spielrein is filtered through idealized expectations of feminine beauty, and feminist or not, her appearance is used only to discredit or to degrade her identity.

For instance, when describing Spielrein and Lou Andreas-Salomé, another female psychoanalyst in Freud's circle, historian Alexander Etkind poses two distinct images:

> Lou Andreas-Salomé, a remarkable, cosmopolitan psychoanalyst and a close friend of Freud's, became one of the brightest stars of European modernist culture. . . . Sabina Spielrein . . . the romantic figure . . . returned to Russia in 1923 in order to contribute to the creation of utopia in her homeland—and instead lived the second half of her life alone, in abject poverty and terror.[115]

Even Toni Wolff, Jung's public partner and scholar in her own right, is described: "Toni Wolff, Jung's former patient, who later became his good friend and a psychiatrist."[116] Rather than described as a good friend or a doctor, Spielrein is instead made into a figure of romance and then of despair, which ignores the life lived between her affair and her death. She is conjured here solely to represent the dark foil to Lou Salomé's remarkable radiance. It is also implied that Spielrein was delusional in her professional ambition by translating her desire to establish psychoanalysis in Russia into a "utopian" fantasy. Perhaps because Spielrein was—presumably—Jung's first affair, she must bear the brunt of ridicule that those who came after do not.

Unfortunately, the ridicule does not end there, as she is next presented as a woman with a death wish:

> Did Sabina recall her own discovery of the unconscious death wish during those months between the two holocausts, Communist and Nazi, that she was fated to experience? Perhaps it was the death wish that guided her actions back then, although she had been the first to recognize its existence. We will never know what role Thanatos [the Greek personification of Death] played in her mind: Did her concept of death help her to comprehend the bloody, absurd events that shook her destitute, lonely life in Rostov? Did it help her understand the execution of her brother[s]? . . . Spielrein, who had so skillfully manipulated her own affections and given them such

> an original philosophical interpretation, was tragically unprepared for her collusion with history.[117]

The term *fate* appears, suggesting that because Spielrein had once philosophically contemplated a "death instinct" (and she was not the first nor the only one to do so) as tied to *sexuality*, she somehow sealed her fate to an early and unjust death. The term *fate* also implies that there is such a thing as six million Jews "fated" to be murdered, which again transmogrifies mass extermination into a glorified notion of destiny. Further, Thanatos, or the personification of Death (θνῄσκω) in Greek mythology, is most closely associated with peaceful death, and would not, like his counterpart Keres, be considered in the context of Spielrein's violent end. Similarly, Thanatos is considered by Spielrein as an instinct parallel to Eros, or the personification of love and lust, in the service of physical and symbolic self-transformation.[118] Also, given that to Spielrein death preceded transformation in the service of creation—as in ancestors passing away giving rise to a new generation or two lovers uniting during physical intimacy—there is no reason she should be expected to have understood the "bloody, absurd events" of the two holocausts.

To be clear, Spielrein's development of a "death instinct" does not mean that she desired or was supposedly "guided" by her concept to participate in her death willingly. The suggestion that she could have anticipated her "collusion" with history also implies that she is somehow to blame for her death by not being clairvoyantly prepared for it. Etkind reinforces—with labels such as "destitute" and "lonely"—Spielrein's image as *The Ever-Patient* and suppresses her actual voice and experience as a woman and mother in the midst of war.[119] Most suspiciously, she is given credit for her work on the "death instinct" when being accused of literally wishing to die, but she is not credited for the concept in academic contexts, where it was—and still is—credited to Freud.

In *Bloodlands: Europe Between Hitler and Stalin*, Timothy Snyder reminds us: "Jewish women suffered in particular ways. Despite regulations against 'racial defilement,' some Germans quickly developed a taste for rape as prelude to murder."[120] These atrocities are noted to challenge the questions that scholars have repeatedly asked of Spielrein, notably whether or not she wanted, was sacrificing to, or was guided by an image of Death at the time of her and her daughters' murder. Spielrein's limited publishing during her later years has also been questioned, though one wonders if such a position in the middle of communism and Nazism helped to contribute to the relative cessation of her writing, when to do so would have put her life in jeopardy, which, of course, would be evidence that she was *not* in fact suicidal.

Nevertheless, Jungian analyst Thomas Kirsch argues in his article "Two Pieces on the Movie: *A Dangerous Method*": "At the end of her life [Spielrein] was a broken woman, hunched over, and appearing as if she were an old woman. . . . To what extent she had lived out Thanatos, the death instinct, we will never know."[121] While there is legend that Spielrein actually died accosting and berating the Nazis, Kirsch mimics the constructed narrative of Spielrein: that she, by being murdered, was living out a "death instinct," which wholly ignores the sexual and metaphorical connotations of the term that *she originated,* as have been briefly discussed. In addition, given that Spielrein was also one of the first, if not *the* first, psychoanalyst to focus extensively and exclusively on children, there is no reason to assume Spielrein did not die actively protecting her daughters. Regardless, Kirsch's insensitive and irresponsible portrayal of her seems overwhelmingly due to her gender.

Strictly speaking, the description of Spielrein as "hunched over" is also mere speculation (and again, highly insensitive to the circumstance), as is the idea that she was "broken," unless Kirsch is implying that she never recovered from her affair, attempting to fix her yet again in the role of Jung's patient and mistress at a time when she was fifty-seven years old and a mother of two. The fact that her age is under scrutiny, described as "appearing old," is a subtle attack and devaluation of her agency as an adult woman; how should she have appeared during her city's occupation? Kirsch thus reduces her solely to her death, or to her "death instinct," and thereby interprets every facet of her life through the lens of death.

Brian Skea also perpetuates the image of Spielrein as self-destructive: "There is obvious truth in [the] depiction of Spielrein as self-sacrificing, if not self-destructive, from her adolescent descent into near-psychosis . . . her impulsive marriage to a man she barely knew, to her tragic death at the hands of the Nazis."[122] Is there obvious truth in this depiction? To blame Spielrein's descent into "near-psychosis" on a self-sacrificing tendency is to dismiss the actual cause of her descent, namely the death of her younger sister Emily. Additionally, she is considered here from the vantage point of adolescence, which in turn entirely stigmatizes the body of personal and professional work completed subsequent to her discharge from the clinic. The cause of her death then arbitrarily resurfaces as being part of a lifelong destructive tendency, akin to self-inflicted participation, while the primary perpetrators of the Holocaust—the Nazis—remain unchallenged.

Casually, Skea (above) lists her marriage alongside her murder, as if to equate the two in terms of "impulsive" behavior. While too little is known about Spielrein's husband to make such assumptions about their marriage; to list her marriage in the same category as her death is to, again, dismiss the thirty years in between the two events, primarily her own maturation as a woman, a mother, and a scholar. There is simply too little known about Spielrein's personal life at the time of her murder to make such stigmatizing claims. One wonders, though, if she spent the last few years of her life as she spent her previous years: as a committed, passionate, and intelligent woman in search of mythic and psychological meaning.

Author and Jungian analyst Gottfried Heuer, in his review (2012) of the film *A Dangerous Method*, proclaims that Spielrein's psychological state was "stuck" in a form of male violence that "ultimately murdered her," asserting that Spielrein, on some level, was responsible for her own death.[123] Heuer also blames Jung's behavior in the affair on Spielrein: "We might easily imagine that Spielrein (un)consciously invited her analyst to abuse her."[124] While Heuer includes Jung in this list of male violence, he ignores the fact that Spielrein was the one to assert her agency to exit the relationship, "so that I do not have to suffer because of others . . . I hope with all my heart that my friend [Jung] deeply respects me and loves me and that he may realize, just like I do, that we could be dangerous for each other."[125] Spielrein left Jung precisely because she recognized her own suffering and did not wish to remain "stuck" in a dangerous relationship, even though it was incredibly difficult for her to make this decision. Additionally, while Heuer assumes that her relationship with her husband was violent, it has been described via Nina Scheftel as extremely caring and enduring after their reconciliation in the 1920s, especially when Spielrein cared for him during his fatal illness.[126]

In Heuer's characterization of Spielrein, he writes that her psychology asked for abuse ("invited it"), on an unconscious level, which is tantamount to suggesting that she *wanted it*. He thus glosses over the reality of the cultural normalization of violence against women—or the normalization of violence in general—and frees the perpetrators from blame, when it may have been they who were "stuck" in a pattern of violence. That being said, having an unconscious desire still does not excuse the external actions of others, nor does Spielrein's personal love life have anything to do with the Holocaust. In short, Spielrein's psychology did not kill her; Nazis killed her. By constructing Spielrein's narrative as *The Ever-Patient*, "stuck" in a form of pathology (or "sacrifice"), Heuer disregards the thirty-year interim between her intimate relationship with Jung and her death, thus confining her role in history solely to her encounters with men.[127]

> Forces beyond your control can take away everything you possess except one thing, your freedom to choose how you will respond to the situation. You cannot control what happens to you in life, but you can control what you will feel and do about what happens to you.
>
> —Harold Kushner, Man's Search for Meaning

I will not try to unpack the complex particularities of communism and Nazism here because their scope far exceeds this book's primary issue.[128] However, a short pause is necessary to examine the conditions Spielrein may have been under at the time of her death, considering that she has been charged with both lacking the understanding and "inviting" her own murder. As iterated by Theodore S. Hamerow in *Why We Watched: Europe, America, and the Holocaust*: "[We] were inclined to view reports of the Holocaust with suspicion. Those reports seemed no more credible than the horror stories that opposing sides had been hurling at each other for almost thirty years."[129] Violence and murder were understood, to be sure, as a part of war, but as Hamerow underscores: "Systematic genocide? That was hard to believe."[130]

According to *The Black Book: The Ruthless Murder of Jews by German-Fascist Invaders*, only one week prior to the massacre, Rostov citizens had been told that the German soldiers were there to protect them and "guard their safety."[131] Terribly, on August 11, 1942, "Jews were directed to gather in the indicated points," and were then "ordered to strip. Their belongings were set off to the side. They were shot in the Zmiev Ravine (Snake Ravine) and immediately covered with clay. Small children were thrown live into the pits. Some of the Jews were killed in the gassing truck."[132] Many of the Rostov citizens trusted that they were safe to remain in town, even if under German order. Those who did not believe they were safe found it especially difficult to successfully vacate, which must also be assumed for Spielrein.

What seemingly began in the 1920s with Adolf Hitler's determination to reinstate German national pride ended in mass genocide. On the Russian front, what started as a socialist proletariat movement of the oppressed ended in purges, executions, and a search for ultimate control and power over the people. These are the circumstances that Spielrein is being challenged to have understood and psychologically desired. This, rather than a love triangle, was the situation Sabina Spielrein was *between*.

The construction of Spielrein's narrative is perhaps a Rorschach test for all scholarship, including mine. I have attempted in this chapter to question the existing narrative of Spielrein as a "hysterical" and "broken" woman who invited her own murder and posit that such characterizations demean and degrade her character and her body of work. In the following chapters, a new narrative around Spielrein will be constructed, utilizing her own words, while examining her treatment, diaries, letters, and scholarship in closer detail. Also examined is the continued suppression of her voice from history and to that end, in the following chapter, the narrative of Ovid's "Echo and Narcissus," where the nymph Echo is cursed with silence, aids in the interpretation of Sabina Spielrein.

2

Trauma, Transference, and Suppression

Sabina Spielrein and the Myth of Echo (and Narcissus)

There is a voice that doesn't use words. Listen.

—Rumi

Introduction

Because I am reclassifying the "affair" between Spielrein and Jung as a destructive transgression rather than a romance, a brief examination of transference—a patient's feelings for his or her therapist—is necessary. Freud "discovered" transference, though his definition strictly referred to a female patient's feelings for her male analyst: "Essentially, one might say, that the cure is effected [*sic*] by love. In fact, transference provides the most cogent, indeed, the only unassailable proof that neuroses are determined by the individual's love life."[1] While Freud defined transference by equating a "cure" with "love," nowhere does he recommend physical or romantic entanglement as necessary to the process.

Still, scholars have used Freud's "love cure" to describe the affair between Spielrein and Jung, as Alexander Etkind reflects on their relationship: "So it was stated: a cure is effected through love."[2] However, though often ignored, Freud did not agree with their involvement and clearly encouraged Jung to maintain professionalism, as will be demonstrated. Indeed, the term *transference* is not actually an apt description of the affair, since it far exceeded the symbolic realm of feelings into physically and psychologically disruptive realities.

Therefore, while her healing was clearly affected by therapy, the fact that their subsequent affair has been touted in scholarship as a romance, or a "love cure," remains under scrutiny in this chapter.

In *Alchemy*, psychologist Marie-Louise von Franz situates therapy within the imagery of alchemy and, in particular, with images of physical union.[3] In its chemical aspect, alchemy refers to the process of creating gold out of base metal, but in its philosophical aspect, alchemy represents attaining spiritual enlightenment and wisdom (gold) out of the mire of one's life experiences. Alchemy is often depicted in images of a life/death/life cycle through male and female eroticism, signifying the path to unifying so-called oppositional aspects of one's psyche. However, Jung specifically related alchemy to transference to the degree that the primary images of physical union are still considered "symbolically expressed" through the therapist-patient relationship: "This bond is often of such intensity that we could almost speak of a 'combination.' When two chemical substances [therapist and patient] combine, both are altered. This is precisely what happens in the transference."[4]

While alchemy may be understood symbolically, there exists a danger in literalizing such erotic imagery, meaning sexual union, especially in the therapeutic setting. As von Franz warns: "Something wants to come up from the unconscious, but there is a short circuit and it appears as a sexual urge, because there is some sort of difficulty in getting on further. . . . Delay."[5] Creative energy can often be misinterpreted as sexual energy, which is not necessarily problematic, unless within the bounds of therapy where trust has been cultivated, payment accepted, and authority exerted. Von Franz is not puritanical in her methodology and she goes on to say that individuals are perfectly free to carry on an affair if both are also free to consent to do so. Yet it is debatable whether or not it is possible (if one is "free") to give consent in a therapeutic setting where financial, psychological, and emotional dynamics of power are clearly upheld.

Indeed, while the relationship between Jung and Spielrein eventually grew into a collegial one, it is generally accepted that a physical affair lasted for the duration of her outpatient treatment (1905–09), and possibly began during her institutionalization.[6] By normalizing their physical relationship in therapy as part of "transference," rather than as a violation of responsibility, the ethical and emotional ramifications that actually occurred have been suppressed. Such a sexualized notion of therapy, assumed into a modern conception of a "love cure," contradicts the fact that such instances are not isolated in the past; the idealization of this affair may in fact contribute to the perpetuation—or at least the tolerance—of similar abuse.

Through a few of Spielrein's letters to Freud, we will investigate the psychosocial effects of the affair on her own life as well as question the classification of their affair as a "romance" in scholarship, which I argue is possible only by dismissing Spielrein's own reflection on the experience. For simplification, the chapter consists of two parts; in Part I, the concept of female suppression is extended beyond Spielrein and interpreted through Ovid's mythic narrative, "Echo and Narcissus." In Part II, Spielrein's treatment and relationship with Jung are explored vis-à-vis subsequent re-categorization of the affair. To clarify, Echo is utilized here as a "meta" narrative for Spielrein and the suppression of female expression and speech; hence, I will not be attempting a line-by-line or a direct comparison of Echo with Spielrein's life or work. Additionally, the myth functions as an origin story of female exclusion writ large; it lends itself to an archetypal and cultural understanding of the suppression of Spielrein.

Part I: Echo and Narcissus

> Myth is not fiction: it consists of facts that are continually repeated and can be observed over and over again.
>
> —CG Jung, *Answer to Job*

A Note on Translation

As Susan Sellers writes in her introduction to *The Hélène Cixous Reader*: "No translation is ever faithful, since the translating language will inevitably erase, add to or alter the meanings of the original. . . . The translator is forced to obliterate, invent, distort, producing a version of the original."[7] This aptly applies to Spielrein's work, originally written in German (or French or Russian) as well as to the many translations of Ovid's "Echo and Narcissus," originally written in Latin. There is no real way around it.

Why Myth?

In *Narcissus Transformed: The Textual Subject, in Psychoanalysis* and *Literature,* Gray Kochhar-Lindgren defines myth as "a story that renews itself through interpretation."[8] She then employs Kant's understanding of the mythic aspect of the imagination, meaning "[the] blind but indispensible function of the soul."[9] Mythic texts bring images and experiences of the human condition into a tangible and understandable medium: narrative, wonderfully summed up by Laurence Coupe in his slim but informative *Myth*:

> "Mythology"—the body of inherited myths in any culture—is an important element of literature, and that literature is a means of extending mythology. That is, literary works may be regarded as "mythopoeic," tending to create or re-create certain narratives that human beings take to be crucial to their understanding [and experience] of their world.[10]

Regarding the practice of hermeneutics, or the practice of interpreting narrative, Richard Palmer lends his definition in *Hermeneutics*: "[It is] an interpretation of a particular text or collection of signs susceptible of being considered as a 'text' . . . [such as] symbols in a dream or even the myths and symbols of society or literature."[11] Within this definition of myth, "literature" and "text" can be extrapolated to include Spielrein's history, diaries, letters, clinical notes, and those mythic texts that extend beyond religion, such as Ovid's "Echo and Narcissus." This particular myth allows appropriation and postmodern recreation outside of any set dogma or doctrine. As Coupe says of postmodern literary critique, "[It is] to blur the distinction between history and myth," and works to destabilize existing constraints, which here includes the concept and practice of female suppression.[12]

To give a brief overview of popular practice of hermeneutics, let's turn to Palmer one last time: "There are two very different syndromes of hermeneutics in modern times: one, represented by Bultmann's demythologizing, deals lovingly with the symbol in an effort to recover a meaning hidden in it; the other [i.e., hermeneutics of suspicion in Marx, Nietzsche, and Freud] seeks to destroy the symbol as the representative of a false reality. It destroys masks and illusions in a relentlessly rational effort at 'demystification.' "[13] There is perhaps a hermeneutical reconciliation to be found in "Echo and Narcissus," by interpreting what may be *one possible* "hidden meaning" (understanding) of the myth while destroying, or slightly dismantling, the literalization of this myth when enacted upon culture as the suppression of Echo, or a gendered reality of female exclusivity affecting women like Spielrein.

When speaking of the place of a woman in narrative structure, Aristotle stated in *Poetics*: "Even a woman may be good, and also a slave; though the woman may be said to be an inferior being, and the slave quite worthless."[14] The influence and reach of this sentiment on women's representation needs a bit of unpacking; Celeste Schenck in *Life/Lines: Theorizing Women's Autobiography* concludes that *Poetics* is the text "which made taxonomy [classification] the very praxis of poetics, system its very theory," and as a result, "Mixed, unclassifiable, blurred . . . genres, like impure, anomalous, or monstrous genders, have traditionally offered up problems" to academic canonization.[15] Since Aristotle was expounding on preexisting theater and creating what has become, for all intents and purposes, the modern guidebook for successful narrative structure, one might say that a hierarchy of gender has rested, even unconsciously, behind subsequent creations of narrative. Such a gender bias appears inseparable from narrative's mythic manifestations since even the current social climate (especially in film, both on screen and behind the scenes) can still feel ramifications of this exclusion.[16]

"Echo and Narcissus" is employed, then, as noted by Wendy Doniger, "because myths are at hand, available . . . and using them is easier than creating from scratch, and because they are intrinsically charismatic."[17] We must bring women's voices as they appear in myth into the current age: "Let us now consider, among the many competing voices in multi-vocal myths, the voices of women, regarding them, from the standpoint of cultural morphologies [the structure and study of narrative], as a social group whose most basic shared interests span cultures."[18] The primary themes I want to explore in "Echo and Narcissus" focus on Echo's violation (curse) of speech as well as on her autonomy in a myth that has primarily been interpreted through the male character's (Narcissus) perspective.

But first, we must confront an inherent obstacle within mythology: Simone de Beauvoir, in *The Second Sex*, argues that there is a particular myth of Woman, and that this "Myth of the Woman" functions in mythology as an inferior and subjugated narrative due to the fact that myths were written predominately by men.[19] Beauvoir asserts that myths are actually harmful to women because they describe them in set categories: seductress, mother, lover, sister, wife, or intellect, rather than as whole human beings. In this way, she contends that women in myths have become "male deficient" characters rather than autonomous Subjects: "The more women assert themselves as human beings, the more the marvelous quality of Other dies in them. . . . They have neither religion nor poetry that belongs to them alone."[20]

While mythic figures are, at times, aspects of an individual (i.e., archetypal) and not intentionally designed to represent the whole range of human capability, female figures may still be included and interpreted, or reinterpreted as the case may be, as figures of depth. Clearly, feminist critique has progressed from Beauvoir's text, not through a rejection of myth, but through reclamation of woman-as-subject within myth. If women are not seen as a subject, it is not because myths do not have female subjects, but because they have not been interpreted as such.

Similarly addressing the fact that the majority of mythic texts were not written by women, Doniger affirms, rather succinctly: "There are women's voices in men's texts," which is to say quite simply that female experiences can still be and should be recovered from history and literature.[21] The task of selective epistemology (from the Greek *episteme,* meaning "knowledge"), then, is to more fully interrogate the dismissal of women's voices like Spielrein's, retrieve those voices, and integrate found knowledge. Hélène Cixous and Catherine Clément, in *The Newly Born Woman*, elucidate this problem of selective knowledge succinctly: "Somewhere every culture has an imaginary zone for what it excludes, and it is that zone we must try to remember *today*."[22] This "zone" seems to act as the exclusion of women's expression and experience (narrative), though it is not just a matter of so-called women's stories—which is to acknowledge that there is no such thing as a universal woman's story—so much as it is about a more inclusive *human* story.

In reference to utilizing the myth of Echo as a feminist reclamation narrative, theologian George Stroup, in "Between Echo and Narcissus: The Role of the Bible in Feminist Theology," outlines:

> To some extent, the two figures of Echo and Narcissus represent the task and the problem which confront feminist theology. Above all else, feminist theologians [and, by extension, feminist mythologists] . . . are determined to liberate Echo from her bondage and her curse. No doubt some feminist[s] . . . find it appropriate that Echo is female, for she represents the history of the daughters of Eve—condemned to speak only when spoken to, never allowed to initiate ideas or conversation, banished to the wilderness, not a voice in her own right (and hence not really a person) but only a reprise. [One tries to] liberate Echo and all her sisters and daughters, to return to them the power of speech, to demand that the world hear their voice and come to terms with their experience of the world.[23]

While Stroup's article relates Echo to male domination within the Judeo-Christian traditions, and even as Stroup repeatedly condescends to the "feminist" task, his categorization is the closest to our use of hermeneutics here, since the myth is extended beyond the imaginal or pathological and into the realm of gender equity. In relation to Spielrein, the task becomes to view her not simply as a stigma (hysteric), but as a woman with voice and vision, even and in fact because her work has been suppressed in history. Because of her suppression, it becomes critical to examine in what ways her body and voice may have been exploited, misinterpreted, or rejected, and to note how or if these patterns continue in scholarship today, as we have already begun to see.

Similarly, Echo is forced to the periphery of her own story; in the myth, Narcissus mistakes his image for an objective reality, while Echo, suppressed in her ability to speak, recognizes immediately an other in her desire to communicate, but is ultimately excluded. Hence, there is a threefold "feminist" program for reclaiming female agency, inspired by theologian Rosemary Radford Ruether: "Naming androcentrism (phallocentricity), disclos[ing] the history of women [by] interpret[ing] narratives from that particular perspective, and [the] reconstruction of traditional narrative through an inclusive lens."[24] These steps are termed "feminist liberation theology," though such a framework applies to fields beyond theology, given that many traditions and histories are susceptible to a phallocentric past.

Therefore, I believe *feminist liberation mythology* may be a more precise description of the methodology applied to Ovid's text in this chapter as well as to the reading and interpretation of Spielrein's history, where this approach becomes an attempt at liberating a voice that has existed in depth psychology, but has often been excluded from the field's reflection. Cautiously, Stroup also speaks to the necessity of a hermeneutics of suspicion within feminist critique, challenging the essentializing notion that there is a norm of female experience, which is duly noted. Since I am specifically relating female experience through the suppression of Spielrein (and, to a lesser degree, of Echo), the challenge stands.

Relatedly, feminist theologian Elisabeth Schüssler Fiorenza, in *But She Said: Feminist Practices of Biblical Interpretation*, concurs: "A *hermeneutics of suspicion* [explores] the liberating or oppressive values and visions inscribed in the text by identifying the androcentric patriarchal character and dynamics of the text and its interpretations . . . it seeks to investigate *how* and *why* the text constructs the story."[25] Such interpretation is meant to take into account and question any institutional or systematic tactics of exclusion. In short, since Spielrein's suppression is being examined, the figure of Echo represents a possible mythic (archetypal) *how* and the concept of androcentricism represents a psychosocial *why*.

What we want is to promote women's full humanity: to reconstruct a narrative that speaks more fully to the female experience *as well as* (not replacing) the androcentric perspective that nevertheless dominates much of the mainstream. This means that whatever does not promote the full humanity of women does not reflect the existing and "authentic nature of things."[26] Obviously, there is no one mode of feminist interpretation, and defining the term is often unclear and muddled with assumptions of sexuality, biology, and identity. Still, by simply creating a means of interpretation that seeks to emphasize what has been systematically de-emphasized, or worse, pathologized, is perhaps an acceptable way into the fray, as Doty underscores: "Feminist archetypal criticisms are overcoming some of the more egregiously patriarchal aspects of earlier archetypalism," the latter being related far too frequently with outdated gender stereotypes.[27]

The Myth: A Summary of "Echo and Narcissus"

> If some fine day it suddenly came out that the logocentric plan had always, inadmissibly, been to create a foundation for (to found and fund) phallocentrism, to guarantee the masculine order a rationale equal to history itself. . . . So all the history, all the stories would be there to retell differently; the future would be incalculable.
>
> —Hèléne Cixous

The Roman poet Ovid (43 BC–AD 17) wrote the Latin epic *Metamorphoses* (*Metamorphoseon Libri*, or books of transformation) in AD 8 and based his text on the mythic tales of the Greco-Roman pantheon. Interestingly, the popular myth "Echo and Narcissus" does not actually begin with either of the titular characters. For Narcissus, it begins with a sea nymph Liriope, whose future child has been prophesied to die if "he ever knows himself."[28] Liriope is then raped by the sea god Cephisus, who viewed her "and had his way" with her, and she later bore Narcissus.[29]

Echo's story, on the other hand, begins with a curse from the goddess Juno, the Roman equivalent of Greek goddess Hera, because: "Time after time, when Juno might have caught / her Jove [Roman Zeus, ruler of Olympus] philandering on the mountaintops / with young nymphs, Echo, cunningly, would stop the goddess on her path."[30] Juno, notoriously jealous of her husband's extramarital affairs, punished Echo by limiting her ability to speak when she is discovered to be distracting Juno during Jove's liaisons. According to Christine Downing in *The Goddess: Mythological Images of the Feminine*, Juno is the embodiment of female subjugation to patriarchy, as she is solely "viewed by men," and as such is transfigured into an archetypal image of repressed sexuality and "un-fulfillment" in her adoption of the role of jealous wife.[33]

While Downing then attempts to reclaim and revision her within a feminist framework, this first image of Juno lends itself to an understanding of her anger against Echo, since the latter is blamed for Jove's actions. Downing states that Juno is so "defined" by her role that "her anger is played out against women" and inverted against herself, rather than against Jove.[32] Following that image, Echo may be interpreted as a manifestation of Juno's inability to communicate her own unhappiness. She is then violated and cursed to perpetuate female suppression in her inability to initiate conversation and in her rejection by male-centric society, reflected in and embodied by Narcissus.

Echo's character in *Bulfinch's Mythology* (1855) is viewed as "failing" in personality *already* (before Juno) due to the fact that she loved to speak: "She was fond of talking, and whether in chat or argument, would have the last word."[33] In this depiction of Echo, her curse is much more clearly related to her previous power and possession of speech: "You shall forfeit the use of that tongue with which you have cheated me, except for that one purpose you are so fond of—reply."[34] In her grief, Echo retreats to the forest, and spies Narcissus, a handsome youth with whom she wants to speak: "O how she longed to address him . . . and win him to converse! But it was not in her power."[35] Here, Bulfinch deemphasizes Echo's desire as sexual, but instead underscores her desire to communicate.

Since she cannot initiate speech, when a frightened Narcissus declares upon their meeting: "I would rather die than you should have me," Echo can only reply, "Have me."[36] While the power dynamics of speech as related to gender will be discussed shortly, it is important to note the fact that Echo's words still carry subjective meaning different from those spoken to her. Still, in her attempt to foster communication she is "shunned" by Narcissus and excluded from his reflection, where he "falls in love" with and becomes obsessed and transfixed by his own image to his own self-destructive and mortal peril.[37]

Echo's not being allowed to speak due to her female "nature" begs exploration: "But she cannot begin / to speak: her nature has forbidden this."[38] Susan Griffin in *Woman and Nature* ponders the "nature" of women through history: "[Man] says that woman speaks with nature. That she hears voices from under the earth. . . . But for him this dialogue is over. . . . He sets himself apart from woman and nature."[39] As Griffin recounts the history of "Woman" in the world's mythology, she asserts that because women have been made synonymous with matter (nature), they have been excluded from the "male" domain of speech and "abstract knowledge."[40] Historically, Griffin claims: "*Our speech is unholy,*" which implies that women's speech has been made synonymous with *unworthy*.[41]

Likewise, Echo is forbidden to relay her thoughts in words and shunned even in her attempt. She is not merely rejected, but shamed in her expression: "So scorned and spurned, she hides within the woods / there she, among the trees, conceals her face / her shame."[42] When scorned and forced to conceal herself, Echo becomes "Other" and the shame acts as paralysis upon her body until she is (fatally) consumed by the suffering of exclusion.

Without the ability to initiate or to be accepted in the speech she was once so "fond" of: "Her form faded with grief, till at last all her flesh shrank away. Her bones were changed into rocks . . . still ready to reply to any one who calls her, and keeps up her old habit of having the last word," though her words are characterized as idle "chatter."[43] Here, her so-called habit of speaking is devalued, perhaps because enjoying the last word implies a certain amount of confidence and agency. Further, Bullfinch's account makes clear the relation between being cursed and being suppressed, for when Echo's previous power (speech) has been taken away, she becomes hardened—turned into rock—in response, though her voice remains ever in search of reception.

Without the ability to initiate speech, Echo becomes an objectified body before her body disappears completely. For example, when Narcissus states: "May I die before you enjoy my body," Echo replies: "Enjoy my body."[44] Mandelbaum translates the original lines: " 'I'd sooner die than say I'm yours!' and Echo answered him 'I'm yours.' "[45] Similarly, in Lombardo's translation, when Narcissus cries: "I'll die before I let you have me," Echo answers: "Have me."[46] In yet another translation, Narcissus states: "I would sooner die before I give you power o'er me," and Echo replies: "I give you power o'er me."[47] Since she is demonized in her fragmented desire, any of Echo's attempts at inclusion are halted and her words, in their actual meaning, fail to find response.

This interplay of exchange is a power dynamic that Narcissus holds and Echo does not. In *This Sex Which Is Not One*, philosopher Luce Irigaray asks:

> Must this multiplicity of female desire and female language be understood as shards, scattered remnants of a violated sexuality? A sexuality denied? . . . The rejection, the exclusion of a female imaginary certainly puts the woman in the position of experiencing herself only fragmentarily, in the little-structured margins of a dominant ideology, as waste, or excess, what is left of a mirror invested by the (masculine) "subject" to reflect himself, to copy himself.[48]

While Irigaray emphasizes rejected sexual desire, her use of mirror imagery applies to the possession of power, whether in body or in speech, that Narcissus—rather than Echo—maintains. Further, her association of fragmentation to the female experience directly relates to Echo's ability to speak in "scattered remnants." Still, while Echo's words may be "shards," they *mean* something entirely different from Narcissus's, so that her speech is not so much repetition as it is an inversion of language that withers upon reception. Echo's words reflect her female experience even if excluded from the dominant narrative, even if she is turned away from the mirror. Instead of being understood on her own terms, she is considered or judged as derivative and her fate defined and confined "to parrot the last few words of the many spoken by / others."[49] Alternatively, perhaps her fate has been to be understood only on another's terms, as the mouthpiece for Narcissus.

If Echo is not repeating language but recreating it, then as Judith Greenberg in "The Echo of Trauma and the Trauma of Echo" suggests, "Echo manifests how she can alter a mode of discourse or narrative patterns" when her perspective is included in the reflection.[50] For example, in the *Hymn to*

Pan, Echo is already known for her ability to transform "song into dirge" and "rejoicing [into] mourning," since her expression actually disrupts the tone of conversation; her words disrupt a male-centric narrative.[51] Of Echo, literary professor John Brenkman asserts: "[Echo] is no longer secondary or derivative since [she] is heard as the voice of another consciousness, another subject or character."[52] She is not an accidental character nor a secondary character, but a second subject in the story.

On the other hand, in *Narcissus Transformed: The Textual Subject in Psychoanalysis and Literature*, Gray Kochhar-Lindgren contradicts: "Echo, the voiced other of the myth, remains unheard and out of sight."[53] However, Echo, as principal a character as Narcissus, does *not* actually remain "out of sight" of the text, which indicates that she instead remains out of sight only to Kochhar-Lindgren. She then asks: "Cannot we employ Echo as a representative for the other that, by setting the dialectic of symbolization in motion, frees Narcissus from the mesmerizing gaze of Thanatos [Death] disguised as desire?"[54] The problem with turning Echo into a "representative" (an Other) for Narcissus is that it positions Echo as a secondary and submissive character instead of a figure with her own parallel narrative. Moreover, Echo here becomes an idealized image of feminine salvation, in that if Echo "frees" Narcissus, which she does not do, she aids in his self-realization instead of her own.

In Jerrine Greer's doctoral work, *From Echo to Embodied Voice as Song of the Soul: Finding Voice as a Midlife Woman*, Echo is a figure in her own right because she refuses to become something else in order to be reflected in what Narcissus would consider an "acceptable" female image.[55] In this interpretation, Echo is not only rejected from reflection, but is rejected due to her inability or unwillingness to conform to a specific standard of "femininity." As Hillman warns to analysts in *Myth of Analysis*: "Rather than in danger of becoming a cold mirror, we are in the new danger of becoming image-makers."[56] This idea extends to the image of women, who when excluded from the societal "mirror" are subjected to images being made for them, as filtered through a dominant male reflection. Influenced by Irigaray, Greer then demands: "A new language is needed to convey women's experience."[57] Yet it is not necessarily a new language that is needed, but an inclusion of the words being spoken by those marginalized from their own stories, such as Echo, and by extension, Spielrein.

Alternatively, Greenberg is suspicious of the credit given to Echo's "mimetic inversion of power," noting that so-called "Echo-reading" is an "abdication of a power that feminist critics never possessed and too easily relinquish."[58] However, Echo does in fact possess the ability to *attempt* to foster communication, whether it is accepted or rejected and, before her curse, she was very much in possession of the power of speech. Feminist critique, or "Echo-reading," is then at least a similar attempt to foster discourse.

As Lya Chapman illuminates in her study, *Revisioning Echo: The Mythical Figure of Echo and Her Importance to Clinical Depth Psychology*, Echo is found in multiple narratives, as she is a messenger in Pindar's poetry and her voice travels through caves in the work of Aristophanes.[59] Echo, in all of her narratives it seems, is a figure of communication, without which there remains only, according to Chapman, "psychic death."[60] Rather than a figure of simple appropriation, Echo is similar to prominent feminist figures such as Hélène Cixous and Catherine Clément, who are described as "consistently taking what they need from a body of knowledge which they refuse to recognize as anyone else's 'property' and make it serve their own purposes."[61] Greenberg likewise admits: "Echo repeats the final words of others in order to manufacture her *own* talk."[62] Even under a living curse, there is communication in these aforementioned myths because of Echo.

Poet and mythological scholar Dennis Patrick Slattery, in his article "Narcissus, Echo and Irony's Resonance," defines Echo's speech as a kind of irony that fails to find a response in Narcissus, since her meaning is not synonymous with words that have been established previously.[63] Her suffering occurs then because Narcissus fails to understand her means of communication, meaning he fails to understand *her* and her experience. Slattery considers Echo's grief as a personal *pathos,* meaning a kind of "suffering."[64] The etymology of *pathos* is "a quality which evokes pity or sadness," which is often translated as "passion" or feeling, and Echo, in her limited speech, represents the passion of archetypal suppression.[65] Incidentally, when musing on *pathos* in her diaries, Spielrein reflects: "To those whose thoughts have been born of prolonged suffering, their thoughts are much more important than glory."[66]

On the other hand, in "A Psychoanalytic Interpretation of Ovid's Myth of Narcissus and Echo" (1992), Echo is seen as a pitiful character, a "victimizer" (abuser), and an "indifferent" figure lacking empathy.[67] To the author, Maryanna Hannan, Echo is an "exploiter" because she distracts Juno from Jove's cheating, though we should not forget that Echo was not responsible for Juno's unhappiness nor was she accountable for Jove's cheating. Hannan interprets her "chatterbox" nature as "shrewd" manipulation and as an attempt to control Narcissus.[68] She is categorized as "parasitic" because she forms her speech from preexisting words, while her ability to recreate language is demeaned into only a "twist."[69]

Even Echo's body becoming rock is seen by Hannan as an allusion to her "obdurate" nature worthy of her own shame and concealment.[70] She describes Echo as heartless, "obsessed," and—interestingly—then as a symbol of female "transference."[71] In other words, Hannan equates female patients in therapy, such as Spielrein, with obsessed and manipulative exploiters shrewdly preying on unassuming analysts. Any notion of female violation has been dismissed as Hannan imprints the image of a femme fatale seductress onto Echo, a role often applied to Spielrein.

Offering his clinical interpretation, William Shullenberger, in "Tragedy in Translation: The Lady Echo's Song" (2003), suggests that Echo's body withers because of her inability to be heard and understood, which acts as internal starvation. He posits that because Echo remains "imperceptible" to the status quo, meaning Narcissus's reflection, her body begins to physically disappear into a "bodiless fantasy."[72] However, Echo is viewed by Shullenberger as merely a "feminized narcissism," which is to say a feminine version of Narcissus, or a deviation from the accepted norm, instead of as her own individualized entity.[73] Of course, in Freud's *On Narcissism*, where narcissism begins in relation to psychodynamics, women are not even seen as capable of true communication or connection with an other, as they "love only themselves with an intensity comparable to that of the man's love for them."[74] For Freud, women represented only an aspect of a central male subject, an idea seemingly perpetuated in the above interpretation of Echo.

He also implies that Echo turns her anger inward as a sort of a destructive solipsism, though Phyllis Chesler, in *Women and Madness*, relays that women have been conditioned to internalize anger as a result of not having the freedom to act out anger in public, as it is seen as a masculine attribute.[75] As Cixous says of such social conditioning in "Laugh of the Medusa": "Insidiously, violently, women [are led] to be their own enemies, to mobilize their immense strength against themselves, to be the executants of their virile needs. They have made for women an antinarcissism! . . . They have constructed the infamous logic of antilove."[76]

Similarly, in Patricia Berry's *Echo's Subtle Body: Contributions to an Archetypal Psychology*, Echo is not seen as a figure in her own right: "If anyone has an identity, Narcissus has it."[77] Berry asserts that Echo has a "poor sense of identity . . . lacks an identity . . . [and] never originates."[78] On the contrary, it is known from the myth that Echo is a well-defined chatterbox before her curse and that she continues to communicate her desire well past her ability to do so. She does not originate speech, but transforms the meaning of given words, even if that meaning is not subsequently understood or accepted. Lacking the ability to express one's identity is not synonymous with lacking an identity, as she is still able to originate *thought*. Her body's dissipation would seem almost a natural response to an external world that views her as a being so lacking.

Echo and Abuse

> If I keep your images and you refuse to give me back mine, your self . . . is but a prison. Love of you but a paralysis.
>
> —Luce Irigaray, *Marine Lover of Friedrich Nietzsche*

Much of Echo's demonization and infantilization in scholarship mimics the character assassination often imposed on the narratives of female survivors of violence, which are frequently subjected to mass scrutiny, mined for credibility, or doubted entirely. Ultimately, Echo points beyond the myth itself, representing a reclamation to what is lost within rejected female narratives, like Spielrein's, which will be thoroughly explored shortly in Part II. Echo is not a figure that fails to be loved by Narcissus, but one that fails to find in him a response, a dialogue, and an "acknowledgement of another"—note "another" *not* an "Other."[79] If we grant Echo autonomy from Narcissus in the narrative, she is then granted her own parallel story.

In Latin, Echo is described as "*garrula non alium*," or "talkative, unlike another," meaning the power of speech was hers until it was violated.[80] This concept of violation is crucial when further considering that Echo is present in another well-known narrative, featured as a lover of Pan, the virile nature faun/god of classical mythology. As described in Longus's second-century *Daphnis and Chlöe*, Pan pursues Echo, and when she denies his sexual advances, he tears her limb from limb "to pieces" and in her dismemberment she becomes a memory within the earth and rock.[81]

Luce Irigaray speaks of female dismemberment in relation to a woman's body being "owned" and subjugated in pieces, and therefore rarely considered as a whole: "My whole body is divided up into neatly ruled sections. Each of them allotted to one private owner or another. Which belongs to whom?—shrieks such and such a part. And no one replied, for each man claimed the whole."[82] Whether or not Irigaray meant to evoke Echo, the latter's dual relationship to the demonization of female expression is emphasized: when assertive, Echo is denied by Narcissus and shamed; when resistant, she is dismembered and dominated by Pan.

This myth of Echo with Pan is an early and archetypal degradation of abuse being transformed into and perpetuated as a tale of so-called lovers. Michael Snediker, in "In the Echo Chamber" (2012), concurs: "The shape of duress—refracted in Echo, reflection—fails if held to the narrative of romantic resolution," though he still goes on to stigmatize her in the image of a "broken" woman.[83] To Chapman, Echo's dismemberment is poetically transformed into an image of "singing limbs," because Echo's voice lingers in the air and in the earth after fleeing from Pan.[84] Contrarily, this image of Echo's "singing limbs," a wailing of sorts, calls to mind the poet Stevie Smith's line, "Not waving but Drowning," wherein she writes that flailing out at sea is seen as waving, though the person in the poem is actually drowning.[85] Similarly, Echo's "singing" after her dismemberment may also be interpreted as a kind of lingering cry rather than as a joyful song—she has, after all, been said to turn song into dirge.

Berry maintains: "Echo's beauty is equally a suffering and a certain passivity."[86] Gendered connotations arise in describing qualities of suffering and passivity as "beautiful" when applied to a female figure, especially in light of violation, as it reinforces stereotypical characteristics associated with so-called femininity. As has been said, Echo does not solely represent a figure of "passivity" but also one of active attempt to communicate (Narcissus) as well as active resistance (Pan). Still, for Berry, Echo is a character that "no one wants to be."[87] Even her desire to speak is turned into pathology in Paul Johnston's doctoral work on the figure of Echo, *Echo: An Aspect of the Archetypal Dependent Personality,* where he fashions her into an emblem of "dependent personality disorder."[88] However, it is Echo who understands the difference between real and reflection and it is she who, when assertive, is either cursed or torn apart.

In "Echo in the Darkness" (2005), scholar Dean Davis relates the plight of Echo to female patients in analysis who have fallen into a social construction of *perceived* passivity, rather than actual passivity, when women's words fall upon the deaf ears of analysts.[89] Unsurprisingly, during a web search on a psychological database, he states that more than 2,200 hits resulted in the search for "narcissus not echo" but only *one* hit returned on the search for "echoism," or Echo "without" Narcissus.[90] This seems like the successful severing from and subordination of a central figure in her own mythic narrative.

In *Marine Lover of Friedrich Nietzsche,* Irigaray again evokes, intentionally or unintentionally, a more holistic interpretation of Echo: "I am no longer the lining to your coat, your—faithful—understudy. Voicing your joys and sorrows, your fears and resentments. . . . Almost nothing to let me rediscover my own becoming beyond your sufferings. All that was left—barely—was a breath, a hint of air and blood."[91] If Echo is not seen as an independent personality, and indeed one who has suffered violation, it is because she is not being seen as a subject. If she is not viewed as a subject in her own right, Beauvoir's assertion that myths are harmful because female figures represent male-deficient "Others" holds true. Echo, if interpreted only in relation to Narcissus, becomes an understudy, understood as repeating only his joys and sorrows instead of her own. In this view, she dissipates into empty air and is not heard as a voice in search of dialogue.

Similarly, Sabina Spielrein has been severed from her place in the narrative of depth psychology, seen primarily as an understudy, or worse—mistress, to Jung. Asserting her own experience, she used the language of psychology to speak of sexual, spiritual, and physical transformation within the context of a male-dominated arena though she was continually dismissed and diminished, with little credence given to the actual meaning of her words. Additionally, her experience amidst a destructive affair has since been twisted into a "love cure." Therefore, like Echo, the suppression and dismissal of Spielrein's perspective will now be examined.

Part II: The Connection Between Sabina Spielrein and Suppression

When speaking of the myth of Echo and Narcissus, James Hillman, in "From Mirror to Window: Curing Psychoanalysis of its Narcissism," explains that analysis is in itself narcissistic and begins to hate itself so that clients may break free, though the essay is without reference to Echo in its examination of Narcissus: "Narcissism is now the rage, the universal diagnosis."[92] He also comments on the "self-gratifying" nature of analysis and relates the myth to the "obsession of analysis today, transference."[93] Hillman further elucidates the problematic nature of transference:

> The horned dilemmas of transference, including the analyst's stare into the mirror of his own counter-transference, the feelings of love and hatred, this agony and ecstasy and romantic torture convince the participants what is going on is of intense importance: first, because these phenomena are expected by the theory and provide proof of it, and second, because these phenomena re-enact what analysis once was in its own childhood in Vienna and Zurich, analysis in primary fusion with its origins in Breuer and Freud and Jung, in Dora and Anna and Sabina. In other words, transference is less necessary to the doctor and the patient then it is to analysis by means of which it intensifies its narcissistic idealization, staying in love with itself.[94]

While Hillman discusses the nature of transference, the *problem* of transference in general is again seen through the perspective of the analyst (or from the perspective of Narcissus) while Anna (Breuer), Dora (Freud), and Sabina (Jung) become the torturous, eroticized, and disembodied objects of analysis. If transference is viewed as "romantic," Spielrein remains tied to her role as a patient serving the narcissistic idealization of analysis. Also, in order to "stay in love with itself," Hillman's idea of analysis excludes the larger psychosocial issues concerning abuses of power, overt demonstrations of authority, and the stigmatization of expressed female sexuality. That is to say, it is the women who become the mistresses, temptresses, or femmes fatales rather than the analysts. Hillman's remark further implies that if therapy remains stuck in this narrative, female patients will continue to be the casualties of such "love." Neither that transference is "necessary" because it is demanded by therapy itself nor that it is expected due to its history seems justification for its current perpetuation of objectification.

Sabina Spielrein: Adolescence and Institutionalization

In his article "Sabina Spielrein: Out from the Shadow of Jung and Freud," Brian Skea notes the "sado-masochistic relationship" Spielrein had with her father that occurred when she was young, though it could be argued that Spielrein was not capable of consenting to such a "relationship" with her father as a child, nor was she capable of participating in the role of a "masochist."[95] As Kerr says of a patient with "identical" symptoms to Spielrein in *A Most Dangerous Method*: "Her father loved her, sexually [and] it struck her as a child that he, besides other evidence of tenderness, slapped her in a peculiar way . . . and indeed only in the absence of her mother."[96] In a seeming attempt to justify abuse, Kerr states: "It was rather commonplace observation that some men derived sexual pleasure from delivering blows to the 'nates' and furthermore that some men—also some women—derived pleasure from receiving them."[97] That it was normalized does not make the suggestion that Spielrein's father received sexual pleasure from hitting her any less incestuous or abusive.

Also, if Spielrein subsequently became emotionally confused concerning sexuality, as it is accepted that she did since she could not stand to see her father during in-treatment,[98] it would again not be appropriate to then define the relationship as "commonplace." Kerr is hesitant to define Spielrein's relationship with her father as abuse because, he notes somewhat strikingly, it did not deter her from her academic pursuits nor did it in any way "interfere" with her intelligence.[99] One wonders how much "interference" is allowed in life before such behavior can be defined as abuse. Kerr's diminishing of her childhood trauma only serves to normalize and justify her father's behavior and demeans her subsequent reaction to it.

In Jung's clinical notes, he relates another "commonplace" experience: "He [her father] has hit [her] and she has had to kiss his hand in return."[100] Again, merely because this action was commonplace, it in no way excuses the harrowing psychological effects of those exposed to it. Still, Kerr tries to maintain that "there is no evidence" of sexual abuse in Spielrein's childhood;

though when speaking of a patient with near-identical concerns to hers, Jung notes a similarity of the father loving his daughter "sexually" and that Spielrein "became ill chiefly because she had been brutally beaten by her father."[101] Jung writes that her father frequently threatened suicide, and would "tyrannize" the household for days on end.[102] While it is noted that she then made threats of suicide while institutionalized, undoubtedly mimicking the behavior she had grown up with, such threats stopped after contact with her father ceased per Spielrein's wishes. It should be reminded that Spielrein's symptoms also coincided with the death of her sister whom she had loved "more than anything in the world."[103]

However, Spielrein is described as in need of institutionalization because of her *reaction* to her father's abuse, which began at age four, rather than because of the abuse itself, due to her complex feelings of disgust at the "sight of humiliation."[104] In adolescence, she became withdrawn and quick to anger, though her symptoms (such as nervous tics) were attributed to a case of general hysteria. Yet Jung further writes of Spielrein during treatment: "many piano lessons . . . intellectually very advanced . . . particularly enjoyed natural science . . . wanted to study medicine."[105] In addition, in her article "Transforming At-one-Ment: Spielrein, Jung, Bion" (2004), Janet Sayers observes that Spielrein "helped with word association research at the hospital" and quickly regained a sense of self and academic ambition.[106] After ten months in the Clinic (August 1904 to June 1905), she was deemed cured and continued acting as such.

Scholar Bernard Minder cites in "A Document: Jung to Freud 1905: A Report on Sabina Spielrein" that while Spielrein intermittently suffered from childhood trauma and depression, she was nonetheless "recovered" enough to attend university and acquire an apartment of her own, though she continued as an outpatient for about four more years.[107] While Angela Graf-Nold differentiates between "recovered" and "cured" in her article "The Zurich School of Psychiatry in Theory and Practice: Sabina Spielrein's Treatment at the Burghölzli Clinic in Zurich," I do not; Jung clearly details to Freud that he has "cured" Spielrein from her case of hysteria, though much of modern scholarship has since retroactively rediagnosed her. While the validity of the diagnosis "hysteria" is questioned in chapter 6 in relation to the history of women's forced institutionalization, the entirety of her clinical history can be found—as can full-length versions of the intimate letters—within *Sabina Spielrein: Forgotten Pioneer of Psychoanalysis*. I am choosing not to dwell on the intricacies or details of her treatment, but instead to question how her relationship with Jung may have affected her personal life and how it has been interpreted subsequently in scholarship as a "romance," and almost exclusively from the perspective of Jung. Similarly, I will not repeat the vast majority of biographical facts that have already been well documented in John Kerr's *A Dangerous Method.*

Analysis and "Affair"

> We shall make a new start, rewriting psychology's history in our own way, a modest attempt at psychological hermeneutics . . . because we are not so much writing history as we are writing psychology.
>
> —James Hillman, *The Myth of Analysis*

When considering the validity of upholding Spielrein's affair as a romance, it must be questioned whether or not she, under the authority of a trained professional, was actually capable of consenting to an erotic relationship, given that even she saw it as a perpetuation of life with her father, and noted in a 1909 letter to her mother: "I fell in love with a psychopath [Jung], and is it necessary to explain why? I have never seen my father as normal."[108] Spielrein further says to her mother that she and Jung "acted" at times as caretakers for each other and that Jung's behavior of raging, weeping, and jubilant prostration mimicked her own experience of her parents: "Remember how dear daddy was apologizing to you exactly in the same manner!"[109] Her equation of Jung to her father perhaps belies a subtle allusion to her experience of the affair as a form of continued abuse.

Carotenuto puts forth that Spielrein lost grip of reality and that in her transference: "It is not *as if* the analyst were the father; he *is* the beloved father."[110] Not so; it is evidenced by Spielrein's letter that she clearly grasped the fact that Jung was *not* her father, but that he was *like* her father, and that at times they would become, metaphorically, parental in their interaction with each other. It is also interesting to note that it is not Jung who leads her to such an understanding. Additionally, at the time of this letter, she was not an institutionalized patient, but an outpatient completing her doctoral work, and her reflection on the matter may be understood without the assumption that she has fallen out of line with reality.

Transference

> A warring peace, a sweet sound, a mild evil.
>
> —John Gower

René Major, in her article "Love for Transference and Passion for Signifiers: Between Sabina S. and Anna G.," presents Spielrein's history in light of what Freud considered the "stumbling block of analysis" (transference), or those actions of a woman when she "gives unmistakable clues . . . that she has fallen in love with the doctor who is analyzing her."[111] Immediately, Major uses Freud to emphasize the patient's behavior instead of the analyst's, implying that it was Spielrein's one-sided "clues" that led her into an affair. Incidentally, Freud undermines his own description of the feelings that emerge in therapy: "There can be no doubt that the outbreak of a passionate demand for love is largely the work of resistance."[112] The demand for love is not the same thing as love, nor does it justify Jung's acquiescence to a presumed demand given his authoritative role.

When discussing the affair, Major's language becomes extremely opaque:

> It could be said that Freud, at least in the case of this affair, considers that Transference love consists of the love that eludes love. There would be no end to undoing the folds woven by Freudian paradoxes around this question, which remains central for psychoanalysis, since it so clearly reposes the question of its origins, even of the non-origin of origins, and it implies nothing less than this: that the analytic tie is rooted in such an asocial, atransferential, auto-analytic radicality, that it can both untie any previous tie and come untied itself.[113]

Jargon aside, it is difficult to unpack this paragraph, but since there are pieces in it that are left open to interpretation, it is important to consider the constructed narrative of Spielrein being left in the role of a lovesick *Ever-Patient*. First, to state that transference love is a "love that eludes love" only serves to transform Spielrein's psychological state into an abstract romanticism while it confuses physical desire with professional ethics. We recall that Spielrein and Jung were not actually in the middle of *only* a transference, since they were engaged in a physical affair between doctor and client, the latter of whom suffered the vehemence of her own family as well as from Jung's wife and an academic history that has since viewed her as a scandal. Second, Major concludes that analysis defies all rationality, being so rooted in "radicality," though this excuse is used to justify blurred boundaries, which in turn become tied to and rooted in a philosophical and conceptual "non-origin of origins." If the relationship in analysis can become so easily untied, as Major posits, it may be appropriate to question the efficacy of the knot.

Spielrein's entire life is then characterized only in relation to Jung: "How can Spielrein find the privileged signifier that will support her desire? . . . From the passion that transference left in a state of suffering."[114] Major strips her of any autonomous control over her ability to love another man and insinuates that it was "transference" that left her in a state of suffering, rather than her physical involvement with Jung. In this image, Spielrein is stuck as *The*

Ever-Patient, always in search of a fill-in for Jung, instead of positioned as a woman who rose from such suffering to create a name for herself in academia. Lastly, the assumption that she was in search of a "Signifier" suggests that she is the supporting figure in her own narrative, a woman signified only by a central male figure in her life.

When Carotenuto defends his bringing Spielrein out from the underground, he does so by reassuring his audience that Jung's behavior need not be challenged because Jung cannot be "measured by a common yardstick."[115] A colleague of Jung's apparently concurs: "As trainees, we always knew when Jung was with Toni [Wolff], because his car was parked in front of the house she lived in. . . . You don't understand. *He* lived on a completely *different* level."[116] Jung is subject to a separate set of rules and to a separate set of ethics in order to maintain an idealized image.

Yet a danger arises in such idolatry, when no room is made for alternative perspectives, especially if one of those perspectives is being entirely dismissed, like Spielrein's. As Beauvoir iterates in *The Second Sex*: "Replacing value with authority, choice with drives, psychoanalysis proposes an ersatz morality: the idea of normality."[117] While opinions of Jung or of his prolific work need not change, it is equally irresponsible to completely diminish Spielrein's experience and her work in order to normalize a "transference" affair.

Carotenuto continues to justify the notion that there was a sexual affair during her treatment: "Jung was forced to behave in an abominable way," due to Spielrein's "attitude."[118] Stating that Spielrein forced Jung to behave a certain way immediately places the onus on her, while exculpating him of any blame. It also implies that a woman's "attitude" justifies "forced" and "abominable" behavior, while the specifics of what constituted her "attitude" remain completely and dangerously open to personal interpretation. She is also called "psychotic" because of her feelings toward Jung, which entirely ignores Jung's encouragement or participation in those feelings.[119]

While Johannes Cremerius challenges Carotenuto's view of Spielrein as a "psychotic," he maintains that the affair was her "cure" due to her later success.[120] However, it becomes problematic if her treatment, when considered to involve a physical affair, is viewed as a "cure" instead of as a professional transgression, solely on the grounds that she then became successful. That is to say, abuse appears tied to whether or not a patient becomes successful in later life and leaves one wondering how her treatment would be defined had Spielrein not gone on to find success. Her success after the affair—or the abuse of power, depending on interpretation—is not the same thing as having found success *because* of that experience. Further, as Cifali notes, the affair led to Spielrein's need to renounce the relationship since it caused her " 'soul [to be] torn with wild grief.'"[121] Again, it is possible to view her achieved success ("fruit") as occurring despite, or at least incidental to the affair rather than as resulting from it.

The idea of enacted transference—a love cure—as a form of abuse is not meant as an argumentum ad hominem, but a necessary inclusion of female expression into the reflection of depth psychology in relation to Spielrein's "transference," transparently veiled in the myth of Echo. Peter Rutter, in his article, "Lot's Wife, Sabina Spielrein, and Anita Hill: A Jungian Meditation on Sexual Boundary Abuse and Recovery of Lost Voices," asserts that women in history and myth who challenge patriarchal superiority are often suppressed, while subsequently they are maintained as "conniving, seductive women who use their sexual power to overwhelm the man."[122] He then adds that such rejection of female perspective is linked to "psychological patterns of abuse that persist in our culture today."[123] Building on Spielrein's perspective as a young woman, the next chapter continues to analyze the relationship between her and Jung in light of such stigmatization with the aid of a selection of her early letters to and from Freud and Jung.

3

An Affair Misremembered

Sabina Spielrein and the So-Called Love Cure

I want to be a wife and mother, and not just a plaything.

—Sabina Spielrein

Introduction

Though the exact dates of the affair have been debated, when Spielrein writes to Freud in June 1909, she remembers: "1½ to 2 years ago, a closer erotic relationship between us was not yet discussed."[1] This timeline illuminates a letter that Jung wrote to Freud in 1907 asking for advice on his (cured) patient: "A lady, cured of obsessional neurosis, is making me the object of her sexual fantasies. . . . Should I continue the treatment . . . or should I discharge her?"[2] No definitive action was taken at the time, though in 1908, while still writing to Freud about the "problems" of his patient, he was simultaneously writing to Spielrein about the torrential feelings that a photo he kept of her induced:

> I regret a great deal and regret my weakness and curse fate . . . .Will you forgive me that I am who I am? That I am thereby offending you and forgetting my duty as physician towards you? . . . My misfortune is that I cannot live without the joy of stormy, ever-changing love in my life. . . . Since the last scene I have completely lost my sense of security towards you. . . . Give me at this moment something back of the love and patience and unselfishness that I

> was able to give to you during the time of your illness. Now I am the sick one.[3]

An intimate relationship likely began prior to 1907 but physically intensified during this year and continued until the cessation of Spielrein's outpatient treatment. Obviously *something* happened between them that caused Jung to regret his behavior, admitting clearly that he forgot his "duty" toward her, signifying that he did think himself her physician at the time as he blurs the distinctions between analyst and client in this letter. Jung urgently demands to be given love, and though it remains ambiguous whether his "stormy" passion and "lost" sense of security refer to physical or emotional need, it would seem to indicate both.

In fact, in 1919, Jung said to Spielrein upon reflection of the relationship:

> The love of S. for J. made the latter aware of something he had previously only vaguely suspected, namely a power in the unconscious which shapes one's destiny. . . . The relationship had to be "sublimated," because otherwise it would have led to delusion and madness. . . . Sometimes we must be unworthy to live at all.[4]

This affair was not a simple matter of platonic sophistry, nor was it purely a matter of Spielrein's "transference." Apropos of this observation, James Hillman speaks to such an entanglement in *The Myth of Analysis*: "Transference, can no longer be bound to a prescribed ritual called the analytical method, in a special therapeutic place for a certain pair of persons, one 'ill' and the other 'well.' "[5]

Recollection through Letters

In late 1908, a conflicted Spielrein wrote to her mother: "He has fallen in love with me . . . he starts reproaching himself endlessly for his feelings, for example, that I am something sacred for him . . . 'poetry' again as usual, will I ever in my life forgive him what he had concocted with me?"[6] She further wonders if she should surrender to the affair or commit herself to her career and future desire to be a mother, since she deems the affair ultimately futile. "Poetry" has generally been accepted as a euphemism for sex, though it has also been considered, by Zvi Lothane in particular, along the lines of touching, kissing, embracing, and "swooning," as Spielrein notes in various letters.[7] However, Lothane claims that the affair should not be considered sexual, meaning consummated, due both to his interpretation of "poetry" as well as to the fact that Spielrein refrained from explicit details in letters to her mother, though very rarely did young Russian women in 1909 detail their sex lives to their mothers.

He further claims in his article "Tender Love and Transference"—already a bias is apparent in his view of a love cure—that Spielrein was "principled," and therefore not sexually active, which implies that "principled" women refrain from sex, dichotomizing and degrading female sexuality into the categories of Virgin and Whore.[8] Lothane here employs a limited definition of female sexuality, defining it exclusively in terms of male penetration, and thus excludes the spectrum of physical contact, including touching and kissing for instance, that may still be considered sexual, and at the very least could be considered irresponsible therapist-client contact.

On the topic of sexuality, Cremerius states that Spielrein "allowed herself to be seduced by [Jung]. . . . Jung want[ed] to extricate himself from the relationship because a public scandal threaten[ed]."[9] Yet in another account Jung is described as being infatuated with Spielrein while she is depicted as planning his seduction.[10] Paradoxically, she is blamed both for being seduced as well as for planning his seduction. Either way, her therapeutic relationship is dangerously transfigured into a sexualized game that she brought upon herself.

In *Uncanny Modernity: Cultural Theories, Modern Anxieties*, Jung's fear of a scandal is made apparent in a letter reproduced; he writes to Freud in March 1909:

> A woman patient whom years ago I pulled out of a very sticky neurosis with unstinting effort has violated my confidence and my friendship in the most mortifying way imaginable. She has kicked up a vile scandal solely because I denied myself the pleasure of giving her a child. I have always acted the gentleman towards her, but before the bar of my rather too sensitive conscience I nevertheless don't feel clean, and that is what hurts the most. . . . But you know how it is—the devil can use even the best of things for the fabrication of filth. Meanwhile I have learnt an unspeakable amount of marital wisdom for until now I had a totally inadequate idea of my polygamous components.[11]

Here, Jung clearly blames Spielrein for the entire conflict and indicates rumors of a scandal, ironically creating those rumors by writing about them. He implies sexual relations by alluding to a "child," since it has already been demonstrated (see chapter 1) that his "gentlemanly" behavior was contradicted by Jung himself in a letter to her mother when he asked to be paid for his services should she desire him to act the gentleman. He had also been writing to Spielrein, as detailed above, lamenting his capacity for passionate love, which perhaps contributes to his not feeling completely "clean." Also, "polygamous components" may be interpreted in its sexual connotation and not simply as a sterile metaphor, as is evidenced by his admission that by denying her a child he also denies himself a certain pleasure.

Though he feels violated, it seems to be due to a violation of pride in confronting the surfacing rumor, rather than because of any truth behind it. In *Women and Nature*, Griffin muses on the historical conflation of woman and vengeful seductress: "Her body is a vessel of death. Her beauty is a lure. . . . Her voice is deceit. . . . She plans her seduction. She cannot help herself. Her mind is a theater of seduction. She is incapable of other thought. Her body was made for seduction. . . . Behind her suppliant flesh is a maw, a devouring hole, an abyss. Death. Destruction."[12]

Jung writes on June 21, 1909:

> I have good news to report of my Spielrein affair. . . . After breaking with her I was almost certain of her revenge and was deeply disappointed only by the banality of the form it took. The day before yesterday she turned up at my house and had a *very decent talk* with me, during which it transpired that the rumour buzzing about me does not emanate from her at all. . . . When the situation had become so tense that the continued preservation of the relationship could be rounded out only by sexual acts, I defended myself in a manner that cannot be justified morally. Caught in my delusion that I was the victim of the sexual wiles of my patient, I wrote to her mother that I was not the gratifier of her daughter's sexual desires, but merely her doctor, and that she should free me from her. In view of the fact that the patient had shortly before been my friend and enjoyed my full confidence, my action was a piece of which I very reluctantly confess.[13]

Jung is disappointed only by the "banality" of Spielrein's revenge, implying that he expected, or at least thought his behavior worthy of, revenge. Of course, it is already known that Jung did not write to her mother that he was "merely" her doctor and so the allusion to "full confidence" would seem to qualify the point Jung stresses about being a sexual gratifier. Though he realizes it was not Spielrein acting as a seductress, but only his own escalation of a relationship to a point he *perceived* to be only "rounded out" by sexual acts, the fact that he feels it necessary to confess to Freud at all suggests that his involvement with Spielrein contributed to the scandal already circulating about his involvement with female patients and students.

Further, he continues in this same letter: "I seriously discussed with her the issue about the child . . . I convinced myself that I was 'hypothetically' speaking, while there was certainly a lot of Eros behind it. I basically shifted all other hopes and desires to my patient."[14] Perhaps Jung did not realize the extent to which he was intensifying the relationship, but his words illustrate the very real nature of their affair, meaning it extended beyond pure symbol into the physical space of Spielrein's womb. Therefore any so-called "fantasy" (as Jung terms it in his previous letter) she may have had about a child, which will be further analyzed when we come to her diaries and letters, cannot be viewed without also acknowledging his encouragement—and possible suggestion—of the idea, where he definitively crosses the professional line with his "patient."

This letter also illustrates how Spielrein's character and diagnosis is dictated by the passing whims of Jung, as he, in his earlier letter, constructed an image of her as the spurned seductress only to free her of that image upon his own confession. Freud's acceptance of such a character construction is evidenced when he notified Jung of her attempt to weigh in on the matter herself: "I too have had news of the woman patient through whom you became acquainted with the neurotic gratitude of the spurned."[15] That her speaking out is interpreted as slander, neuroses, and as a desire for revenge rather than as a credible perspective or account of the affair is an unfortunate display of gender politics and unwarranted character assassination.

In an examination of transference, André Haynal, in *Psychoanalysis and the Sciences: Epistemology—History*, reproduced Freud's reply to Jung after the letter of confession:

> Such experiences, though painful, are necessary and hard to avoid. Without them we cannot really know life and what we are dealing with. I myself have never been taken in quite so badly, but I have come very close to it a number of times and had a "narrow escape." . . . But no lasting harm is done. They [female patients] help us to develop the thick skin we need to dominate "countertransference" [feelings for a patient by a therapist] which is after all a permanent problem for us; they teach us to displace our own affects to best advantage.[16]

In stating that "no harm" has been done, he means that no harm has been done to Jung and does not admit the female experience into the scenario. Admitting that transference and countertransference are "permanent problems" for the practice is insightful, but Freud seems to insinuate that they are only problems for an analyst and not a patient. He suggests that Spielrein (and all women patients?)

are teachers rather than clients, existing only to tempt and train analysts out of their own desire. However, she is portrayed as an ideal patient for providing Jung with the necessary tools to "dominate" his own feelings. In this way, women are typed as bringing problems *for* analysis instead of *to* analysis, which transforms them into potential *femmes fatales.* Still, Freud does seem objectively detached enough from female patients to advocate professionalism, though in the same letter he goes on to say that he only escaped such a trap because of his elder age, rather than due to moral or ethical obligations.

From Spielrein's perspective, it is known: "On May 30 1909, Spielrein assertively wrote to Freud requesting an audience," in order to express her point of view on the affair and her experience of being blamed by Jung for rumors of a scandal.[17] Freud denied her such a meeting. However, upon receiving Jung's letter exculpating Spielrein, Freud wrote to her: "The fact that I was wrong and that the lapse has to be blamed on the man and not the woman, as my young friend himself admits, satisfies my need to hold women in high regard. Please accept this expression of my entire sympathy for the dignified way in which you have resolved the conflict."[18] While Freud views Spielrein as a representative of the entire female gender, she did not exactly resolve the conflict, as even by speaking with Jung without "revenge," it still took Jung's writing to Freud to absolve her of blame.

Sabine Richebächer details the affair in *Sabina Spielrein: Forgotten Pioneer of Psychoanalysis*, though the entirety of her research remains in German. Richebächer recounts Spielrein's reply to Freud's initial brush off: "But you are quite clever, Professor: 'Let the other side be heard as well.' First, you should have given me an audience without the slightest resistance. But one would like to be spared an uncomfortable moment, right? Even the great 'Freud' cannot always overlook his weaknesses."[19] Spielrein understands that her reputation has been maligned and in speaking out against a known entity (Jung), she has been ignored by another "great" man (Freud) in power.

Actually, she is not simply brushed off by Freud in the beginning of their correspondence, but is disbelieved and even encouraged to change her story so as not to cause trouble: "Dr. Jung is my friend . . . I think I know him . . . and have reason to believe that he is incapable of frivolous or ignoble behavior. . . . I would urge you to ask yourself whether the feelings that have outlived this close relationship are not best suppressed and eradicated."[20] Perhaps Freud diminishes and invalidates her experience due to being confronted by something that he does not want to accept, which is to say Spielrein must be proven wrong in order for Freud's ideal of Jung to remain intact. Unfortunately, by stating that Jung is "incapable" of such behavior, he stigmatizes Spielrein, as if she must have been entirely mistaken or hysterical to put forth such an accusation—common practice in the context of the time.

Still, she does not remain silent. Instead, she continues to provide him with details of their relationship, which implies that she did not feel anything to be resolved, regardless of Jung's subsequent confession: "He [Jung] told me he was going to the theater, and I was forced to ask about it. He laughed: 'A stupid story: *The Rape of the Sabine Women*' (My name is Sabina). Of course I was quite taken aback."[21] Beauvoir illuminates the myth of the Sabine women: "The legend that claims that the ravished Sabine women resisted their ravishers with obstinate sterility also recounts that by whipping them with leather straps, the men magically won them over into submission."[22] If one were to conclude anything from this, it could be determined that Spielrein indeed felt violated, or at least confused by her relationship with Jung and by the subsequent rumors, given that she relates so intimately to the story. She would later write in a 1910 diary entry: "Actually, my love mostly caused me pain; there were only a few moments, when I rested my head on his chest, that allowed me to forget about my pain."[23]

Of being accused of circulating rumors, she further (1909) wrote to Freud: "Tolerating this mockery from a man whom one loved above all else in the world for 4–5 years, to whom one gave the best part of one's soul, to whom one offered one's maidenly pride and whom one has allowed to kiss, etc. for the first and perhaps the last time in my life."[24] She states that Jung "could not take it anymore and wanted 'poetry' . . . I could not and did not want to resist for many reasons . . . suddenly this was supposed to mean he was too gracious to me."[25] Her pain is especially apparent when she speaks of the sacrifice given to her ideal of love that she feels has been betrayed. That she did not want to resist indicates a sense of sexual autonomy that has also been betrayed, as if Jung was only humoring her (by being "too gracious") rather than participating in the reciprocal relationship she believed it to be. Clearly, Spielrein alludes explicitly to her lost "maidenly" pride and the kissing, "etc." would imply that their affair was sexual even if they restrained from intercourse, contrary to Lothane's definition of the intimate relationship. Indeed, that the affair has been questioned at all in terms of sexual consummation only emphasizes the phallocentric bias imposed upon female sexuality and the dismissal of Spielrein's words regarding her own experience.

Even so, Covington and Wharton are among the multitude of scholars who maintain: "While it is debatable whether their relationship was actually consummated, it bore fruit for them both."[26] Again, the term *consummated* is misleading if it is equated with penetration, when there was an unequivocal erotic and sensual relationship between the two. For example, in 1909, Spielrein remarks that Jung watches her undress in her apartment "[and] kisses me and bawls . . . he pulled the comb out of my hairdo and loosened my hair, whereupon he became jubilant."[27] Spielrein was affected emotionally, physically, psychologically, and mentally, regardless of whether or not there was "consummation." Moreover, to define the affair as sexual solely on terms of penetration may become a dangerous yardstick for measuring what "counts" as sex, or as sexual abuse, specifically in regard to a therapist-client relationship.

When tension was still rising between the two after the so-called affair, she writes to Freud of her disillusioned sexual awakening on June 13, 1909: "If I wanted to hold everyone in high esteem, I of course, soon had to realize: 'All is a swindle, all is a comedy, all people are stupid and false,' etc. The artistic way of viewing the world comes only with age, with the awakening of the sexual component."[28] Simone de Beauvoir, when expounding on a similar line from her own memoirs, "I'm swindled," echoes Spielrein's sentiment: "Life has made me discover the world as it is, that is, a world of suffering and oppression . . . things that I didn't know when I was young and when I imagined that to discover the world was to discover something beautiful."[29] Still, Lothane cites the affair as Spielrein's cure and her "healing," though what transpired between her and Jung also provided her with a fair amount of unanticipated hurt and a tarnished reputation in need of, as Lothane's "In Defense" article title suggests, defending.[30]

In the same letter, she relates:

> I know, even if there had been consequences, my parents would say nothing because these are my personal affairs and I am living exactly the way I want to live. I was not ashamed, but facing my father would be impossible, as I am forced to remember: the man whom I so deeply loved and so highly praised behaved this way and that.[31]

The term *consequences* is used by both Jung and Spielrein in various letters, and considering the previous talk of a child, it would seem to imply pregnancy. She attempts to conceal Jung's letters to her wherein he writes of anything "more" than friendship, but relays a particular passage to Freud: " 'If one has already married, it is better to commit the lie only once and then atone for it' . . . I think that's clear enough," though she continues to cite Jung: " 'If the love for a woman is awakened in me, I first feel concern and pity for the poor woman who dreams of eternal fidelity and other impossibilities and is in for a painful awakening.' "[32] One can comprehend from Jung's earlier letter chastising himself for his passionate love that her account rings true to life. The implications of lying and doing penance for one's actions seem to be Spielrein's way of describing the affair to Freud in terms she deems appropriate and not overly explicit.

Strangely, Lothane writes that Spielrein "gave up the love affair [with Jung] without a fuss," excepting the fact that the two had an argument that escalated to Spielrein's drawing a knife on Jung after a heated accusation that she felt Jung to be maligning her reputation as well as stealing her academic ideas.[33] This incident perhaps provided the action that their previous "banal" conversation lacked, as Bettelheim recounts:

> Not realizing what she was doing, [she] had hit Jung in the face in a fit of desperation over his defamation of her, and that when she did so, she had been holding a knife in her hand, not knowing what she intended to do, Jung grabbed her hand and she ended up bleeding, her left hand and forearm covered with blood . . . to escape from it all and get a grip on herself, she left Zurich for the country.[34]

It would appear that Spielrein and Jung were deeply troubled by their relationship to the point of violence, challenging both the notion that she walked away silently without a "fuss," and the idea that only fruit was born from their involvement. In fact, when news of the fight broke out, her mother thought her child to be in mortal danger and her father, in reaction to Jung's behavior, encouraged Spielrein's physical response.[35] Years after the affair, in an attempt to reconcile Freud and Jung, after forgiving the latter herself, Freud declines and suggests to her: "You have not brought to light the hatred he merits."[36] Such hatred would not be warranted from an amicable split or from mere "transference." These details are important to redefine an affair that has been considered a "love cure" rather than a professional transgression, in an already ambiguously defined therapeutic relationship that appears to have caused immense harm.

When writing to Freud after the knife incident, she is deeply distressed by the entire relationship:

> I, however, want to separate from Dr. Jung completely and pursue my independent path . . . when I can either forgive him for everything or murder him. It haunts me constantly. . . . I would be happy if someone could show me that he is worthy of love and that he is not a villain. For over three months I have analyzed everything, I retreated into nature in attempt to save myself and my ideal; I finally spoke with a colleague about him . . . and the result was that I felt much lonelier than before, because my beloved could not be saved, and the thought [entered] that he might be a good-for-nothing, and that he just used me for his first experiments, etc. etc.[37]

This reflection reveals the necessity of parting from Jung. Though she would like to be proven wrong, her experience of him does not allow her, at the time of this letter, to be convinced that she has not been treated cruelly. Her mental health has also been disregarded by the person whom she trusted with her entire psychological well-being. Though he played into her image of a beloved, that image has been shattered now, and their intimate relationship unravels. She relays that she is destroyed and that she "had respect neither for him nor for myself."[38]

She is led to the idea that she must, figuratively speaking, murder him from her psyche in order to begin to heal from the relationship, and so she retreats, like Echo, into the woods for a time of self-reflection. However, she returned to Zurich to complete her doctorate knowing Jung would continue to act as dissertation advisor until 1911. A shift in their relationship is apparent after this incident as she, though still emotional (as we will see through her diaries) became determined to succeed on a collegiate level with him as well as with Freud. She and Jung then kept an intermittent correspondence until a complete severing of their relationship a few years later.

Lothane, in a 2003 addendum to his previous scholarship on Spielrein, believes that viewing her in light of sexual transgressions is placing her in a role of the helpless woman: "The myth [of an affair] has also inspired a sizable feminist literature, especially in Germany," a literature under the so-called myth of "male power."[39] Lothane trivializes the "sizable" amount of feminist literature by equating its foundation with a myth, by which Lothane means a lie. It is unfortunate that to simply uncover an alternative version of history, specifically with Spielrein's perspective in the forefront, "feminist" authors are automatically believed to be under a mass delusion of male dominance, a notion that turns them into de facto hysterics. Lothane immediately positions feminist literature *against* male literature, though given the topic it is to also pit Spielrein against Jung, with no reconciliation between the two perspectives. Therefore, one must be seen as the dominant truth, and historically, it has been Jung's perspective and experience that has garnered the most attention.

I should state for the record that I accept the term *sexual relationship* regardless of the ambiguity around the term *consummation*. Clearly, there existed a sensual relationship between the two at a time when Spielrein was Jung's intermittent patient. This is not a "myth," as Lothane would have it, but a fact evidenced by both sides. There is also no "myth" of male privilege, as in this specific historical context women were not even allowed to vote, which demonstrates a social and political male advantage. Acknowledging this need not be seen as an attack, but as a general understanding of dynamics of power, autonomy, and exclusivity within history.

This perspective does not make Jung an "evil seducer" as Lothane argues, nor does it make her a "helpless" victim.[40] Violation is not about helplessness, which demeans female agency, but about being subjected to a certain exertion of power (an assumed privilege), whether that power is exercised psychologically, physically, or emotionally. Lothane emphasizes a "mutual attachment" between the two, which is no less true merely because ramifications of that attachment are questioned from an additional perspective.[41]

Lover, Beloved, Analyst, Father, Confusion

> You are to me not only a you but that in me which is you-directed, which comes into being as it is shared with another, a you apart from whom I cannot imagine myself.
>
> —Christine Downing, *The Goddess*

As has been noted above, Spielrein commented on the dynamics of her relationship with Jung as bordering on the parental, and at times, in the roles of mother and father. An analyst then must be aware not of what he or she "is," but of what he or she may become for the patient. What is real and what is fantasy may blur within transference, especially if an analyst literally enacts a fantasy role for the patient, as Jung did for Spielrein. As she reflects on the affair and her experience of betrayal in a letter to Freud, Spielrein evokes poet Erica Jong when she likens Jung to someone who has been "my highly revered friend, doctor, beloved," and also a father figure and a personal poet.[42] Jong, in her poem "Autobiographical," suggests that archetypal Love appears in and through the entwined figures of analyst, father, son, lover, husband, and "maybe even Death."[43] Rosemary Balsam, too, terms Jung to be Spielrein's "ex-analyst/mentor/lover/friend."[44]

Contrary to Spielrein and Balsam, James Hillman remarks in *The Myth of Analysis*: "The analyst is neither lover, nor daimon, nor creative demiurge, nor embodiment of culture. . . . Moreover, analysis presents only one example of the creativity of any psychological relationship. It is . . . fatherless."[45] The difference between the female and male interpretation of the analyst is striking in its opposition. It is clear that to Spielrein, Jung indeed became the embodiment of many roles, as happens with figures in positions of power, though she appears to have remained conscious of her own projection during the relationship. It may be said that analysis is not "fatherless," as it remains very much rooted in its male (e.g., Freud and Jung) pioneers of the field, though repeatedly excludes its fore-*mothers*—which is not to conflate womanhood and motherhood—of the field, Spielrein being only one of the early female contributors.

In *The Pregnant Virgin*, Marion Woodman relates to a female client's experience, specifically in an emotionally charged therapy dynamic, and notes how an analyst becomes the figure of the "beloved. Here is where her [the client's] intimate intercourse is. . . . The model of the alchemical vessel, involving harmonious cooperation . . . is tailor-made for her. And tailor-made for her destruction if the male analyst becomes frightened, is seduced, or misappropriates his power."[46] Woodman comprehends "intercourse" as it may also be recognized in relation to Spielrein, contrary to the debate about consummation. Woodman underscores that psychological intercourse can be as equally destructive when it is utilized as an abuse of power. Still, while Spielrein was not destroyed, and actually succeeded in rewriting the concept of destruction into a narrative of resurrection (her 1912 article "Destruction as the Cause of Coming into Being"), the potential for her emotional destruction is evident in her diaries and letters.

Lasting Effects of the "Love Cure"

Carotenuto claims that "only a man could help" Spielrein and that the dissolution of treatment following a sexual liaison was destiny.[47] He also underscores his gender bias in relation to therapy: "A man placed in this situation can, at least for a short while, do what he likes, for he is actually in a very strong position with respect to the woman he has saved. He can . . . permit himself anything, but precisely because he has this unlimited power, his moral integrity and feelings ought to be absolutely steadfast."[48] Kerr similarly maintains that Jung may have permitted himself anything, given that he often did not charge Spielrein for services, though the nature of pro-bono work and ethical obligation has already been discussed.[49]

It is problematic that a male therapist is thought to be able to "do" anything he likes to a client in regard to her body, merely because he is helping her. This objectifies a female client and equates an analyst's psychological strength with sexual manipulation. It is also disturbing that the healing process is considered by Carotenuto to be a time of ultimate physical domination and that only "steadfast" integrity, rather than respect, is what he deems necessary to maintain boundaries with a female client. This opinion implies that though Jung was not morally absolute, Spielrein, as a female, walked into a relationship where her boundaries were already considered elastic.

Carotenuto writes that though a woman might suffer within sexualized therapy, it is how she, like Spielrein, learns to "grow up and become a woman."[50] While certain suffering has the potential to lead to personal growth, it is not causally related (and thus justified) to a woman's maturation, especially when such suffering is equated with sexual misconduct in therapy. Also, suffering in this context has the potential to re-constellate previous trauma, which is rarely considered necessary to becoming a woman, and implies that a woman only grows up in relation to the external actions of a male figure. It seems as though this claim—that Spielrein matured due to the pain she endured—is made in order to suggest that any pain Jung may have inflicted was done for her benefit.

When speaking of her treatment, Carotenuto further states:

> I doubt that a patient can suffer any blows more savage than [Jung's]. The analytic situation of seventy years ago is the same today. The analysand cannot imagine that the powerful analyst could be mistaken . . . if these [trusts] are removed, as happened in this case, there is again the possibility of a retreat into illness. But here the patient was Sabina Spielrein, a young woman steeled by suffering, and therefore capable of doing battle.[51]

If Spielrein had not been "steeled," she still would not be to blame for having trusted her therapist. It is disconcerting that she is supposed to have been capable of doing "battle" during therapy, as her job was not to prepare for such a battle but enter into a therapeutic environment of healing. It was not her duty to suffer, nor was it her duty to rise above said suffering. It is also doubtful that she would be regarded in Carotenuto's favor if she had retreated into an "illness," as if that would have signified a personal failing on her part. I find it disheartening that she is praised for her suffering and acceptance of such "blows," which implies that it was her responsibility as a patient to steel herself against abuse and reinforces stereotypical notions of female passivity. Still, perhaps most unsettling is his notion that nothing has changed in the dynamic between therapist and client.

Interestingly, sexual exploitation as a whole is often diminished in order to justify the affair. For example, Jung states that he was "[a] victim of a sexual assault by a man I once worshipped."[52] However, Kerr immediately minimizes this recount by transforming it into something other than a violation: "For the record, the 'assault' happened in Jung's adolescence, when he was already of fairly imposing size, it was therefore more in the manner of seduction."[53] While downplaying the significance of the event, it is unclear whether Kerr is suggesting that the assault was acceptable because Jung was a teenager and not a child, or that because Jung was tall, he was therefore immune to sexual assault. Either way, assault is turned into seduction and then used to cast doubt on whether or not Spielrein's "seduction" should be redefined along the lines of abuse. Sadly, Kerr's tactic continues to pervade current rape culture: to twist an admission by a victim of assault into hyperbolic exaggeration, while implying that he or she *really wanted* it. When these two things are done, abuse is erased and "seduction" is then cemented into the narrative.

Contrarily, Balsam extrapolates:

> [This] account presents their clinical and personal alliance as the prototype of a *folie à deux* between a needy, self-involved therapist with poor boundaries and a compelling but possessively consuming patient, leading to severe ethical violations on the part of the therapist. Psychoanalysis and the understanding of erotic transference were, to be sure, then in their infancy. However, Jung was a sufficiently seasoned hospital psychiatrist to be aware that he was exploiting Spielrein's youth and patienthood.[54]

Despite the slightly demeaning characterizations of Spielrein and Jung, Balsam highlights the fact that their affair was an act of exploitation, though she defines it as an ethical violation, rather than a physical one. Further, she notes the prototypical nature of the affair, which is to say that the phenomenon of sexual exploitation in therapy did not end with this affair, but actually began with it, in terms of depth psychoanalysis. Though the concept of transference was in its "infancy," Jung had already had enough contact with his superiors at the clinic to be well aware of the acceptable role of an analyst.

Similarly, psychologist Gary Schoener, in *Breach of Trust: Sexual Exploitation by Health Care Professionals and Clergy*, views Spielrein as an "example" of exploitation distinctly because she was the first in a long line of sexually exploited clients, not only by Jung, but in the general field of psychology.[55] The purpose of referencing her in this context is to underscore the fact that exploitation has since been perpetuated in practice, though it remains a marginalized and suppressed shadow of the field. We might say that this perpetuation remains possible when such breaches of trust are maintained as "seduction" or "romance" in scholarship.

Carotenuto contributes to such exploitation when he further refers to Spielrein: "A thing which is not liked or desired generally requires no prohibition."[56] Aside from objectifying Spielrein by turning her into a "thing," he disturbingly assumes that if Jung did not physically "desire" her, she would have been safe, as if to say that women who fall outside of a male definition of desire are in no threat of violation and conversely, that women who do fall within such a definition are automatically under threat. Spielrein, here considered desirable, is thus implicitly blamed for Jung's lack of prohibitions.

On the other hand, Peter Gay, a biographer of Freud, says of Spielrein: "[She was] one of the most extraordinary among the younger analysts [who had] gone to Zurich. . . . She fell in love with her analyst, and Jung, taking advantage of her dependency, made her his mistress. After a painful struggle in which Freud played a minor but not admirable part, she freed herself from her involvement and became an analyst."[57] This is one of the rare instances where Spielrein's agency is demonstrated, as Gay describes her as having actively freed *herself* from the relationship, though she is still classified as a "mistress," a label in direct conflict with reference to an abuse of power.

However, here is Bettelheim's defense of Jung's behavior:

> Whatever may be one's judgment of Jung's behavior toward Spielrein . . . one must not disregard its most important consequence: he cured her. . . . In retrospect we ought to ask ourselves: what convincing evidence do we have that the same result would have been achieved if Jung had behaved toward her in a way we must expect a conscientious therapist to behave toward his patient? . . . True, Spielrein paid a very high price in unhappiness, confusion, and disillusion for the particular way in which she got cured, but then this is often true for mental patients who are as sick as she was.[58]

Bettelheim comes very close to stating that Spielrein deserved Jung's behavior, as if by being institutionalized, she practically asked for it by wanting to be "cured." He dismisses her suffering, her "unhappiness," and her pain altogether, since it is seen as having served the treatment, which evokes Hillman's earlier statement about women in therapy serving analysis's narcissistic aspect. Yet it is possible that she would have gained the same ground without Jung's entering into an affair with her. Perhaps the fact that Spielrein succeeded in spite of the affair is more important than assuming she could not have succeeded without it.

Ultimately, the idea that she could only have been cured through an affair and that it is to be expected is a dangerous path, for it suggests that sexual involvement between client and therapist may be necessary for the former's future success. Bettelheim insinuates that Jung could have done whatever he deemed necessary, as long as Spielrein emerged from treatment still able to function in society, which dismisses the fact that most scholars interpret her later years as a broken woman, pining for Jung in a never-ending cycle of suicidal wishes and unrequited love. In fact, her narrative thus far has been highly regarded as a woman who remained ill, rather than a cured woman of high academic success, personal achievement, and intelligence. Repeatedly, Spielrein is thought cured only when attempting to justify the methods of her treatment ("love cure") with Jung.

As Gottfried Heuer states: "Metaphorically speaking, the scalpel of the soul-doctor may well become a dangerous weapon when he betrays his art and commits 'soul-murder.' Actually, it is not really the method that is dangerous, but rather the analyst who abuses it."[59] It is at least apparent in Heuer's title, "'Soul Murder' and 'The Birth of Intersubjectivity' in David Cronenberg's *A*

Dangerous Method," that the question of violation has been raised regarding Spielrein and Jung, though Heuer notes that the affair must be considered on an archetypal level. By that he means one must consider those involved as mythic characters, or as "angels wrestling" out their own complexes.[60] However, by turning Spielrein into a symbol (or an angel), she is divorced from the psychosocial reality of her historical person. He also maintains that whatever the method, which apparently includes sexual abuse, Spielrein was "cured," though he does not actually question the validity of hysteria itself, from which she was so quickly cured.

Additionally, Heuer's statement, discussed in chapter 1, is recalled: "We might easily imagine that Spielrein (un)consciously invited her analyst to abuse her."[61] The context of that statement will not be repeated here, though it may be restated that a so-called unconscious wish, like her claimed desirability, is not the same thing as an invitation. Peter Rutter, in *Breach of Trust*, challenges such an assumption based entirely on psychological jargon:

> The very structure of the sentence, "She really wanted it," is a boundary violation—because a man has decided that he has authority over the inner reality of a woman. This attitude, in only slightly less direct language, has been institutionally adopted by certain circles of psychodynamic psychology, in the only recently challenged idea that, when women complained of sexual contact with their therapists, they were having psychotic transference fantasies. "Wish fulfillment" has been a crucial psychodynamic concept. But this is just the same old message, "She really wanted it," in modern-day psychological language. This message still exists . . . after all, the image of the temptress, our culture's version of the archetype of the feminine seductress, appears just after the Creation. In the image of the seductress is the projection onto the woman of power over [a] sexual boundary that men actually maintain; it is a way of disowning that power and placing it in the woman. This disowning usually occurs when something goes wrong for the man—for instance, when his secret is told. The real seductress certainly exists. Our dysfunctional culture has quite successfully produced many such women, driven them mad, in a sense, with their own sexuality being objectified and turned against them.[62]

This is not to say that patterns of violence are not perpetuated in later life, but that Spielrein is not responsible for, nor is she the cause of another's actions. Rutter contradicts Carotenuto's theory that a man has absolute power over a woman in therapy and may permit himself what he wishes, by re-categorizing assumed psychological power into the language of patriarchal entitlement. He also challenges the reframing of a narrative of violation into one of seduction and views Spielrein's story as relevant for today's culture as ever, given that patients, particularly those marginalized, are still vulnerable to abuses of power and subsequent character maligning. By speaking in the very real and physical terms of exploitation and abuse, Rutter does not divorce material reality from archetypal scrutiny.

Practicing Jungian analyst John Haule speaks of Spielrein and Jung within the context of romantic love in *The Love Cure* as he equates female patients in therapy with "sirens."[63] Haule's gendered characterization implies that women exist in therapy to seduce a male therapist, thereby objectifying female clients and turning them into mere sexual distractions, rather than as humans in need of guidance. Given that Haule directly references Spielrein in relation to her so-called seduction of Jung, it is clear that the notion of abuse is disregarded in favor of perpetuating the image of a siren.

He further muses: "When the issue of 'sexualized therapy' comes up, we tend to freeze. Our language gets fuzzy. We speak in generalities as though we might be led into loosening our hold on the hottest of ethical guidelines. We are 'fundamentalists' on the question of sex in connection with therapy."[64] Unfortunately, while Haule attempts to de-moralize sexualized therapy (where it is, he is clear, the woman being sexualized), "guidelines" are already in place to protect both patient and therapist from potential harm. He also uses the term *love cure* in relation to Spielrein and Jung, a term that is dismantled by Phyllis Chesler in *Women and Madness*, as she equates such a "love cure" in therapy with "rape," sidestepping any romanticized euphemism.[65] It is as though Spielrein and Jung's relationship is used to justify continued practices of abuse, in that to cite this specific affair does not evoke just *any* transference, but one clearly ambiguous, erotic, physical, and, by Jung's own admission, near-madness-inducing. It is, bluntly, to equate abuse with a cure.

Haule attempts to level the playing field between client and therapist within the boundaries of therapy:

> The love cure. . . . According to the maxim of the persona field, the patient is always a weak, vulnerable, easily damaged neurotic whose fantasies of sexual involvement with her therapist stem inevitably from her "woundedness" and "lack of boundaries." The therapist is always powerful and overly influential, and the patient is a potential victim in an unbalanced power differential. Prematurely closing off these questions reinforces the inequalities.[66]

However, it is not prejudicial to examine power inequalities and authority when stating a simple fact: those without training seek guidance from those who have had training and are assumed experts in the field. Under normal circumstances, that is usually where the healing begins. This is a power differential because it hinges on inequality of experience, not an arbitrary hierarchy imposed to erase an individual's civil liberties. There are ethical "boundaries" in place that do not "reinforce" inequality but in fact protect potential victimization on either side, often because a patient *is* vulnerable and an analyst *can* be influential, which need not be interpreted as demeaning or negative. Incidentally, while he warns of creating a power dynamic, he also states in earnest that a patient is often vulnerable with "poorly defended wounds" opposed to a therapist's more "integrated" personality, which implies that a power differential indeed already exists.[67]

Haule continues: "An *a priori* attitude does not allow for the possibility that this particular unique individual may be an exception to the general run of patients [sex]. It stuffs her into a pigeon-hole labeled 'patient in need of protection from her sexual self.' "[68] To imply that the therapist should not engage in sex with a patient to protect her from herself undermines the power that a patient does have to sexually engage with another person outside of therapy. Again, a woman's "sexual self" is here heteronormatively viewed only in relation to her male analyst, which greatly restricts the spectrum of sexual intimacy (as previously discussed) and turns sex in therapy into a woman's liberation. Though Haule quantifies that only a few patients, such as Spielrein, might be qualified to engage in such a "love cure" with an analyst, an a priori rule is literally already in place, both legally and ethically, and it is not set up to protect a female patient from herself but from a therapist and vice versa. Additionally, to state that there need not be any a priori laws protecting a woman's body from objectification is ill-advised and rather counterintuitive to cultural and social realities.

Again citing Spielrein's transference, Haule excuses the affair by invoking Kerr to normalize it: "Jung was scarcely the only person to become involved with a patient. Gross' exploits were legendary, Stekel had long enjoyed a reputation as a 'seducer,' Jones was paying blackmail money to a former patient," while noted colleague Otto Rank famously began an affair with his patient, Anaïs Nin.[69] While listing other "seducers" is supposed to justify Jung's behavior, it only serves to cast a dark shadow onto the field of the named psychologists. Chesler draws attention to the fact that abuse is transformed and commonly "present[ed] as either necessary for the 'cure' or as a unique instance of 'love.' "[70] Hence, using Spielrein as a figure of seduction in the attempt to ethically blur the lines of sexual misconduct seems an irresponsible use of her narrative. While scholars continue to use the terms *cure* and *seduction* rather than *abuse,*

RAINN, the Rape, Abuse, & Incest National Network, states: "Sexual contact of any kind between a helping professional and a client [is] . . . exploitation," a definition widened in its conception of sexuality to include more than just phallocentrism or the use of force.[71]

The fact that there are exceptions to an accepted practice of therapy, meaning that some women find later success after a sexualized affair, seems to be used for validation on multiple accounts, as Lothane also argues: "It ought not to be judged by its seeds, as Sabina's transference and Jung's countertransference, but by its fruit: the good it did for both. Nor should it be regarded as pathology, but as an issue in the politics of marriage and the double standard."[72] It is not actually about the politics of marriage, but about the merits of a profession. While Lothane would have the ends justify the means, one might ask just who is being sacrificed as the means, since the "fruit" born—again—could easily be compared to the pain it caused both involved. Also, Jung's "fruit" has been widely accepted within academia, whereas Spielrein's has not. In short, viewing the affair only within the context of "fruit" seems possible only when her personal experience and her words are largely dismissed.

Still, Haule again equates sex with a love cure:

> To stop at the fact that our present-day preoccupation with the issue of sex in psychotherapy has a long ignoble past, would be to see only the superficial aspect of the issue. It deserves more serious consideration. We need to grasp how it is that therapists from Freud onward have been fascinated with the idea that *the cure is effected by love.*[73]

First, almost every individual is "fascinated" by sexual attraction and love, not just Freud and his brethren. Second, to see sex in therapy as superficial wholly denies the real-life consequences that may bring upheaval and emotional turmoil to those involved, while it dismisses the very "serious" matters of abuses of power and subsequent suppression. The inclusion of Spielrein's experience (or other previous patients' experiences for that matter) might actually account for "serious consideration" being given to the issue. While Haule accepts the definition of "love cure" as being synonymous with "sex in psychotherapy," it may be reminded that Spielrein was not initially "cured" by an affair but by Jung's employment of Freudian talk therapy.

Chesler's *Women and Madness* details accounts of women who felt exploited by engaging in sexual acts with a therapist, and their language is strikingly similar to Spielrein's own account of the affair. For instance, Chesler elucidates the idea of "femininity" being forced upon gender in relation to symptoms occurring after therapist abuse, such as introversion, depression, anxiety, and self-blame, as opposed to anger or revenge, which have been socially perpetuated as "masculine" characteristics: "They were the most vocal advocates of 'pity' and 'understanding' for the therapists. . . . They insisted *they* were to blame; that *they* were the real seducers."[74]

Upon reflection of the affair in 1910, Spielrein admitted: "We were supposed to be working but instead we spoke of the sexual instinct/death instinct . . . of the world of the ancestors. We just could not stop. He [Jung] listened to me excitedly. . . . He was quite taken by the parallels in our thinking and feeling. He told me that this realization makes him afraid, because it is the way I win his love. . . . He admitted that he did not want to love me. But now he must."[75] In Carotenuto's translation, Spielrein has been told that she "made" him fall in love with her simply by existing and the decision to resist (or not) appears entirely in Jung's power. In relation, seventy years after Spielrein's affair, a woman in Chesler's account reflects: "I think that he just finally couldn't resist me any more. I think I just put too much pressure on him."[76] Another anonymous woman claims her therapist, while sleeping with her, continued an emotional detachment: "He'd interpret everything I said as 'transference love.' "[77] Clearly, a "love cure" still carries the weight of an ambiguous "transference," which in turn evokes sexualization, and the term has only served to perpetuate the exploitation and suppression of Spielrein's actual experience. Like Echo, when Spielrein is excluded from reflection, this narrative remains incomplete.

> I inquire, I do not assert; I do not here determine anything with final assurance; I conjecture, try, compare, attempt, ask.
>
> —Motto to Christian Knorr von Rosenroth, Christian Cabalist

Spielrein's experience has been largely dismissed in favor of the "love cure" narrative because her success challenges an accepted male-centric image of power in history. However, by examining Spielrein's own words, a recreation of her perspective is possible. Through her diaries, chapter 4 continues to explore the language of a woman being brought forth by longing, passion, scholarship, ambition, and betrayal. In addition, historical context of female autobiographical writing and its stigmatization will be provided. In the following chapter, Sabina Spielrein comes closer into being.

4

Writing as a Way of Coming into Being (Sabina Spielrein's Diaries)

> Yes, I would like to be free! Where will I go? Where will I start? All banal questions. For the time being—work!
>
> —Sabina Spielrein

Introduction

In *Mythography: The Study of Myths and Rituals*, William Doty coins the phrase *individual mythohistory*, referring to "[the] self-crafting of autobiography. Most autobiographies have at least an implicit mythostoried account of the person's origins, strongest and weakest suits, and individual features . . . [they are] automythological."[1] While this chapter will not dwell on autobiographical theory, the placement of women's writing outside of the academic canon will be briefly addressed before Spielrein's writing is explored in light of Doty's definition of mythohistory. Since she has been excluded from the field's larger academic conversation, there remains "No mirror of *her* era," as Bella Brodzki and Celeste Schenck relate in *Life/Lines: Theorizing Women's Autobiography*, where the history of enforced marginalization of women's voices is recounted.[2]

It follows, then, that the lack of societal significance imposed upon women's writing contributes at least in part to the suppression of Spielrein's personal and professional writing. Apropos, integral to this chapter is her diary, which spans the years 1909–1912. Unfortunately, various pages remain unavailable (at times entire years are missing), as they sit unpublished at the estate of Georges de Morsier in Geneva, Switzerland. Also, many entries have been sacrificed due to constrictions of copyright—Carotenuto's edition is the preeminent English translation—and cohesion of narrative. To that end, while certain "Jung-heavy" passages will be reproduced, entries where her voice seemed most alive have been specifically chosen, which at times do not intersect with Jung but instead with her dissertation, her future husband, or a haunting dream image.

In fact, specifically because her dream imagery has been used as evidence of psychosis, the mythic significance of a few of her dream images will be explored so as to offer an alternative (to the clinical) interpretation. As Robert Ellwood says of Jung in *The Politics of Myth: A Study of C. G. Jung, Mircea Eliade, and Joseph Campbell*: "The psychology of C. G. Jung rests on psychic biography . . . the narrative of the subject's inner life, above all as it is expressed in dreams and fantasies."[3] Spielrein's words are also related to the emotional intensity of other passionate and often stigmatized writers such as Sylvia Plath, Anaïs Nin, Simone Weil, and the Portuguese Nun, in order to show how her writing contributes to the underrepresented field of female autobiography. By reading her diaries (and work) in this way, rather than through the lens of pathology, her personal experience may be further illuminated.

Defining "Women's Writing"

> [Writing is] an act that will also be marked by woman's *seizing* the occasion to *speak,* hence her shattering entry into history, which has always been based *on her suppression.*
>
> —Hélène Cixous, "Laugh of the Medusa"

As Estelle C. Jelinek reminds us in *Women's Autobiography: From Antiquity to the Present*: "It is from women . . . that we have the earliest extant diaries, an ancient tradition . . . [which] became a highly cultivated form written by women of the sophisticated courts of Japan during the tenth and eleventh centuries,"[4] Though personal diaries and letters have now been accepted as forms of autobiography, Shari Benstock asserts in *The Private Self: Theory and Practice of Women's Autobiographical Writings* that, academically, the line between theory and practice in so-called women's writing continues to blur because the subject in question is tied to "[a] selfhood that is always under examination."[5] Women's autobiographical writing is frequently overlooked and delegitimized specifically because the (female) self as revealed in personal writing represents a self that has rarely been given social autonomy.

Relatedly, when referring to the "fathers" of autobiographical theory (Georges Gusdorf in particular), Carolyn Heilbrun contributes in *Life/Lines* that autobiography has historically been defined as "expressing a concern peculiar to Western men" dependent upon who has been considered socially "significant."[6] Consequently, the significance of women's writing has been relegated to the margins of the academic canon. Further, while Gusdorf maintains that autobiography reflects man's image "back to himself," psychoanalyst Jacques Lacan believes that one must first come to know one's image through the "cultural mirror" in order to attain self-knowledge (qtd. in Benstock, 15; qtd. in Benstock, 16).[7] If it is assumed that the cultural and/or dominant mirror *does not* reflect a woman back to herself ("no mirror of *her* era") then women are unintentionally excluded from similar self-knowledge.[8]

Therefore, any attempt to reveal Spielrein's "self" in her diaries and letters is to confront a history of suppression of women's writing:

> To be able to theorize women's writing practices, including women's critical writing practices, is to make women's writings somehow legitimate within the academy. The costs of such a legitimacy are always an issue when discussing forms that have traditionally been considered illegitimate [such as women's] diary, letter, and memoir writing.[9]

Since women's writing tests the limits of genre by defining a self that has been psychosocially stigmatized, Benstock argues that it is then "submitted to the violence of a theory that merely registers its effects . . . such writing may fare the worst in both worlds: it is overlooked or misrepresented by 'theoretical' critics and denied careful attention" in the literary or mythological fields to which it belongs.[10] Still, in an attempt to honor the particularities of selfhood, she admits: "Women's writings are as individual as women themselves, and they often resist easy classification," though such a broad term as *women's writing* is simply the easiest (even if problematic) semantic shorthand when defining this specifically overlooked genre.[11] Actually, because Benstock asserts that women's writing defies genre, she also avoids binaries such as "male/female, soul/body, public/private, gender/genre, [and] letters/literature."[12] While this study similarly examines specific characterizations applied to gender that have been used to stereotype and suppress, it does so through Spielrein's specifically female-identified experience.

Creating a Self with Words

> In the heart of the Looking-Glass country . . . Alice comes to the center of the labyrinth of language. This is also the center of her journey, of her dream, and of the game in which she as a white pawn plays and wins in eleven moves. On the wall of the labyrinth sits Humpty Dumpty, poised over the abyss of the meaning; he thinks himself the master of

> language . . . [Alice states] "The question is . . . whether you *can* make words mean so many different things" [and Humpty replies] "The question is . . . which is to be master—that's all."
>
> —Teresa de Lauretis, *Alice Doesn't: Feminism, Semiotics, Cinema*

Like Lewis Carroll's Humpty Dumpty, autobiographical theory has similarly evolved into a critique on the mastery of language instead of an exploration of the individual asserted within the language. As such, Gusdorf iterates that autobiography represents the "expression of individual authority in the realm of language."[13] Per contra, if authority in language has already been deemed inferior (as in the case of Echo), or pathologized (as in the case of Spielrein), then such a definition of academic power is both disrupted and challenged by women's autobiographical writing. For instance, Spielrein's diaries, wherein she discusses topics such as sexuality, motherhood, and academia, have been primarily used as so-called evidence of mental illness rather than as an example of literary, historical, or social importance.

Alternatively, Benstock professes that female autobiography "serve[s] as a means by which to create images of a 'self' through the writing act, a way by which to find a 'voice'—whether private or public—through which to express that which cannot be expressed in other forms."[14] Brodzki and Schenck believe that in order to retrieve women's voices, a "feminist re-appropriation of the mirror" is necessary by "locat[ing] the female subject in spite of the postmodern campaign against the sovereign self," and while Echo (as discussed in chapter 2) is not mentioned in their text, a mythic parallel is obvious.[15] Without falling into essentialism then, the task of this chapter becomes to historically locate a cis-female-identified subject, as Spielrein is located and explored through her own words.

Yet the notion of retrieving a self is to assert that a self exists within a text, a somewhat contradictory notion to the postmodern critique of any kind of localized "self," as noted above by Brodzki and Schenck. As Katherine Goodman stresses in *Life/Lines*: "Barthes's and Foucault's analyses [deconstruction of selfhood] dissolve the very interiority of the autobiographical subject into a pose, or, at best, a role and nothing more. . . . Feminists, however, know that it makes a great deal of difference who is speaking."[16] That is to say, before a self can be de-localized, one must first be granted the authority and equity of an "I," an agency that has often been denied women. It is then assumed—for the purpose of this book—that Spielrein does recreate a piece of herself in her writing, and it is this self that is examined vis-à-vis subsequent stigmatization.

Further complicating the intersection between women and writing, Gusdorf renders autobiography "not possible in a cultural landscape where consciousness of self does not, properly speaking, exist."[17] Conversely, in her article "Women's Autobiographical Selves," Susan Friedman reveals her distrust in Gusdorf's precondition for autobiography: "The model of a separate and unique selfhood that is highlighted in his work and shared by many other critics establishes a critical bias that leads to the (mis)reading and marginalization of autobiographical texts by women and minorities in the processes of canon formulation," where one's concept of selfhood may already be influenced by the shared consciousness, or experience, of a subjugated group.[18] Hence, one can simultaneously be an "I" and a "We." In short, while Spielrein is here viewed as autonomous, her identity remains inextricably intertwined with a shared sociopolitical position.

Additionally, as Friedman argues, "[Gusdorf's] emphasis on separateness ignores the differences in socialization in the construction of male and female gender identity," a statement supported by Spielrein's interest in personal transformation through union, a topic discussed both below and at length in chapter 5.[19] Likewise, she proclaims that women's writing is largely linked, by hook or by crook, with a desire to communicate through relationship, though psychological maturity has been readily defined, following Freud and Lacan, as "[a] process that moves away from fusion and toward separation."[20] Such a limited definition of relatedness denies and deems inferior other avenues of individuation, expression, and socialization within the world.

In other words, the classic definition of autobiography does not work when: "[A woman] is always aware of how she is being defined *as woman*, that is, as a member of a group whose identity has been defined by the dominant male culture."[21] That being said, the intricate paradoxes of gender theory are far too complex to continue to address here.[22] While the aforementioned understanding of women's writing may not be applicable to the entirety of the genre, it is certainly relevant to Spielrein's writing where she attempts to reconcile her private and public selves within the confines of a repressed post-Victorian society and, of course, in her diary.

Sabina Spielrein's Diaries

> Remembering my journal that looks like a Beethoven manuscript—blots, blue ink, red, yellow and green, pages torn by an angry pen, smudged with tears, leaping with joy from exclamation marks to dashes that speak more than the words between, my journal that dances with the heartbeat of a process in motion. . . . How can a woman write from her authentic center without being labeled "histrionic" or "hysterical"? Splat!
>
> —Marion Woodman, *The Pregnant Virgin*

In his description of Spielrein's diary in *A Secret Symmetry*, Aldo Carotenuto remarks: "The diary depicts her emotions and feelings toward her analyst, seen sometimes as a devil, sometimes as a hero. Any girl who keeps a diary about her analysis would very likely use similar language."[23] However, he then goes on to say that the language she uses is evidence of her "schizophrenic" personality and revelatory of "psychosis," which irresponsibly equates "any girl" in therapy who keeps a diary with a schizophrenic psychotic.[24] In *The Pregnant Virgin*, Marion Woodman counters this sentiment by stating that literalizing one's personal writing is akin to "[a] demonic parody of the creative imagination."[25] She further points out that such stigmatization of women's writing, as is apparent in Carotenuto's assessment, is how women become "trained to silence."[26] Nevertheless, while Spielrein's language has been pathologized, it is still possible to read her prose through a depth psychological and mythological lens.

It should also be pointed out that at the start of her diary, her analysis (as well as her relationship) with Jung is near its end, which means her diary is not merely "about her analysis," but about her life. For example, in one of the first available entries in August 1909, she wonders how to reconcile her past and present ambitions:

> What about the noble idea of my youth—to roam the earth surrounded by students like ancient Greek philosophers, while teaching my students in harmony with nature [and] the great outdoors? I wanted to teach them about sincere love for all living things. I had visions of us sitting outside in the sunset between spikes of grain rustling in the wind, enjoying a simple supper of bread. . . . "Not pomp . . . not divine splendor; only love may be blessed with happiness and suffering." I would say now—may it be boisterous, may it be delicate, may it be calm and equally wide; but I do want to teach my students about great and true love. Is there Someone who understands where I am coming from? When life requires you to follow the silliest of formalities in order to sustain it? . . . I was unable to bring up the main issue and that is that my friend [Jung] loves me. More about that later.[27]

At twenty-three years old, she expresses a romantic ideal of love in its many forms, from her desire to find kindred spirits and students to her eagerness to teach a personal form of mystical animism. Her description of the rustling grain underscores her authentic rather than forced sentimentality, as she spins what could be considered a simple occurrence into an image of spiritual awakening within nature. Even as Jung remains the "friend" that loves her, he is no longer the focal point of interest in this entry as much as is the abstract "Someone." In effect, she is a yearning nomad in search of new experiences and new people, though settled in her adopted intellectual lineage of Greek academics.

It is unclear whether or not she inserts a piece from her own poem when she refers to the "pomp" and "divine splendor" of joyous and sorrowful love, but an exact match could not be found, which leads one to believe it is an original piece. Nevertheless, these lines once again recall Wordsworth's "Intimations of Immortality" (as in her Last Will, chapter 1), evoking a kind of ephemeral beauty in her youthful exuberance for life. That being said, her voice is not one of nostalgia, like Wordsworth's, but an urgent plea to an unknown and open future.

On August 28, 1909, she explains: "I was unable to fully cherish the peaceful life within the circle of family. I am afraid of complete quietude. I need ambitious people around me; I need to partake in the lives of others; I need to be inspired by deep and profound emotions, and I need to be surrounded by music and art. In truth, it is impossible to satisfy me."[28] Her hunger to surround herself with inspirational people remains at the forefront of her thoughts, while the intensity in her voice highlights a desperate need to actualize her life's passions, which pull her in various directions throughout her diary, from art and music to mythology and motherhood. Her poetic sensibility is similarly mirrored in the work of Cixous, in a reflection on living: "I need to feel myself quiver with living: I need to call myself into living and to answer myself by living . . . I need double-living . . . I write celebrating living: I need to accompany living with music."[29] Likewise, Anaïs Nin wrote in a 1932 diary entry: "I felt I was gifted for living many lives fully."[30] Spielrein, longing to express multiple facets of her personality, speaks with the same celebration for life as Cixous and Nin in her dreams of artistic reverie.

The immediacy of her writing is owed in part to one of her literary inspirations, *Julie's Diary*. For example, on September 21, 1909, Spielrein admits: "I saw it described most beautifully [the joy and pain of life] in Peter Nansen's *Julie's Diary*. The book brought me much enjoyment. At the same time, it plagued me that I cannot write as well. . . . My mind is still youthful and fresh, my intellect is already very old."[31] *Julie's Diary*, as it is still known, was originally written as fiction in the late 1800s and republished in 1908, though one can imagine certain passages gripping Spielrein, such as these opening lines: "I am going to write all my thoughts and everything that happens in my life . . . I intend to write down the good as well as the bad. In this way the diary will be a truthful mirror. But I wonder when the book is finished, if it will tell the tale of a happy or sad life?"[32] Clearly influenced by *Julie* at the advent of her writing and torn between innocence and experience, Spielrein probably sought to create a space that allowed exposure to her own "truthful mirror."

When writing of her relationship to Jung during the break of the "scandal," before anger became the dominant emotion, her tone is a cry for resolution:

> Mother says it is impossible for my friend and me to remain friends after we have given one another our love. A man cannot tolerate pure friendship in the long run. . . . This made things hard for me, very hard! Oh God, what do I want? If I could summon Fate, if I could be sure that my entreaty spoken in front of witnesses could be fulfilled in any way, then I would request this: Fate, make it so that my friend and I are exceptions, that we will always meet each other in radiant joy, that we will support each other in happiness and in pain, and that even at a distance, we will form one soul, that we will give each other a hand in striving for "higher, farther, and further," or as my friend says, "for the good and the beautiful," and that we will support those who are weaker. Make me his guardian angel, his inspirational spirit that drives him onward to something new and wonderful. Perhaps I want too much?[33]

Only in hindsight is it possible to view this passage with such pathos, knowing that a destructive force is rearing like an ill wind about to blow apart the rest of her semester and preoccupy her mind with disbelief and grief, as is evident in her letters to Freud noted in chapter 3. Her depth of connection to the mythopoeic is vivid here as she calls on Fate in a manner similar to Percy Shelley urging the heavens to "Be thou, Spirit / fierce, / My spirit! Be thou me, impetuous one!"[34] Her words are also met with clarity, knowing that in her exaggeration she probably "asks too much" from Fate in the midst of this particular extramarital affair (or, abuse of power). Still, she holds a dramatic ideal of "good" and "beautiful" love and seeks to swear to the role of Muse with a holy oath, if only to be rescued from a heartbreak she is too terrified to predict. This was the last time she would write with such unabashed hope in the "radiant" fervor to love and to be loved, pleading with Fate to retain an untarnished image of Jung that once shattered becomes, for her, irreparable.

During this time, she is also panicked about releasing chapters of her doctoral dissertation to her advisor, Dr. Bleuler, and relays on September 23, 1909: "I was dreaming that I was with Father and Mother . . . and heard the words of my father say that I have come to the world to do something great, [and] I should just work quietly and patiently."[35] As she links her dissertation to an accomplishment of "something great," anxiety about work begins to dominate her personal writing. She frequently ponders future success and becomes concerned about maintaining a balance between her personal and professional lives. Though Jung later figures into this entry as a dangerous presence looming in the distance, the emphasis is clearly on her own academic ambition, which she views as a kind of heroic destiny. Even if patience and calm are mildly ironic words to describe her emotional state at this time, she does attempt to integrate her dream into her waking life by reaffirming her commitment to her work.

There is a yearlong break in the diary before she emerges again on September 8, 1910, though one can imagine that she remained preoccupied with her dissertation and continued processing her relationship with Jung. Now, her writing is more reflective and begins to show signs of slight disillusionment:

> Why this unrest again? Why this pain? Unfortunately, I had to continue with my work [dissertation], i.e. the "exam chase." . . . I also went to my colleague to recover and to console her in her weariness with life. . . . Is this youth, the strength and bloom of humanity? Is it also possible that I will never enter a different milieu among people who love life as much as I do, who understand how to find beauty in everything and do not always jeer at everything. . . . What do I want? . . . I had hardly mentioned my concerns about the fate of my [dissertation] . . . when the wish was fulfilled. . . . He [Bleuler] asked me whether I would like to publish the work in a Freudian journal. . . . And now: will it actually be printed? . . . Speaking honestly, my work contains a few interesting and exciting things, and therefore it is good that it will be read.[36]

Nearing twenty-five at this point, her primary concern is her future reception as a scholar, while also fearing judgment by the field for her first publication. Though she has been reassured by Dr. Bleuler, she continues to doubt the validity of her work while still craving to make a name for herself in academia. It appears she is restless to move forward in life and find her true pack, or those that similarly revel in the "beauty" of life rather than lethargically sit in "ennui." Her greatest disappointment is also revealed, possible perhaps only because she is still in it: youth. She has been let down by her own expectations of youth and by others' seemingly lackluster response to her own zest for living, though she retains the freedom of age to ask: "What is it I want?"

There is a tonal shift in this passage to the sarcastic and slightly overwrought (involving "agitation" and "pain"), and it should be noted that at the request of Dr. Bleuler, she has allowed Jung to become an additional dissertation advisor, thus entwining their lives once more. Still, bored by a perceived monotony, she again evokes Anaïs Nin in her desire to find a group of peers lit by the same internal fire: "I go out into the world to seek life, and the experience I want is denied me because I carry in me the force which neutralizes it."[37] Though minimal, a fracture between the younger and older Spielrein is apparent, as scarcely an entry is written without reference to her dissertation and to her growing need of independence.

Indeed, even as she recalls her relationship with Jung, it is largely placed in the past tense, as she begins to separate the memory of herself in therapy (and in the relationship) from her present life. For instance, though she endeavors to see him as "noble" after his "horrid behavior," she pauses for a brief moment on an image of a shared embrace before brushing the memory aside and defining the affair as a "wild power," stating, "Yes, it was a lot!"[38] She further reflects upon a specific therapy session:

> "These intelligent eyes," he sighed sometimes, or tears would come to his eyes when I would tell him something, for example something about the psychological music of Wagner (still unpublished). And I was prepared to die for him, to give him my honor. It was my first youthful love. Life without him, or at least not for him, for the child that I wanted to give him ["Siegfried"], seemed impossible to me. I wrote poems for him, composed little songs about him, I thought only of him.[39]

She details her past behavior with a cathartic purge not evident in earlier entries, as if trying to relay a depth of emotion accessible only through memory. There is a sadness to her ruminations that reveals a previous life now lost to time and irretrievable after the scandal. An older self is also apparent in her reflection on the infatuation she felt when she was younger, before she would come to see the affair through the lens of "horrid behavior" and as a source of her own suffering. Additionally, music permeates this passage in the references to her compositions as well as to her poems, which she often scored to piano, and to Wagner's opera, the latter of which would inspire her to expound upon the concepts of sacrifice and sexuality in her dissertation and in her development of the "death instinct."

In late September (1910), rather than remain in a romantic idealization of the past, she slowly progresses into anger around the affair:

> In the language of society I might be called immoral, mistress or perhaps "maitresse." He can openly appear in public with his wife, while I have to hide from public. . . . However, the fact that I had to hide still always hurt me. As a matter of fact, he wanted to invite me into his house and make me his wife's friend. It is

> completely understandable that his wife did not approve of this idea. . . . But really; should I want this? Could we be happy? I think none of us could . . . because the thought of his wife and children would make us miserable. . . . She has been the reason for my suffering many times; in my thoughts, I often asked her for forgiveness for the pain I caused her family! Actually, my love mostly caused me pain.[40]

Her ambivalence in this passage must be considered vis-à-vis the authority (and trust) Jung could have exercised as a figure of power as her previous therapist, which undoubtedly led to her confusion and self-blame on the matter. Here, Spielrein actively grieves the memory of being asked to enter into a polygamous arrangement that she believes would have produced nothing but misery. Even considering the situation continues to wreak tremendous emotional havoc as she comes to terms with how living with his wife (Emma) would actually make her feel. Obviously still empathetic, she finally confesses to and assesses her own pain. She also continues to ask herself, on her own terms, what it is that *she* wants.

Moreover, she realizes that as a woman she would only be further subjected to the shame and stigmatization, as "mistress," that has left her feeling isolated and ostracized from the public. Even so, she ceases to rationalize the affair and refuses to be granted reprieve from the harm she believes was caused to his family solely based on a romanticized notion of "love." That is to say, the rose-colored glasses have seemingly been lifted as she admits to some of the darker, less comfortable realities of the relationship that caused everyone involved a significant amount of suffering.

On September 11 she reorganizes her thoughts around the reality of her position:

> How could I hope for new love with a child in tow? In addition, my scientific goals would suffer significantly if I made such a decision. I would not be accepted anywhere with a little boy. That would be the best-case scenario. . . . So, I will try to fall in love with someone else if at all possible. I want him to love and respect me; I want to merge my life with his so I do not just have a meteor who causes current and subsequent agony, so my female pride does not suffer constantly and I do not have to suffer because of others.[41]

As if awakening from a fog, she readjusts to her own authentic path of scientific scholarship. Realizing her deeply felt "agony" as a socially shamed woman ("mistress"), it is of note that even when reflecting on her past desire to have a baby with Jung, she pictured herself alone and in search of a new love while encumbered by a child. Further, she speaks to the difficulty of retaining autonomy and acceptance at work when a woman is also a mother, a still-present societal stigma she would challenge after the birth of her first child in 1913. Though clearly still healing, she reaffirms her own desire for a steady and reciprocal relationship by pointing to the future and claiming what she wants from a partner: love, respect, companionship, and union. Her image of a meteor perfectly encapsulates the tension within this passage as it unconsciously conjures the image of a burning and destructive crash. The message is clear: she is resolved not to suffer.

A New Direction

> Some parts of my work delighted him. . . . Oh, God, if he had any idea how much I have suffered and am suffering because of him! . . . I am ashamed that I wasted so much time. But courage! Oh yes—courage!
>
> —Sabina Spielrein, 1910

Her anger slowly evolves during the time Jung is invited to edit her dissertation. In a fragment from late September (1910), she more fully realizes her interchangeability in relationship to Jung when speaking of a female patient:

> Being one of the many who pine for him and receive his kindly glance and a few nice, friendly words. Looking up to him from below and fulfilling all of his wishes in order not to draw his ire onto oneself! Not enough accommodation has been made for his vanity, and so one must atone for this severely: he takes on a very cold tone, and who suffers the worst from this? Not him, of course: a bit of annoyance can be driven out with work, the love for one can be replaced with love for another. Then one is certain that this woman will end up humiliating herself, and she will become the dumb little girl. . . . [Jung] recommended that I publish my second work alongside his. . . . He found the idea "sexual instinct/death instinct" thoroughly worthy of working on. I clung to my scientific work and imagined scenes of my future success and thereby forced myself back to "reason."'[42]

The more emotional distance that is maintained, the more her determination to succeed finds an outlet, and the clearer she becomes in her scholarship. She relates how she was once that "dumb little girl" who was tormented, and is perhaps still tormented, by Jung's behavior and speaks profoundly to the experience of humiliation and anxiety that can accompany heartbreak. She also provides an unflattering description of Jung's gaze when cast upon female patients, viewing them as commodities continually traded in for newer models. It is interesting that in her stream of consciousness she links her reflection on love to her work on the "death instinct," assertively channeling her energy into her own life and future rather than propelling into memories of the past. Being at her most self-critical, she continues to acknowledge the negative impact the affair has had on her emotional state, so that any lingering idealization of Jung is replaced by her belief that she has merely been "one of the many."

Speaking of a different patient who has developed feelings for Jung, Spielrein writes with a caustic tone:

> She loves him and believes, that he loves her. "Blessed is [s]he who believes." . . . And now I come early in the morning and am weak and tired because I must renounce love, meanwhile she hopes and glows from passion. Who knows: me he considers "dangerous" and takes heed in front of me, and the love he suppresses in my presence may find an object in her. "So you have outlived your appeal," I thought, remembering Mr. Mark's various ladies in *Julie's Diary*. Oh, protective spirit, save me from this terrible experience! I cannot possibly be one of the many. . . . It is necessary for me to know that he has not exchanged me for another girl so quickly.[43]

Because nothing more is known of the "She" in this passage, the woman (Ms. Aptekmann) may be interpreted as a surrogate for Spielrein's own emotional response to the relationship. As "She" is hopeful and in love, Spielrein is depleted, desperate, and bereft of her former encomia. Again she expresses a feeling of being replaced and betrayed because she believes her value has been placed on ephemeral physical attraction, underscoring the equation of women's worth with an arbitrary standard of aesthetic appeal. Her mental state also finds its parallel in her body, manifesting as exhaustion and a loss of vitality. She invokes *Julie* in her identification with the protagonist who similarly comes to "renounce love" after an upsetting end to her own relationship. Love's ideal that courses through Spielrein's earlier entries with an air of splendor is here diminished to delusion.

In late September, after focusing on her work, she reveals a transformative mythic image:

> When I looked in the mirror before going to sleep, I was violently startled: that wasn't me with a rock-gray face and unsettling, glowing, deep black eyes peering back at me: it was a powerful and

> dark Want coldly waiting in the depths, that would not stop at anything. 'What do you want?' I asked myself, frightened. . . . The next morning I was completely changed. The air was cool, and I breathed it in with delight. . . . "Do you want to?" I asked myself. "Oh yes!" I answered, without knowing what it was. I felt myself determined for something great and sublimely above everything.[44]

Her own creative purpose (destiny) continues to well up within her despite any external drama. She asks herself what it is in her depths that she wants, which powerfully affirms her agency as an active participant in her life's journey. She confronts, rather than ignores, this terrifying image within her psyche and stares into it—into herself in the mirror—and speaks to her soul. In *Alchemy*, Marie-Louise Von Franz defines such an inner dialogue as "active imagination," which she considers a staple of depth psychology as it is a "meditation" on an image of the inner self (through dialogue or any artistic endeavor) that leads to "underlying meaning" appropriate to one's life.[45] Anthony Storr notes in *The Essential Jung* that active imagination was taught to be "[a] state of reverie in which judgment was suspended but consciousness preserved. They were then enjoined to note what fantasies occurred to them, and to let these fantasies go their own way without interference."[46] It would appear that not only is Spielrein utilizing her imagination, but also actively engaging with the core of her being, to which she answers in a rapturous "Yes."

There is debate about whether or not the word reads "wolf" (*wolf*) or "want" (*Wollen*) due to the original document's legibility. Nonetheless, because the wolf figures into her consciousness so profoundly in its mythologized translation, a brief pause on the significance of wolf imagery in relation to mythology and women's psychology is still in order. The American poet Diane Di Prima, when speaking of her own femininity, recites in her poem "DREAM: The Loba ["Wolf"] Reveals Herself" that the wolf acts as a figure of protection, a "great mystic beast" and a "green warrior woman."[47]

Di Prima also refers to the wolf as "Mother" and "Myself," at once a dangerous yet archetypal and life-sustaining "feminine" energy that manifested for her in a meditation on the image of a wolf.[48] In *The Goddess*, Christine Downing relates the wolf to Greek goddess and huntress Artemis, who is referred to as "the Wolf-One," due to, among other things, a "fearless self-sufficiency" and her "utterly uncompromising" and singular personality.[49] She represents the untamed nature of the soul and, in her connection to childbirth, the "struggle to be born."[50] Spielrein's independent spirit and her connection both to child psychology and to the idea of *coming into being* closely align with this image of Artemis, with or without an explicit reference to a wolf on her part.

Similarly, in *Women Who Run with the Wolves*, Clarissa Pinkola Estés posits that "La Loba" ("Wolf Woman") represents both the soul and the power of the unconscious, often synonymous with a woman's wild and radical individuality. To Estés, "She" comes as a teacher-guide, a storyteller, an inspiratrice, and often visits "through night dreams, through events half understood and half remembered."[51] This description directly relates to Spielrein's hazy, disjointed and half-understood memory, though it left her feeling renewed and empowered.

Estés states that when the archetype of the wolf is integrated: "She canalizes through women. If they are suppressed, she struggles upward. If women are free, she is free."[52] Further: "No matter how many times she is forbidden, quelled, cut back, diluted, tortured, touted as unsafe, dangerous, mad, and other derogations, she emanates upward" as affirmation of a woman's instinctual self.[53] The wolf is recognized by Estés as a sexual symbol and dangerous or not (and female or not), the image conjured by Spielrein is one is one that she readily accepts as a darker yet positive part of herself without seeking any literal meaning from it; instead, she trusts her body's assimilation of the image.

Throughout her diary, Spielrein continues to speak to an ambiguous spirit guide, though perhaps it is this inner image of herself that is conjured. Indeed, her resounding "Yes" recalls Molly Bloom in the last lines of James Joyce's *Ulysses*: "Yes I said yes I will yes."[54] In this moment of the soliloquy, Molly sensually recalls the day her husband proposed to her, where her entire mind, body, and spirit acquiesce to an image of life (and a future) that is conjured through the action of saying "Yes." Like Spielrein, her "yes" also seems a reaffirmation and recommitment to her life in the present.

Contrarily, Carotenuto uses Spielrein's dream images as evidence of mental illness as well as an "inability" to confront reality, citing the "uselessness" of her efforts to progress beyond Jung.[55] Yet Spielrein's dream imagery often drips with mythic symbolism, for example, when extremely fatigued and allowing her mind to slowly drift into imagination:

> This produces a hypnagogic figure, a polygon where I "crawl" along the perimeter. . . . [T]he polygon turns into a mesh wire that I want to climb up, but a quiet dark-haired girl grabs me by the foot every time and pulls me down. . . . [Then] I see a beetle climbing up a spider's web and I touch it with my finger. Each time it has to start over again or at least go back a good part of the way.[56]

Seemingly out of the blue, Carotenuto states that this dream points to Spielrein's clinical "anal fixation."[57] While he believes this dream to be a product of institutionalization, Spielrein herself refers to the above as a current and recurring image (since 1904) in a letter to Jung dated in 1917. She goes on to relay that her images are symbolic and appear from the "side-conscious," resulting in part from her own complexes and ambitions. It is strange that Carotenuto completely dismisses her own analysis (written when she was a competent clinician) in favor of a stigmatized "anal fixation." Instead of examining this dream through the lens of psychosis, it may be helpful to trace the mythic relevance of a few of these images in relation to the context of Spielrein's life. Though the entirety of the dream cannot be analyzed in detail in this chapter, I would like to offer an alternative and mythic interpretation of some of her images: the beetle and the spider.

In Egyptian mythology, the Sungod Ra is renewed every night after a confrontation with the underworld, where he is transformed into a beetle before rising with the sun each morning. As further detailed by Theodor Abt in *Knowledge for the Afterlife: The Egyptian Amduat—A Quest for Immortality*: "The Sungod is like a prototype of a well-functioning human ego that is able to connect to the life-giving forces of the unconscious night-world and is not destroyed by them. . . . It enables consciousness to be once again in tune with . . . supportive but also potentially negative forces" of the psyche.[58] Metaphorically speaking, it is the tale of the "reunion of soul and body" that must take place in order for "new life" to grow.[59] This journey, as depicted by Abt, marks a transformation of self that utilizes depth psychological language and is amplified by stark mythic imagery, like those found in Spielrein's dream. For instance, the beetle may signal an underworld journey of her own, where she is "seized" and pulled down by "dark" unrecognizable forces (a shadow self?) to encounter less-comfortable and "potentially negative" inner realities.

Though the image of the beetle signals a time of "panic," it ultimately leads to personal relief and "rebirth."[60] Ra represents a "quest for renewal" expressed in the depths of the dream world and after much distress, "in the form of a scarab," he rises with the new dawn.[61] R. T. Rundle Clark's *Myth and Symbol in Ancient Egypt* further relates: "The beetle is . . . master of eternity."[62] Von Franz likens the scarab to "the secret of sexual generation" as well as to the "re-creation of the world."[63] It is possible then that the image of the beetle in Spielrein's dream mimics such a confrontation and process of transformation and rebirth. In fact, hope of renewal is given in the dream as she attempts to help the beetle begin its climb "over and over," as she similarly determines to "scramble up" on her own despite being repeatedly dragged down.

Since she "crawls" along the edge of her dream before turning to a central web image, the spider must also be given attention. Von Franz does not hold the spider's web in high regard, and states instead that it is a "negative illusion" as well as a dream symbol of "Maya, weaver of a fantasy world."[64] Yet other cultural traditions connect the spider and its web to "feminine spirituality," and as recounted in Chevalier and Gheerbrant's *Dictionary of Symbols*, it is a "Lunar manifestation, weaving . . . reminiscent of that of the Fates. . . . Divination through spiders is still practiced in the former Inca empire," where Maya is not only considered a goddess of illusion, but one of "beauty and creation."[65] Additionally, in West African folklore, the spider is a figure that "[p]repared the material from which the first humans were made and created the Sun, the Moon, and the Stars."[66] Therefore, while Von Franz labels it a negative image, the spider also brings with it positive amplifications.

That is to say, the context of Spielrein's life determines her relation to these mythic images; they cannot be solely defined by an abstract pathology. Hence, when analyzing the dream, her past trauma, her desire for independence, and her ongoing fascination with death and resurrection should be considered in relation to the image of the beetle. Also, her hope to produce worthwhile material in the field of psychology seems especially relevant to the spider's connection to female creativity. While this analysis is somewhat speculative, it is as mythically appropriate to Spielrein as "anal fixation" appears clinically appropriate to Carotenuto.

Spotlight: Siegfried

Night of annihilation,
let your mist fall!
Siegfried's star
now shines upon me:
he is mine forever,
always mine,
my inheritance, my own,
my one and all:
radiant love,
laughing death!

—Valkrie Brünnhilde,
The Richard Wagner Libretti

In October, she reflects on her doctoral work, her religion, and muses: "It was . . . it was . . . a wonderful dream, coming to me in the words of the little song I composed. Yes. And this dream was my Siegfried."[67] She continues to explain that this mythic figure has become a symbol for the manifestation of her dissertation as well as her "higher purpose," even though she is worried that her work might not amount anything out of the ordinary.[68] She also speaks of birthing Siegfried, and though she was encouraged by Jung to interpret the figure as a real baby (as noted previously), he is here made synonymous with her own creativity and used in relation to a musical composition rather than interpreted as an actual child. Her strong connection to Siegfried, specifically as rendered in Wagner's opera, begs a deeper exploration due to his connection to the motifs of destruction and creation, which permeate future diary entries as well as her own academic research.

Richard Wagner's opera *The Nibelungen Lied*, or the "Ring Cycle" (1876), revivified interest in mythic prose and poetry for decades after its initial performance. In the closing movement of *Siegfried*, as noted in the opening quotation to this section, the Valkyrie Brünnhilde recounts the birth of love that is paradoxically brought about by the destruction of herself and her lover, the Norse god Siegfried. According to W. C. Sawyer's 1904 *Teutonic Legends in the Nibelungen Lied and the Nibelungen Ring*, the opera was a source of German pride: "Not only the lovers of music, but the students of folklore and of general literature, are thus stirred to the pursuit of the old myths which so illustrate the peculiarities of our race and the history of our moral development."[69] German nationalism was clearly afoot within the works of Wagner, but it is in the opera's mythopoeic aspects that the figure of Siegfried is considered here to be the story that so intimately captivated Spielrein's soul.

While detailing Wagner's entire work would reach far beyond the scope of this book, suffice it to simplistically say that Siegfried and Brünnhilde reside in Norse mythology and folklore, and in the summation of Sawyer: "Wagner's *Nibelungen Ring* [Ring of the Nibelung, a king of dwarves], consists of four operas . . . dealing with the struggle for the possession of a magic ring. . . . *Das Rheingold* [an introduction] . . . *Die Walkure* (The Valkyries) . . . *Siegfried*, and *Götterdämmerung* (Twilight of the Gods)."[70] According to Freda Winworth in her 1897 work *The Epic of Sounds*, Siegfried is recognized as a sungod defined by his union with his lover: "When inspired by the secret of Love, imparted by Nature, proves [him]self equal to all tasks."[71] Sadly, Siegfried is overtaken by lust for power and betrays, if unintentionally, his love of Brünnhilde, an act that destroys the realm of the gods.

However, in the final scene of the opera, the lovers are united through Brünnhilde's own bodily sacrifice on Siegfried's funeral pyre. Actually, annihilation of the old gods is necessary for the birth of new earthly creations, and as Winworth notes, their deaths bring about the supposed "Reign of Love."[72] This reclamation of relationship is defined as "Love's Redemption," and makes possible a new era of beauty and truth.[73] Sawyer characterizes the opera as "emphatically moral" due to the guiding principle of the work residing in: "Loyalty of lovers to one another."[74] As Bulfinch iterates in his *Mythology*: "The gods have broken moral law, and coveted power [the ring] rather than love, gold rather than truth, and therefore must perish. They pass, and a new era, the reign of love and truth, has begun."[75] These motifs illuminate the power that Siegfried held as a personal image for Spielrein when she dreamt of birthing (or being) such a hero, when she longed for a passionate romantic relationship, when she became intoxicated by ambition, or when she felt her scholarship to be similarly bound by labors of love and sacrifice.

The idea of destruction in service of creation can also be clearly traced throughout Spielrein's dissertation as well as in her paper "Destruction as the Cause of Coming into Being" (1912), both of which will be further examined in the next chapter. Still, it may be quickly pointed out that to Spielrein, the surrender of the self (ego) during sexual union is represented by images of death or sacrifice, as in Siegfried and Brünnhilde, though such temporary destruction ultimately brings about transformation and new creation—whether metaphorically, artistically, or physically in the form of a child. This equation of one's sexual impulse with destruction and creation is what she termed the "death instinct."

Love and Death

In late October, she begins to delve deeper into her own psychological makeup when reflecting upon past experiences with religion and idolatry:

> Until the age of 13 I was extremely religious, despite some contradictions and despite the scorn of my father, I dared not abandon a belief in God. Detaching from God was extremely difficult for me. A void was created, though I retained my "protective spirit" [or "guardian spirit"]. When I dreamt of a girl friend in my loneliness, I always imagined a Jewish girl, who would be first in the class after me. And there was such a girl. . . . I loved her with all the tenderness of filial love . . . then I was disappointed and chose a Christian girl as my best friend. . . . Later I distanced myself people in general; it was in the 6th grade, after the death of my little sister, when my illness began. I fled to solitude and let my two friends develop a deep friendship amongst themselves. . . . I united them and then continued on my own."[76]

This is the only time she speaks of her sister or of her sister's death, which she links directly to her "illness," seemingly dispelling the notion of congenital hysteria, as Jung previously diagnosed. She also underscores her withdrawal as a necessary isolation in order to more fully experience her grief, which coincides with her loss of faith in God. To compensate for her loss of religion, she cultivated relationships with de facto representations of Judaism and Christianity, possibly to help find solace within the "void." Yet academia is never far from her reflection, as even her childhood longed-for friend would be only second to her in class.

With striking similarity, Simone de Beauvoir is described in the 2010 introduction to *The Second Sex* as a girl of "singular brilliance . . . [who] lost her faith as a teenager, her dreams of a transcendent union . . . shifted from Christ to an enchanting classmate."[77] Since Spielrein's future work focused heavily on the union of the physical and spiritual elements, perhaps her friends acted as embodied complements to abstract religious theory, which she admits to processing all too cerebrally in its literal "contradictions." However, that was not the last time she would try to foster friendship between Jew and Christian, as she later attempted to reconcile the theories of Freud and Jung.

Interestingly, her reflection on God leads to an anecdote about an early male muse, and while she retains a sense of skepticism when speaking of religion, she would come to embrace a kind of pantheism in her mythic and symbolic study of religious figures:

> My history teacher [in high school]: Christian . . . he wins me with his high intelligence and the serious, sad look in his black eyes. . . . Later I learn to control myself when my interest in science opened up a whole new world. At the same time, my infatuation awakened in me and got even stronger, opening a great world unknown to me until now. I want to sacrifice something to him, I want to suffer for him. . . . I choose to increase my knowledge about various religious viewpoints. At this time, I was vividly interested in the psychology of religion. I took hours of lessons in old Hebrew in order to read the Bible in the original. I was looking for a friend with whom I could express myself completely. . . . I considered him [Hebrew teacher] a deity.[78]

Her personal attachment to an other is again defined by the other's tie to religion. While an appreciation for her high school teacher gives way to a passion for knowledge, it is his embodied presence that acts as representation for her metaphysical experience, which in turn opens up a new and deeper world of communication with her "crush." Her attraction seems to lie in being challenged on an intellectual level, and specifically in the mutual love of learning, which twice in this description evokes an erotic charge with an other. It becomes clear that from an early age she desired relationships stimulated by an academic inspiration that spilled over into an inflamed lust for life. Yet her conflation of divinity and individual must be held within the context of a reflection of the past. This passage is a reminder that there is distance between the younger and older Spielrein, and that as a scholar whose self-professed interest in the psychology of religion began years ago, she is here attempting to understand (or at least, to describe) the mythic power of sexual attraction.

Still, an inkling of her future scholarship is apparent in her desire to "suffer" for the teacher with whom she was infatuated. Her teenage experience recalls the religious ecstasy and passion of praised Catholic nun Julian of Norwich (1342–1416), who shares in the want to suffer for an idol: "I desired . . . more knowledge of the bodily pains of our Savior . . . for I would be one of them and suffer with Him. . . . I should have the more true mind in the Passion of Christ."[79] Like Julian, Saint Teresa of Ávila (1515–1582) expresses in *Interior Castle*: "This is a delectable death, a snatching of the soul from all the activities which it can perform while it is in the body; a death full of delight."[80] In their sublime adoration, Julian and Teresa yearn to experience Christ's bodily pain in order to demonstrate devotion. They equate love, religion, and closeness with imagery of pain, sacrifice, and death. By relating her memory, Spielrein speaks to this same idea that self-destruction is somehow connected to desire and union, a motif that would reemerge in "Destruction as the Cause of Coming into Being."

To End Is to Begin

> I'm in love! I'm not in love!
> I'm crazy! I'm not crazy!
>
> —Sappho, 615–571 BC

Clearly shifting away from Jung as a love interest (November 1910), she instead fears he will steal ideas from the research he has been reading:

> The first goal that I want to achieve is that my first work is so well written that it guarantees me a place in the psychoanalytic association [e.g. Vienna Psychoanalytic Society, VPS]. Even more important to me is my second work, 'On the Death instinct,' and I must confess that I am greatly afraid that my friend [Jung], who wanted to reference my idea in his article in July, with a mention that I have rights of priority, . . . now wants to refer to in January. Is it unjustified mistrust on my part? How could I worship a man who is lying, stealing my ideas, who is not my friend, but a petty, cunning rival? And love? . . . I love him and I hate him.[81]

It is known that her dissertation reveals her theory of archaic (ancestral, or what she terms "phylogenetic") components of the psyche as well as her initial development of the "death instinct." In the above passage, because she esteems her contribution to the field as innovative enough to be stolen, Jung is considered her rival rather than her confidante or therapist, even though her attachment to him is still in flux. Be that as it may, her trust and respect in him wavers and she views herself as a future colleague and peer instead of a patient or a subordinate scholar.

Gone is her idealization of Jung upon the realization that her work might be in danger from a man whom she had previously never questioned. Additionally, she once again evokes the emotional contradiction demonstrated by her beloved Julia in *Julie's Diary*, who expresses: "When I ask myself, if I love you, the answer is no—and yet—if at this moment you entered the room and asked me if I would be your wife, I would say yes without hesitation" (Nansen, 7). Spielrein mimics the equivocation felt in heartbreak when love and hate collide and subsequently devolve, at least for her, into bitter suspicion.

In December, Spielrein definitively turns toward hope for a relationship with someone other than Jung, who has fallen back into the "Don Juan role" which she finds "repugnant":

> He said that I should belong to the category of women who are not made for motherhood, but for free love. What can I say? I blush deeply at the memory . . . I was terribly depressed. . . . I want to love someone with all of my soul, one who can reciprocate my feelings with the force of youth . . . I want him to see what I am capable of and what I am worth. I want him to love me madly and I want to defy him. I want him to see how I can love and how I can lift myself. . . . Where is the man whom I could love?"[82]

Here, being a mother is juxtaposed and dichotomized against being a sexual woman, though Spielrein distrusts this notion and is clearly upset by Jung's seeming manipulation of her sexuality. She actively seeks a man whom she could love and who could love her in return and asserts her own need to be valued for her worth as a woman capable of intense feeling, intellect, and independent spirit.

The passage recalls her previous love-hate vacillation and expresses a sentiment akin to the Portuguese Nun, whose sixteenth-century letters to a departed lover lament: "I have to hate you like poison. . . . I was young, I was naïve . . . I owed to you the graces and beauty you found in me" (*Letters*, 45).[83] In parallel, Sylvia Plath underscores analogous emotions toward her husband, whom she discovered having an affair: "How much of life I have known: love, disillusion, madness, hatred, murderous passion . . . now the horror of primal feelings, obsessions"[84] While voicing similar conflicting passions, Spielrein ceases to fixate on a man whom she realizes does not embody the qualities deemed necessary for a partner.

In February 1911, she calls to the gods in preparation for her doctoral exams:

> I resist, because I have something noble and great to accomplish and am not made for the mundane. It is a struggle between life or death. . . . If there is a God-Father: may He hear me: no pain is unbearable to me, no sacrifice is too great to fulfill my sacred destiny! Before my final exam I call out: "Help me, Fate, because my mind is directed toward the good and my will—divine will!" . . . As a descendent of several generations of holy men, I believe in the psychic powers of my unconscious. One can in fact be so close to this "God" that one can speak with Him and find out what He wants, which is what is most useful for the sum energy of infinite generations that one calls an individual. So what do you want, God? Or, perhaps more correctly, what have you, Gods, decided in your common council?[85]

Here, Spielrein comes closest to expressing mythic pantheism with signature dramatic flair, as she recognizes the plurality of images available in her unconscious (psyche) that manifest as "Gods." In a prayer-like manner, she calls upon the gods with the force of a mystic lineage whose generational energies she considers coursing through her unconscious, supplying her with archetypal council. She deems these images accessible owing to her Jewish (rabbinic) background and believes it allows her an immediate and direct spiritual connection to the divine, which she calls upon for her exams rather than for an abstract beloved. Her source of confidence, like her religious proclivities, appear to manifest through academic verve and she thus remains "defiant" as a woman in her inability to settle into anything societally expected of her (or "routine"). Like Spielrein, the poet H.D. would later reflect (1927) in her autobiography that she could not predict at the time of her youth that "[her] entire failure to conform to expectations was perhaps some subtle form of courage."[86]

Almost a year later in early 1912 (the interim entries are missing or nonexistent), she has earned her PhD, moved away from Zurich, and notes that material from her dissertation is being prepared for publication. She briefly speaks of Freud, the VPS (to which she has now presented), her teaching, and of her ever-present desire to find a partner who may understand her own flaming soul: "My first work was very successful. In fact, because of my dissertation, I am now a member of the [VPS]. . . . All that I wished for to date has been fulfilled, with the exception of one: Where is the one I could love, whom I could make happy as a wife and mother of our children?"[87] For Spielrein, achieving success and practicing as a psychoanalyst is only complemented, rather than replaced, by becoming a wife and mother.

As if anticipating curiosity from an audience, she notes: "A reader would ask 'What happened?' There was nothing final, though much occurred, and yet no conclusion. Traveled from Zurich to holiday in Montreaux . . . from there—to Munich for its art history, and here [Vienna], where in isolation I completed my work, 'Destruction as the Cause of Coming into Being.' "[88] Simply, she has continued to move on with her life. Acknowledging a potential "reader" suggests that she may have intended to have her own diaries read, like those of her celebrated *Julie*, perhaps wondering how she would be viewed in her own attempt to reflect an image of truth. Excitedly, she writes about growing interest in her "death instinct": "Professor Freud, who has become dearly fond of me, is very enthusiastic and is telling everyone about my 'superb work.' "[89] With eagerness in her future endeavors and assurance in her intelligence, she focuses intently on contributing something to the study of psychology and mythology, though she now remembers Jung as "[the] one who crushed my whole life," and refers to herself as a woman "healthy, vigorous, intelligent, and equipped with a soul of burning love."[90]

After another short break in the diary, in the last available entry (July 1912), she briefly states that she has married Pavel (Paul) Scheftel, with whom she would have two children. After recalling a dream about serving tea, the diary's final thought trails off with ellipses, possibly unreadable to its translator, but nevertheless unfinished: "At night—'Freud' . . ."[91] As a reader, one is left with no real conclusion to her journey, though there remains a slight anticipation of her emergence as a scholar in her own right. Indeed, where her diary ends, her career begins—a picture completed with the aid of her available research and letters. While the diary only represents Spielrein from ages twenty-three to twenty-six, there is still a sense of the passing of time in a younger and an older self, a before and an after treatment, a before and after her dissertation, and an overarching endurance and dedication to life that is recreated and reconstructed in words.

> Writing is working; being worked; questioning (in) between (letting oneself be questioned) of same *and of* other without which nothing lives; undoing death's work by willing the togetherness of one-another, infinitely charged with a ceaseless exchange of one with another . . . a course that multiplies transformations by the thousands.
>
> —Hélène Cixous

Spielrein's diaries, which constitute only a piece of her personality, should be treated as such, and not merely taken as grist for the clinical mill to be used against her as diagnosis, though Carotenuto labels her diaries "schizoid," while Rosemary Balsam accepts the diagnosis of "borderline personality."[92] Yet Adolf Guggenbühl-Craig, in his article "From the Wrong Side: A Paradoxical Approach to Psychology," defines the depth psychological approach to life as having:

> [A] mythological background. A large part of our therapeutic work is rooted in mythology. We assist our patients in finding the mythic qualities of their lives, in shaping and forming their personal mythology. . . . We transform the meaningless chaos of their lives and suffering into meaningful mythological stories, novels, and dramas—into tragedies, yes, into comedies. . . . An incomprehensible life begins to take on the nature of a biography.[93]

Ironically, though Spielrein has often been treated as *The Ever-Patient*, she has not been given the same mythic treatment. Instead, her writing has been interpreted outside of the depth psychological framework even though she understood transforming "meaningless chaos" into "meaningful mythology" as early as 1911 in her doctoral work, as noted in chapter 1. Furthermore, she clearly saw her own life as material made for meaning and frequently spun confrontations with heartbreak, betrayal, ambition, success, and suffering into a personal mythopoetic narrative.

It appears that her writing has not been interpreted as an extension of mythopoiesis due to character stigmatization, and her potential contributions to multiple fields within academia have since been dismissed. However, her diaries reflect the experience of an intellectual woman who yearned for a muse as well as motherhood, and who reached for and achieved success in the midst of restrictive gender expectations in a male-dominated arena. It is thus with her written self in mind that attention is turned to her academic publications and to the development of her "death instinct."

5

Sabina Spielrein in Academia

Destruction and Transformation

> [Due to] mythological formations known to us from cultural psychology . . . we commit a generalization with every expression of a thought . . . because words are symbols that serve the precise purpose of forming that which is personal into the generally human and comprehensible.
>
> —Sabina Spielrein, "Die Destruktion als Ursache des Werdens"

Introduction

The development of Spielrein's pivotal contribution to academia, the "death instinct," can be found in her seminal work on the topic, "Destruction as the Cause of Coming into Being." Her concept is here traced through a draft document/letter to Jung previously dated 1907, but coincides much more with her intellectual interests and disintegrating relationship with Jung circa 1909–10. For example, much of the text is devoted to an emerging idea that is mentioned in a 1909 letter to Freud: "This demonic power is by its very nature destructive (evil) and is yet simultaneously also the most generative of forces, as from the destruction (of 2 individuals) a new individual is created. That is the sex drive, which is essentially a destruction drive . . . for the individual."[1] Also, in a diary entry from October 19, 1910, she writes: "Secretly germinating is my new work, 'On the Death Instinct,' [*ueber den Todesinstinkt*]."[2]

Since the undated document is in three segments, each perhaps written at a different date, the portions regarding the "death instinct" are explored in this chapter, while the remainder, concerning her personal relationship, is discussed in the next chapter vis-à-vis her correspondence. Notes from her presentation to the Vienna Psychoanalytic Society (VPS) in 1911 are also briefly referenced, as is her dissertation, before her publication is viewed in detail. While parts of her scientific understanding are considered outdated and at times heteronormative—though it should be remembered that she was theorizing female sexuality at a time when it was largely considered a symptom of hysteria—there are still mythological and philosophical gems worthy of further inspection.

Most crucially, her article is explored in relation to Freud's *Beyond the Pleasure Principle*, which has been given the academic credit of originating the "death instinct" through the figure of Thanatos, the Greek god and embodiment of Death. However, nowhere in his 1920 work does the term *Thanatos* appear, while it is explicitly referenced in Spielrein's. Lastly, the stigmatization of her work will be analyzed, since it has been widely demeaned as pathology and dismissed by prominent scholars in the field as a possible influence on Freud's work. Alternatively, I offer a reading of her article as a foundational work in the fields of comparative mythology and depth psychology, specifically as put forth by a woman and a scholar.

Development of the "Death Instinct"

> Let's not confuse the two: I refer to the degree of love that a person is capable of, not a passing attraction.
>
> —Sabina Spielrein

"Unedited Extracts from a Diary" has been dated "1906/7?" by French psychoanalyst Jeanne Moll, largely based on the fact that Spielrein had been traveling to Lago Maggiore (Switzerland) at that time and references the location in her writing. Yet in a letter to Freud, she wrote that she took (or quite possibly, dreamed) a trip to Lago Maggiore to prepare for her exams in 1908.[3] She also mentions a 1909 publication of her own within the text, leading me to attribute this later date to it. Further, it is somewhat inaccurate to call it a diary since she clearly speaks to Jung in the latter segment of the text and even asks him to return her letter in order to work out later the ideas contained within her writing.[4]

In Segment I, entitled "Two Speakers," Spielrein writes a fictionalized dialogue in order to shed light upon her theories: "One reaches the summit of his art only when he gives himself up to passion: it is a passion that warms his brain into life, irrigates it and forces his spirit to show its strength. The other . . . sometimes tries to present his case passionately, indeed violently and thunderously."[5] Though "the other" mentioned above has been attributed to Jung, her comments on the dual nature of passion may be understood metaphorically irrespective of literal "speakers." She uses descriptions of each unknown speaker to give voice to the charged and interdependent dynamic between art and passion, which she then relates to the intimacy of a romantic relationship. Her claim that surrendering to one's life purpose can be as nourishing as it can be dangerous also sets the stage for her later conceptualization of sexuality.

She continues: "From the point of view of the preservation of the species . . . it is impossible to understand why these endless tortures should be brought about by a person . . . what really is this abominable thing called love?"[6] Here she seeks to reconcile the emotional, psychological, and biological experiences of love, a recurring motif in her personal and academic work. Moreover, she pauses to question the existence of passion, which she feels only detracts from the (assumed) instinct to procreate, meaning the "torture" of love seemingly contradicts the body's urge to merely preserve the species. She offers no answers but instead goes on to write of a woman's discriminating choice in a sexual partner who fits an ideal image, since women's sexuality so frequently tied them to childbirth.[7]

Later in this segment she states that marriage does not solve the problem of lust for man or for woman and reasons that biology is therefore not the only instinct at play in sexual attraction.[8] She relates one's desire to experience the ineffable in a relationship to the romantic notion of a pathetic fallacy, or the "similarities between the storm in nature and the storm in one's own heart," which in turn, she posits, gives rise to longing for a spiritual "beyond."[9] She believes that every encounter with an other acts as a "mirror" for a self that secretly (or unconsciously) seeks transformation, and defers to Nietzsche as a reflection of human nature at once destructive and creative: " 'Rejoice . . . in our madness so as to be able to rejoice in our wisdom.' "[10]

She then turns from a macrocosmic perspective to a more intimate discussion on love: "We see our own pain in the soul of the other . . . hence the relief. . . . Every complex looks for its twin. . . . Shared sorrow is easier to bear."[11] In *Reflections on the Art of Living*, Joseph Campbell speaks to this sentiment when relating the key to his own marriage: "Suffering with, feeling another's sorrow as if it were your own . . . it is an immediate participation in the suffering of another to such a degree that you forget yourself and your own safety and spontaneously do what's necessary."[12] The notion of surrendering the self (ego) specifically when in the presence of a beloved, both in its positive and negative connotations, is what Spielrein labels the "death instinct."

To her, this instinct expresses itself like art, as it is similarly a complex, or an energy, that "wants to be transformed."[13] She explains that it may appear as something destructive, but "simply wants to emerge" in the outer world.[14]

She writes that the "death instinct" contains within it a psychic energy that may be literally, rather than symbolically, manifested and thus negated of its sacred element: "Elevated instincts [may] present themselves as murderous instincts . . . [and] that is how young people, completely transformed by their desires, strike magnificent poses, torches in hand, pathetic speeches on their lips, and leap to their death."[15] Contrary to literalisms, she urges us to look past death into the "culminating point of love. . . . It is when it is placed beyond death that a complex attains the sublime."[16]

Repeatedly throughout her writing, she refers to one's yearning for this so-called beyond equated with the realm of the sublime, and believes that such an experience may be achieved through sexuality.[17] To understand what she means by the "sublime," it is useful to turn to Immanuel Kant's "Analytic of the Sublime" from *The Critique of Judgment*: "The sublime . . . is to be found in [the] formless . . . for this directly brings with it a feeling of the furtherance of life, and thus is compatible with charms and with the play of the imagination."[18] He continues by stating that the imagination is at once being enticed by pleasure and repelled by it, which may lead to a felt experience of "violence to the imagination" that is paradoxically "judged to be only the more sublime."[19] Kant's description of the sublime as both imaginally and emotionally engaged yet potentially destructive/violent perfectly illustrates Spielrein's use of the term in connection with the "death instinct."

Her frustration toward sexual demonization in religious traditions also becomes apparent, albeit briefly: "Sexual power is considered to be demonic power, a destructive force; the sexual act is a sin! Where does that come from? How is it that everyone always puts up so much resistance to sexual feelings? Why are they hidden, why are they felt to be unbearable, why can they be expressed only in a sublimated or symbolic form?"[20] Rather than attempt to answer these questions, she instead meditates on the significance of one's desire for a union where "two individuals [are] fused into one," which is experienced, in her opinion, as a temporary loss of self, often accompanied by images of death and resurrection.[21] Hers would be a useful perspective to add to the works of Georges Bataille or Camille Paglia, both of whom expanded upon this theme in the later twentieth century, in *Tears of Eros* and *Sexual Personae* respectively.

Spielrein considers this giving of the self the "most sacred knowledge" in the world and utilizes Siegfried and Brünnhilde, specifically from Wagner, as mythic representations of the "death instinct," demonstrating "[the] domination of the idea of love."[22] As Freda Winworth further explicates in *The Epic of Sounds*:

> Jubilantly they [Siegfried and Brünnhilde] surrender themselves wholly to the influence of the exultant, overpowering feelings in their hearts, though this passion bears in itself the element of

> destruction, both for themselves and for the gods . . . she surrenders herself willingly, and calls down the night of annihilation on all that she once held sacred. . . . With an exulting cry of "Shining Love, laughing Death," they fall into each other's arms. The joyous Motive of Love's Ecstasy resounds triumphantly.[23]

The motif of dying into and being resurrected by love is certainly not new to Spielrein and is clearly present in poetry and literature far predating her, as evidenced in Winworth's 1897 work above. Instead, Spielrein's contribution to the motif of destruction and creation is the infusion of psychological and physiological analysis. Rather than seen as something shameful, she grounds her concept in the body and elevates sexuality to a path of interpersonal transformation, something she will repeat in her publication.

She also asserts that sexuality, and female sexuality in particular, carries with it an instinctual desire to be embraced by a beloved, which she equates with sacrifice and "annihilation."[24] In *Sufism: The Transformation of the Heart*, Llewellyn Vaughan-Lee reflects on the death of Shams, the poet Rumi's beloved, and the latter's subsequent *annihilation*: "Inwardly [Rumi] united with Shams. . . . He had walked this road of annihilation, the sacrifice of the self that leads to union with the Beloved."[25] Spielrein's "annihilation" touches upon this same sense of mysticism, and though hers is distinctly embodied, she later expresses: "It is not the sexual feeling . . . it is the instinct of transformation which every complex possesses . . . the sexual complex also possesses a transformation instinct; and the sexual act is but a particular aspect of this transformation."[26] Here, the "death instinct" and "transformation instinct" are made synonymous in her personal writing, as they will again be made synonymous in her article.

She continues to ponder aspects of individuality in relation to her concept and argues that there are coexisting instincts of resistance and attraction integral to one's sexual identity, summarizing: "Nobody really knows what makes up an individual. A person consists of feelings and counter-feelings . . . positive and negative emotions."[27] She then goes on to provide examples of conflicting love/death images; for instance, she lists *Le Vaisseau Fantôme* (*The Ghost Ship*) as prime representation of the "death instinct," a French opera by Pierre-Louis Dietsch set to Wagner's poem "The Flying Dutchman" about a phantom ship condemned to eternally sail the seas with no living crew aboard. The ship and its apparitions are ultimately saved by an act of female sacrificial—defined by Spielrein as "destructive"—love that is capable of pointing "beyond" death and into the realm of redemption and union with the beloved.[28] It should be pointed out that this narrative is defined by Spielrein as symbolic of a human instinct for union and transformation and is not tied to gender.

According to Sarette Zecharia in *Mysterium Coniunctionis: The Meeting Ground of the Masculine and the Feminine*, mystical roots of transformation also reside in a Kabbalistic image of holy union with the divine: "*Shekhinah,* which denotes the feminine aspect of the Divine . . . is in search to reunite with the masculine aspects of the Divine."[29] This spiritual union, she illuminates, is embodied and reflected in our relationships: "[The] alchemical process of the coniunctio . . . sexual union . . . is the actual union of [for example] man and woman in marriage," where the divine archetype of the *Shekhinah* is enacted in the physical world.[30] Spielrein, already known to be influenced by the mystical aspects of her Jewish background, states that her position would be ideologically similar even if "[she] had not known the essence of the sexual act."[31]

Her hypothesis of reaching the "beyond" through the sexual act evokes what Martin Buber in *I and Thou* (1923) calls the I-Thou relationship: "The primary word *I-Thou* can only be spoken with the whole being . . . I become through my relation to the Thou; as I become *I,* I say *Thou*. All real living is meeting."[32] I-and-Thou establishes a "world of relation" where "He, She, or It" is transformed into a sacred "meeting" between two individuals.[33] Spielrein's "death instinct" may be interpreted through this lens of Buber's, where relation to an other is heightened by an instinctual desire to dissolve and transform through this "meeting" with a beloved in a moment when s/he becomes "Thou."

As Buber further expounds, perhaps influenced by the "death instinct" himself: "The moments of the *Thou* appear as strange lyric and dramatic episodes, seductive and magical, but tearing us away to dangerous extremes, loosening the well-tried context, leaving more questions than satisfaction behind them, shattering security."[34] Spielrein speaks to such *Thou* moments: "The sight of two magnificent grey eyes may accentuate the sympathy . . . they are linked to a certain powerful emotional complex . . . [and] besiege the psyche" with the potential to destroy the "I" as much as lead to its rebirth.[35]

In *Preludes: Essays on the Ludic Imagination, 1961–1981*, Christine Downing praises this manner of relating as "[a] long-awaited complement to Jung's emphasis on individuation, on the self," where instead interpersonal transformation is emphasized.[36] Spielrein reaffirms in her concluding remark (of Segment I): "It is clear to me that . . . the alpha or omega, of feeling is the transformation instinct, which could eventually be satisfied by the sexual act."[37] To Spielrein, such transformation is possible, as noted in the opening quotation to this section, when one gives of love as much as one is capable, rather than in a "passing attraction," the duration of which may last a moment or a lifetime.[38]

In her article "Transforming At-One-Ment: Spielrein, Jung, Bion," Janet Sayers iterates: "Spielrein . . . emphasized intersubjectivity . . . self-loss with another in love. . . . Today, therapists and psychoanalysts are often much more friendly to the notion of losing oneself in oneness with another as means of healing transformation. But they scarcely, if ever, credit Spielrein for pioneering this idea."[39] Indeed, Spielrein asserts that all psychic energy "makes use of all possible ways to get transformed" whether that be through art, religion, or relationship, but reminds us that her particular interest relies on the interdependence between sexuality and symbols of destruction.[40] Prior to her conclusion, she also differentiates her own research from Jung's by claiming intellectual agency and independence on the topic of sexuality: "There is a fundamental difference between your concept and mine . . . this is what *I* think."[41]

The "Death Instinct" in Her Dissertation

In her 1911 dissertation, *Concerning the Psychological Content of a Case of Schizophrenia*,[42] she formulates her own theory on the occurrence of mythic imagery within the unconscious. After extensive dream interpretation and interviews with her patient, she states in her conclusion:

> The parallel to the mythological mindset points to a special relationship between the dream mechanism and archaic thinking. This impression immediately came to mind when I examined [the] patient. . . . While Freud and Jung initially established a parallel between neurotic and dream phenomenon with the emergence of schizophrenia, I believe I can add a significant contribution to the Freud-Jung concept based on my phylogenetic approach . . . i.e. our own personal experiences and our inherited ancestors' experiences. My collection of material can offer researchers who analyze similarities between dreams, psychosis and myths considerable evidence.[43]

Brought into academia by German biologist Ernst Heinrich in 1866, "phylogenetic" is defined by the Oxford English Dictionary in an evolutionary capacity as "the historical relationship of a group of organisms." Spielrein injects the term into the field of mythology, where she relates ancestral ("archaic") symbols to current experience and emotion (and dreams), an area of study only now reaching scientific prominence: "[The] unconscious provides information pertaining to current personal conflicts and conflicts of the phylogenetic past, through which the personal experiences emerge, and perhaps it provides information on future developments, because the future is built based on the past."[44] Though she would later expand her understanding of mythic imagery as available to the psyche at large rather than confined to so-called neurotics, it is here that she begins to more concretely develop an idea she believes to be a vital contribution to the field.

Spielrein then continues to refine her definition of the "death instinct" as "[the] representation of sexual activity by death symbolisms [*Todessymbolik*]" and through further analyses of her patients' language: "In my opinion, the cause for the occurrence of such symbols lies in the essence of the sexual activity itself, more precisely in the two antagonistic components of sexuality."[45] While she defines sexuality by "antagonistic" components, it would be false to categorize her instinct as merely oppositional or binary, since she considers destruction and attraction two sides of the same coin, and would later adopt the terms Thanatos and Eros, respectively, as representational shorthand. In any regard, her scholarly formulation of the "death instinct" in published form begins at the end of a dissertation devoted to the language of schizophrenia.

Reception at the VPS

> There is absolutely no other free act which it is given us to accomplish—only the destruction of the "I."
>
> —Simone Weil, twentieth-century Christian mystic

Though she first mentioned her work on death and transformation during a meeting on November 15; it was on November 29, 1911, that Spielrein delivered her evolving research to the VPS in a lecture entitled "On Transformation," based on her dissertation and the work that would become "Destruction as the Cause of Coming into Being"—written during 1911, published in the 1912 *Jahrbuch*—and presented to such members as Paul Federn, Sigmund Freud, Otto Rank, Wilhelm Stekel, and Victor Tausk.[46] Rank, secretary of the society at the time, notes:

> Taking as her point of departure the question of whether a normal death instinct exists in Man (Metchnikoff), Dr. Spielrein endeavors to prove that the component of death is contained in the sexual instinct itself; inherent in that instinct is at the same time a destructive component which is indispensable to the process of coming into existence.[47]

She was undoubtedly influenced by leading Russian biologist Élie Metchnikoff (1845–1916), who was the first to popularize a "death instinct" as associated purely with the cessation of life, as Todd Dufresne concurs in *Tales from the Freudian Crypt*: "According to the Minutes of the Vienna Psychoanalytic Society, Spielrein, herself a Russian, couched her discussion of a death instinct explicitly in terms of Metchnikoff's biological speculations."[48] During her presentation, she expanded her notion of destruction (*Thanatos*) into a desire for transformation and linked it to the preservation of the species, evoking the content of her earlier draft letter.[49] Freud, not particularly encouraging, offered a few words of suspicion: "The speaker attempted to base the theory of instincts on biological presuppositions."[50] Ironically his own "death instinct" would amass similar criticism, as will be discussed shortly.

Contrary to Freud, Tausk argued that her stance was "very close to the realm of metaphysics" and thus of interest to an individual's psychological makeup.[51] He maintained: "From this point, as the paper has indeed shown, one comes by deduction to all these questions to which in psychoanalysis one has come by way of induction. . . . The point of view that resistance to sexuality stems from the destructive element is a valuable one."[52] Stekel, reminding that he had already mentioned Thanatos as related to "death anxiety," granted Spielrein's point of departure into mythology and sexual union, presumably because she specifically cited his influence in her paper.[53]

She also provided images to support her concept, noted in the *Minutes of the Vienna Psychoanalytic Society*: "In numerous mythological conceptions the need for destruction is even directly expressed: Death is the way in which any transition to another state is conceived . . . the mythological concepts of life and death are then pursued into the symbolics of earth and water."[54] She continued a matrifocal line of thinking, as the transition between destruction and rebirth is interpreted through the image of a woman's body:

> Man has a need to come into existence and to perish. . . . Sacrifice is represented as an analogue to being transposed into the mother's womb, the dying individual, too, is transferred back into the mother and then reborn. . . . Destruction is thus the cause of coming into being; the old must be destroyed for the new to take shape. There is, therefore, no absolute concept of death, and what for the old mold signifies death, for the new one means life.[55]

Here she evolves her idea of the "death instinct" in relation to lover and beloved into images of dissolution and (pro)creation in mythic narratives at large. Though Freud failed to rein in the eventual disapproval she received by the end of the night (regarding its "mystical" nature), he still encouraged the submission and publication of her full article in the 1912 *Jahrbuch*.

Destruction as the Cause of Coming into Being

> A considerable part of this speculation has been anticipated in a work which is full of valuable matter . . . Sabina Spielrein.
>
> —Sigmund Freud, *Beyond the Pleasure Principle*

In her article "Destruction as the Cause of Coming into Being," her first publication following her dissertation, at age twenty-six, Spielrein provides psychological interpretations of her patients' dreams before introducing images of death and resurrection in mythology.[56] She is also quick to assert her own perspective (and bias) as a female scholar before elucidating images of female sexual fantasy: "I quote Jung's words so thoroughly because his remarks correspond the most with the results I have had in that he makes reference to an unknown danger that lies in erotic activity. It is additionally very important for me that a male individual is aware of a danger that is not solely social."[57] Also aware of the zeitgeist around this particular theme, she notes that Stekel's research on "[a] wish to die . . . had not yet appeared when I wrote this paper," though his work regarding "Thanatos" had been circulating, which is why she clearly cites him as influential throughout her paper, as will be seen.[58]

She begins her article by acknowledging the so-called negative feelings such as "anxiety and disgust" that can at times accompany sexuality, owing to the fact that sex is seen in society as something "dirty" or taboo.[59] She then turns her attention to "[the] sexual wishes [that] are associated with images of death," referencing Stekel's postulation that the sexual dynamic is one of "moral issue."[60] However, she soon counters Stekel's assertion, especially in regard to women, and instead views death imagery as pointing not to a "moral death" but to a "sacrifice" of self when confronting the unknown.[61] Of women's sexuality in particular, and drawing from her experiencing working with girls, she states: "A feeling of anxiety is normal and moves to the forefront of repressed feelings. . . . You might ask: Is this all? Is this the high point with nothing more beyond?"[62] Evoking her draft letter, she again seeks to reconcile physical experience with the desire to reach the "beyond," meaning a point of transformation, specifically after consummation has been long anticipated. The "destructive component" is then briefly made analogous to being consumed in the arms of a beloved.[63]

To ground her "destructive component of the sexual instinct" in myth, she relies on Stekel's terminology: "Specific erotic fantasies even influence the choice of the manner of death (e.g. suicide). Poets had repeatedly discussed such ideas and philosophers often have illuminated the relationship between Eros and Thanatos."[64] However, while Stekel remains in the realm of violence, Spielrein expands the concept, anticipating research in object relations, and suggests that rather than being diametrically opposed to Eros, one's "self-destruction" or may be relieved figuratively through the image of or union with one's "external love-object."[65] She also notes that to literalize the image of destruction, such as in cases of extreme sadomasochism leading to physical death, is a "derangement of the sexual life" and leads to the loss of the transformative potential of Thanatos: temporary dissolution in the beloved.[66]

This *Eros-Thanatos* relationship brings yet another examination of female Catholic ecstasies as noted in the last chapter, which reveal the so-called dark side of the "death instinct" when tied to an image of one's Beloved. For instance, Julian of Norwich in *Revelations* recalls: "God sent me a bodily sickness [so] . . . that I might have the more knowing and loving of God and bliss of Heaven. . . . I should desire the second wound of our Lord's gracious gift: that my body might be fulfilled . . . of his Blessed Passion."[67] Julian then wishes for further illness, where death is thought a welcome "delight" and perceived as a blissful union with God.[68] She frequently describes her joy in God as a surrender to "marvelous pains" felt in her body as well as her soul.[69]

Similarly desiring to suffer for a beloved (in this case the man who has been conflated with God), The Portuguese Nun writes in her *Letters*: "Never accept that my feelings have been passionate enough! Be harder to please! Require me to die for love of you."[70] Though these experiences and expressions are not labeled "derangements," such ecstatic declarations highlight Spielrein's "death instinct"—the desire to reach the sublime/to transform—when associated with images of love, infatuation, and destruction. Additionally, in *Erotism: Death and Sensuality* (1957), Georges Bataille, who specifically explored nuns' ecstatic visions, asserts: "Eroticism . . . is assenting to life up to the point of death" and also claimed that all eroticism has within it a realm of surrender and death.[71]

In Michael Freze's *They Bore the Wounds of Christ: Mystery of the Sacred Stigmata*, various nuns are referenced throughout the centuries (a seemingly disproportionate number in the twentieth century) as being "miraculously" covered with physical wounds such as the stigmata, blood-soaked eyes and hands, as well as scars on their torsos and legs.[72] While Freze considers the likelihood of self-infliction, he also underscores the spiritual and "sacred" relationship they had to their wounds, experienced as "ecstasies" and "passions."[73] Freze then provides images of such nuns in their ecstasies lying bloodsoaked in bed but smiling as they "receive" their wounds from God.[74] Though Freze reports that many of these women died from excessive blood loss, a great number are still considered saints, mystics, and Doctors of the Church.

Actually, as Caroline Walker Bynum explains in *Fragmentation and Redemption: Essays on Gender and the Human Body in Medieval Religion*: "Women's mysticism was more historical and incarnational—more fleshly and bodily, if you will—than ordinary Christian piety. The Eucharist as body, flesh, meat, was a central focus of female religiosity . . . [the] religious goal was seen to be union with the physical body of [Christ]."[75] This phenomenon contextualizes the darkly sensual connection to *Eros-Thanatos* present in Spielrein's "death instinct" when the desire to dissolve into a beloved is met with actual self-destruction, a phenomenon she herself tried to illuminate.

While her entire article cannot be discussed, there are a few passages from her analyses of patients' dreams that should be highlighted. In her clinical observations, she states that the unconscious presents "ancient" images, one example of which she interprets:

> The Earth is the original mother in the conscious or unconscious perception of everyone. . . . It was not for nothing that Greek philosophers, such as Anaxagoras, sought the origin of *Weltschmerz* [when reality falls short of one's ideal] in the differentiation of that which exists from the original elements. This pain is made up of every particle of our being yearning for a transformation back into its origins, out of which proceeds a new coming-into-being.[76]

Spielrein compares this image of a seed to a universalized impulse to transform out of a place of wounding where the old self gives way to the new, and cautions that one must be able to understand the image metaphorically. She also admits that the "death instinct" is only one of many possibilities: "I should note that we could just as readily derive everything from the nurturing instinct rather than from sexuality."[77] She then proceeds, as in her draft letter, to make "destruction" synonymous with a drive for "self-preservation" as well as a "desire for transformation."[78]

Her familiar mystical leanings appear again when she situates her theory within psychology: "The closer we approach conscious thought, the more differentiated our images become. The deeper into the unconscious we delve, the more general and typical the images become. The depth of our psyche knows no 'I,' but rather only its summation, the 'We,' " and it is this "We" that she believes may be activated by sexuality.[79] Following this, she puts forth the idea that each individual is comprised of "dividual" parts, affecting each person in varying degrees.[80] Astutely, she argues that it is the "We" that overwhelms the ego without respite in her schizophrenic patients, meaning the "I" can no longer be found among the collective, which similarly occurs in individuals whom she believes have an "increase in sensitivity." She then states forcefully: "I must resolutely defend the viewpoint that the psyche is driven in the unconscious by impulses that lie deeper and which are not at all concerned with our feelings or reactions to the demands they place on us."[81] To her, this "deeper" impulse, like her earlier formation of the "sublime," creates the desire for union as well as the desire for the "I" to experience a moment of the "We," and subsequently be transformed by it.

Pulling from dreams of patients "overwhelmed" by archetypal imagery is how she comes to realize the depths of potential in the mythic dimension: "The ego-differentiated images are assimilated . . . and transformed into universal images that are typical, archaic, and collective."[82] She further points out that a resulting transformation instinct may burst forth inside an individual and s/he will then become "Inundated with new, more richly adorned images. . . . We see this most beautifully in artistic productions."[83] This realm of images and mythic thought, though relayed through her patients, is something she later regards as available to all through dreams and experiences of love and death:

> Experiences with dreams in schizophrenia patients teach us that our psyche harbors perceptions [images] in its depths that do not correspond to our current conscious way of thinking, and which we cannot directly understand. We do, however, find these perceptions in the consciousness of our ancestors, which we can conclude from mythology and other products of the mind. According to that [mythology], our unconscious corresponds to the conscious way of thinking of our ancestors . . . [our] inherited images.[84]

By ancestral and "archaic," mimicking the language used in her dissertation (phylogenetic), one can grasp her archetypal meaning.

She also opens up her discussion to a more general public: "Close to our desire to maintain our present condition, there lies a desire for transformation" which she equates with a felt death.[85] To elucidate her concept, she again uses the image of a seed transforming into a tree, where the seed must "die" in its destruction, which gives way to the new iteration of a tree that has originated "at the expense of the other."[86] She then focuses exclusively on her central theme of the ego's tie to death and sexuality, stating her thesis explicitly: "This phase of the reproduction (transformation) drive, which is most dangerous for the ego, is accompanied by feelings of delight because the dissolution (union) takes place in the beloved (i.e. in love)."[87]

She lingers on the ecstasy of love before turning to what she deems the masochistic tendency of the soul when concretized and directed at the self, asserting that one's own destructive impulse is necessarily tied to Eros when a feeling of loss (of love) overwhelms the ego: "Through complete denial of the external love object, the self becomes the libido's object and this results in self-destruction."[88] Spielrein refers to enacted violence, or literal death, as regressive, but a mythic and psychic reality nonetheless rendered in countless literary narratives from Siegfried and Brunnhilde to Tristan and Iseult.

She continues:

> Pain, in and of itself, is strongly defined by aversion because pain corresponds to a damaging of the individual against which our

> self-preservation instinct strives. Within our depths there is something that, however paradoxical it may sound *a priori*, desires this self-damage. Joy in pain is, however, thoroughly incomprehensible if we take only the ego into consideration, which only wants desire.[89]

In *The Myth of Analysis*, James Hillman categorizes soul phenomena in a similar manner: "Masochism shows that pleasure and pain are not ultimate opposites. . . . The psychic qualities, eros and suffering . . . all psychic phenomena, also refers to one's death . . . imagined as an ecstatic release . . . exquisite enjoyment."[90] On the other hand, in *Beyond the Pleasure Principle*, Freud states that "destruction" and "pain" are diametrically opposed to "life-sustaining Eros."[91] Apropos, while Hillman states that it was Freud who introduced Thanatos into psychology and Jung who "saw that [it] has an imaginal aspect, a mythic factor," Spielrein also early understood the symbolic relationship between Eros and Thanatos.[92]

For example, she compares one of her patient's (Frau M.) dreams of being "reborn through dying in Christ" to sexual union.[93] To Spielrein, in studying mythology, it becomes apparent that death symbolizes an "impregnation" and eventual rebirth: "Death is necessary for the advent of life."[94] Thus, in her opinion, the dream signaled a time of transformation for her patient. She then meditates on the plurality of dream symbols at large: "Every sexual symbol in a dream, as in mythology, possesses the significance of a life-and-death-bringing god."[95] She also argues, when writing of male and female desire, that the "boundary is not so sharply drawn [because] every human is bisexual."[96] She subscribes to the notion that individuals possess psychological androgyny, a concept similarly invoked by Jung in that year's *Symbols of Transformation*.

Incidentally, when speaking of (Freud's) "death instinct," Hillman assigns Dionysus to the term, the life-and-death-bringing god of transformation and sexuality whom he believed embodies both Eros and Thanatos: "Death and bisexual consciousness are what Dionysus involves."[97] Hillman attempts to liberate the "death instinct" from gender, since to Freud "The female principle was passive and masochistic, so that woman was . . . death," while Eros ("life") was male, "opposed" to death.[98] Alternatively, in Spielrein's paper, she utilizes Gogol's *The Inspector General* to assert that sadism, where one seeks to "destroy the love-object," may be understood as a psychological instinct irrespective of gender: "Therefore, if the female is sadistic, the male is masochistic."[99] Though her article is not free of heteronormative assumptions in relationship, passivity (and Thanatos) is not limited to a "female principle" nor is activity (and Eros) confined to a male principle.

After extant dream interpretation, she returns to poetry, perhaps pulling from her draft letter: "The most loved life-bringing sexual animal may turn into a source of death. It is remarkable how often passionate poets die in their compositions."[100] She goes on to discuss the motif of love and death in literature and continues: "White-hot passion may develop when hate . . . releases previously unavailable images. This passion, because it is so strong, must destroy in order to be contained within the limits of self-preservation."[101] However, she argues that "complete annihilation" may be replaced by attachment to family, "nature worship or religious symptoms" where one is also able to experience a sense of release, surrender, and transformation.[102] She argues that because such images of destruction are uncomfortable to confront, we "readily . . . overlook the death instinct within the sexual instinct."[103]

She then expounds:

> In love, the dissolution of the ego into the beloved is simultaneously the strongest self-affirmation: a new ego life in the person of the beloved. If love is not present, then this idea changes within the psyche or body of an individual, who is under the influence of a foreign power such as the sex act, into the image of destruction or death.[104]

This passage provides a clear summation of her ideas of the beloved, the positive and negative losses of "I," mystical oneness, and the possible violent complications of love's shadow: the difference being destruction in the service of transformation rather than destruction in the service of cessation of life. In *Reflections on the Art of Living: A Joseph Campbell Companion*, Campbell defines his marriage in similar terms of destruction and transformation: "There must be disintegration of ego for the two to combine. The uniting process involves fermentation, amalgamation, disintegration, and putrefaction in their psyches. When I married . . . I felt it was a crucifixion . . . it's a reciprocal crucifixion. . . . You are sacrificing yourself to the relationship."[105] If Campbell observes dissolution of self in the service of transforming through the beloved, then the potential for "psychic alteration" in the face of failed love is expressed in feminist scholar Ginette Paris's *Heartbreak: Recovering from Lost Love and Mourning*: "Your Beloved is your executioner!"[106] Spielrein's "death instinct," while dependent upon context, contains both.

In her summary, entitled "Life and Death in Mythology," she expands upon mythic images of death and transformation to include the Christ narrative as a chief example of destruction in service of creation. She repeatedly defines Christ as a mythic symbol to be interpreted rather than understood as a literal figure, possible perhaps due to her Jewish and admittedly agnostic background: "Christ is a symbol of mankind. The Tree of Life is a source of death for Christ, as it is for men."[107] She later, following Freud, compares

Christ to "the savior prototype" who allows individuals to bring about death "in remembrance," through mythic identification, thus fulfilling, in her words, "the necessary sacrificial death that will bring [one] to resurrection" in the physical world.[108]

Additionally, she gives an example from the Biblical narrative of Adam transforming into a tree upon his death to exemplify her "death instinct" and reaffirms: "Adam came into the world as a new being."[109] This image is linked to the impregnation of the earth and eventual resurrection possible only by a necessary "destruction."[110] Further, she transforms the expulsion of Adam and Eve into a symbolic narrative demonstrating "injury to the individual; because the reproductive drive requires destruction of the individual, it is entirely natural that images of punishment so readily incorporate a sexual coloring."[111] Here, reproduction is made synonymous with the "death instinct" due to its potential to create new life from the "old" parents, and is freed from sociopolitical ties to the subordination of gender. This link with reproduction may also be influenced by the threat of maternal death during childbirth, based on Spielrein's involvement with pregnant patients: "One is destroyed during pregnancy through the child that develops . . . at the mother's expense."[112] Sayers similarly remarks that Spielrein highlighted "[o]neness and transformation with women and mothering" in a manner that would not return to mainstream conversation until the rise of feminist hermeneutics in the 1960s.[113]

Relying again on Siegfried and Brünnhilde to portray the mystical component of her thesis, she states that the figures "Replace the sun and the earth . . . in Wagner, longing for death is often a desire for dying in love."[114] She notes that their "merge" is most poetically rendered in Wagner's opera where "they sacrifice themselves to their love and die" (*Liebestod*), thereby paving the way for a new era of love to which Spielrein exclaims: "Death is a victorious song to love!"[115] Relatedly, in a chapter entitled "The Love-Death" in *The Masks of God: Creative Mythology*, Joseph Campbell also utilizes opera in his examination of the "romantic . . . cult of *amor*."[116] Campbell defines *amor* as "Love's meeting of the eyes, to love's pain, love's rapture, and on to death" and terms the theme (following Wagner and Spielrein) a "Death for Love Motive."[117] This theme is earlier evoked by Spielrein in her diaries when she speaks of her high school teacher's power to "win" her and is again recalled in her draft letter when referring to being "besieged" by the psyche at the sight of two "magnificent" eyes.[118]

To be sure, Campbell also agrees that this motif is not literal, but symbolic of "anamorphosis," meaning "to form anew," evoking Spielrein's concept of coming into being.[119] He relates the "dual sense of love and death" to an "allegory of the soul" that may be found in countless mythic narratives (of which he provides examples, one being Tristan and Iseult) of lovers who are transformed by their ecstasy, merged in "eternal death" and subsequently transformed "anew."[120] While Spielrein also recognizes this allegory, she speaks of self-transformation explicitly in relation to physical and sexual union as additional expressions of soul.

Near the close of her article, Spielrein affirms: "This cry [of life] is a death wail. . . . Death's source lies in life itself and vice versa."[121] She repeats that symbolic destruction may be found in mythic images (like Christ) that "figuratively" suffer with an individual: "Self-destruction can be replaced by sacrificial destruction."[122] Here she elicits her earlier notion that one may replace one's so-called annihilation through an attachment to religion or religious symbols. She also progressively reasserts that Christ, rather than ascending to a masculine God, represents a "re-implantation of Mother Earth. . . . Resurrection is rebirth," eliciting an image of transformation that relates Christ to earlier matrifocal harvest mythology.[123] She then implores the necessity of death consciousness: "Without destruction, coming into being is impossible!"[124]

She analyzes her most quoted author, Friedrich Nietzsche, especially his *Zarathustra* and what she interprets as his longing for love, as well as *Romeo and Juliet*; Wagner's *Tristan and Isolde*; suicide; castration; childbirth; and vaginal self-gratification before summarizing: "This chapter has shown that coming into being [or, becoming] emerges from destruction. . . . Death in itself is gruesome; death in the service of the sexual instinct, i.e. its destructive component (which leads to becoming), is salutary."[125] She also references Wagner's *The Flying Dutchman*, harkening back to her draft letter, as representative of "erotic death"; she then concludes:

> In this second part, I have limited myself to a few examples with the goal of illustrating the applicability of the observations on mythology developed in the first part. . . . A more thorough and deeper-delving study will be required here to prove the destruction component of sexuality in individual psychological or mythological formations. I believe, however, that my examples clearly show that the reproductive drive, corresponding to biological facts, is comprised psychologically of two antagonistic components, and that it as just as much a coming-into-being drive as it is a destruction-drive.[126]

After citing Freud, Jung, and Stekel in her notes, she reaffirms one last time the inseparable nature of Eros and Thanatos within the "reproductive" instinct, by which she means the power of the sex drive. Clearly, her paper was never meant to be the final word or even a comprehensive view on her theory, but more an introduction to the connection between life, death, sex, birth, and transformation represented in mythology, biology, and psychology.

Freud's "Death Instinct"

> I remember my own defensive attitude when the idea of an instinct of destruction first emerged in the psycho-analytic literature, and how long it took before I became receptive to it.
>
> —Sigmund Freud, *Civilization and Its Discontents*

Succinctly outlined in Carly Knapp's doctoral work, *Eros and Thanatos: A Figuration of Death as an Imaginal Presence in Dialogue with Depth Psychology*, Freud's "death instinct" in his 1920 *Beyond the Pleasure Principle* (*BPP*) can be summarized as "[An] aggressive . . . instinct opposed to life in his dual instinct theory."[127] Freud also contributes: "Organic matter [desires] return to a prior inorganic state," a biological assumption about death's inevitability that Knapp admits has since been challenged.[128] While she cites Jung as expanding upon the idea to include "[the] connection between death and love" in 1961, Knapp argues that it was Freud who "introduced" the instincts of Eros and Thanatos into psychology, though "Thanatos" has only been retroactively applied to his work, since the term is absent from his text.[129] Indeed, in *BPP*, death is viewed as physical cessation of life, rather than as a mythic or transformative experience in service of creation.

In brief, as this chapter is not an analysis of his work, Freud focuses primarily on Eros as a "pleasure principle" in opposition to a "death instinct."[130] However, he ventures into Spielrein's territory once when speaking of the potential loss of a "beloved" and asserting that an individual "would prefer that his life be forfeit[ed] to an inexorable law of nature, the sublime."[131] Though one may view his relation of the sublime to the love/death motif that so frequently appears in Spielrein's work, Freud uses the term without romantic or mystical connotation and instead as evidence of one's desire to die (or lose a beloved) naturally rather than by "a mere accident."[132] Contrary to Spielrein, Freud, in *BPP*, refrains almost entirely from mythological narrative and makes no mention of eroticized death imagery.

Indeed, Freud expands on "the burden of existence" and what he views to be the strange laws of "natural death" that seem to "elude" science.[133] He grounds his theory in biological organisms and cellular speculation, as Spielrein does at times, though the "death instinct" of one's ego in Freud's text—meaning the drive toward, or inevitability of one's physical death—is pitted against sexuality and against one's "life instincts."[134] In this way, he entirely severs the idea that Thanatos is inherent to sexuality. In fact, in a seemingly direct challenge to Spielrein's work, he asserts: "We were prepared indeed to reckon even the alleged self-preservation instincts of the ego among death instincts, a position which we have since corrected and withdrawn from."[135]

Further, he states that his "Libido theory," wherein the sexual instinct is tied to the "life-instinct" alone, is built upon "the transference-neuroses forced on our notice," alluding perhaps to both Spielrein and to her development of the idea.[136] Within the "death instinct," he examines pleasure and pain in propagation, one's discomfort with tension, childhood repression, neurotic stimuli, and like Spielrein, explores sadomasochism, although in direct opposition to Eros.[137] Though Spielrein has been said to rely too heavily on biology (e.g., by Freud at the VPS), her research clearly relies more on mythic imagery than Freud's *BPP*.

Another striking polarity demonstrated in the two works reinforces the idea that Freud is responding to Spielrein if only to offer a rebuttal to her theory; for instance, he states, "The goal of all life is death."[138] Spielrein once declared, "The aim of all death is life."[139] It seems likely that this is more than a mere coincidence on Freud's part, especially since he attended her first presentation to the VPS in 1911 and proceeded to publish her article in the *Jahrbuch*, presumably recognizing its merit even if he disagreed with its thesis. Moreover, in a fact often disputed, as will be discussed, he cites Spielrein by name as anticipating his own research in *BPP*: "A considerable part of this speculation has been anticipated in a work which is full of valuable matter and ideas but is unfortunately not entirely clear to me: Sabina Spielrein."[140] The two works are not synonymous; they offer significantly different insights into sexuality, and whether or not Freud was actually confused by her work, her influence is still clear, as he himself acknowledges.

According to Jessica Benjamin in *The Bonds of Love: Psychoanalysis, Feminism, and the Problem of Domination*, Freud's "death instinct" is a drive toward "nothingness" in its battle for "omnipotence," and thus, in its search of total domination, is devoid of erotic transformation.[141] Unaware of Spielrein (presumably), she gives a feminist interpretation of the term where "losing oneself" in creative work as well as in erotic union affirms "[a] fundamental experience of attunement."[142] In "Thanatos and Existence: Towards a Jungian Phenomenology of the Death instinct," (Freud's) "death instinct" is described by scholar Mark Welman as "[the] darkest and most stubborn riddle posed by the legacy of psychoanalysis."[143] However, it is referenced only in regard to Freud and Jung, and only the latter is credited with infusing Thanatos with a "poetic" sensibility, while Spielrein is mentioned only in passing as Jung's "lover."[144] As Knapp reminds us, it is French historian and anthropologist Jean-Pierre Vernant, who is generally credited with having "updated" Freud's theory into one where "Death [is] inseparable from Eros."[145]

Further weighing in on either side of the merit of the "death instinct," modern thanatologist Ernest Becker relegates it to "the dust bin of history" while, conversely, psychoanalyst Jean Laplanche purports it as "[the] most fascinating and baffling [work] of the entire Freudian corpus."[146] Like Laplanche, psychologist Ernest Jones claims it to be the most "profoundly philosophic" work in Freud's opus.[147] In this discussion, Spielrein is not referenced as a scholar on the "death instinct," but is instead referred to pejoratively as Jung's "illicit lover" as well as a "dangerous" pawn between Freud and Jung. Of course, the fact that Freud never actually used the term *Thanatos* is thought "odd," though according to Knapp (and Kerr in 1994; and Dufresne in 2000) it is assumed that he refrained from using the word solely because Stekel previously introduced it, and Spielrein's use of the term and the concept to which it refers are entirely dismissed.

In *The Denial of Death*, where the "death instinct" is expanded into thanatology, or the study of death and dying, Ernest Becker asserts that Freud relied too heavily on biological instincts at the expense of the symbolic, though he refrains from discussing Spielrein's contribution to the topic: "[Freud] seems to have been unable to reach for the really direct existentialist level of explanation."[148] He then goes on: "No one explained this dynamic more elegantly than [Otto] Rank [1929, *Will Therapy*]: 'The death fear of the ego is lessened by the killing, the sacrifice, of the other; through the death of the other, one buys oneself free from the penalty of dying.' "[149] It may be recalled that Rank was the secretary at the VPS during Spielrein's presentation in 1911 where she explicitly referenced her theory of sacrificial destruction and resurrection.

Like Becker, Welman argues that Freud's "mistake," and one that Freud also accepted, was in turning to biology "for his conceptual ground . . . formulated as that of literal death," and censures his statement that the goal of all life is death, void of symbolic meaning.[150] However, Spielrein states the exact opposite in her article, declaring instead that death's aim is life and attempts a mythological understanding of the instinct in addition to the biological. Still, Welman cites modern Freudians as responsible for "fixing" the theory: "Some psychoanalytic theorists have made significant contributions to a hermeneutics of death by re-visioning Freud's theory in a poetic light . . . that the goal of Thanatos is not of literal destruction but rather a metaphoric death, referring to the 'deconstruction' of the literalist ego."[151] A similarly significant contribution may also be found in Spielrein's article wherein Thanatos is synonymous with a drive for transformation.

In addition, Welman looks to Jung's *Symbols of Transformation* as having introduced thanatology, the very work (1912) discussed in the last chapter that led Spielrein to believe her ideas were being stolen, as she felt owed the rights of priority in publication. Indeed, after confronting Jung about it in a letter, he replied on March 25, 1912: "Your study is extraordinarily intelligent and contains splendid ideas whose priority I am happy to acknowledge as yours. The death tendency or death wish was clear to you before it was clear to me. . . . I express myself so differently from you in my work that no one could imagine that you had borrowed in any way from me."[152]

Be that as it may, he then backtracks: "Perhaps I borrowed from you too; certainly I have unwittingly absorbed a part of your soul as you doubtless have of mine. What matters is what each of us has made of it. And you have made something good . . . .I hope you will be able to represent my new ideas."[153] While at first praising her work and granting her the rights of originality and priority, he then tries to take possession of her ideas by claiming them as his own. Also, in moment of seeming duplicity, having called her work "extraordinary," he would write to Freud about it, paraphrasing Horace's line in *Ars Poetica*, which originally reads: "What is a beautiful woman in the upper part terminates unsightly in an ugly fish below"[154] Still, the clarity of the "death tendency" is here admitted as Spielrein's, regardless of the intimate details surrounding their relationship.

Sabina Spielrein and the Debate of Influence

> When Plato attempted to encompass the soul, he was driven to myth as much as to careful rational thinking. He needed two ways. Freud, too, used two ways. His rational language is interspersed with mythical images. . . . That grand vision of Thanatos, worthy of the pre-Socratics.
>
> —James Hillman, *The Myth of Analysis*

Knapp underscores the fact that Herbert Marcuse utilized the "philosophical and sociological implications" of the "death instinct" in his own writing, specifically in *Eros and Civilization*, and critiqued Freud's theory as "patriarchal" in its rejection of a maternal image for the concept of death and rebirth.[155] Interestingly, Spielrein couched her presentation to the VPS specifically in images of the Mothers from *Faust*—she believed them to be representations of the unconscious and archetypal maternal image—demonstrating the relation between death and rebirth through the symbol of the womb, as discussed in chapter 1. This connection of Spielrein's has been ignored and has actually been deemed evidence, as has her writing, of "borderline personality disorder" in modern scholarship, also referenced in chapter 1.[156]

Yet the same idea returns in her publication in relation to surrender and transformation: "Mother is also simultaneously the image of the depths of the unconscious that exists out of time. . . . In the unconscious, all places merge with one another."[157] At the time, Spielrein's theory of "merging" with Mother (Earth) was invalidated and dismissed by the VPS upon reception, as noted in the *Minutes*: "The interpretation of sacrifice as union with the mother would be valid only for the era of the matriarchates."[158] The debate surrounding an "era of the matriarchates" aside,[159] since she presented to what may be historically defined as a patriarchal context, affecting both men and women, Spielrein's matrifocal image was instantly discarded.

A few critics have even claimed that a "death instinct" never appears in her paper. For example, according to John Kerr in *A Most Dangerous Method*: "In the end, Spielrein's was a curious literary fate, to be known for a theory she did not hold. 'Destruction as the Cause of Coming into Being' . . . there is no 'death instinct' in it. Neither the term nor the idea in Freud's sense appears there."[160] While Kerr (and Dufresne in 2000) argues that she never uses the term *death instinct,* it is clear that she does, as has been discussed in detail.[161] Actually, in the original German publication, Spielrein writes of a *Todesinstinkt,* which literally translates as "death instinct," as well as a *Todesvorsellung,* meaning "death imagination," and references "the death instinct within the sexual instinct," which she believes related to the desire for transformation, or the *transformationswunsch.*[162] Unfortunately, such doubt has led to a debate among scholars, seemingly because the merit of her article has been made dependent upon its influence on Freud rather than sui generis.

Whether or not the term and its concept exist in her article appears irrelevant, as does the fact that Freud explicitly names her as an influence, though both are true; rather, the crux of the debate relies on whether or not Spielrein's concept exists in "Freud's sense," a curious notion given that her work predates his. Nonetheless, let us gain insight into what might constitute "Freud's sense," Hillman elucidates in *Suicide and the Soul*: "In Freud's sense, Thanatos is ever-present . . . death resides in the soul."[163] Surely, Death's ubiquitous soul presence can definitively be "sensed" within both works.

Contrary to Kerr, in "Sabina Spielrein: Out from the Shadow of Jung and Freud," Brian Skea mistrusts those who claim to misunderstand her thesis: "Erotic attraction, with the image and feeling of two persons merged as one, is both euphoric in terms of transcending the limits of the ego boundary, yet also threatening to its integrity and independence."[164] However, suspicious of her own mental health, he then proceeds to fall into the pattern of degrading her contribution to psychology at large by asserting that her work is relevant primarily to psychotics.[165] Additionally, the only other woman present during Spielrein's presentation to the VPS, Margarete Stegmann, who happened to agree with Spielrein's theories, has also since been said to be speaking solely through "borderline psychopathology," seemingly only to fit the need to align Spielrein's work with so-called psychotics.[166]

In Todd Dufresne's *Tales from the Freudian Crypt; The Death Drive in Text and Context,* Freud's contribution is lauded, while Spielrein's is further demeaned; he first introduces the topic: "The idea of a death drive [*trieb*] seems immune to criticism. . . . It is as though the metaphors of *Beyond the Pleasure Principle* have become . . . those of our culture."[167] By that logic Spielrein's theories should be similarly immune to criticism, though he agrees with the "fundamental debate about her importance for the development of Freud's death-drive theory," meaning he does not believe in her importance, thus spurring the debate.[168] He says instead: "It is possible that Freud acknowledged his debt to Spielrein precisely because she was not a real competitor in the world of analysis. Or perhaps he used Spielrein to put his followers off the scent of his true debts [Stekel]."[169] He asserts that even if Freud did owe a debt to Spielrein, it was tied only to his "complicated relationship with Jung."[170]

By stating that Freud's acknowledgment of her work amounts only to a political slight, Dufresne exposes who he believes to be the "real competitor": other male scholars. Kerr perpetuates this notion when he wonders why Freud did not instead "acknowledge Stekel" rather than Spielrein, though one wonders why both Spielrein *and* Stekel cannot be regarded as equally influential.[171] Despite the fact that Spielrein's work is not actually examined by Dufresne, she is still objectified as something to be "used" and is subsequently defined—again—solely as Jung's "lover."[172]

Dufresne also seems to overtly snub her work when he refrains from citing her as one of the few psychologists to adapt the "death-drive . . . to clinical ends," such as examining children's fantasies of death, and instead cites Melanie Klein.[173] While Klein is a pioneer in the field in her own right, Spielrein began doing exactly that as early as 1912; one of her last references to a "death instinct," before focusing exclusively on child psychology, appears in her article "Contributions to the Knowledge of a Child's Soul," wherein she interprets the dreams of child (and adult) patients. In the article, before turning to interpretation, she also associates her own childhood fantasies and fear of death with the German folktale manifestation of Death, the Erlking: "My 'Erlkönig' was God."[174] After reciting a few lines from Goethe's "The Erlking," she then proceeds to examine imagery and symbols of death in dreams.

Further condescension ensues when Rosemary Balsam states that it was "gracious" but unnecessary of Freud to acknowledge that Spielrein anticipated his own work in *BPP*.[175] Unlike Hillman's praise of Freud's vision of death that he deemed worthy of the pre-Socratics, Balsam says of her article, even while recognizing her marginalization: "Spielrein's ideas seem today like flights of unconscious fantasy organized around the binary pair of life and death . . . I think this reflects her still raw and unrequited love for Jung."[176] Mireille Cifali, though sympathetic, similarly notes Spielrein's work as being only a manifestation of "[her] transferences, always with somebody else in mind" and "out of the sufferings of her own life."[177] Spielrein's academic work is rarely examined without stigmatized reference to her personal life, which diminishes the importance of the mythological imagery and erases its potential. In addition, Spielrein's concept of Eros and Thanatos are not binary per se but inherent to the same instinct.

Even if one were to deem her paper a "fantasy," it may be worthwhile to interpret the work per Hillman's urging: "A psychological approach means what it says: a way through the psyche into myth, a connection with myth that proceeds via the soul, including especially its bizarre fantasy and its suffering . . . myth begins with the exegesis of oneself, soul-making."[178] Regardless of whether or not her personal life influenced her research, as it very well did, the content of her work reaches beyond subjectivity in order to make such a "connection with myth." Certainly, she was not Jung's lovesick patient at the time of her publication, but a PhD and a practicing analyst.

On the other hand, Spielrein scholar Victor Ovcharenko, in "Love, Psychoanalysis, and Destruction," grants Spielrein originality in her work:

> There are various ways of looking at the personality of Sabina Spielrein and her creative achievements. But in so doing it has to be admitted that, at the time, and in the judgment of the psychoanalytic élite, hers was an original, significant and forward-looking concept . . . and touching upon the most fundamental problems of the psychoanalytic picture of man.[179]

While Ovcharenko awards Spielrein the recognition of her progressive and cutting edge research, he is quick to warn the reader of Spielrein's "many faults."[180] Hence, her work is pitted against her personal history once again, as if one must overcome or bypass her personality in order to read her work, which would not be necessary if her character was not already maligned. Ovcharenko also slyly demotes her accomplishments by defining her publications and achievements as "creative" rather than as academic and scholarly work.

In *The Discovery of the Unconscious: The History and Evolution of Dynamic Psychiatry*, Henri E. Ellenberger asserts:

> Among psychoanalysts, the concept of a death instinct had been occasionally expressed. Sabina Spielrein had written on "Destruction as the cause of becoming." Rank's theory that every man longs to return to the mother's womb was considered . . . as an anticipation of Freud's concept of the death instinct. . . . The classical pairs of opposites were *Eros-Neikos* (Love-Strife), and *Bios-Thanatos* (Life-Death), but not *Eros-Thanatos*. . . . Freud first brought forth his concepts as hypotheses, but in later writings he showed that he firmly believed in them.[181]

Freud was not the first to propose *Eros-Thanatos* as explicitly relating to the "death instinct." Rather, it was Spielrein who continued to build on the psychological theory of *Eros-Thanatos* and more than "occasionally expressed" it, as her article is considered her seminal work. In the entire discussion in Ellenberger's text on death in psychoanalysis, mention of Spielrein is limited to the above sentence before examination of Freud's *BPP* begins. Granted, this text was published before Carotenuto's, but that in no way precluded access to her publication, as he references it himself, and in fact would have made him more susceptible to read her work unencumbered by later stigmatization.

Spielrein's work is discussed in Ronald Britton's *Sex, Death, and the SuperEgo: Experiences in Psychoanalysis* (2003), in a chapter entitled "Hysteria (III): The Erotic Countertransference." Yet Britton asserts that her article must be read through the lens of a "patient . . . at the height of their disturbance . . . hysterical psychosis. . . . Hers is a death wish in hysteria" and he proceeds to label her a "schizo" and a "borderline."[182] These labels are used to completely delegitimize her work and to purport that she was still a patient at the time of her publication, which she had not been for years. Rather than grant mytho-psychological insight to her paper, she is further pathologized and demeaned as only Jung's lover, "obsessed" with—rather than interested in—the concept of death.[183]

Since the affair is not categorized by Britton as an abuse of power, Spielrein's writing is once again labeled as "transference" and the label is superimposed onto her later work, constricting and limiting the article's ability to transcend subjective history.[184] Also, though clearly out of chronological order, her diaries are used by Britton against her paper, and her professional writing is regarded as a matter of her "own complexes" without value to the larger field.[185] Even her interest in sexuality is seen as a female hysteric's libido gone awry, using material deemed (by Britton) "arousing" and "stimulating," as if Spielrein was not completely qualified to venture into the subject both personally and professionally.[186]

Contrarily, in 1913, criticism of her work refrained from such pathology. Paul Federn, a fellow member of the VPS, wrote a review of Spielrein's article in the *Zeitschrift*, one of the oldest German psychology journals of review, where he repeatedly describes her as a "mystic" (*Mystiker*).[187] In a lengthy review of her article, he finds immense intrigue in her "*selbsterhaltungtriebe,*" or the instinct for self-preservation.[188] He states that her article is "A contribution . . . to the analysis of the mystical modality of thought that is so significant for humanity," though he wonders if she perhaps relies too heavily on her "intuition."[189] He then refers the reader to her original publication for her discussion on "Life and Death in Mythology."

Federn continues to discuss her transformation-instinct (*Transformationstrieb*) that arises out of images and "thoughts of death" (*Todesgedanken*), which, he notes, Spielrein relates to sexuality and is open to her idea that "An individual may come into being [literally and metaphorically] through the sexual drive."[190] Although he concludes that her theory is too grandiose, "contrary to all rationality," and too "wide-ranging" in its scope, he repeats: "[It] reminds, perhaps without the author's knowledge, of the works of the great mystics."[191] Where Freud admonished her for being too rooted in biology, Federn critiqued her "mystical modality," neither allowing her reconciliation between the two.

That being said, Federn acknowledged her philosophical insight as significant to the field. Likewise, Otto Gross, an influence on both Freud and Jung in the early 1900s, in his seemingly directly influenced 1913 article "On the Symbolism of Destruction," examines "Why the symbolism of 'destruction' in Sabine Spielrein's [*sic*] sense regularly forms" in dreams related to sexuality.[192] Before going on to discuss the dreams of female patients, he states: "Spielrein's provocative study begins with this problem [of destruction]. With these words, the deepest question is broached that modern psychology has to offer."[193] Clearly influencing later assessment of her work,[194] Gross early recognized the potential of her paper and its relevance to psychology.

Additionally, in *Eros of the Impossible: The History of Psychoanalysis in Russia*, Alexander Etkind restores Spielrien's contributions to the history of psychology and includes her in a discussion on the philosophical connection between love and death popular in Russian culture: "A similar intuition led Sabina Spielrein to her discovery of the attraction to death as the obverse of the two-sided sexual instinct. . . . The three greatest thinkers of the epoch, Solovyov, Rozanov, and Fyodorov, likewise focused on the interaction of sexual love, the struggle against death, and the idea of rebirth."[195] It is quite plausible, as Etkind believes, that Spielrein was familiar with these Russian thinkers when writing on the topic, given her literary background and familiarity with Russian intellects.

Similarly, in Adrian Carr and Cheryl Lapp's *Leadership is a Matter of Life and Death: The Psychodynamics of Eros and Thanatos in Organisations*, Spielrein's origination of the "death instinct" is accepted, as is the nuance of her idea, especially in reference to Freud's challenge in 1911: "Spielrein did not accept Freud's dual-instinct theory involving two classes of instinct. Instead she preferred consideration of death as part of the destructive/dissolution component of the sexual instinct."[196] Carr and Lapp highlight Spielrein's attempt to free her instinct of dualisms and instead reconcile and integrate the mythic realities of Eros and Thanatos.

Though Spielrein is still considered within the context of a seductress in John Launer's *Sex Versus Survival: The Story of Sabina Spielrein, Her Life, Her Ideas, Her Genius*, "Destruction" is viewed as extremely progressive and anticipatory of evolutionary biology: "A description of the biological events of sex. . . . She also draws parallel between these physical events of sex and the feelings that surround it."[197] For example, Spielrein notes in her paper:

> A unification of the female and male cell takes place in procreation. Every cell is thereby exterminated as a unit, and out of this product of extermination, a new life comes into being. Some lower living creatures, such as the mayfly, give up their lives and die off with the production of a new generation. Creation for these creatures is simultaneously destruction, and destruction, considered on its own, is the most horrific thing to a living being. If this personal destruction is in the service of new creation, the individual longs for it.[198]

Launer then compares: "Modern evolutionary theory says: 'The imperative for all living organisms is the replication of their genes by direct or indirect means in the face of individual extinction.' "[199]

Alternatively, psychoanalyst Gottfried Heuer attempts to dismiss Spielrein's idea of the "death instinct" as entirely outdated in ""Soul Murder' and 'The Birth of Intersubjectivity' in David Cronenberg's *A Dangerous Method*:" "Current neurobiology cannot support the concept of a primary bloodthirsty human, driven by an aggressive drive."[200] While Heuer argues that her theory falls outside of scientific research as well as modern psychology due to its "aggressive drive," it may be recalled that it was Freud who posited the "death instinct" as bloodthirsty and aggressive, and not Spielrein. Etkind reminds us of her thesis:

> For something to be constructed, Spielrein argued, what came before has to be torn down. Therefore every act of creation implies a process of destruction. . . . The attraction to death is an inseparable element of the attraction to life and life's continuation in a new human being. . . . Sexuality and death. The flip side [shadow] of love was the desire to destroy the object of desire; every birth was a death and every death a birth.[201]

While Launer's attention is focused on the biological aspects of the paper, rather than the mythological or psychological importance, he notes the significance of Spielrein's work: "As she clearly understood, all the discoveries of reproductive biology pointed in exactly the same direction. The genes we pass on to our children and our descendants are not of our choosing. In a profound sense they are no longer 'us.' "[202] At the same time, he does not find her conclusions wholly consistent with modern science, ostensibly because she extends into mystical dissolution of the "I" and mythic narrative, failing again to fall decisively into the category of *mythos* or *logos*. Still, Launer argues that had her peers been more collaborative "[and] less pathologising the victim," perhaps her theories could have been expanded upon much earlier.[203] At the very least, she may have continued her research on these fertile topics, as she urges others in the conclusion of her article.

> She is very bright and well organised; there is meaning in everything she says.
>
> —Sigmund Freud to C. G. Jung re. Sabina Spielrein, 1912

Personally concerned with the image of death and resurrection, specifically as tied to sexuality, Spielrein would go on to name her first daughter *Renata,* meaning "rebirth," discussed in more detail in the next chapter. Renata (Renate) constellated many of the theories explored in her publication, both symbolic and literal, though such significance is lost when Spielrein is read solely through the lens of psychosis. Further, if thought such a subordinate scholar or a "seductress," her career is seen as an anomaly, and her work hinges on her sexuality rather than on her scholarship. As Patricia Hampl aptly points out when speaking of the work of female writers in her autobiographical *I Could Tell You Stories*: "Our [Western] culture is not prepared to see its central myth played out by a female protagonist. . . . Death-and-resurrection is a male role."[204] It is possible then, that Spielrein's formulation of death and resurrection is viewed as an uncomfortable trespass into a male academic landscape.

Nonetheless, Spielrein retains her relevance to current culture. For example, in a 2011 article on sexual motifs in cinema, "Women, Sex, and Death—From Vampires to Psychoanalysis," Lynn Stuart Parramore writes that *A Dangerous Method*, the 2011 fictionalized film about Spielrein and Jung, marks a rise in the cinematic motifs of "dangerous female sexuality," "dark passions," and "remembrances of death" that "peak" in vampire fiction and film franchises such as *Dracula* and *Twilight* respectively.[205] Parramore then explicitly refers to Spielrein's article: "[She] points out that young women often have dreams of lying in a coffin, symbolizing a desire to return to the womb (the tomb) . . . Spielrein noted that the essential desire for transformation is often constructed as death."[206] Parramore insists that the death drive as tied to sexuality is very much alive in culture, especially for female figures in film, quipping: "We'll have to be damned creative to avoid the destruction."[207]

Contrary to Parramore's wit, Spielrein did not advocate avoiding destruction. Rather than repression of death, she frequently acknowledged its power, its transformational potential, and its necessity for creation. Coincidentally, during a meeting of the VPS in 1911, Spielrein was part of a discussion on vampires: "The legends of the dead themselves are tormented by the libido. . . . According to [Rudolf] Kleinpaul, the belief in vampires has its origin in the experience of 'wet dreams.' "[208] Thus, Parramore is not reaching when she ascribes Spielrein's work to vampire lore and its portrayal of "dark passions" in connection to sexuality, and female sexuality in particular. According to Texas Tech professor Erin Collopy, such films hinge on being "a metaphor for our own anxieties and desires" experienced specifically through an awakening female, a phenomenon that Spielrein's paper anticipates in its discussion on female sexuality, death, and transformation.[209]

She in fact offers a new fluid vision of a united *Eros-Thanatos*, an image patterned on primordial carnality that we find across centuries of poetry, prose, film, mythology, and religion. Destruction, to her, was also expressed on a sacred level: physical union as capable of reaching the realm of the sublime, in all of its glory and terror. This is manifested in physical union resulting in the survival of the species (childbirth) on one level, as well as in a union darkly sensuous and possessive, which harbors blood, vampiric dissolution, destruction, and psychological transformation. Hers is an attempt at exploring love as a *danse macabre.*

Speaking of a *danse macabre,* renowned filmmaker and fellow Russian Andrei Tarkovsky situates the understanding of love and sacrifice as a particularly "Russian" personality characteristic and, when speaking of his final film *The Sacrifice*, expounds:

> In this film I deal with one of the aspects of this struggle for anyone living in society: [the] concept of self-sacrifice. If one has never known such a feeling, never experienced such a desire, then, as far as I am concerned, one cease[s] to be a man, one begins to revert to the animal condition and becomes a strange machine, an object to be experimented with by society and the state. On the other hand, if one acquires a moral autonomy, one may discover within oneself a capacity for self-sacrifice.[210]

Perhaps Spielrein's Russian sensibility contributed to her interpretation of Eros as a simultaneous experience of dissolution—or at the very least, a loosened grip and disidentification with the ego in order to experience something larger than the self, an embodied psychology rendered in the image of a beloved and a "death instinct."

The image that her "death instinct" has inspired in recent artistic productions is almost another story entirely, running parallel to the academics that have supposedly found her article incomprehensible. Writers and filmmakers devoted to Spielrein's story have not only found her work comprehensible, but have, incredibly and independent of each other, used different Gustav Klimt images of *Judith* to highlight the unity of Eros and Thanatos throughout her writing. See Figures 1 and 2 below:

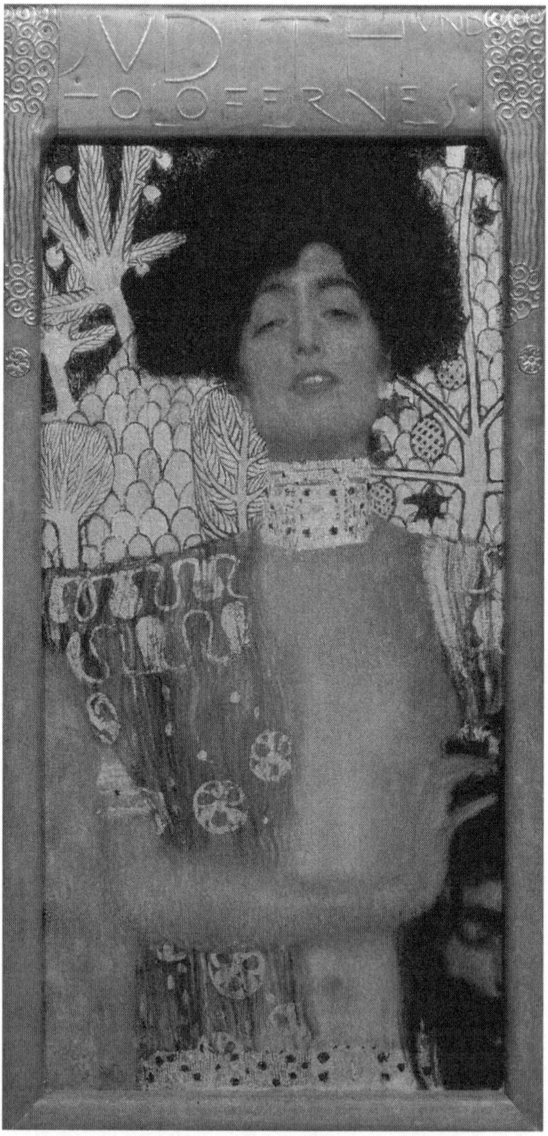

Figure 1. *Judith I (und der Kopf des Holofernes* [and the head of Holofernes]). Gustav Klimt. 1901. Galerie Belvedere, Vienna. Public Domain.

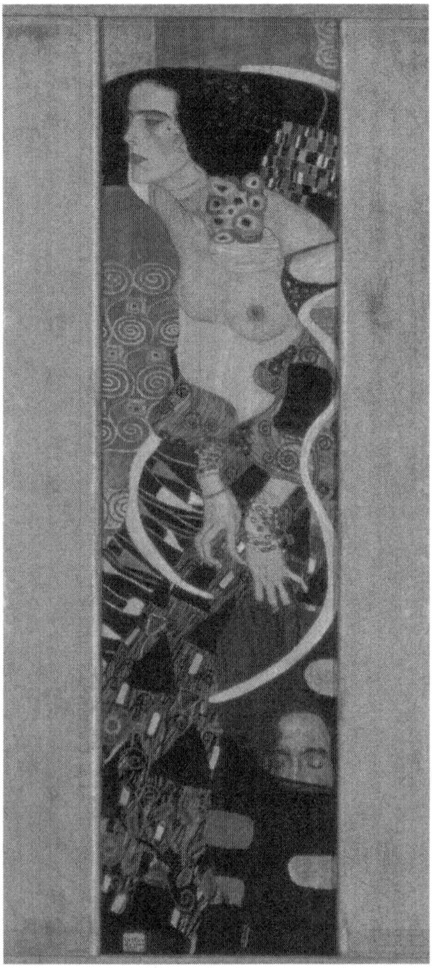

Figure 2. *Judith II (Salome)*. Gustav Klimt. 1909. Musei Civici Veneziani, Venice. Public Domain.

Amazingly, even though Judith is mentioned only once and in passing in a letter to Freud, *Judith I* is featured on the cover of Christopher Hampton's play *The Talking Cure*, a fictionalized and highly sexualized account of Spielrein's early treatment with Jung that was used as inspiration for the 2011 film *A Dangerous Method*, starring Keira Knightley and Michael Fassbender. Incidentally, *Judith I* is also featured on the Penguin edition of Leopold von Sacher-Masoch's *Venus in Furs* (1870)—the author from whom we derive *masochism*—wherein the protagonist's vision and desire for an Aphrodite-in-the-flesh to exert her will on his heart is realized. *Judith II* is featured in a scene in the Italian film *Prendimi L'Anima*, a provocative study that depicts Spielrein's adult life and career in the years she lived post-Jung. Of course, the film—and the play for that matter—may have also been insinuating that Spielrein herself was a kind of "Judith" to Jung, or a *femme fatale,* rather than using the image to reflect her work, though this seems unlikely given the sensitive and profound portrayal of Spielrein in the film as a pioneering woman in history.

Briefly, in order to provide context to Klimt's *Judith*: the story of Judith in *The Book of Judith*, Deuteronomy, underscores sexuality, death, and the various forms of being consumed by a lover. Judith is an Israelite savior, having beheaded the Assyrian conqueror and general Holofernes, who in his drunken vulnerability is seduced by Judith and decapitated. While interpretations abound, this scene may be read as aggressive female sexuality and carries with it visual connotations of orgasmic death, since the entire scene occurs in the "bedroom." Judith is also above identified with the Biblical Salome, whose figure in Mark and Matthew is never directly named, but she is most identified in her artistic representations as the daughter of Herod whose seductive dance was gifted, at her behest, the head of John the Baptist; Eros is again released through the lens of Thanatos. While *Judith I* and *II* are certainly provocative images representing the "death instinct," Judith must not be confused with Spielrein.

It must be mentioned that her article is not without its faults. Spielrein ventures into biological and gendered assumptions without deeper explanation, and her scope is far-ranging and varied, leaving the door open to an array of vastly disparate interpretations. Under the umbrella term *death instinct,* there exists idealization of the beloved and its shadow, sexuality, dissolution, transcendence, the survival of the species, impregnation, birth (and rebirth), mythology, biology, idolatry, religious sacrifice, shame, sadism, and death. It is an amorphous and speculative term that points to more questions than answers. That being said, it remains a mythic reflection and analysis on sexuality and the struggle of coming into being, and signals a time of destruction in the service of creation in its many forms.

Her work was always meant to be carried forward, as she herself urged quite clearly. While Freud would later sever Eros and Thanatos as diametrically opposed and Jung would emphasize the psychological rather than physical elements of Eros and Thanatos; Spielrein's unique contribution has been unequivocally ignored. As Freud says of his own work, he was simply "giv[ing] oneself up to a line of thought."[211] The same may be said of Spielrein. On that note, we turn to her personal letters, which give insight into her burgeoning academic career, from the point of pre-"Destruction" to the early 1920s.

6

Sabina Spielrein's Correspondence and Traps of the "Feminine"

They used my own pen to probe at my wounds.

—C. S. Lewis, *Till We Have Faces: A Myth Retold*

Introduction

In her article "Female Rhetorics," Patricia Meyer Spacks affirms that letters, like diaries, define the genre of autobiography: "Letters . . . construct or reveal a self, they encourage readers to acknowledge a personality so compelling as to constitute selfhood, [but] the notion of direct self-revelation and self-assertion would conflict with ideas about femininity deeply inscribed in the culture."[1] Spacks argues that such self-assertion depends on whether or not a writer feels free to "claim" material "for herself" against stereotypes of feminine docility. Sidonie Smith, in *A Poetics of Women's Autobiography: Marginality and the Fiction of Self-Representation*, concurs that female self-assertion is often viewed as a facsimile of so-called male and phallic characteristics.[2] Though old relationship woundings resurface in Spielrein's correspondence, she repeatedly confronts and questions the right she has to "claim" for herself her own ideas and interests amongst societal constructions of "femininity," even when this puts her, at times, at odds with both Freud and Jung.

She also filters concepts through her own interpretation of psychoanalytic theory, though at the time, scholarly ambition was considered highly unfeminine. For example, Freud himself believed that a woman's drive toward a professional career amounted to nothing more than penis envy: "The wish to get the longed-for penis . . . may contribute to the motives that drive a mature woman to analysis, and what she may reasonably expect from analysis—a capacity, for instance, to carry on an intellectual profession—may often be recognized as a sublimated modification of this repressed wish."[3] His sentiment reveals the male-centric atmosphere that failed to fully integrate female psychology and sexuality into culture, which in turn directly affected both Spielrein's personal and professional lives, which will be further explored in this chapter.

Following Freud, philosopher Jacques Lacan gives voice to women's historical exclusion when speaking offhand about "feminine" nature: "There is woman only as excluded by the nature of things which is the nature of words."[4] He continues in *On Feminine Sexuality*: "Woman is a signifier, the crucial property of which is that it is the only one that cannot signify anything, and this is simply because it grounds woman's status in the fact that she is not-whole. That means we can't talk about Woman," but only about how she "reflects" others.[5] According to Joanna Russ in *How to Suppress Women's Writing*, fellow Freudian Karl Abraham believed that women who were unable to "fulfill the role [of] womanhood," equated here with motherhood, were the same ones interested in "masculine pursuits of an intellectual and professional character," and often labeled homosexual.[6] Spielrein, relegated to a simultaneously male-deficient yet "masculine" role, embodies the difficulty and tension of pursuing academia as a woman in Europe in the early twentieth century.

This perpetuation of gendered power is critiqued in *Undoing Gender*, in which Judith Butler asserts that women have been historically defined by their so-called Other-ness, and subsequently positioned "in the negative," while at the same time held to idealized images of passive "femininity."[7] She also points to psychoanalysis, utilizing examples such as Freud and Lacan, as being constrained within this social construction of "existing differentials of power."[8] On the other hand, Hélène Cixous offers an understanding of what has been psychosocially accepted as "positive," or accepted within the phallocentrism of assigned masculinity, meaning the "plus-value of virility, authority, power, [and] money."[9] Spielrein highlights this notion of women's existence as a shadowed reflection of man excluded from both language and wholeness when writing in her diary about Jung's degradation of her reputation in public: "Perhaps I am his tragic negative? Accursed!"[10]

This chapter, aided by the content of Spielrein's letters, seeks to examine the conflation of gender with constructions of "femininity" through epithets used against Spielrein such as "Jewess," "hysteric," and "anima." As Spielrein wrote in 1912: "One can associate many things to the word 'woman' since it requires associations only to the substance [body] of 'woman.' "[11] Because a few of her letters both to and from Jung have been referenced in previous chapters in relation to the "love cure," they will not be replicated here. Rather,

her correspondence to Jung from the years 1909 (her draft letter) and again from 1917–18 will be explored in closer detail as they relate to her emerging autonomy, as will her letters to and from Freud—which are dated 1909 to 1923—as they reference her personal life and professional career. Again, like with her diary entries, many letters have been necessarily sacrificed in order to preserve the cohesion of narrative and constrictions of space and copyright.

Sabina Spielrein's Letters

> O, I believe very firmly in the existence of love. . . . How beautiful love is when one can devote oneself completely to the feeling, when one has another person, if only for a short while, utterly to oneself.
>
> —Sabina Spielrein, 1910

Returning to the draft document/letter discussed in the last chapter, these latter segments represent what translator Jeanne Moll calls "Female confronting the male."[12] Similar to her "Destruction" article, the idea of love in association with death is presented, though she declares that her idea that sexual energy " 'wants to be transformed' (my words)" is distinct from Jung's theory that the instinct wishes to " 'express itself fully' (your words)."[13] Theologian Carol Christ evokes Spielrein's idea in her article "Mysticism and Feminist Spirituality," when she defines sexuality as an "embodied embedded mysticism" and relates it to a "sensing through the body of connection to the larger whole or web of life of which we are a part and to the divine power that is the ground and sustainer of all being and becoming."[14]

Spielrein's interest in "embodied embedded mysticism" is complemented by her study of evolutionary biology as she ponders (but does not answer) the questions: "Why does love exist and not only coarse sexual attraction? Why are species which are more intellectually developed more discriminating in their choice? . . . Does this conform to the point of view that everything tends to promote the preservation of the species?"[15] To her, "coarse sexual attraction" is always discussed in light of its corresponding emotional and existential aspects in her evolving theory on an individual's drive to procreate, which is present here in its infancy. She also notes that the more singular or "differentiated" a person is, "the more fatal the story becomes" in finding a partner, which may allude to her own experience of societal ostracizing subsequent to the so-called scandal.[16]

She briefly muses on "biological" attraction to female forms in relation to animal instincts before concluding: "Beauty does not have to be linked to value. . . . There is no absolute beauty."[17] In direct opposition to the notion of a formulaic standard of beauty, she uncouples female aesthetics from human worth, in speaking directly to Jung in the process. She also touches on projection in romantic relationships: "One loves one's ideal in the other. . . . One prefers to remember the ideal image. But the ideal is nothing other than that which is deeply anchored in the psyche as a result of an infinity of circumstances."[18] A few years later, Jung would write something similar in *Psychological Types*: "This person is the object of intense love. . . . The influence of such a person is immediate and absolutely compelling because it always provokes an affective response . . . [in] the person representing the soul-image."[19] Both speak to the process of separating an individual from one's idealized version of that person, which, as Spielrein recognizes, is rooted in an infinite number of personal and ancestral circumstances.

Importantly, she confronts questions of love and sex through her own perspective and thus as *human* instincts rather than as specifically male or female. She also seeks to recognize the various kinds of love that do not harbor sexual attraction. Presumably due to her disintegrating relationship with Jung, her writing centers on abstractions, as summarized by Cifali: "What differentiates the love of a woman from that of a man? . . . How can these essentially human feelings be distinguished from sexual attraction? . . . What enables us to renounce it?"[20] As previously noted, she often poses questions without answers in an attempt to understand her own psychological and physical presence in the world.

Referencing her own clinical history with Jung, she proceeds to a more critical analysis of transference, reminding that one looks to one's doctor "to be free of a complex" and urges: "It's not . . . necessary for one to react with a sexual complex," possibly reacting to the sexual overtone of her own treatment.[21] Actually, she directly scrutinizes their "dreadful" relationship before proclaiming: "I shall be free!"[22] Bemused by her own analysis, she quips that she has been dubbed "somebody who thinks."[23]

Again speaking from personal experience, she writes that especially for "hysterical" patients, one should "prevent as much as possible the excitement of a psycho-sexual expression," and wonders, in response to her own emotional state at the time, "Will I be able to come out of it safe and sound?"[24] She admits that it is difficult for her to speak in such a "frank" manner but sarcastically offers: "Should I play the ambitious one? Or the role of the righteous, offended woman? . . . The complexity of the situation makes me adopt the unnatural role of the man and you the feminine role."[25] Highlighting prescribed gender roles of the era, she resolves to continue addressing him regardless of how "unfeminine" she appears. In fact, she later quotes a line from Aleksandr Pushkin's play *Boris Godunov* laying claim to her "justifiable rage" which she equates to having " 'blood-spattered before my eyes.' "[26] The line is also found in Pushkin's poem, "The Captive," reading: "Then, leaving the blood-spattered morsel, his eye / He fixes on me with a dolorous cry."[27]

Troubled by the affect that sexual concretization in therapy has had on her life, she also explains that "transference" may be present in any human relationship and that it contains within it the possibility for "non-sexual transformation."[28] Reflecting years later in 1918, Spielrein again states her opinion on the matter to Jung, based on her own experience of falling into relationships of greater and lesser erotic impulses: "I see absolutely no difference between transference to a doctor and every other kind of transference: when giving one's own personality, one takes on the personality of the other person whom one loves."[29] In *The Myth of Analysis*, James Hillman would similarly free transference from its historical and gendered setting: "We are in transference wherever we go, wherever a connection means something to the soul."[30]

However, both Spielrein and Hillman differentiate between sexual and nonsexual relationships, ostensibly referring to boundaries between relationships in and out of therapy respectively, as Spielrein would further write to Jung on January 6, 1918:

> Analysis of the "unconscious," depending on the patient's personality and in particular the doctor's, can deprive the analyzed material of energy or "soak it with blood." It is probable that, as recommended by Freud, a neutral attitude on the part of the doctor is best for the average patient because: if the doctor shows disapproval, then he increases defenses and repression; if he shows too much joy, he encourages the patient's inner desires and "soaks them with blood." These two extremes are especially dangerous in analysis among different sexes.[31]

While borrowing a phrase from Jung ("soak with blood") written in an earlier letter, she still claims adherence to Freud, who had previously written on the necessity of maintaining neutral boundaries within therapy.[32] She, too, warns of potential problems inherent to the therapeutic setting where two individuals may become dependent upon each other. Her own experience may be viewed as one such example of "risky" behavior.

Returning to the draft letter as well as to the subject of Siegfried, Spielrein states that her love for Jung was originally "without the least thought of a child," claiming the figure had always held a heroic interpretation for her: "My wish has never been formulated thus: 'I want to bear you a child.' "[33] Verily, the fact that Siegfried became a symbol for a creative "child," before it became a symbol divorced from Jung completely, is evidenced in another letter written to Jung during her doctoral research, at a time when her anger had subsided:

> Receive now the product of our love, the work which [is] Siegfried. It was a tremendous effort, but nothing was too hard for me if done for Siegfried. . . . Then I will be free. The work goes far beyond me and my life, which is why I am so scared. . . . Siegfried has an unholy drive to create, even if he is granted a shadow existence in the realm of Proserpina. . . . I don't want to cause any trouble or disrupt your rest: on the contrary, the [dissertation] is intended to give you the greatest possible satisfaction. . . . The mythological part is probably much better than the rest, because there, I was alone with Siegfried.[34]

Proserpina is the Roman equivalent of the Greek figure of Persephone, and according to Christine Downing in *The Goddess: Mythological Images of the Feminine*, she is "Goddess of the realm of the dead . . . of the power and beauty of the dark moments in our life," as well as the ruler of "mystery."[35] Spielrein's relationship to Proserpina reveals her journey through the dark process of coming to terms with Siegfried while creating her dissertation, the act of which literally freed her from any residual ties to Jung, being that he was one of her dissertation advisors. Siegfried, birthed in the form of her writing, was then "free" to infuse other aspects of her life from psychiatry to motherhood to teaching. This underworld experience represents a time of transition from Spielrein's attachment to Jung to her growing intellectual and emotional autonomy.

An intriguing note on the figure of Siegfried comes from Claire Douglas's *Translate This Darkness*, wherein to Christiana Morgan, a patient and colleague of Jung's, he is quoted as saying: " 'You are like Brünnhilde. You have never been broken in. There ought to come to you a Siegfried who would break through your ring of fire—who would make you into a woman.' "[36] Douglas then comments: "With this loaded image, Jung consciously or unconsciously intimated that he . . . would make the only suitable lover for Christiana Morgan."[37] While Jung used Siegfried on more than one occasion in analysis, which undoubtedly led to some of the confusion surrounding the symbol, it must be remembered that Spielrein's identification was not with Brünnhilde but with Siegfried, and may thus be viewed through the lens of a hero rather than through a figure of martyrdom.

At the close of her draft letter, after lashing out at the "lies" spread about her during the scandal, she exclaims: "I cannot allow you to defend yourself by humiliating me."[38] In a non sequitur, she then relays the entire history of the Russian Tsar Boris, seemingly as a parable, when she speculates that he achieved power through the murder of innocent youth.[39] She warns:

"Fate takes its vengeance on the Tsar."[40] Possibly viewing herself as a youth sacrificed for Jung's gain, she admits to her own guilt of "borrowing" Jung from his wife in the past and sadly states: "My soul has lost its softness."[41] Be that as it may, she reclaims her academic ambition and states that she "had to write it!" regardless of how she would be perceived by him and reflects: "I do not exclude the possibility that I may fall in love with somebody else."[42] She then prepares herself to move beyond his influence and continue her research.

Defecting

And what is it, the "present"?

—Sabina Spielrein, 1917

The years directly following her draft letter saw Spielrein's graduation and induction into the VPS as well as her emerging analytical practice, publications, marriage, the birth of her first daughter, and her increasing interest in child psychology. In 1914, after Jung's resignation as editor of the *International Psychoanalytic Journal* (*Internationale Zeitschrift für Psychoanalyse*), Freud wrote to Spielrein:

> Please let me know if you want to appear on the masthead of our journal. If so, then it will be done in the next issue. . . . We shall shortly be removing all Zurich names and addresses. It would be the clearest sort of partisanship if your name was placed on it now. . . . Don't stand on ceremony, but whatever you decide to do, do it unreservedly. . . . There will be a warm welcome for you if you stay with us here, but then you will have to recognize the enemy over there.[43]

While this letter is certainly a challenge to Spielrein, it has been seen (as noted in chapter 2) as Freud's attempt to use Spielrein against Jung. However, it is known that multiple prominent psychologists, such as Alfred Adler, had been kicked out of the VPS when seen as apostates from pure Freudian methodology, and Freud's request for Spielrein to "recognize the enemy" may also be seen in this light.[44] Furthermore, he would not have extended a legitimate offer to her if he did not also hold her scholarship and character in high esteem, considering she was at this time not merely a previous patient of Jung's, but an accomplished and published doctor who had little contact with Jung at this time.

Still, even adhering to Freudian psychology, she refused to choose sides:

> I did resent his behavior toward you, Professor, but I don't disregard him. . . . The position J. took on our society I could forgive even less than I could for my personal matter. I saw him only once after my marriage, but after all, I'm not the father, but the sister. I still like J., despite his aberrances, and want him back on our side. You two belong together much more than one would believe. . . . This fervent wish is not a betrayal of our society! Everyone knows that I declare myself a member of the Freudian Society, and J. cannot forgive this.[45]

In her diplomacy, when condemned at this time by Jung for turning to Freud (as will be shown), she firmly stands her ground with the latter and, unprecedentedly, is not excommunicated from the society as a result. Further, Kerr asserts (and maintained by Rosemary Balsam in her article "Women of the Wednesday Society") that Spielrein remained stuck "in the role of the protective, self-sacrificing mother," and it appears she actually felt an allegiance to Freud as the de facto father of psychology, while she viewed herself as a sister, or on equal footing, to Jung.[46]

Interestingly, a few years later, in 1919, perhaps attempting to make up for his past stubbornness, Freud wrote to her:

> You may remain our member and our debtor for as long as you wish. . . . I also feel that I have no right to dissuade you from participating in the translation of Jung's writing, the less so since you write that you enjoy doing it. . . . I would naturally like very much to have you as translator of my own psychoanalytic books. . . . Please send your promised contributions direct to the publisher (Rank).[47]

Feeling an obvious affinity for Spielrein, Freud not only trusted her with his own texts, but also frequently encouraged her contributions to the *Journal.* In fact, according to Alexander Etkind in *Eros of the Impossible: The History of Psychoanalysis in Russia*, she was often regarded as "meticulous" and "pedantic" in her standards of translation for both Freud and Jung's works, and was displeased with the quality of other translations.[48]

On October 17, 1917, letters between Spielrein and Jung increased both in number and disagreement, as her attempt to reconcile his theories with her own Freudian understanding of psychology was interpreted as hostile. They argue over symbology, and Spielrein attempts to explain her developing theories on November 27, 1917:

> Will to Power or Sex Drive? . . . And the feeling of power? What else is it if not the desire for more attention and love? And the feeling of inadequacy?—One suffers from feelings of inferiority, because one feels [s]he has less claim to recognition and love, and then one cannot continue to exist or reproduce; this applies both to the unsatisfied repressed wishes and to their sublimated products.[49]

As she does in her "Destruction" paper, she connects the psychological aspect of one's sexuality to one's instinctual need for love (and transformation), so that the hunger for power is thereby interpreted as a superficial sublimation of the former. She also differentiates her theory of power from Adler's and seeks to integrate Freud's position with Jung's on the matter: "It is very instructional for me that you and Freud accuse each other of the same [thing], namely, a biological conception of psychology."[50] On his part, Jung implored to be left in peace "clinging to my runes" as someone "mocked" by outside circles.[51]

He also readily disregards her ideas: "You are proceeding from the outset . . . that there is only the instinct for the preservation of the species. . . . With this assumption, however, you do violence to the psychology of the subject. . . . It is inadmissible. . . . You must read Adler or Nietzsche."[52] Jung's condescension is unwarranted, since it is well known from her published work that Spielrein was very familiar with Nietzsche, and she very clearly references Adler in a discussion of his theory in the above letter. That Jung reduces her line of thinking to merely the "preservation of the species" also dismisses the mythic importance that underlies her entire emphasis on sexuality and death, as evidenced by her previous presentations and articles. Even though Spielrein intellectually embodies a symbiosis between Freudian and Jungian methodology, she is repeatedly censured for it in her correspondence.

In another letter, dated December 15, 1917, she defines Jung's terminology of "extravert-introvert":

> It seems quite natural to me that your "introverted type" is the one in which the will to power is prevalent, while the need for self-surrender [or, devotion] is stronger in the extravert. . . . In ordinary language, the need of self-surrender is called "love." . . . In my opinion, the introvert also has feelings, but they are primarily in contrast to those of the extravert: while the extravert, who strives for self-surrender, projects his personality onto others and is aware, first and foremost of "empathy," so the introvert's approach must

> be the opposite of this rapport. . . . I have made two schema for the Extra + Introverted types.[53]

In these diagrams (Appendix B), she defines introversion as "withdrawing from the object" on the threshold of consciousness, which she terms, and coins, "side-consciousness," to the dismay of both Freud and Jung.[54] On the other hand, she compares the extravert to the "need for self-sacrifice (becoming one with the object)," harkening back to her earlier images of dissolving into and uniting with a beloved.[55] To her, the "need to be absorbed in love (self-surrender) may be felt so deeply that it replaces the will to power."[56] Here one gains an insight into her previous letter's emphasis on the sexual instinct rather than the desire for power, which to her infuses the psychology of introverts and extraverts to varying degrees dependent upon personality.

In "Transforming At-One-Ment: Spielrein, Jung, Bion," Janet Sayers asserts that it is in this letter that the theory of the subconscious emerged in the field of psychoanalysis: "With this [concept of self-surrender] she developed a new theory—of the subconscious."[57] While psychologist Pierre Janet had used the term previously, Spielrein's equation of the term to "side-consciousness" was completely original, as further elaborated in her December 15 letter:

> Later I saw that you and Freud understood [the unconscious] in completely different ways. A certain "urge," "need," "wish," in us, which is connected to our darkest and deepest instinctual lives, seeks to dissipate (live out) its energy in dreams by using subconscious symbolism to represent wish fulfillment. This whole "reshaping" of the subconscious world of ideas takes place in the pre-conscious, because the dark "repressed" wishes may not even occur in the subconscious ("side-conscious").[58]

Spielrein would continue to use the term *side-consciousness* to differentiate her understanding and interpretation of mythic imagery within the psyche from Freud's or Jung's. She continues to develop it in a letter dated December 20, 1917: "The sublimated symbols are more general and archaic than the equivalent conscious thoughts. . . . This is my view."[59] To her, "side-conscious" imagery, or "all the ancestral wisdom which is not known to us," differs from instincts and images completely censored from one's psyche, as the former infuses the dream-world and the latter forms a distinct part of the sub/unconscious.[60]

She includes an additional diagram of her mental construct and speaks of "body feelings" corresponding to psychological states, an early observer of somatic psychology.[61] She concludes by observing: "One thinks in terms of symbols."[62] To be sure, she further posits that symbolic imagery is available to a greater and lesser degree, dependent upon how conscious an individual is, and by how much one is influenced by his or her own schema of body sensation, symbol formation, and instinctual nature. In response to her lengthy explanation, Jung curtly replies: "Your conception of the unconscious seems arbitrary to me."[63]

In defiance of Jung's dismissal, she replies that it is her determination to understand her "vocation" and sees the potential of an analysis that emphasizes discovering one's personal destiny (Jung) as well as one that emphasizes one's childhood trauma (Freud): "This method would be one of the greatest human discoveries with exceptional value for both the ill and for the healthy. Therefore, I had the intention of understanding your method in a practical manner."[64] She admits that she has only had the chance to experiment with Jung's method of dream interpretation and amplification on herself, but she warns: "The subconscious can also deceive."[65] Spielrein's method is thus distinct from both Freud's and Jung's, since it was from the beginning inherently pluralistic.

In response to Jung having claimed she could "not understand" him when Siegfried had been reintroduced into the discussion, she replies on January 19, 1918:

> You believe that I can never understand your letters, which makes any conversation useless. I assume a pragmatic standpoint . . . does this bridge tell us anything? . . . My heroic attitude toward the world has never been a secret even in my childhood years and I would have been aware of it without any type of psychoanalysis. Without your advice, I would have believed, like all laymen, that I dreamt of Siegfried because I carry around heroic fantasies, be it through conscious expressions or be it in the shape of "heroic psychological attitutdes." I am and I have always been, a person who is mystically-minded. I strongly resisted the idea of Siegfried being a real child and, merely based on *my being mystically-minded,* I believed it was my fate to live a grand and heroic life and that I would have to sacrifice my life for an epic creation. I could not interpret my dreams in which my grandfather and father [both of them rabbis] blessed me and said, "Your life will be marked by a powerful fate, my child," in any other way. . . . According to Freud, the Siegfried fantasy is "merely" wish fulfillment. I have always rejected the word "merely" . . . I am personally more inclined to believe that I portray the "heroic attitude" in music and the "religious feeling" in science. . . . You assume that music is merely a bridge for me, an expression of the religious feeling. Is my work as a doctor also merely a bridge? If not—why is music merely a bridge for me?[66]

Even though some of her letters leading up to this response are lost, it is clear that she feels defensive of both her Siegfried symbol as well as of her love of music. She disagrees with both Freud's and Jung's interpretations of Siegfried—reducing the figure to a wish or a bridge respectively—and clarifies that she has always harbored a mystical element rather than a tie to a literal child. She also rejects the notion that her role as doctor or musician is a "bridge" to something else, since they are both integral to her psyche and expressed in her life as "religious" and "heroic." Without allowing either Freud or Jung to define Siegfried, her relationship to it, or its manifestation in the outer world, she reaffirms that both scientific work and music are her personal paths.

That being said, Jung continues to reorganize Spielrein's thoughts around his own: "You are always trying to drag the Siegfried symbol back into reality, whereas in fact it is the bridge to your individual development. . . . You are rejecting dreams and seeking action," and laments that she "cannot understand" him.[67] Jung devalues her connection to Siegfried by implying that she is "drag[ging]" it into reality, and misses the point that for Spielrein, Siegfried *is* her reality, having used the figure at various times as metaphor for her writing, profession, pregnancy, and instinctual nature, as will be further demonstrated. Also, in none of her letters does she "reject" her dreams, though she does attempt to illuminate their symbols, albeit on her own terms rather than in direct agreement with Jung.

Still, he continues: "I am underlining all the passages in your letter where you are thinking concretely and, typically, misunderstanding the symbol. . . . In relation to this world you have to be real, either a musician, or a doctor, or a wife and a mother. But your task is not completed when you do that. Those are mere functions."[68] Granted, Jung does not attempt to dissuade her from becoming either a doctor or a musician, but states that either is still a "function" of her life rather than its expression. Moreover, he underscores gender expectations of the time by implying that she must choose between being *either* a working professional *or* a wife and a mother. Spielrein is rarely afforded her own opinion on the topic.

On January 27, 1918, Spielrein's tone becomes rather acerbic because the two have once again entered into a debate on Freudian methodology: "You are so extraordinarily valuable to me that I would not want you to become so self-interested. . . . Freud has accomplished an extraordinary amount in his lifetime. . . . You, however, are still capable of development."[69] She reproaches him for being too "one-sided" and does not understand why her attempt to reconcile the two respective theories is met with such resistance: "You see neurosis primarily as a regression process. Freud primarily sees an arrested development. If adopting this general definition, both are decidedly right."[70] She feels Jung owes his success in large part to Freud, but she continues to encourage him to carve out his own path without disparaging Freud, whose legacy she believes to be exemplary.

Defiantly, she returns to elaborate on Siegfried, again through her own perspective:

> A sexual problem can often be of a "higher" power because it is also part of God's required life task. . . . My Siegfried problem, for example, could be a real child as well as a symbolic Aryan-Semitic child, for example, a child from the union of your and Freud's teachings . . . [Siegfried] soon was a candle (light) . . . then a book . . . Wagner's *Siegfried*, then music, then prophetic dreams and prophecies that only in analysis [with Jung] turned "Siegfried" into a real child.[71]

This passage cuts to the heart of her personal symbol that was for a time confused with her relationship to Jung. Here, Siegfried retains his malleability, tied as much to her creative path as a musician as well as to her interests as a psychoanalyst. It seems as though Siegfried is a reflection of any part of her life that touches upon her own personal ambition and interests. Apropos, referencing her heroic aspiration: "Soon I had become Siegfried."[72] In addition, she challenges the assumption that sexual impulses are less elevated than psychological ones, since they are also "of God" and lead (for her) to the preservation of the species. Predating World War II, she speaks in terms of reconciliation between Aryan and Semitic polarities, which have been constellated in Jung and Freud respectively.

She then begins to reflect on her own psychological state after the birth of her first child, reclaiming the right to interpret the figures within her dreams as she sees fit: "I almost lost my daughter simultaneous to or due to a mighty Siegfried dream during pregnancy. Finally, the child triumphed in reality and I called her Renata."[73] "Renata," meaning rebirth, evokes her "Destruction" paper in relation to sexual transformation and destruction in service of creation, here equated with the birth of her daughter, and in turn, a rebirth of herself. In a moment of profound honesty, she acknowledges that reconciling her "heroic" image of Siegfried with the physical state of pregnancy and prospect of motherhood resulted in an existential and anxiety-filled search for integration of all of her self-described vocations. In his reply, Jung does not recognize the fact that Spielrein's reflections are contextualized in the past, and further diminishes her experience by arguing: "Your inner world is chaotic."[74]

In her last available letter to Jung, from late January 1918, she replies with a resounding affirmation of her own passions, represented again in Siegfried:

> I consider it an equivalent "higher power" to provide "Siegfried" as a bodily or spiritual child and due to various considerations and decisions, he is now an intellectual child. . . . The more I work on musical compositions—the more I am pulled in despite all the opposition and criticism. I am making rapid progress. . . . Music for me is the most soulful and immediate need, even an intellectual necessity, and because I understand more and more, it brings me high spiritual joy.[75]

She resigns herself to her scientific "vocation" and refuses to choose between her profession, motherhood, or music: "Giving up music . . . I cannot do it: it would be like tearing out a piece of my soul, and the wound would never close. . . . Please be so kind and send the letter back to me."[76] Recalling her draft letter, she again asks Jung to return her letter so that she can continue to analyze its material. In this way, she determines with a vigorous effort to confront her own psyche as well as to reconcile disparate perspectives for her own use. As iterated by John Kerr in *A Most Dangerous Method*: "Her letters are unique in the entire surviving documentary record of psychoanalysis. If anyone else made such an intensive attempt at integration during this period, their efforts have been lost."[77]

The year that Jung's letters fade away from Spielrein, in 1919, Freud's letters to her resurface (or have been made available) when he asks her to become translator of his own works and discusses various topics concerning the Vienna Psychoanalytic Society. In 1922, he asserts, recalling his previous enthusiasm: "The people of Geneva are each and every one of them dilettantes to whom you must gradually transmit something of your analytical training. [Édouard] Claparède is no exception. Saussure,[78] when he returns . . . will probably be the only expert apart from you."[79]

At this point, Spielrein had moved to Geneva, where she taught and practiced before ultimately deciding to move back to Russia. Freud's esteem in her abilities is evident in his ranking of her as an expert alongside Raymond de Saussure, who helped to found the Paris Psychoanalytic Society. Freud's tone remains kindred, though he is often impatient regarding the absurd analysts from Zurich.[80] Still, he continued to welcome her contributions to the *International Journal* and his last letter to her indicates genuine concern for her return to Russia: [February 9, 1923] "Your plan to go to Russia seems to me much better than my advice to try out Berlin. . . . These are difficult times for all of us. I hope to hear from you soon."[81]

"Othering"

> . . . I am his star, rising above the Burghölzli
>
> dead: ex-patient, Persephone, proof a "schizophrenic"
> child who lives out whole her fairy tale, needs only
> heroic hands, to lift her fingers from her eyes.
> . . . .
> You men stick tight, you *Doktors*. Who in the world am *I*
> to complicate your bond? A naughty, little, girl, hysteric.
>
> —Pamela White Hadas, " 'Jung and
> Easily Freudened': Sabina Spielrein's Analysis"

LITTLE GIRL

After her first presentation to the VPS, Freud wrote to Jung: "Fraulein Spielrein read a chapter from her paper yesterday (I almost wrote the ihrer [her] with a capital 'i'). . . . I have hit on a few objections to your [Ihrer] (this time I mean it) method of dealing with mythology, and I brought them up in the discussion with the little girl."[82] Jung returns in kind, referring to her as the "little authoress" and musing on the "errors" of her interpretation of myth.[83] One of the problems that arises here is that Freud does not even credit Spielrein with the work of her own paper when he "almost" writes "your paper" to Jung, implying that her article was without original contribution on the part of the author. Yet the very fact that Jung finds fault with her work is evidence that she was not merely his mouthpiece.

In "Sabina Spielrein: Another Picture," Mereille Cifali justifies the use of the term *little girl* by both Freud and Jung as being due to her age, equating it with a term of endearment.[84] However, such an endearment is used when she is twenty-six years old and a doctor. Regardless of intention, the term is condescending, infantilizing, and belittling to Spielrein's position as a colleague and an equal member in the VPS at the time. It also positions her as a *little girl* among *grown men* as it would be equally as demeaning to refer to Jung as a "little boy," when he was a married man with children. Aldo Carotenuto also repeatedly refers to Spielrein in *A Secret Symmetry* as "Sabina," "little girl," and "the poor sick child," even when speaking of her adulthood, while Freud and Jung are afforded the respect of last names.[85]

Likewise, in Ronald Hayman's *A Life of Jung*, Spielrein is only ever referred to as "Sabina," and she is introduced as a woman with "big dark eyes" whose importance is defined by " 'an aspect of his [Jung's] anima.' "[86]

To Hayman, Spielrein is simply another manifestation of Jung's ideal: "He then projects this image [anima] onto the female companion [Spielrein] he has chosen because intuition told him she would be capable of receiving this projection."[87] Additionally, in André Haynal's *Psychoanalysis and the Sciences: Epistemology—History*, she is referred to as the "Young, dark-complexioned, black-haired hysterical woman."[88] It is of note that Johannes Cremerius is one among only a handful (Covington and Wharton in 2003; Heuer in 2011) to acknowledge the aforementioned remarks as disparaging.[89]

JEWESS

> This bitterness did not result from your dissertation . . . but from earlier, from all the inner anguish I experienced because of you—and which you experienced because of me. . . . Approach him [Freud] as a great master and rabbi, and all will be well.
>
> —Jung to Spielrein, 1911

Though her gender informed Spielrein's reception as a scholar, her self-identification as a Jew also created an element of exoticisation and sexualization as an "Other." To that end, in October 1910, she wrote in her diary:

> [Jung] tells me that he loves Jewish women, and that he would love a black-complexioned Jewish girl. Also in him is the desire to remain close to his religion and culture, as well as the desire for refreshment through a new race, a desire for liberation from his paternal obligations in an unbelieving Jewess.[90]

She clearly understood the image she held for Jung as well as the stereotypes being projected onto her persona. It must be understood that referring to herself as a Jewess is not the same thing as being exoticized or fetishized by Jung because of it. In "The Image of the Hysteric," cultural critic Sander Gilman illuminates the societal view of the "Jewess" at the time: "The Jew is the hysteric; the Jew is the feminized Other; the Jew is seen as different, as diseased."[91] Similarly, in *The Politics of Myth*, Robert Ellwood agrees: "Jews were alien, dark shadows on the margins of social reality. One could praise them, do business with them, resent them, hate them: whatever the attitude, they were regarded as different, other, and so a problem or potential problem."[92]

Actually, as early as Jung 20, 1909, Spielrein notes her own interchangeability in a letter to Freud: "The girl was deeply embedded in him, and she was my prototype."[93] She refers to the fact that Jung confided to her that he had loved a "Jewish girl" before her, and Spielrein now suspects that she may already be a "psychosexual" replacement of transferred affection for another young Jewish woman: Freud's daughter Anna.[94] Jung admits to this prototype and confirms to Freud: "The Jewess popped up in another form, in the shape of my patient [Spielrein]."[95] Spielrein is not granted a full humanity, but is instead reduced to a projected image of Jung's own making, based on the idealization and generalization of Jewish women.

Interestingly, during the mounting distrust between Freud and Jung a few years later, as reproduced in Alexander Etkind's *Eros of the Impossible: The History of Psychoanalysis in Russia*, Freud relayed to Spielrein: "We are and remain Jews. The others will only exploit us and will never understand or appreciate us."[96] If any allegiance to Spielrein is felt in Freud's letter, it appears in the alliance between two "Others." Simone de Beauvoir gives voice to this historical exploitation in *The Second Sex*, specifically in regard to women: "Objectified as the Other in ways that were both overtly despotic and insidious . . . [women's] particularity as human beings was reduced to a lazy, abstract cliché (the eternal feminine; "the black soul"; the Jewish character) that served as a rationale for their subjugation."[97] As we know from Spielrein's diary, she soon saw herself as "one of the many" who would periodically fulfill this role for Jung and subsequently disengaged from him because of it.[98]

Her ethnicity never ceased to be a point of complex contention, and in 1918, Jung directly confronts her marginalization: "There is a part of the Jewish soul which you are not yet living . . . you still have your eye too much on the outside. That is—"unfortunately"—the curse of the Jew: the aspect of his psychology which . . . he calls "infantile wish-fulfillment," he is the murderer of his own prophets, even of his Messiah."[99] Exactly whose Messiah was "murdered" aside, Spielrein replies in a calculated manner, speaking as much to Jung personally as to religion generally:

> Messianism is quite interesting in Christianity. If one understands this religion in the form in which it is presented to us in school, it is of course nonsense and actually, quite harmful. If we penetrate deeper into the nature of Christ—a question appears: has the redeemer already been to earth, or is it a thoroughly justifiable claim that he will not come until the end of the world, as the "unbelieving" Jews claim. Christ is the symbol for the union of Heaven and Earth, the transitional stage from man to God, the most perfect symbol of the sublimation process, since the "higher" life and "spiritual" salvation will be attained after overcoming all animal and selfish impulses. For *mankind* Christ has not yet come, for the complete realization of Christian ideals, meaning complete self-denial (self-negation of animal and selfish impulses), would

> lead to the extinction of the world . . . if Christ has not yet come in this realized form, he does live in all of us as a tendency as a reaction against our basest instincts. . . . You accuse us Jews, along with Freud, of viewing our deepest spiritual life as infantile wish fulfillment. To this I must reply that there is hardly a nation so inclined to see mysticism and the promise of fate in the world as the Jewish people.[100]

Spielrein validates the mythic power of Christianity and responds to Jung's denigration of her own "unbelieving" tradition, while at the same time she challenges religious dogmatism. She instead identifies as a mystic within a "prophetic" heritage and questions the biological reality of a Christ realization, pragmatically noting that such complete abstinence and negation of the body would result in the extinction of humanity. In doing this, she again evokes her "Destruction" paper, wherein Christ is interpreted as a symbol of transformation and a spiritual aspect of the self. Years later, in *Answer to Job*, Jung repeats this idea when, during a discussion on the literal reality of the "symbol" of Christ, he states: "If everyone were converted to this point of view, man as a species would die out in a few decades."[101]

In *Lingering Shadows: Jungians, Freudians, and Anti-Semitism*, Adolf Guggenbühl-Craig argues: "The anti-Semitism of Jung was a sheer banality, part and parcel of the collective he belonged to. Jung displayed positive and negative sides. He was, for instance, an appeaser. . . . Again, this was a typical collective attitude."[102] Acknowledging Spielrein as her own autonomous person outside of Jung's conception of an "unbelieving" Jewess is noted in order to question how this "collective" perspective affected millions of members of a particular group. For instance, Spielrein's felt interchangeability was not a "sheer banality," but a belief system based upon degradation and generalization that led to her own emotional duress as well as to her murder in Rostov years later.

HYSTERIC

> There is a good principle that created
> order, light, and man
> and a bad principle that created
> chaos, darkness, and woman.
>
> —Pythagoras

Susan Griffin explains in *Woman and Nature*:

> The word "hysterical" is taken from the word *hyster*, meaning womb, because it is observed that the womb is the seat of the emotions (and women are more emotional than men). That crying is womanish . . . that women have the defect of "inordinate affections and passions" and overlively imaginations.[103]

In Lisa Appignanesi and John Forrester's *Freud's Women: Family, Patients, Followers*, Spielrein is first introduced and mislabeled as Freud's patient and as a hysterical woman "cured" by his suggestion of marriage: "Freud hoped, indeed trusted, [she] would be cured by marriage."[104] Instead of a scholar, she is then viewed in relation to Jung as "[the] classic instance of a woman becoming the means of communication between Freud and another analyst. . . . She was not only Jung's first analytic case. She was also his first analytic muse and mistress."[105] In the little said about Spielrein, objectified in a string of "Freud's Women,"[106] she is defined by her role of mistress, one that completely disregards Spielrein's own reaction to the relationship. Also, while she is viewed as a "means" between Freud and Jung, the only active reconciliation she pursued was between the two respective theories in her correspondence.

Speaking specifically to women in psychoanalysis in *Trauma and Recovery: The Aftermath of Violence—From Domestic Abuse to Political Power*, Judith Herman argues that while Freud saw a link between hysteria and childhood abuse, he later dismissed his patients' testimonies as not credible: "Out of the ruins of the traumatic theory of hysteria, Freud created psychoanalysis. The dominant theory of the next century was founded in the denial of women's reality. Sexuality remained. . . . But the exploitative social context in which sexual relations actually occur became utterly invisible."[107] The eventual distancing of Freud from underlying roots of hysteria is further pondered by Carolyn Heilbrun in *Life/Lines: Theorizing Women's Autobiography*: "The desire to remember only the good things is perhaps not unconnected with Freud's ultimate conclusion that memories of childhood sexual assault were merely the fantasies of the women who recounted them."[108] While Spielrein's symptoms were labeled "hysterical," one may remember the abuse suffered at the hands of her father and the death of her sister that ultimately resulted in such "symptoms."

Unsurprisingly, in her article "Hysteria, Feminism, and Gender," Elaine Showalter asserts that not just sexual exploitation but also sexual suppression caused similar "symptoms" of hysteria, like "aggression" and hostility, which signaled "a disruption of femininity" and with it, a disruption of patriarchal[109] order resulting in diagnoses of so-called mental instabilities.[110] Alternatively, according to Mari Jo Buhle in *Feminism and its Discontents: A Century of Struggle with Psychoanalysis*, psychoanalysis is responsible for developing a safe space for women, and hysteria is defined as "a new language to express female selfhood."[111] However, the language spoken by women must be juxtaposed with how seriously that language is accepted into the culture at large.

For example, in Helen King's *The Disease of Virgins: Green Sickness, Chlorosis and the Problems of Puberty*, hysteria is further defined by associations with "selfish" and "manipulative" characteristics of femininity, including the terms "passive, weak, innocent [and] victim," for which as late as 1908, "a good spanking" and "threats of burning" were considered effective forms of treatment.[112] Showalter attests:

> That hysteria became a hot topic in medical circles at the same time that feminism, the New Woman, and a crisis in gender were also hot topics . . . does not seem coincidental. During an era when patriarchal culture felt itself to be under attack by its rebellious daughters, one obvious defense was to label women campaigning for access to universities, the professions, and the vote as mentally disturbed.[113]

That Spielrein has retained the labels of hysteric, schizophrenic, borderline, and seductress makes clear that such stigmatization has not disappeared. According to clinician Mark Micale, in his study, "On the 'Disappearance' of Hysteria: A Study in the Clinical Deconstruction of a Diagnosis," hysteria was not wholly disregarded as a diagnosis until the 1970s, when it was then subsumed into the diagnosis "borderline personality disorder."[114] As argued in "The Scarlet Label: Close Encounters with 'Borderline Personality Disorder' " by Drs. Jacqueline Simon Gunn and Brent Potter: "The label is a cultural-historical construction typically foisted upon women with a history of . . . stress."[115] Gunn and Potter further assert that this cookie-cutter diagnosis has been divorced from its social narrative in its inclusion into the psychiatric *Diagnostic and Statistical Manual of Mental Disorders*.[116]

Similarly, since the label of schizophrenia is in direct opposition to the opinion of this book, analysis will not be given to its constructs. Still, since it has been clearly retroactively assigned to Spielrein, let this summary by R. D. Laing in *The Politics of Experience* suffice:

> The term "schizophrenia" was coined by a Swiss psychiatrist, Bleuler [Spielrein's dissertation advisor]. . . . In using the term schizophrenia, I am not referring to any condition that I suppose to be mental rather than physical, or to an illness, like pneumonia, but to a label that some people pin on other people under certain social circumstances. . . . It is clear, at least, that some people come to behave and to experience themselves and others in ways that are

> strange and incomprehensible to most people, including themselves. If this behavior and experience fall into certain broad categories, they are liable to be diagnosed as subject to a condition called schizophrenia.[117]

It seems as though the term has been broadly associated with Spielrein based on certain assumptions of her behavior as "strange," possibly due to the intensity of her personal writing. Still, while her challenge to gender limitations of the time may be interpreted as progressive, they need not be seen as "incomprehensible." Perhaps the confusion of this label has arisen due to the fact that Spielrein wrote on the topic of schizophrenia for her dissertation.

In Greg Mogenson's *The Dove in the Consulting Room: Hysteria and the Anima in Bollas and Jung*, Spielrein is again mentioned in passing as "the hysterical patient" even at the time of her first publication, which occurred three years after her outpatient treatment had ceased: "A hysterical patient with such powerful insight into the rupture in the soul should have served as the sign stimulus that activated the archetypal libido latent in Jung's unconscious."[118] She is viewed as something to use, or as a "stimulus" in service of Jung's psychology, rather than as a fellow analyst. Her letters are then further diminished by Mogenson as "transference neurosis" and defined as the "speech of the hysteric."[119] That is to say, her letters are interpreted only in relation to a tenuous pathology thought to be cured years before the majority of her letters were even written. In her article "Dismantling the Animus," Lyn Cowan speaks to this discrepancy: "Woman herself is not locked within this profound struggle [being "activated"], she is only the catalyst for man's struggle with himself. It is never too certain that woman has any self at all."[120] (13).

Additionally, Spielrein is equated with two other women in the field's history, Josef Breuer's patient Anna O. and Freud's patient Dora (discussed in chapter 3), with no distinction made by Mogenson that Spielrein, unlike the other two mentioned, went on to earn her doctorate, raise a family, and practice as an analyst. Instead, she is dismissed as an "anima" figure for Jung and a reflection of his ideal: "Hysteria is the anima, or Madonna even . . . the soul of a man."[121] Yet it must be remembered that Mogenson is referring to an actual historical person whose importance does not rely on being an unfleshed "anima" figure.

ANIMA

> You could indeed have it [the child] if you wanted to, but it would be such a shame.
>
> —Freud to Spielrein, 1913

The term *anima* is often debated in postmodern feminist scholarship, and while that debate far exceeds the limits of this book, specific salient arguments will be highlighted in regard to the term in its historical context as it affected—and continues to affect—Spielrein. William Doty offers a brief explanation of the term in its current use in *Mythography*: "Many literary studies have used Jungian analytical categories (notably . . . the anima/animus, [meaning] the contra-sexual component of the unconscious, male for females, female for males) as a means of exposing the dynamics of works of poetry and fiction."[122] Actually, in *Alchemical Psychology*, James Hillman names Spielrein alongside a few other patients as being historically responsible for the term: "Sabina, Babette, Miss Miller. In fact, it was only at the culmination of this development of ideas, refined through confrontation with the dramatic expressions and mystifications of these women and their symptoms, that the idea of anima itself appeared and could be distinguished from actual women."[123]

The term's relationship to psychology was thus paradoxical from the beginning in that it was both born of and divorced from "actual women," though related specifically to a male-gendered creation. Incidentally, Hillman is responsible for freeing the term from its gendered connotations in *Anima*, as interpreted by Susan Rowland: " 'Women do not bear the anima or soul for men. They have souls of their own and, like males, should develop psychologically through the cultivation of the culturally neglected feminine anima. Similarly, both women and men have equal access to animus, or 'spirit.' "[124] Hillman envisioned the anima (and animus, or "the masculine") as a purely psychological "soul image" available to individuals irrespective of gender-identity. Contrarily, because even the labels "feminine" and "masculine" have so frequently been conflated with gender stereotypes, especially in the early 1900s, the term *anima* and its relation to those stereotypes must nevertheless be questioned.

For instance, *logos,* or rational thinking was at the time arbitrarily assigned by Jung to "masculinity" and therefore a quality that women were assumed to "lack."[125] On Freud's side, a woman's destiny was determined "through beauty, charm, and sweetness."[126] Also, as illuminated by Jo Collins and John Jervis in *Uncanny Modernity*, to Freud: "Women . . . represent the vanishing point of logic, sense, and meaning, they are symbolised by the genitals which encapsulate their ascribed 'lack.' "[127] At least psychologically, women were then defined by their "lack" of so-called masculinity.

Spielrein did not wholeheartedly agree with such a characterization, and on June 13, 1909, she wrote to Freud: "I spoke [to Jung] of equality concerning the independence of women, to which he claimed I was an exception, while his wife on the other hand is an ordinary woman and, accordingly, is interested only in what interests her husband."[128] Simultaneously, she promotes the intellectual independence of women while alluding to the gender inequity of the time, being considered herself an "exception" to a rule of general female vacuity. Once expressed by Jung: "In women . . . Eros is an expression of their true nature, while their Logos is often only a regrettable accident."[129]

In order to gain insight into just what the "feminine" meant, at least psychoanalytically during Spielrein's early career, Jung elaborates in *Aspects of the Feminine*,[130] wherein a range of publications and public presentations on the topic of "anima" from circa 1912–1927 are included. He begins by stating that modern male individualism began with "worship of the woman, which strengthened the man's soul very considerably as a psychological factor, since the worship of woman meant worship of the soul," which he then conceptually equates with "anima" as envisaged by man.[131] However, the "erotic impression" of anima is then made synonymous with "mother and woman as desirable maid."[132]

Sexually, women are viewed here as either mothers or tempting maids, which produces "[the] psychological need which drives a man to prostitutes and to the mere business they make or are forced to make of love."[133] Stereotypes of womanhood are further conflated with living women: "As a rule when a girl marries she wants a child. . . . A marriage without children has no special attraction for a woman."[134] Also, a woman's logic, considered a garbled attempt at masculinity, is summarized by Jung: "The astonishing assumptions and fantasies that women make about men come from the activity of the animus, who produces an inexhaustible supply of illogical arguments and false explanations."[135] One can see clearly why Spielrein earlier muses on being labeled "somebody who thinks."

Speaking to the era's "Woman Problem," or the taking of social and political positions by women in post–World War I culture, he states:

> Unless she is prepared to sacrifice her whole erotic life, she again stands in some essential relationship to man. In numerous ways woman is indissolubly bound up with man's world. . . . Neither politically, nor economically, nor spiritually is she a factor of visible importance. If she were, she would loom more largely in man's field of vision and would have to be considered a rival. Sometimes she is seen in this role, but only as a man so to speak, who is accidentally a woman.[136]

To be clear, a woman who acts "as a man" must sacrifice her sexual life as well as her associations with womanhood to become a visible figure in society, albeit then only as a "rival." Cowan provides insight into the perpetuation of Jung's sentiment: "Some masculine qualities are desirable (such as rationality, objectivity, self-discipline), but others are not because they make woman appear less sexually attractive, or as what men perceive as 'competitive' (which is the derogatory for 'equal') . . . 'unfeminine.' "[137] Arguing against epithets often applied to the *anima,* Cowan proceeds to question whether "masculine" and "feminine" have ever been conceptually equal.

As if prescriptive, Jung urges: "Woman is . . . passivity . . . it fits in with her nature to keep her ego and her will in the background, so as not to hinder the man in any way, and to invite him to realize his intentions with regard to her person. This is a sexual pattern."[138] Here the equation of the feminine in principle and the female gender is made clear. He admits that by being in "masculine professions," such as politics, women concede to a "masculine psychology:" "No one can get around the fact that by taking up a masculine profession, studying and working like a man, woman is doing something not wholly in accord with, if not injurious to, her feminine nature."[139] Thus, masculine traits are defined by omission as everything oppositional to a passive feminine nature. Nevertheless, at the time of these remarks, Spielrein continued "studying and working like a man" as she pursued both motherhood as well as a career in academia.

However, in his article "Memories, Dreams, Omissions," Jungian scholar and translator Sonu Shamdasani debates over whether or not Spielrein should even qualify as "Jung's anima," rather than as someone wholly unimportant to the history of psychoanalysis, upset it seems over the fact that Spielrein has been "hyped" up and integrated into a "bearer of . . . personal myth . . . [that] has had disturbing implications for the understanding of Jung."[140] Because her relevance does not depend on being or not being Jung's anima, as she has her own personal myth, it may still be argued that rather than erasing her from history in order to avoid a "disturbing" reading of Jung, she may instead be remembered as an autonomous presence in (and out of) Jung's early career as an analyst.

Spielrein has been further abstracted into a seemingly random image of femininity in recent scholarship; for example, Gottfried Heuer, in his response to the film *A Dangerous Method* (2011), states that her enduring power hinges on the fact that she *ended* as an exemplary image of the feminine ideal in her capacity to "relate and love" and for her "empathy, [and] forgiveness."[141] In this way, Heuer transforms Spielrein's legacy into one of superimposed docility. Also, while he views her as having embodied love and forgiveness, given her diaries and letters it is in reality debatable how much of these qualities can be extracted from her writing.

Carotenuto invokes a similar image of Spielrein as he discusses her in her maternal role: "This unhappy woman, obsessed by disgust and the notion of the feces that everywhere surrounded her, became a graceful feminine image."[142] His degrading misrepresentation of her early institutionalization aside, the notion of a "graceful feminine image" is one constructed out of his own ideal as he proceeds to define her as a "typical" image of the anima archetype. Both Heuer and Carotenuto define Spielrein's life achievement as fulfilling an anima image, which subtly implies that a woman may be considered crazy or irrelevant until she fulfills a predetermined role of feminine "grace." Ironically, the "feminine" image that she did fulfill, aside from motherhood, was that of practicing analyst amid Communist oppression and threats of Nazi invasion.

Apparently, Spielrein was aware of the psychological projections of the "feminine" placed upon her by Jung at the time, and wrote to him in an undated fragment: "It is striking that with the analytical qualities that you possess you were not aware of the pathological constructions you assigned to me."[143] Indeed, from the beginning of their relationship Jung attempted to construct Spielrein into his own ideal: "Ugly clothes give me pain. You have given that up now, thank God. Don't be angry with me for writing to you about such things again. I want you to be beautiful both inwardly and outwardly for such a thing alone is natural."[144] Such sentiments undoubtedly affected the remaining years of their correspondence during which Spielrein repeatedly attempted to approach Jung as a scholar rather than as a former patient or as an idealized image of feminine "beauty."

In *The Woman in the Mirror: Analytical Psychology and the Feminine,* Claire Douglas compares a scene from the film *The Unbearable Lightness of Being* to the experience of Jung's female contemporaries:

> The actual mirror that holds and frames a supposed anima-woman, Sabina [character], is now beneath her on the floor. She centers herself on the mirror on her hands and knees and slowly serves her own body. . . . Sabina seems to be drawing libido . . . out of herself and up from its mirroring. . . . She is weighed down by his ignorance of her and by these attempts to interpret her from his perspective. She serves her own sense of being so truly that, finally, she escapes the man's patriarchal limitations of her and his denial and repression of her power . . . [and] leaves.[145]

The coincidence of the name "Sabina" aside, Douglas perfectly outlines the trajectory of Spielrein's autonomous unfolding, both personally and professionally. Bluntly, she untangled herself from a mere abstraction and began a life and career in her own right. Douglas encourages, following feminist theorists Ann Belford Ulanov and Irene Claremont de Castillejo, a reaffirmation of the qualities deemed unfeminine, rather than a complete abandoning of the jargon altogether, and reorganizes the term *anima* in accordance with social equity revolving around "reclamation and reinterpretation."[146]

Likewise, Estella Lauter and Carol Schreier Rupprecht in *Feminist Archetypal Theory: Interdisciplinary Re-Visions of Jungian Thought* urge a "re-visioning" tactic to "elucidate [female] counterstructures" regarding terms applied to gender.[147] They continue: "Revision . . . is especially important when a theory does not fit the facts of experience it was constructed to explain."[148] Similarly, if the narrative that has been constructed around Spielrein is revisioned, she may be spared from further confinement according to Collins and Jervis in *Uncanny Modernity*, to her "shadowy and disavowed role" in the history of the field.[149]

We all end up telling our own stories.

—Sabina Spielrein, undated

Rather than examine Spielrein's letters as evidence of hysteria, this chapter sought to explore the autobiographical qualities of her personal writing in light of the changing social dynamics of the time, as a testament to her own capabilities as a woman and as a scholar. Her letters were also interpreted through her perspective as a teacher, mother, musician, and intellect, rather than as simply Jung's "student," as she is positioned in John Kerr's *A Most Dangerous Method*.[150] In addition, Siegfried was analyzed not as a mere "love child" but as a spiritual heroic and malleable emblem for Spielrein's personal life.[151]

According to Karen Pechilis in "Devotional Subjectivity and the Fiction of Femaleness: Feminist Hermeneutics and the Articulation of Difference," reclaiming female narratives is accomplished by "de-centering" patriarchal assumptions within "[a] hermeneutics of recovering."[152] Therefore, aspects of Spielrein's narrative are recovered by de-centering stereotypes about the "feminine" in relation to her representation in scholarship. The next and final chapter examines Spielrein's contribution to female sexuality, her important article on child psychology, and her role in Russian intellectualism during revolution, war, Stalinism, mounting women's liberation, and Nazism.

7

Sabina Spielrein

Coming into Being

> The Jewish women in Freud's psychoanalytic circle belonged to a generation which grew up surrounded by anti-Semitism and limitations due to gender, and found in psychoanalysis a refuge. . . . Among the women in Freud's circle, Jewish women such as Sabina Spielrein, Helene Deutsch, [and] Anna Freud became central contributors.
>
> —Alison Rose, *Jewish Women in Fin de Siècle Vienna*

Introduction

Spielrein began teaching in Geneva, Switzerland, after a tour of Berlin in the 1910s and returned to Russia in 1923 to teach, lecture, raise her daughter, and co-direct the Moscow (State) Psychoanalytic Institute. According to Alexander Etkind in *Eros of the Impossible*, while she was based in Switzerland

> [s]tudents at the Rousseau Institute in Geneva were asked to think of the three most important questions they could ask God, fate, or some other higher power. A week later the experiment was repeated, this time the students sat with their eyes closed for two minutes before beginning . . . In 1931, Spielrein used a different experimental procedure in Rostov-on-don to pursue the same key issue of the relationship between conscious, social, adaptive thought and unconscious . . . thought.[1]

During this period, she began to focus primarily on child psychology, and her articles "Contributions to the Knowledge of a Child's Soul" (1912) and "The Origin of the Child's Words 'Papa' and 'Mama'" (1922) are explored in closer detail in here.

In *Uncanny Modernity: Cultural Theories, Modern Anxieties*, Jo Collins and John Jervis label Spielrein the "New Woman" of psychology: "She also signals the subversive potential of a particular kind of femininity: the educated and assertive 'New Woman.' This kind of woman was increasingly more visible in journals, newspapers, and visual representations, and a few (such as Spielrein) found their way into psychoanalysis."[2] The "New Woman," specifically in Russia, emerged during a time of societal unrest, challenging preconceived notions of "femininity" as a whole: what it meant, how to define it, and who could embody it. This chapter explores Spielrein as a "New Woman" figure, one that presented to the Vienna Psychoanalytic Society (VPS) on female sexuality, contributed to the field of child psychology, and emerged as a fearsome scholar of the Russian intelligentsia before her death in 1942 during World War II. Additionally, I look at the political climate in Russia, initially discussed in chapter 1, in order to contextualize Spielrein's return to Rostov.

Confronting "Female" Sexuality

> How daring a feat, how great a transgression it is for a woman to speak—even just open her mouth—in public.
>
> —Hélène Cixous, "The Laugh of the Medusa"

Referring to the historical positioning of the woman in the "negative," Jessica Benjamin elaborates in *The Bonds of Love: Psychoanalysis, Feminism, and the Problem of Domination*:

> Woman's renunciation of sexual agency [penis-envy] and her acceptance of object status are the very hallmark of the feminine. And though we may refuse this definition, we are nevertheless obliged to confront the painful fact that even today, femininity continues to be identified with passivity, with being the object of someone else's desire, with having no active desire of one's own.[3]

Even so, during a meeting of the VPS on January 24, 1912, Spielrein spoke directly on the topic of sexuality and eroticism in the society's Fourth Discussion on Masturbation: "Spielrein, referring to the question of psychic masturbation, remarks that a woman in love imagines herself in her lover's place, and thereby becomes excited; the transition from this psychic masturbation to physical masturbation takes place as the result of the fact that the woman imitates this . . . a special form of female masturbation."[4] In February, it is also noted that she interjects her opinion when the meeting turns to images of the Madonna and a woman's "narcissistic" capacity to love: "Spielrein maintains that man, too, loves at first narcissistically."[5]

As the only woman in the room, Spielrein put forth images and ideas of an embodied eroticism at a time when women's sexuality was labeled (by Freud) the "dark continent" of psychology, and female orgasms were categorized into two groups: clitoral, or "infantile," and vaginal, or "mature."[6] The clitoris itself was equated with an "amputated penis," its stimulation considered a form of penis-envy, and lest a woman achieve satisfaction through "penetration," she was often diagnosed with a case of frigidity or hysteria.[7] Contrarily, right or wrong, Spielrein here attempts to give voice to the "special" nature of women's arousal without degrading its manifestation or filtering it through a range of neuroses. She purports only a difference in its form, meaning that she believes female masturbation coincides with psychological stimuli and fantasy as well as in the act "imitating" and "imagining" the desired lover.

On March 20, 1912,[8] prompted by previous meetings, Spielrein gave her second presentation (the first being material from her "Destruction" article) to the VPS during the Eighth Discussion on Masturbation: "Spielrein is inclined to ascribe to all artistic activity the auto-erotic and heterosexual aspects mentioned before in relation to music. . . . The creative act can be reduced to a re-differentiation of all auto-erotic elements, which are then adapted to the external world."[9] While Spielrein tried to open the erotic principle up to artistic endeavors by relating sexual pleasure to creativity, both Stekel and Tausk argued against "two kinds of music," or one that could be used to erotic ends, and she was discouraged from continuing her line of inquiry.[10] Not one to be deterred for long, when it was postulated that men react to masturbation with a sense of shame, she reminded the room, "The sense of guilt is regularly linked with religious ideas," here meaning dogmatism, and related it just as quickly to "female auto-eroticism."[11] Again, she fought to include women's experiences into the emerging psychological theories of sexuality.

Most strikingly, she discusses eroticism and Freud's castration theory, reflected in the meeting's minutes:

> [Spielrein] further mentions that genital masturbation changes to other forms (hand-rubbing; tearing one's hair, etc.), and that psychic masturbation (heroes of novels) plays an important role. . . . The fact that in the woman (who is generally more erotic), anything can serve as a means of stimulation . . . special attention is called to a form

> of masturbation that occurs while listening to music. . . . Spielrein considers woman's application of the castration fantasy to man as an analogy to man's castration fantasy. A woman patient suffered from a continuous fear that her hand would fall off; another patient had strangulation fantasies. Mention is made also of the superstition that "one's mind is being sewed up."[12]

Whether or not her ideas are conducive to modern gender theory, she asserted the belief, through clinical research with multiple female patients, that women were more erotically charged, that erogenous zones vary depending on psychological stimuli, and attempts to define a woman's "application" of the castration fantasy that does not revolve around male genitalia. Also, again evoking her previous comments, she connects physical arousal to experiences of music and literature. Paradoxically, she follows Freud in her methodology, since she also proceeds to link eroticism and breastfeeding, but transforms polymorphism—sexuality not centered solely on the genitals—from its so-called "infantile perversion" (Freud) into a more inclusive view of adult eroticism.[13] Historically speaking, this is one of the first instances of a woman publicly introducing theories on female sexuality to the VPS.

Although she reorganizes a woman's "castration fantasy" around biologically female body parts, it is further noted:

> Freud does not consider it useful to try in every way to find in the woman an analogue to the castration fantasy that has the same meaning for her as the castration fantasy has for the man. The woman has no need of this fantasy, since she has come into this world already castrated, as a woman. Later on, she may simply give her sanction to this fact by producing the fantasy that her penis has been cut off.[14]

While Spielrein attempted to interject, she was promptly dismissed.[15] Coincidentally, Susan Rowland's *Jung: A Feminist Revision*, illuminates Judith Butler's concept of body fluidity, wherein Butler "removes the . . . phallus from its binary opposition masculine/feminine by challenging the assignation of the male body's castration anxiety to the wholly discursive yet uniquely privileged phallus . . . [it] may be transferable to other, multiple body parts, since castration anxiety need not be limited [to the phallus]."[16] Spielrein then, anticipates this countertheory by almost a century when she reorganized castration around female strangulation and a woman's fear of the loss of her hands, respectively. Moreover, according to Rosemary Balsam in her article "Women of the Wednesday Society [meaning the VPS]," Spielrein observed that female fear included losing the ability to be "genitally open" as presiding over an obsession with the "lack of penis she never had."[17] Though speaking here through biological absolutes—as were they all, Spielrein was painfully ahead of her time.

On March 27, 1912 when other members began to discuss the "death instinct," Spielrein reminded them that this was an idea of hers "now in print," asserting intellectual ownership of the concept that she previously brought to the VPS in 1911.[18] On the subject, she affirms:

> The problem of why the individual defends himself against sexuality can be approached on the basis of the fact that the sexual instinct is bipolar: it contains one component that calls for the dissolution of the ego. . . . Every psychic reaction has a tendency toward dissolution of the ego into its phylogenetic past; the second factor is that of projection and adaptation to the present.[19]

Although the entirety of the notes cannot be reproduced, she maintains her position on the "death instinct" and continues to discuss what she understands as the problem of sexuality in relation to both male and female masturbation and to his or her desire to dissolve into a beloved.[20] In these few months, she introduces the notion of female psychology as existing outside of and unrelated to penis envy. On the contrary, her second presentation is significantly loaded with images of female sexual fear and arousal.

For example, Spielrein also equated the dream symbol of a snake with female sexuality, but was "corrected" by Freud: "[He] corrected her view of symbols, specifying the difference between the sexual and the genital."[21] Freud believed that Spielrein was misguided because, as a genital symbol, the snake *appears* masculine, and in equating it with female-ness, she challenged the social phallocentricity of the symbol at the time. Still, his devaluation of her work is a testament to the discrimination faced by Spielrein as a woman in the early years of her career. Contrary to Freud, and according to Jean Chevalier and Alain Gheerbrant in *The Dictionary of Symbols*, a snake retains multiple interpretations throughout various cultures: "The serpent [may] discard its male appearance to become female, coiling up, entwining around, squeezing, throttling, swallowing. . . . Ever ambivalent, it toys with its own sexuality; it is both male and female."[22] Since the snake has been an important mythic symbol for millennia, representing everything from a "womb" to a cosmic ouroboros, it is perhaps this latter interpretation that Spielrein meant to evoke at the meeting.[23]

In her automythological "Uses of the Erotic: The Erotic as Power" from *Sister Outsider*, Audre Lorde lends insight into female eroticism's struggle for recognition:

> In order to perpetuate itself, every oppression must corrupt or distort those various sources of power within the culture of the oppressed that can provide energy for change. For women, this has meant a suppression of the erotic as a considered source of power and information within our lives. We have been taught to suspect this resource, vilified, abused, and devalued within western society. On the one hand, the superficially erotic has been encouraged as a sign of female inferiority; on the other hand, women have been made to suffer and to feel both contemptible and suspect by virtue of its existence. It is a short step from there to the false belief that only by the suppression of the erotic within our lives and consciousness can women be truly strong.[24]

In her presentation, Spielrein speaks of such an "energy," specifically in the lives of women, and attempts to free female eroticism from its vilified suppression, though Freud would go on to confine Eros to an exclusively male "life force" and define the realm of femininity as passive "death."[25] Lorde's equation of strength and suppression is reminiscent of the *anima* figure that, according to Jung, must sacrifice her erotic life in order to be seen as a true "rival," or equal, in society, as discussed in the last chapter. Aside from Spielrein's theories, her own eroticism has also been used against her in scholarship as an attempt to turn her into a seductive hysteric and tempting Jewess.

Emerging Child Psychologist

On December 20, 1911, Spielrein presented to the VPS on the topic of child psychology:

> Spielrein finds . . . the child is incapable of being aggressive and may perhaps for this reason identify himself with his powerful parents in order to gratify himself by way of the parental role he has assumed. . . . Lying, for instance, as well as the urge for truth, may often be brought on by the fact that the parents have concealed the sexual questions from the child; the thirst for the truth, for the why and wherefore of all things, may develop out of this, just as, on the other hand, it may also provide the child with an occasion for lying and spinning fairy tales. This compulsion of the child to ask questions appears later as a fear of asking questions . . . [and] the desire to ask about something forbidden.[26]

Spielrein offers her contribution to this discussion a few years before the birth of her first child, though her early interest in child psychology is evident. Probably pulling from her own experience, she questions how a child comes to consciousness through his or her "urge for truth," in a growing interest in sexuality and identification with or fear of his or her parents. In later articles she often references her own past to support her evolving research on child psychology and its connection to sexual embodiment.

On February 7, 1912, she contributed the following:

> Spielrein believes that all children go through a period of neurosis. In some cases the neurosis remains latent in its course; in others it breaks through. Almost all children have anxieties. Besides, there is a period when the child is at an in-between age that usually coincides with that of religiosity. If it is generally believed that masturbation, if harmful, one may expect there to be some reason for this belief [religiosity]. Some patients show a clear need for guilt and expiation—a trait connected with the destructive component.[27]

Here, evoking the work in her "Destruction" paper, she begins with childhood anxieties and quickly expands to a discussion of shame, religion, masturbation, and adolescence. While sexual curiosity is related to "guilt," to which she attributes religion as a possible underlying cause of the emotion, she also notes one's psychic desire for "expiation"—atonement. This desire results from her conception of a "death/destructive instinct" that harbors not only the desire to dissolve into and transform through a beloved, but also the violent potential for emotional and physical sadomasochism, especially when seeking forgiveness from whatever is considered wrongdoing. These aforementioned comments from 1911 and 1912 are some of the first contributions to the VPS on the topic of child psychology introduced by a female scholar.

In stark contrast, in *A Secret Symmetry*, Carotenuto undermines Spielrein's contributions to the society and argues that, during this time, "It is hard to judge Spielrein's mental state."[28] Carotenuto also turns her first article on child psychology into an admission of guilt: "From early childhood . . . she thought of herself as a goddess, sovereign of a powerful realm, and felt herself in possession of a great strength," which he relates—egregiously—to early onset mental illness.[29] Yet in the article, "Contributions to the Knowledge of a Child's Soul" (1912), wherein she examines the dreams of her young patients, Spielrein states in no uncertain terms regarding her childhood play:

> I had a great imagination. I was a goddess and reigned over a mighty kingdom. . . . I was able to reach every goal and know everything.

> Although I did not directly believe in the reality of my imagination, it was too beautiful to not believe. . . . At that time, I was not interested in listening to fairytale stories. I was fully capable of producing my own fairytales. I have always been a critic who knew the difference between reality and imagination.[30]

Carotenuto's dismissal of Spielrein's identification of the goddess also seems to undermine the twentieth-century feminist reclamation movement of Goddess religion[31] outlined by Christine Downing in *The Goddess*, wherein she identifies with and has deeply spiritual experiences with archetypal Greek goddesses during different periods in her life: "We need images and myths through which we can see why we are and what we might become. . . . My search for Her led me to the goddesses of ancient Greece, but the original *She* is the one we discover by returning to more archaic mother-goddess traditions."[32] Downing relates her own imaginal relationship to the "Goddess" in way that lends insight into what Spielrein, in her youth, may have been experiencing, since she admitted in her diary that she ceased believing in one monotheistic God-image during adolescence, as we have already seen. If nothing else, she was simply a child with an active imagination who very clearly understood the line between "reality and imagination."

She then recounts her own childhood memories of an existential nature:

> Who made God? I was told that God has always existed. I also knew that man was created from earth and God gave breath to man. My mother had proven this to me by rubbing her hands together and creating soil. I wonder how I combined the birth and the earth theories? Was it perhaps that only the first human was made from earth? Otherwise, as far as I can remember, I believed that God created a baby in a mother's body without any human action, merely by wishing for a child. It was my ardent desire to create a living human being, just like God did. That is why I was the omniscient goddess in my fantasies, capable of everything. I tried to create humans from earth, clay, and all other available materials; however, I was unable to make them come alive. . . . One time, an uncle who was a chemist showed us an experiment that delighted me. He dipped a small, cut zinc rod into a lead-salt solution and created a complex formation of branches just like a real tree. It dawned on me that chemistry is the force that creates miracles! I became an alchemist. . . . I cannot forget the mixed feelings of delight and fear I felt. . . . I kept my "secret" liquids in bottles

> and "wonder stones" and other things of which I expected the great "creation."[33]

In his assessment of the above, Carotenuto argues that Spielrein was merely "pretending to be an alchemist."[34] On the other hand, her identification with alchemy may be understood to infringe upon a male role, as Jung states in *Mysterium Coniunctionis*: "I am speaking here of masculine psychology, which alone can be compared with that of alchemists," while the woman is associated only with an image of the male mind.[35] Claire Douglas iterates in *The Woman in the Mirror*: "Jung's blindness to women alchemical writers, women alchemists, and the whole feminine half of the alchemical opus—except as it pertains to men's psychological development—closes Jung from an entire area of women's experience."[36] Spielrein, speaking here with vivacious pathos, imagination, and passionate curiosity may be included among such alchemical writers transfixed from an early age by life, death, and (re)creation.

In this same article she offers an interpretation for her child patients' dreams and relates their dream images to an emerging fear of death. First, she reveals her own childhood fear of being abducted by the *Erlking*, an elf-king in Scandinavian and Germanic folklore who preys on small children: "My Erlkönig was God."[37] She then recites lines from Goethe's poem "Der Erlkönig" and interprets the Erlking as a representation for death consciousness in childhood:

> "My father, my father, and do you not hear
> What the Erlking promises me so softly?"
>
> . . . .
>
> "I love you; I'm charmed by your beautiful form;
> And if you're not willing, then I'll use force."
>
> . . . .
>
> The father shudders, he rides swiftly,
> He holds in (his) arms the moaning child.
> He reaches the farmhouse with effort and
> Urgency.
> In his arms the child was dead.[38]

She proceeds to relate the images evoked in the poem to the dreams of a child patient who has admitted to being "constantly worried about being attacked."[39] She also asserts that children may be able to confront and interpret images of death when also "applying a birth fantasy," since to her, as we know, death signals the creation of something new.[40] While the rich mythical allusion and dream interpretation in her article cannot be reproduced further here (see Appendix

B), she invokes *The Magic Flute*, the Egyptian myth of Isis and Osiris, fairy tales, sexuality in mythology, destruction as preceding creation, and an image of a melting clock in analyses of her child patients' dreams, giving utmost validation to the material of their imaginations. While her article adheres to the Freudian associative method, she never strays far from mythic amplification.

She muses further on a child's desire to separate from his or her parents before concluding: "Real objects can be replaced with imaginary objects. One wants to leave the parents' home to become a god, a king or a queen. One is fascinated by religion (in fact, God and angels), the fairytale world in which heroes travel to faraway places, followed by a passion for travel adventures."[41] Strangely, Carotenuto wonders why, in this academic paper published in the *Jahrbuch*, Spielrein omits reference to her institutionalized "analeroticism," as if that would have been at all appropriate.[42] Though Carotenuto attempts to peg her as *The Ever-Patient* rather than a serious scholar, Spielrein provides only salient and on-topic reflections in her article.

Sins of the Mother

In one of Spielrein's early papers on Russian folk and fairytales entitled "Mother-in-Law" (1913),[43] she explores the relationship between daughters and "negative" mothers, often represented in narrative by a mother-in-law or stepmother figure. Struggling with gender constrictions of the time, Spielrein first states that while the "biological" role of the woman often leads to motherhood, "Women [are] by no means less intelligent or creative than men," but have "failed" to appear as a dominant force in the arts because of such ties to maternal responsibilities.[44] She writes that even under the assumption that women are predominantly "empathetic," as opposed to the assumed logos-centered man, "I do not know how valuable it would be to make women believe that a man's way of feeling is 'superior.'"[45] She continues to analyze the notion of a self versus a self-in-relationship, specifically tied to the "mother-daughter relationship:" "The modern world almost exclusively talks about the mothers-in-law of men," but reminds us that "young women also" have a psychological impression of this image.[46] She then explicitly refers to this relationship in terms of "object-relations"—again, one of the first to do so—and compares the love of a parent to the love from a beloved.[47]

While this short article remains rife with contradictions, it is among the first forays into child consciousness in the field as she ponders the positive and potentially negative psychological effects on girls by women in the role of Mother. She also attempts to examine "little children" and their relationships with mothers who are seen as "god-like" authorities: "In the depths of the soul, one always sees his or her own mother as young and beautiful."[48] In doing so, she foreshadows by almost seventy years the theories of Nancy Chodorow in *Feminism and Psychoanalytic Theory*: "It is not because she knows she is a female that a girl or woman experiences her self in relationship . . . her self in relation is a developmental product, tied to her mother's sense of self, [and] not only to gender identity or gender-role learning."[49] Chodorow further argues that such a "re-centering of the self" through the mother challenges classical psychoanalytic theory, and Spielrein was doing exactly that in 1913.[50] Similarly, in her article "Contributions to the Knowledge of a Child's Soul" (1912) Spielrein acted inclusively when she stated: "Female lover and at the same time daughter, just like male lover and son: these connections are common in mythology as well as in a child's psyche. Eve was, after all, Adam's daughter and wife at the same time."[51]

On the Development of Speech

At the Psychoanalytic Congress of 1920 in The Hague of South Holland, Netherlands, Spielrein spoke on child psychology as well as on Russia's psychoanalytic movement, championing the inclusion of her native land to the International Society. Spielrein took the floor to demand that "summaries of Russian research be published in the journal. . . . Freud stood up, and recognizing the seriousness of the issue, promised to do something about it in the future."[52] Upon the Moscow Society's admittance, an amendment was supported to "unite local groups operating in member states."[53] At the time of her presentation, she was a member of three primary societies: Berlin, Moscow, and the International Psychoanalytic Association:

> Spielrein attended the International Psychoanalytic Congress at The Hague in September 1920, delivering a paper, "The Origin and Development of Spoken Speech," that revealed a new and seminal line of enquiry. Her interest in children had begun before the war, but now it took a novel form which linked analysis to the development of psychology and linguistics. Her overall framework, as ever dualistic, was the contrast between autistic and social languages (singing, poetry). Speech, she stated, was an intermediary zone between the pleasure and reality principles. She reviewed the theories of language acquisition and put forward her hypotheses about the origin of the words "mama" and "papa," examples of the process whereby first words arise out of the act of sucking, imbued with magical, wish fulfilling qualities.[54]

On the merits of her own research, she also discussed many of the aforementioned ideas with her then-patient Jean Piaget,[55] the famed child psychologist: "The patient [Piaget] questioned . . . and the therapist presented her counterarguments. The famous Swiss psychologist's work continues for many decades to be stimulated by an interest in the key issues set before him by Sabina Spielrein."[56] Interestingly, she declined the congress in 1911, which was at the time interpreted as academic self-destruction (by Jung), though her independent attendance a few years later with a seminal line of inquiry on child psychology would suggest the opposite. Actually, it can be inferred from her diary that she merely wanted to avoid being "one of the many," since Jung is remembered as bringing to the congress his "entourage of women" including Toni Wolff, Maria Moltzer, Beatrice Hinkle, and his wife, Emma.[57]

After her presentation, she developed her material into two published papers: "Analogies between Infantile, Aphasic, and Unconscious Thought" and "The Origin of the Child's Words 'Papa' and 'Mama.'" In "Transforming At-One-Ment: Spielrein, Jung, Bion," Janet Sayers reproduces Spielrein's research at the time:

> [A child's] state of mind or desire through differences is in the rhythm, pitch, intonation, intensity of his cry, in sum in a primitive melodic language. . . . Mothers intuit the little one's psyche, and furthermore find, in the depths of their own psyche, preformed in the preconscious stage of personal development, the material that makes them speak to the child from the drives of the unconscious.[58]

Importantly, Demaris Wehr attributes Chodorow with developing a "corrective" view to psychology's emphasis on the father in *Jung and Feminism: Liberating Archetypes*: "[Chodorow's] feminist studies of the effects of women's mothering . . . offers an indispensible corrective to Jung's view that each child projects onto the parent of another sex. . . . This gives the mother a certain primacy," both in psychological and sexual development for a child of any gender.[59] As underscored by Sayers, Spielrein's work, both in the 1920s as well as in her papers a decade earlier, may also be seen as giving primacy to the mother in a child's psyche.

In her translation of Spielrein's 1922 "The Origin of the Child's Words 'Papa' and 'Mama,'" Barbara Wharton underscores the fact that Spielrein anticipates other notable work in the field, such as Melanie Klein's "Weaning" paper of 1936 on "[the] importance of the infant's relationship to the breast."[60] Wharton points to Spielrein as originating two lines of inquiry: "Whether the child makes his language, or whether he simply inherits it" and "Self, individuality, separateness, and the function and meaning of loss" in a child's relationship to the mother.[61] In the article, Spielrein begins by paraphrasing lines from Moritz Lazarus to highlight a child's relationship to a parent and his or her eventual transformation into an individual: " 'Let us remember that language only exists in society, and therefore man only finds a Self and an I by simultaneously being near other selves and other I's.' "[62]

She then expands on the history of language:

> First of all, the language of melody, music, greatly precedes spoken language in its most primitive form of rhythmics and sound inclination: long before the first signs of spoken language appear, the wail is a proven means of communication between child and caretaker. Attentive mothers and caretakers know very well that their charge screams in very different and specific ways depending on whether he is wet, hungry, feeling pain, or simply desiring the closeness of the caretaker.[63]

She compares the language of music to a baby's developing sounds, relying on her own experience with her daughter, and goes on to assert that music's popularity can be understood once it is realized as an inherently "magical" language: "Even if it began as a means of self-enjoyment, it soon became a method of communication *par excellence*, a call for attention, a prayer, a complaint directed to God or to fellow human beings demanding their involvement."[64] She elevates a baby's developing preverbal sounds, musician that she is, to a divine form of communication that relates a child's desire to the caretaker. This analogy is used to tie a baby's sound to the "magical" appearance of Mother or Father.[65]

Following Freud, she believes that all thought processes lead one back to childhood, though to be more "appropriate," she speaks in terms of the "subconscious" and asks: "Who invented verbal language? Was it the adult or the child?" then answers: "The ancestor sleeps within the child," and vice versa.[66] She believed, rather Platonically, that one can never know if language arises from an adult in a childlike state or within a child accessing ancestral wisdom. She then emphasizes mimicry and ponders the similarity of the words "Papa" and "Mama" across languages and cultures, questioning their association with the meaning of a caretaker.[67]

She reports on the beauty of observing a child creating language to the sound of water, mimicking "Lululu" to a running stream, and demands that more research be undertaken, recognizing an extreme lack of information in child development at the time.[68] Still, she names a few key players in the field, but notes objections to and differences from existing theories.[69] She proceeds to wonder about children "of all races" and their relationship to the words *Papa* and *Mama,* and muses on the possibility that these are not literally the first words spoken by children, but only "generally assumed" to be the first words conceived based on a child's first natural sounds.[70] If so, she believes this to be tied to the societal importance placed upon the relationship between child and parent.

Returning to the topic of existing theories on child development, she characteristically claims intellectual autonomy:

> Now I would like to add my view on psychological preference to these [aforementioned] theories. I want to anticipate here that I would like to differentiate three stages of language development: first, the autistic stage, where language is intended for itself; second, the magical stage, where a word takes on the meaning which evokes its reality [as in "Papa" or "Mama"]; third, the present stage of social language meant for human beings.[71]

She invokes Freud's *Totem and Taboo* for theoretical support and then lingers on the condition of schizophrenia, which she now—and markedly—terms "so-called 'schizophrenia,' " which is characterized by fantasy overwhelm and thus related to early psychological development: "It is enough to think something for it to happen; this thought, however, is always an expression of a wish or a fear. . . . It must be the case that at the earliest age the connection between certain movements and the sensations accompanying them is already laid down."[72] She then illustrates such a bond between desire, movement, and sensation when she connects the sound of "Mama" and its corresponding mouth shape of an "O" to the physical action of suckling and pleasure.[73] She does not claim that a baby retains the information of "Mother," but associates the feelings of "warmth, of softness . . . liquid, of fullness" with "magic" in the mind of an infant.[74]

Spielrein posits that the words *Papa* and *Mama* become differentiated from sensations through time and, speaking directly to early trauma, "If this name [Papa, Mama] is altered or damaged in any way, the psychic content connected with it . . . is also damaged."[75] Though she does not expand on her statement, she clearly anticipates research on verbal-emotional triggers and their corresponding associations with childhood. She then recounts a memory of her daughter experiencing the world differently with her eyes open than with her eyes closed and states that a child exists solely for self-interested pleasure before realizing the world exists even when he or she is not witness to it.[76]

For instance, she outlines a child's relationship to other human beings, where one becomes aware of fantasy and reality and of things existing *alongside* oneself rather than as oneself. In addition, she reflects on a diary entry written years prior that she utilizes for her research:

> "Tomorrow little Renata will be ten months old," it says in my diary. . . ." She is still a little dummy, has no teeth, does not sit up on her own, does not understand what Papa and Mama mean (and these are words that she often babbles in the daytime). I do not know if I have noted it yet, but when little Renata is satisfied, she says 'Papa,' but when is unsatisfied or wants something, she says 'Mama."' Stern also reports of his little daughter that Papa is a symbol of satisfaction and Mama is a symbol of sadness, and I believe this as well.[77]

She also asserts, perhaps in an attempt to maintain originality: "Dr. Hug-Hellmuth,[78] who heard my congress statement, thought that I snatched the words out of her mouth. . . . How could this strange phenomenon be explained?"[79] She admits that she did not know these ideas were so widespread at the advent of her clinical analyses.

She concludes that she is not clear on the "decisive" formulation of sounds, but that the words *Papa* and *Mama,* as well as their physical formations, "suggest a close connection to suckling."[80] However, she cautions: "I am not claiming that it is suckling alone which gives rise to children's speech," and quickly remarks on a child's dependence on a caretaker.[81] Referring to her personal experience as a mother, she offers:

> The small being learns that there is a sanctuary in this outside world that is desirable for him not only because hunger is quenched here, but because it is warm and soft and protected from all danger. If one has ever in felt in life, "Linger, moment, for you are so beautiful," then it was certainly at this time. Here the child learns for the first time in the broadest sense of the word to love, i.e. to feel contact with another being as the highest bliss, even when independent of nourishment.[82]

Rather than suckling and speech, it is relationship, rooted in love and contact with an other, that Spielrein ultimately emphasizes in connection to her child. Yet never completely severed from Thanatos, she has already relayed, somewhat sadly, "This bliss has an end," and in this end, a child also learns of loss.[83]

Spielrein's evolving psychoanalytic work on the image and experience of the Mother is clearly evidenced from the beginning of her academic career. For example, in one of her first presentations to the VPS in 1911, Spielrein commented:

> The unconscious takes away from an event the character of being in the present and transforms it into one that is not tied to any particular time (cf. the Mothers [Faust], for whom all boundaries and times melt into one another). What the unconscious does with time it also does with place and with contrasts. . . . At the deepest level of the unconscious, however, we do not know how to measure time.[84]

In this quote she anticipates the work of feminist philosopher Julia Kristeva, summarized by Susan Rowland in *Jung: A Feminist Revision*: "Against linear time, [Kristeva] sets 'women's time' as cyclical and monumental . . . the time of the maternal semiotic."[85] Kristeva further argues that the "conception of time as linear" begs a feminist re-visioning that de-locates time and space from a so-called patriarchal understanding, wherein the "maternal" principle is given freedom to emerge.[86] "Maternal" is not defined as biologically predetermined, but instead as a state of consciousness, which evokes Spielrein's conception of a timeless "deepest level" tied specifically to images of Mother.

Return to the USSR: The "New Woman" and War

> But not for anything would we exchange
> this splendid
> Granite city of fame and calamity,
> The wide rivers of glistening ice,
> The sunless, gloomy gardens,
> And, barely audible, the Muse's voice.
>
> —Anna Akhmatova

Growing proletariat unrest and protest ushered in a time of great reform in the early 1900s, causing two revolutions in Russia in 1905 and 1917, the latter of which led to subsequent communist rule. According to historian Barbara Engel in *Women in Russia 1700–2000*:

> Long-suppressed discontents finally exploded. Industrial workers, students, professionals, even nobles . . . became caught up in the

> wave of resistance that swept Russia in the wake of Bloody Sunday (January 9, 1905), when tsarist troops fired upon a peaceful demonstration of working-class women and men.[87]

Further, under Russian Tsar Nicholas II (1894–1917), restraining women in traditional roles became almost impossible during rapid industrialization, even though restrictions on women's access to education aimed to subvert radical feminism. However, women's demand for education increased, and with that the desire to earn an independent income as a working professional.

Spielrein's career was always intertwined in Russian politics. For example, according to Martin Miller in *Freud and the Bolsheviks: Psychoanalysis in Imperial Russia and the Soviet Union*, her ties to Russian political figures even penetrated the VPS:

> Tatiana Rosenthal . . . a Russian psychiatrist who had recently become a member of the new psychoanalytic community . . . had joined the illegal Marxist Social Democratic Party in her native St. Petersburg during the revolution. . . . She was accepted into the Vienna Psychoanalytic Society. In January and February 1912, she was accompanied by her colleague Sabina Spielrein at three of these meetings, making these dates one of the few occasions when Russian was spoken in Freud's chambers.[88]

During the revolution, "Women's liberation was inseparable from the liberation of society as a whole," and women's suffrage led to the first political women's meeting in Russia by the All-Russian Union for Women's Equality.[89] Among other gains of the era, the right to vote was granted to women in 1917, while many requested the right to separate from their husbands despite laws that forbade separation."[90] We might remember that in 1915, Spielrein chose to remain separated from her husband in order to pursue her career.

In 1918, Marxist and feminist Alexandra Kollontai wrote and distributed pamphlets on "The New Woman" calling for social equality by questioning the secondary status of women in Russia:

> Who, then, are these new women? They are not the pure, "nice" girls whose romance culminates in a highly successful marriage. . . . Nor are they old maids who bemoan the unhappy love of their youth, just as little as they are "priestesses of love," the victims of wretched living conditions or of their own depraved natures. No, it is a wholly new "fifth" type of heroine, hitherto unknown . . . heroines who assert their personality, heroines who protest against the universal

> servitude of woman. . . . If women emerged in history with features that recalled contemporary heroines, they were viewed as random deviations from the norm, as psychological phenomena.[91]

Kollontai evokes Jung's earlier statement that Spielrein was an "exception" to the rule of women's limited intelligence. Instead, Kollontai outlines an assertive personality wholly outside of the psychological construction of docile femininity. Even popular Russian women's magazines at the time with more than one hundred thousand issues in circulation, such as *Niva* and *Messenger of Fashion*, confronted the Woman Question by championing women's achievements in the field of medicine.[92] Spielrein, beginning her career at a time of such societal reorganization, embodies the tension between a patriarchal culture and a burgeoning feminist reaction to limiting gender roles. Also, though she was sent abroad for her education, her return to Russia as co-director of the Moscow (State) Psychoanalytic Institute clearly benefited from the changes claimed in her absence.

Also affecting Spielrein's return was a wave of anti-Semitism that spread throughout Russia and continued to grow to disastrous proportions in Germany and abroad. For this reason, along with an eruption of anti-Jewish violence, Engel notes that in order to build a sense of community during the years most affected by political and gender upheaval, "substantial numbers of Jewish women participated in intellectual and social movements," many of them pursuing the field of psychology.[93] Alison Rose elaborates in *Jewish Women in Fin de Siècle Vienna*: "Alongside the need to find a way to reconcile bourgeois views of femininity with their . . . desire to assert themselves, . . . Jewish women bec[a]me psychoanalysts . . . [which] provided a framework for negotiating female identity and confronting gender and racial stereotypes."[94]

At the same time, these years were filled with terror. For example, the Russian Empire lost more than three million citizens[95] in World War I, which directly contributed to the 1917 Revolution and the uprising of Lenin-led Bolshevism. In addition, according to Alexander Etkind in *Eros of the Impossible*: "Because of the war, the [Russian] journal Psychotherapy . . . ceased to exist. . . . Many doctors went to the front [and] patients could no longer pay for services rendered. The rapid growth of . . . anti-Semitic sentiment during the war also hindered the development of psychoanalysis."[96] During this second revolution, Spielrein's family lost its financial stability and her father's house was confiscated, which certainly contributed to her vacillation between remaining in Switzerland and returning to Russia.

A long and bloody civil war ensued between the Bolsheviks, or the "Majority," and the provisional government after the execution of Tsar Nicholas II; it ended with the creation of the USSR (Union of Soviet Socialist Republics) in 1922, with Stalin rising to complete power shortly thereafter.[97] In 1923,

Spielrein returned to Moscow to become, in her words, "a great [presence] in psychiatry."[98] Indeed, she worked in three different positions as "a researcher at the State Psychoanalytic Institute, as a doctor and pedologist in a village called Third International, and as a chair of the child psychology division at the First Moscow University."[99]

She also led conferences on child psychoanalysis for the Moscow Psychoanalytic Society and continued her work with child patients at the Children's House-Laboratory. However, rather than positioning her as an imposing intellect at this time, Etkind describes her as using her "feminine charms [to] overtake even the most powerful minds," thereby reducing her accomplishments to her sexuality rather than to her scholarship.[100] On the other hand, Jean Piaget, who left his own analysis with Spielrein due to a trigger of his own mother projection, remembers her as "[a] very intelligent person, full of original ideas."[101]

During this time, Spielrein remained active in child analysis and publishing, and contributed articles to the *International Journal of Psychoanalysis* on dream interpretation and symbology alongside prominent members such as Otto Rank, Hans Sachs, and Anna Freud.[102] At the peak of her career, all seemed aligned to carry her career forward:

> No government was ever responsible for supporting psychoanalysis to such an extent, before or after. . . . [Moscow had a] fully recognized training program . . . [and] an outpatient clinic was established together with the children's home, all functioning on psychoanalytic principles. The extensive publication of psychoanalytic books and articles was proceeding at a level that was difficult to imagine a few years before.[103]

Under Spielrein, the institute also emphasized a less Freudian-centric methodology and welcomed an interdisciplinary curriculum involving literature, science, and the arts. Sadly, under increasing political pressure, the Moscow Institute was closed in 1925, and the International Association had serious reservations and misgivings about their Russian members due to "much fear of the new Soviet state and its communist ideology."[104] In fact, prominent Marxist and Bolshevik leader Leon Trotsky "defended the world of Freud's Russian followers . . . [while] his association with them (however indirect it was in reality) soon became a fatal liability once Trotsky himself fell into political disfavor."[105]

Freud sums up succinctly the paradoxical nature of Marxism as realized in communist practice:

> Any critical examination of Marxist theory is forbidden, doubts of its corrections are punished in the same way as heresy was once punished by the Catholic Church. The writings of Marx have taken

> the place of the Bible and the Koran as a source of revelation, though they would seem to be no more free from contradiction and obscurities than those older sacred books.[106]

The threat to Spielrein's academic position at the institute was similarly regarded by the state as a matter of heresy. Furthermore, her attention to child psychology became forbidden and her decision to return to Rostov ultimately inevitable: "Not only were psychoanalysis and Freud being repressed, but crucial areas of research . . . were also abolished. . . . A ban was imposed on the study of the sexual development of children."[107] Soviet rule was distinctly threatened by Freudian psychoanalysis, ostensibly for its practice of questioning groupthink, and though Spielrein expressed her opinion on the matter in "The Problem of the Unconscious in Contemporary Psychology and Marxism," her article sits unpublished at the Alexander Luria estate.[108]

The following decades saw increased Soviet suppression and the mounting threat of World War II. Though Spielrein went into relative radio-silence, it is known that she reconciled with her husband and later gave birth to her second daughter in 1926. While evidence of her participation is sorely lacking, it is documented that she published until 1931, taught at the university until 1936, and was at least listed as a member of the Russian Psychoanalytic Society until it disbanded. However, the majority of activity had already ceased for all intents and purposes under the period of persecution during the years of Stalin's Great Terror.

As already referenced, in the 1920s and 1930s Spielrein suffered the loss of her three brothers who were intellectually persecuted and executed in the Gulag; she also lost her parents, Freud (d. 1939), and her husband. Even under these circumstances, she is still reported to have continued psychoanalytic practice in sparsely decorated and private blacked-out rooms.[109] When discussing her history and relationship to psychoanalysis, the above narrative is rarely included, because considered as subordinate to her sexual history with Jung.

> Oh, if I'm waking the dead,
> Forgive me, I can't do otherwise:
> I grieve for you as for my own,
> And I envy anyone who weeps,
> Who is able to weep in this terrible hour
> For the one who lies in the ravine's depth.
>
> —Anna Akhmatova

As Barbara Clements elucidates in *Bolshevik Women*, paradoxical and complicated as it was, "Nowhere else in the European world were there so many female lawyers, professors, scientists and artists, as well as judges and party secretaries, as there were in the Soviet Union by 1930."[110] Yet during World War II, stereotypical views of femininity resurfaced and women were, in allegiance with a widespread propaganda campaign of images of domesticity, encouraged to "replenish a society that had been decimated by war."[111] Similarly, out of the number of women who were at one time recruited by the Bolsheviks during the revolution, many were subsequently forced into exile.[112]

Concurrently, in 1941, the Germans seized Leningrad (present-day St. Petersburg),[113] which broke the countries' nonaggression pact and eventually resulted in Rostov's occupation in 1941 and '42. Taylor Allen summarizes the aspect of "racial cleansing" integral to the Holocaust as it related specifically to Russia:

> The war aims of the Nazis can be summed up in the phrase "race and space." . . . The transition from persecution to genocide occurred sometime during the summer of 1941, when Germany invaded the Soviet Union. Special police squads euphemistically called "Special Action Groups" (*Einsatzgruppen*) followed close behind the front. In an action that was officially defined as a police measure . . . these groups engaged in a series of mass outdoor shootings in which a total of about 2 million people—most of whom were Jewish civilians—were murdered. At first, these squads seemed unsure of their orders: some included women and children in their operations, and some did not. By the end of the summer, they regularly killed women and children along with the men.[114]

Actually, the second occupation of Spielrein's hometown on August 11, 1942, was in direct response to infamous SS leader Heinrich Himmler's vision of extermination during the Holocaust, as he recounts in a letter from July 1942: "I herewith order that the resettlement of the entire Jewish population of the General Government be carried out and completed by December 31 [1942] . . . a total cleansing is necessary."[115] As previously noted, 27,000 citizens, mostly Jewish, were murdered alongside Spielrein and her daughters in Rostov that August, their bodies covered in clay in the Snake Ravine.

In the words of Martin Gilbert in *The Holocaust: A History of the Jews of Europe during the Second World War*: "So little is known of the fate and reaction of individuals. Statistics can dull the mind, and examples numb it. Nevertheless, [one] must try, through the records and stories that have survived . . . [so] that the fate of individuals would not be forgotten."[116] These facts are recounted and added to the information in previous chapters to further contextualize her later life and scholarship, which have been greatly overlooked in favor of her participation in a "love cure" to the detriment of her academic reputation and contributions to the field.

Afterword

> Memory, once waked, will play the tyrant.
>
> —C. S. Lewis, *Till We Have Faces: A Myth Retold*

On October 18, 1911, Dr. Sabina Spielrein was the second woman inducted into the Vienna Psychoanalytic Society, because she was known to many of its members; the vote was unanimous.[1] She was the first woman to write a dissertation on the psychology (and mythology) of schizophrenia, under the advisement of Bleuler and Jung, and continued to publish and present on the topics of female sexuality, dreams, and child psychology in the decades following, the bulk of which remain untranslated. She taught and practiced as an analyst in Zurich, Geneva, and Moscow, unencumbered by cultural or linguistic barriers. She was also a mother of two who lived through the loss of her entire family of origin before being exposed to the horrors of anti-Semitism during World War II.

Even so, in *Feminism and its Discontents: A Century of Struggle with Psychoanalysis*, Mari Jo Buhle writes her out of the history of female Freudians, and instead names only Margarethe Hilferding, Karen Horney, Helene Deutsch, Hermine Hug-Hellmuth, and Lou Andreas-Salomé.[2] Quite glaringly, Spielrein is omitted from this list. In scholarship, she is consistently labeled a "hysteric" and ultimately condemned for her participation in a love cure, though the latter is rarely viewed from her perspective, or instead is seen as a breach of professional ethics. Her personal and professional writing has similarly been stigmatized and used as evidence of mental illness rather than explored for their mythopoetic or psychological insight.

In *How to Suppress Women's Writing*, Joanna Russ speaks to such suppression and details the techniques routinely used to diminish a woman's work as perpetuated by both male and female critics (brackets and italics are hers):

> Denial of Agency: *She didn't write it.*
>
> Pollution of Agency: *She shouldn't have written it.*
>
> Double Standard of Content: *Yes, but look what she wrote about.*
>
> False Categorizing: *She is not really she* [an artist] *and it is not really it* [serious, of the right genre, aesthetically sound, important, etc.] *so how could "she" have written 'it'*
>
> Or simply: Neither "she" nor "it" exists. (simple exclusion)
>
> But sometimes it is admitted: *She wrote it.* That is, some "wrong" authors do make it into the canon of the Great, the Permanent, or (at least) the Serious.[3]

Spielrein has been subjected to almost all of these recategorizations in order to devalue the content and primacy of her work: her origination and development of the "death instinct" has been challenged and degraded; her character has been polluted by epithets such as "seductress," "mistress," and "hysteric"; the subject matter of her personal writing has been retroactively mined for qualities of schizophrenia; her publications have been demeaned as derivative; and she has repeatedly been abstracted into an idealized image of femininity with minimal basis in her historical reality.

Jean Baker Miller illuminates the gender stereotypes enforced upon Spielrein in *Toward a New Psychology for Women*: "The present divisions and separations are, I believe, a product of culture as we have known it—that is, a culture based on a primary inequity."[4] For instance, in *A Most Dangerous Method*, when commenting on her death and the decline of psychoanalysis, John Kerr posits that Spielrein's entire life was ultimately tragedy and underscores her looks rather than her scholarship: "And so disappeared a world which had once sent forth an hysterical teenager who thought she was ugly and could not bear to be looked at."[5] Kerr diminishes Spielrein's adult life by defining it through teenage self-consciousness and childhood "hysteria" that was assuredly cured, if one subscribes to the notion that she was suffering from "hysteria" at all. Though her life was touched frequently by grief, it was also full of extraordinary accomplishments.

In fact, even when confronting thoughts of mortality and insecurity in her diary, she always rebounded: "But let this sad fantasizing go. A few years still belong to my life . . . do not despair, rather—'Courage!' "[6] She understood the depths of darkness, from her sister's death to her "affair" with Jung, and transformed her early experiences with Thanatos into a "death instinct" and an academic career as a child psychologist. Dr. Sabine Richebächer laments in "'In League with the Devil and Yet You Fear Fire?' Sabina Spielrein and C. G. Jung: A Suppressed Scandal from the Early Days of Psychoanalysis":

> Spielrein's pioneering achievements in her special field of child analysis have remained unnoticed until today. In the official view of psychoanalysis, Freud's daughter Anna features still, as she always did, as the founder of child analysis. . . . Thus we are faced with the strange finding that, of all disciplines, psychoanalysis, which is founded on a belief in the healing power of memory, stubbornly resists its own history.[7]

Additionally, while her interpretation of motherhood was often romanticized, she was one of the first women to write on the "positive" and "negative" mother image in relation to a child's developing consciousness, anticipating the works of later feminist scholars in the field.

Modern Representation

Nevertheless, though the tide is slowly shifting, the conflation of rumor with historical fact has had unfortunate repercussions for Spielrein's reputation. For example, she appears as a masochistic seductress reveling in being spanked by Jung in the film *A Dangerous Method* (2011). Though based loosely on John Kerr's *A Most Dangerous Method*, conversations within the film between Jung and Spielrein are actually reproduced in near entirety from Christopher Hampton's fictionalized play, *The Talking Cure* (2003). In the film, her academic achievements and adult life are only briefly referenced on the screen in a flash of text before the end credits. Two other notable films, *Prendimi L'Anima* (2002) and *Ich Heiße Sabina Spielrein* (2002), also revolve around her treatment with Jung, but from the perspective of trauma; both films incorporate a more fully integrated narrative and succeed in complementing her early life with her return to Russia.

Still, Jungian analyst Tom Kirsch in "Two Pieces on the Movie: *A Dangerous Method*" (2012) chooses to highlight Spielrein's role as a seductress:

> In 1983 there was another international Jungian Congress. . . . Carotenuto's book had been published and was well received. Joe Wheelwright, cofounder of our Jung Institute here in San Francisco was furious with him. Joe felt that Carotenuto was trying to make a

> reputation for himself, which he did with this book, and he said that the material would be used as either a Broadway play, musical, or movie. . . . It was quite a screaming match. . . . The play, "The Talking Cure" by Christopher Hampton and now the movie are the result![8]

Kirsch uses Spielrein as a comedic anecdote about a rift between analysts, though whether or not the material was subsequently turned into a film or a play is irrelevant to the existence of the material. She did not write in her diary or become an analyst for the sole purpose of contributing to a sensationalized film produced seventy years after her death. Kirsch demonstrates that her diaries and letters have from the beginning been considered an attack against Jung's character rather than as insight into her own and have been used to emphasize her sexuality rather than her personality.

In response to *Ich Heiße Sabina Spielrein*, many of the comments made at the Barcelona Congress (2004) in a remarkable panel held on the "Spielrein affair" are similar to Kirsch's. In his presentation "Sabina Spielrein and the Use of Symbols: Reflections of a Jungian Psychoanalyst," Gert Sauer begins by stating, "Sabina Spielrein has become herself a symbol [of destruction] . . . [a] victim of Jung and Freud . . . a victim to bring psychoanalysis into total disrepute."[9] She is not viewed as an autonomous being, but chastised in a debate about victimhood and blamed as a woman with the potential to entirely dismantle psychoanalysis instead of considered as a psychoanalyst in her own right with a unique perspective to contribute to the field. Additionally, Sauer states quite condescendingly: "Spielrein . . . d[id] not know the battle in herself between the traditional role of woman and that which is creative by giving birth to children, and her scientific spirit."[10]

As is evidenced by her diaries and letters—and to an extent, her academic publications—Spielrein frequently remarked on the inner battle between motherhood and her vocation as a scientist and psychoanalyst, and in fact progressively embodied both. In Marcio Giovanetti's response to Sauer in "S. like Sabina, S. like Sergei: Brief Comments Regarding E. Márton's Film and G. Sauer's Paper," he follows Axel Hoffer's (in 2001) diagnosis of Spielrein as a "textbook" case of hysterical symptoms and states: "This trio [Jung, Freud, Spielrein] shows us the dimension of the human soul," and purports that they therefore should not be discussed in light of historical consequences.[11] While attempting to defend Spielrein, Giovanetti loses sight of the fact that she, while "representing a symbol" or a "dimension" of the soul, was also a historical woman, meaning her symbolic power does not excuse the boundary violation, suppression, or violence she encountered, nor does it appropriately acknowledge her personal and professional accomplishments.

A Voice in the Distance

Spielrein's idealization into a disembodied symbol, as well as her academic degradation, draws us back to Ovid's Echo, the figure through which archetypal female suppression has been relayed and considered as ancestral to Spielrein's own story. It may be recalled that Echo was under the living curse of limited speech, interpreted here as the patriarchal exclusion of women's perspectives, though, as is asserted by Judith Greenberg in her article "The Echo of Trauma and the Trauma of Echo:" "Echo repeats the final words of others in order to manufacture her *own* talk."[12] Likewise, Spielrein took the existing language of her field and helped to pioneer child psychology, the "death instinct," and ideas about female sexuality, even if she has not been remembered primarily for her scholarship or for her personal writing.

As discussed in chapter 2, Echo was abstracted into a "bodiless fantasy," much in the same way Spielrein has been abstracted into an *anima* image and her speech interpreted through a host of tenuous pathologies already entwined with psychosocial gender biases.[13] Echo's suppression is mirrored in Spielrein's stigmatization and exclusion from academia's larger male-centric reflection. This double standard of rejection is further pondered by Pat Berry in *Echo's Subtle Body*: "Maybe the reason we have concentrated on Narcissus to the exclusion of Echo is that Echo's passion is much more difficult. . . . Echo's passion is painful; her longing is unrealizable."[14] Regardless, if a woman's own story in a male-dominated narrative is to be highlighted, we must also be willing to realize the difficulty and pain that may accompany such a confrontation.

One must also be careful when re-visioning a cemented story, though I am encouraged by famed philosopher and mythologist Karl Kerényi: "A Greek God comes to us in such manifold forms, from so many places, out of so many levels of past human life, that we must first of all assemble him as we would a heap of collected bones—which is itself a mythological act."[15] While Spielrein is no Greek God, the re-storying of her narrative is a similar feat, which attempts, with mythic determination, to reconcile and reassemble facts from history and shards from contemporary critique. I am not offering *the* interpretation of her life, but I am offering an alternative interpretation to the oft-accepted existing narrative of Spielrein as *The Ever Patient*. There are still numerous diaries, letters, and articles of hers to be explored through mythic, historical, psychological, and autobiographical lenses. An example of this would be the "death instinct," as distinct from Freud's, which offers unique insights into the mystical aspects of physical union, eroticism, transformation through motherhood, destruction in service of creation (e.g., Siegfried), a specific death awareness anticipating subsequent existential philosophers, and the sadomasochistic potential of consuming love. There exist only a few investigations into history, psychology (child or depth), film, or mythology specifically utilizing the *Spielreinian* method.

Also, much remains unanswered in relation to Spielrein's legacy: Are there any other surviving records of her life in the 1930s that remain hidden in personal archives? Why are her glorious unpublished diaries and letters kept secluded in the vaults of private European estates, when they lend so much to women's literary autobiography? Should the inclusion of her narrative change the landscape of the field? Does the suppression of her work reveal or contribute to the perpetuation of academic inequity? I, of course, was not able to confront every question here, but find the evolving atmosphere encouraging. This book, rather than a sweeping analysis, is meant purely as a reintroduction to Spielrein's personal words (albeit, many through translation), a look at a portion of her work, and a reinterpretation of her history as a participant in a "love cure."

In closing: for a few short years in her adolescence, Spielrein suffered from emotional trauma resulting from a host of personal and social factors. She was then institutionalized and for four years she was an intermittent outpatient receiving talk therapy. In contrast, for more than thirty years she was a doctor, teacher, mother, writer, and a pianist. She was also a woman who lived life with intense passion, intellect, and courage in the midst of continuous social upheaval. In kind, we must remember her achievements and grant her a full and complex humanity in the face of gendered biases and historical silencing. As she reminds us in her Last Will: "I too was once a human being. My name was Sabina Spielrein."[16]

Appendix A

Timeline for Sabina Spielrein as Reflected in *Sabina Spielrein: The Woman and the Myth* with Select Bibliography

1885 Sabina Spielrein born in Rostov, Russia

1900 Spielrein begins demonstrating symptoms of "hysteria" after her sister Emily dies

1904 Treated by C. G. Jung at the Burghölzli Clinic, Zurich, Switzerland

1905 Begins studies at University of Zurich in Psychiatry, ceased being an in-patient and begins outpatient care with C. G. Jung under clinic director, Eugen Bleuler

1911 Earns her doctorate from the University of Zurich

1911 "On the Psychological Content of a Case of Schizophrenia" dissertation published

1911 First Presentation to the Vienna Psychoanalytic Society (Freud's Circle), "On Transformation"/Membership in the VPS accepted unanimously

1912 Marriage to Pavel (Paul) Scheftel

1912 "Destruction as the Cause of Coming into Being" is published

1912 "Contributions to the Knowledge of a Child's Soul" is published (See Appendix B)

1913 Birth of daughter, Renata (Renata), meaning "Rebirth"

1913	"The Mother-in-Law" is published
1913–1922	Teaches in Geneva, Switzerland, intermittently
1914	"The Unconscious Mind" (Article)/"Two Menstrual Dreams" (Article)
1915	Pavel leaves to Russia without Spielrein
1916	"The Appearance of the Oedipus Complex in a Child" (Article)
1920	Presentation to Psychoanalytic Congress in The Hague
1920	"Feelings of Shame in Children" (Article); "On the Origin and Development of Vocalized Speech" (Article); "Repressed Oral Eroticism" (Article)
1921	"Russian Literature: A Report on the Successes of Psychoanalysis 1914–1919" (Article)
1922	"The Origin of the Child's Words 'Papa' and 'Mama' " is published
1923	Return to Russia to co-direct Psychology Institute in Moscow
1923	"A Dream and a Vision of Falling Stars (Article); The Car as a Symbol of Male Potency" (Article); "Time in the Subliminal Life of the Mind" (Article); "Some Reports from the Life of Children" (Article)
1924	Return to Rostov and reunion with Pavel
1926	Birth of second daughter, Eva
1929	"An Abstract in Psychoanalysis" (Article)
1931	"Children's Drawings Done with Their Eyes Open and with Their Eyes Shut" (Article)
1930s	Moscow Society Disbands; Becomes unsafe to practice psychoanalysis in Russia; Loss of Spielrein's brothers in the Gulag; Trail on Spielrein is lost
1942	August 11–12, Death of Sabina Spielrein, Eva, and Renata in Rostov under Nazi occupation

Appendix B

Contributions to the Knowledge of a Child's Soul*

Sabina Spielrein

The magnificent teachings of psychoanalysis, particularly in the field of child psychology, need copious and easily understandable evidence. This is why I would like to quote three cases at this point, regarding two boys and one girl. The analysis of the girl is self-observation and as such, relatively complete. Regarding the first boy, I had to make do with only a fragment, out of respect for the mother, which demonstrates the correlation between fear and sexual perceptions. In the case of the second boy, it was his tender age that complicated the analysis. The little one was just not interested in giving us any kind of information. All three children have one thing in common—they all come from distinguished family backgrounds and were brought up correspondingly.

1. Analysis of a Girl

My parents, well, mostly my mother, were proud of the *"innocence"* and "*naiveté*" of their daughter. My friends did not wish to "*tarnish*" me through sex education. In high school, the insemination of animals was stricken from

*Originally published as "Beiträge zur Kenntnis der kindlichen Seele" *Zentralblatt für Psychoanalyse* 3 (1912). Translated from the German by Annika Romero and Angela M. Sells

the natural sciences curriculum in consideration of the "proper upbringing." In the end, I began to like my "*innocence*" and exhibited a certain shyness toward knowledge that could take my innocence away. Hence, it was not until my enrollment at the university that I participated in lectures about zoology where I learned about sexuality.

During the clinical semesters, I began to notice that I, like many beginners, started to fear diseases. However, I noticed that my fear was very specific. I was only afraid of certain infectious diseases which I personified. For example, I imagined the plague to look like a dark figure with fiery red eyes that glowed. I knew that this fear originated in my childhood. Until I was six or seven years old, I was not afraid of "*any devils*." I was constantly made a role model of courage for my brother and took advantage of this by making fun of my brother and jumping out at him from a hiding place or telling him scary stories. I had a great imagination. I was a goddess and reigned over a mighty kingdom. I had a special power, which I called "partus power," [Partuskraft] which was derived from the French verb "*parter*" = to fly. This non-existent verb is probably a compound product from "partir" = to depart and "porter" = to carry. Hence, a power that carries me away.

With this power, I was able to reach every goal and know everything. Although I did not directly believe in the reality of my imagination, it was too beautiful to not believe. If "*Abraham*" was able to get to heaven alive, then why wouldn't I be able to experience the same miracle? I had so much power inside of me, unbeknownst to others, and must have been God's chosen one. My parents did not know anything about this part of my imaginary life, although I was certain that I was not hiding anything from them. I did not think it was important and I was afraid adults would laugh at me. I have always been a critic who knew the difference between reality and imagination.

At that time, I was not interested in listening to fairytale stories. I was fully capable of producing my own fairytales. I wanted to know the truth. My parents were aware that I liked to scare my brother and one time, my father said to me, "*Just wait, fate will punish you in time. One day, you will be afraid of something and this will teach you how your brother felt*." I don't think I took this threat seriously, but apparently, it had consequences. One day, I was startled when I saw two black kittens on top of a chest of drawers in one of the rooms. It must have been an illusion, but it was so clear that to this day, I can still see the animals sitting together quietly. "*This is death or the plague*," I thought to myself. And suddenly, a period of fear began. I started seeing many horrifying animals when I was by myself in the dark. I felt that an unknown force was trying to take me away from my parents and they had hold both of my hands, trying to pull me back.

With great fear and interest, I wanted to hear descriptions of various diseases, which I would later discover on myself at night and which tried to "*attack*" or "*get*" me in the form of people. A person who is not a psychoanalyst would simply interpret this as follows: the father scared the child; his threat became suggestive and the child became afraid. But for a psychoanalyst, there are many questions, such as, why was the fear introduced in a vision of cats? What kind of "*fantasies*" went through the child's head? Was there no correlation to sexuality, which is completely missing in these descriptions? I have to say that the answer to this question is affirmative. As far as I can remember (I can think back to the time when I was around three or four years old), and this was verified with my parents, I know what nagging questions I dealt with: Where do people (children) come from? What is the beginning of all beginnings and the end of all ends? The thought of infinity was especially unbearable.

I was also fascinated by the diversity of people. Americans especially amazed me because I thought they must be walking on their heads with their feet up in the air, since the world is round. For a long time, I dug holes in the ground and asked my mother repeatedly how long it would take for me to dig all the way through the earth to the other side to pull-up an American by his legs. When it comes to adults, we would interpret this behavior immediately as unconscious birth fantasies, based on extensive experience with individuals and social psychology, but in the case of "innocent children," we do not dare to do so. Therefore, I am going to mention another favorite game for the sake of completeness, the making of balloons and other flying objects out of paper. At the age of five, I knew already that the mother carries the child in her body, before giving "birth." I imagined that the child would somehow be removed from her body, for example, by cutting her open or, like someone told me, by unwinding the belly button to remove the baby without causing the mother any pain.

Where children came from was terra incognita, so I asked about that. I also asked who made the father and mother and who created the mothers' mothers, and ultimately, who made God? I was told that God has always existed. I also knew that man was created from earth and God gave breath to man. My mother had proven this to me by rubbing her hands together and creating soil. I wonder how I combined the birth and the earth theories? Was it perhaps that only the first human was made from earth? Otherwise, as far as I can remember, I believed that God created a baby in a mother's body without any human action, merely by wishing for a child. It was my ardent desire to create a living human being, just like God did. That is why I was the omniscient goddess in my fantasies, capable of everything. I tried to create humans from earth, clay, and all other available materials; however, I was unable to make them come alive.

I spent a lot of time drawing magnificent palaces and invented new animals and plants for my kingdom. One time, an uncle who was a chemist showed us an experiment that delighted me. He dipped a small, cut zinc rod into a lead-salt solution and created a complex formation of branches just like a real tree. It dawned on me that chemistry is the force that creates miracles! I became an "*alchemist*." I think that even before this experiment, or perhaps after, I developed a bad habit to the dismay of my parents. I combined leftovers of foods and beverages at the dinner table, mixed everything up real good and made a mess, because I wanted to find out what it would turn into. I loved watching how colors changed and how new shapes and textures emerged. I cannot forget the mixed feelings of delight and fear I felt when a piece of fabric became paper after it had been treated with an unknown liquid substance. Was this simply a product of imagination? I kept many "*secret*" liquids in bottles and "*wonder stones*" and other things of which I expected the great "*creation*." I constantly nagged my parents to tell me how all kinds of things were "*created*."

Since I could not make a human, I kept myself busy making olives, soaps and whatever else I could create. Once, I asked an older woman if I could have a child, just like my mother. "*No*," she answered, "*you are too young to have a child. At this age, you might be able to give birth to a kitten*." Her joking words had a lasting impact: I prepared for the birth of a kitten and pondered whether a kitten could become as intelligent as a human if I raised it accordingly. That was what I was going to do! Now, here we have the sexual etiology of fear. The kitten that put me into a state of fear was the longed-for child. Actually, I saw two kittens; perhaps I thought unconsciously about my younger brother, my loyal playmate, who had to do whatever I told him to do. The immediate thought during my "vision" was that it was "*death*" or the "*plague*."

Therefore, I perceived the child to be a dangerous, perhaps fatal disease. I often find women describe pregnancy and child-birth similar to a dangerous disease (infectious disease, the plague, especially the bubonic plague), a malignant tumor, or a growth, which seems to be recurrent theme: The woman consciously or unconsciously imagines the new creature to be a creature that grows at the expense of the host. It is quite interesting that we react to this destructive idea somewhat with pleasure, somewhat with fear, and at least with reluctance. My fear of infectious diseases, as mentioned above, was the fear of a child, but not only that. I was also afraid of the abductor or seducer, respectively.

When I was a child, I was clueless as to the sexual role of a father, as far as I can recall. Like most girls my age, I probably assumed that the father existed to be the provider. Hence, I kept searching for the abductor, meaning the man. We once climbed on top of a chest of drawers and prayed with our hands lifted toward the sky. We prayed, "*Oh, dear God, take us with you*" (like Abraham). Our alarmed mother lifted us off the chest. She was not only afraid that we would fall, she was also afraid of the mere thought that she could lose us (through death).

During my anxiety attack, an unknown force was trying to take me away from my parents. I often thought that I could fly away against my will. Animals and diseases, which I saw as living creatures, were trying to "*harm me*" and take me to the incredibly sinister death. This infantile fear of the abductor or seducer, respectively, is described in Goethe's poem "Erlkönig." "*I love you; I'm charmed by your beautiful form; and if you're not willing, then I'll use force.*" The seducer in the poem whispers those lines into a boy's ear. This also implies that the poet fantasized about pederasty. Goethe himself must have experienced this "*fearful desire*" for a replacement of his father, otherwise, he would have not been able to relate to the anxiety experienced by the boy as well as he did. My "Erlkönig" was God. It should be noted that a young uncle embodied my image of "*God.*"

When he was in high school and around 13 or 14 years old, he loved to aggrandize himself in front of us. He sometimes pretended to be God, took us to a dark room, told us scary stories and played the violin. I laughed at him. My brother was afraid, although I tried to cheer him up. I was three or four years old[1] at the time. I consciously forgot the stories about God and my uncle within two to three years. However, my unconscious self was actively thinking about it. The reason why I believe this is because I once dreamed about a giant God, who was dressed like my uncle. Furthermore, I became a goddess and scared my brother, like our uncle used to do (the well-known identification with the lover), and I finally had an "*omniscient Moperl*" (as servant), who was a product of my imagination. The Moperl was also called "*Moskja*" in Russian. It wasn't until my analysis that I remembered we used to call our uncle "*Mosjka.*" (He did not like it when we called him by that name and he gave us candy so we would call him "*Uncle Mossia.*") The fantasy of being taken by God (unconsciously the uncle) was always pleasurable to me; apparently, I unconsciously felt the need to look for a substitute for parental love since my early childhood. Then my father's threat turned lust into fear.

This case illustrates the development of scientific interest based on sexual curiosity. First, each and every individual shows interest in his or her own person and then for objects with which the individual comes into contact. Perhaps the appearance of a new family member causes a child to ponder these questions regarding non-existence and the creation of humans. How are people "*made?*" Where do I come from; where does my brother, my mother, my father, the dear Lord come from? Where is the beginning and the end? Questions regarding inaccessible issues bring up questions about accessible things that one can "*create.*" How does one create all kinds of items, such as olives, soap, and so forth?

A child is surprised to learn that olives grow and carefully observes the development of young plants that grow from seeds. She also observes the development of young animals with great interest. I was especially impressed by the transformation of the small zinc rod that was dipped into the lead salt solution, because it became a "*real*" tree. It was like an artificial creation of life! And this led to the passion for chemistry, just like it does everywhere, first in a primitive way of alchemy. There had to be a supernatural power which made this miracle become a reality right in front of my own eyes.

When I was a student at the university, I loved lectures about inorganic chemistry. It even felt as if I had already known about all this a long time ago. However, this was not the case when considering consciousness. At my all girl high school, the chemistry curriculum was limited to just under two pages of a small text book. That was all I knew, because my high school was more likely to hinder any kind of interest instead of encouraging it. I found an explanation for my strange false recollection by telling myself that we inherit the wisdom of our fathers unconsciously. It doesn't matter if this wisdom comes in the form of imagination or silhouettes which have to be "*soaked in blood*" to become alive in consciousness or in the form of pertinent energy tension which causes us to seek analogue experiences. The most important fact is that we only experience or discover analogue[2] experiences which we correctly perceive as such.

2. Analysis of a Boy

In our society, we believe that nervous anxiety can only be cured by finding the cause. Of course, nobody mentions sexuality in this context. Soon after, the highly intelligent 13-year-old Otto calls me aside and tells me that as a child, he constantly worried about being attacked from behind with a knife or revolver. He asks me what this could mean. I try to avoid his question by stating jokingly that he must have done something forbidden. Otto is relentless and tells me that he experienced a recurring dream when he was two years old (time shifting!) in which an old lady wanted to attack him from behind. He is horrified and runs to his mother, who fights off the old lady. I ask him of whom the woman from this recurring dream reminds him. He immediately thinks of an old, ugly coal merchant. [In the dream] A cook taunted him and told him that the coal merchant wanted to kiss the boy. He often dreamed that the coal merchant attacks him; he tries to scream, but is not able to do so. He wants to run away, but has no control over his legs.

Furthermore, Otto does not know why he is afraid of the woman. She could harm him—and first and foremost, she wants to take him away from his mother, where the boy seeks refuge. The first thing Otto remembers about the coal merchant, without my help, is that she is old, ugly and, as others mocked him, she wants to kiss him. These are all associated with erotic fantasies. In the unconscious, we expect adults to imagine things that are connected to the anatomy of male and female bodies. Until now, I have not explained to the boy the meaning behind his fear. However, I am a little surprised that he told me about another dream that involved an anatomical structure, after describing the aforementioned memories, at his own accord. It is obvious that his imagination in regard to the coal merchant also has something to do with anatomy, otherwise he would not have thought of this dream. The dream goes like this: Otto is located in front of an anatomical building at Währingstrasse, some (in reality three) steps lead into the building. There are bars in front of the entrance. He sees the scary woman and cannot escape because the bars hinder him. For a psychoanalyst, the meaning of this dream becomes immediately clear. The layman should try to envision the following thought process: "*Somebody*" is trying to attack me and wants to stab me; it is the coal merchant. People say she wants to kiss me—this old, ugly woman. The first dream: I flee from this ugly woman to my (beautiful) mother. The second dream: I am trying to flee from this woman into an anatomical [or, Anatomy] building; however, the building is locked (for me).

If we analyze these two dreams objectively, we find that the beginning is the same in both dreams. "I" flee from this ugly woman. In the first dream, I manage to escape. In the second dream, I don't. The first dream is closer to reality; the boy flees to his mother, which might have occurred numerous times on other occasions. In the second dream, the place of refuge is a building instead of the mother, but he fails to enter the building. This is pure imagination and we assume that, based on our knowledge about adults and their dreams, the second dream revolves around the same topic (in this case him fleeing toward his mother), but in a symbolic way, like most other sexual desires. As mentioned before, we expected the association with the "physical structure" in connection with erotic imagination consciously or unconsciously. Instead, Otto gives us the anatomical structure.

What comes to mind is the German word "Frauenzimmer" [chamber of a woman] which is used in German as a synonym for the word "woman." Adults frequently associate buildings with a symbol for females. Even [Karl] Scherner, who was not an analyst, pointed out that we envision our own bodies in dreams as buildings: A professor underwent a skull surgery; when the surgeon used a chisel to open the skull, the professor called out, "*Come in!*" Apparently, he thought of a room when he envisioned his skull. And even in Otto's case, the building represents a symbol of a human body. Particularly the word "*anatomy*," a science that covers the human body, tells us the expected anatomical concept. Instead of running to his mother, as in the first dream, Otto tries to escape into a body, but is not allowed to do so.

Symbolically, the bars stop him from entering the building. Of course, I do not explain this to the boy. The next day, he tells me about another dream from the same time period, according to him. The dream goes like this: Otto enters a room (I will attach a sketch of the room), his governess sits inside the room with her back toward the door, he walks to the window, steals a piece of jewelry, but loses a pearl. Another woman rushes into the room through the other door. He wants to run away, but the door is closed. The woman jumps on top of Otto and, in his own words, crushes him. After that, he wakes up. Especially scary was her mouth, which was wide open with large teeth.

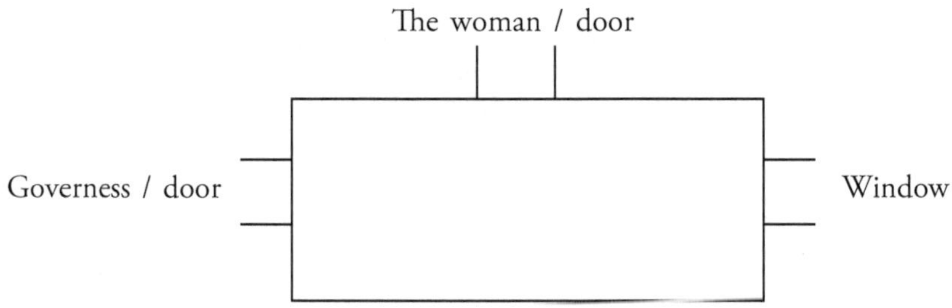

After he finished speaking these words, Otto walks over to the piano: "*I keep thinking about this melody*," he says and plays the melody; it is a choir from Mozart's *Magic Flute*. I ask which part he remembers; it is a chorus to Iris and Osiris, where there are priests with long flutes, and one of them wants to get married.

The dream indicates that he did do something forbidden. Whether this happened in reality or was a product of imagination remains to be seen and is irrelevant to us. Our psychological life only includes products of our psyche—Otto steals the forbidden jewelry, like Adam and Eve took the forbidden fruit. The sexual interpretation of this theft is underscored by analogue symbolism of adults and by Otto's associations. Otto receives the punishment he deserves; he is especially scared of the woman's large mouth and her teeth. Apparently, the woman represents the devil that comes to get him, based on the following religious connotations. The part of the *Magic Flute*, which Otto associates with the dream, reads:

> Chorus of the priests (Sarastro standing in a half circle):
>
> O Isis and Osiris! What delight! The dark night retreats from the light of the sun!—Soon will the noble youth experience a new life,

soon will he be wholly dedicated to our Order. His spirit is bold, his heart is pure, soon will he be worthy of us.

Sarastro (waves to the right)

Two priests (leave toward the right, front side and immediately return with Tamino, who is covered with a veil)

Twenty-second appearance.

The same characters. Tamino at Sarastro's right side.

Sarastro:

Prince! Your behavior till now has been manly and composed. You will now have to wander two dangerous paths. If your heart is still beating for Pamina and if you still desire to once reign as a wise ruler, may the gods be with you. Give me your hand! (He makes a sign to the left)

Let Pamina be brought in!

This shows clearly that inside Otto, the dream touched on fantasies of a young man like Tamino, who is manly, composed, and was able to resist multiple seductions and remain faithful to his bride. *His spirit is bold, his heart is pure, soon will he be worthy of us.* The dream demonstrates the opposite of self-confidence, hence, we have to assume that Otto behaved the opposite way of Tamino. His heart is cowardly (because he constantly tries to flee) and he did something impure. Furthermore, Otto is being taken by the devil, as opposed to Tamino, who is accepted by the gods. Otto is a "sinner" because he steals, and strikingly, steals a feminine item—jewelry—which underscores our thought of sin within a sexual context.

I do not want to go into detail about reasons why Otto decided to equip the priests with flutes instead of Tamino, and neither am I going to discuss what the flutes might mean. When Otto retells the story, he states that the priests play trumpets, and later he mentions "*horns*": it is the well-known uncertainty related to deeply emotional imaginations. "*There is a bridal couple,*" he adds, "*which is initiated by the gods.*" He cannot recall the name of the hero. "*How would you call him? Buffoon? Only dumb people need a God. I do not believe in God,*" he says. While philosophizing, he tells me, "*There is no God. The man consists of a good human, the worm, and the bad human.*" His division of humans into three parts is a consequence of religious imagination, which he just repudiated. Three is a holy number. The strangest part of the human, the worm, should be interpreted in the religious context of a seducer, because a worm pit or snake pit represents hell and the snake is nothing but a large worm.

Otto created this division unconsciously, because he was unable to elaborate on what the "worm" is exactly when I asked him for a more detailed explanation. He had to think about it and told me later that evening that the worm is actually life. According to him, the worm has the same shape as life; it moves like life. The boy demonstrated a serpentine form while explaining this [also, ouroboros]. This is actually the conscious reinterpretation of the imagination that emerged from his unconscious and reveals again that the worm belongs to the religious mindset and is associated with the consumption of the forbidden (sexual) fruit. Otto must have spent a lot of time thinking about the worm, considering that he added it to his categorization of a human and made it an integral part of his own existence. A well worthy of note is the fact that he mentions the worm (= life) as the center part of a human, which corresponds with the anatomical construction of the body.

Otto is fondly attached to his mother. When he was a child, he was dyspeptic and his mother was his main caretaker. He keeps two poems in a notebook that are dedicated to his mother. It remains an open question whether he wrote the poems himself or copied them; his mother believes the latter. Anyway, it is quite interesting to see how he interprets these poems:

One of them is called "*Life*":

> The beginning is the end;
> The end is a song;
> The beginning ends,
> The end wins.

Otto explains, "*Things were better before we lived. When life begins at the time of birth, this happy state ends.*" I ask Otto where one is before one is born, "*Inside a human,*" he replies. I ask control questions and he gives the same answer. Otto adds that he believes the happiest state is right before birth. This belief goes hand in hand with the perceptions of passionate poets, who wish for the greatest pleasure followed by death. In Otto's mind, birth means detachment from his mother and equals death.[3] The end, nothingness, is the most desirable state in Otto's opinion. Otto later adds that it is better not to live if one has been removed from a state that was much better, meaning an existence inside another human [see "Destruction.] This "*womb fantasy*" should be compared to Stekel's "Language of Dreams" and Otto Rank's "Lohengrin

Saga." The latter scientist provided evidence that the aforementioned "womb fantasy" exists in mythology and explained specifically in his work "Myth of the Birth of the Hero" that humans believed in the return to a mother's womb and reincarnation.

And Otto [child] longs for death because he longs for the reunification with his beloved mother; he longs for the time before his birth [see, "Origins."] The same desire was mentioned with respect to his dream about the anatomical building.

Another poem we discussed is called "*The Clock*":

> An old clock stands next to the table,
> It was inherited from family.
> Its job was to
> limit the life of humans.
> Only one understands the clock's oracle;
> It is the Grandmother.
> And I have been longing for the end,
> When my time has come.
> When I became sick one day,
> I looked forward to the judgment;
> But then, Grandmother was gone,
> And I was unable to ask her
> The Question on my mind.

Otto also told me about other women who had taken the place of the coal merchant in his dreams. All of them were elderly women. One of these women becomes his Goddess of Fate, because she understands the oracle of the clock. In Otto's own words, the clock represents the grandmother of two coachman boys with whom he socialized despite the fact that his mother prohibited him from hanging out with the boys. He wanted to ask the grandmother how long he will live. Freud states that children and neurotics live outside of time, because they live in an imaginary world, which is not linked to time.

Stekel writes about "neurotics and their relationship to time"[4] that neurotics will never be able to cope with time because they were unable to deal with their childhood desires. He adds examples of children who constantly calculate, which prove to be a calculation of age differences between the child and his or her parents. Consciously or unconsciously, every child wants to be the same age as the respective parent to enjoy the same rights and pleasures. Otto wanted to know the date of his death, for which he consistently longed. He fell ill and must have enjoyed the great love and care of his mother. Death was nothing else but a culmination point of this love; however, he was not granted the culmination point. The anxious question of when the peaceful moment would arrive remained unanswered because the grandmother = clock became silent.

3. Analysis of a Boy

"*Where did you come from, little one?*" I jokingly ask the four and a half year old Valli. "*From mom's blood,*" replies the little one, laughing mischievously. "*Where does she get the blood from?*" "*From the finger. It comes out when one pricks it,*" he replies. "*How do you know?*" I ask. "*From the fairytale, Snow White. Her cheeks were red, like blood.*" It appears that the little boy combined two fairytales into one: Sleeping Beauty, who pricks her finger and dies,[5] and Snow White, who has cheeks as red as blood. He thereby reinterprets Sleeping Beauty's death by applying a birth fantasy.

In order to avoid suggestive questions, I do not ask questions about the role of the father and instead ask where his father came from. "*He also came from mom's blood,*" replies the little one, "*Mom first made me and then dad.*" The boy wants to be as old and strong as his father, better yet older and stronger, which corresponds with Freud's thesis. We have also seen this in adults. As soon as a topic revolves around a desire that is supposed to be kept secret, resistance emerges, exhibited by "absent-mindedness," ignoring questions, and evasive answers; Valli exhibits the same behavior. "*But why do you call him father?*" I ask. Valli provides the following absurd answer: "*Because he is an agronomist*" (the father's occupation). Another time, I ask him where the plants in the soil come from. Any child from a rural area would be quick to provide the correct answer. It is all the more striking that he pretends not to know the answer, considering that his father is an agronomist and he has seen him work in the garden many times.

When I insist, he finally replies that they come from a cherry. (Note: They are red and round, like a drop of blood.) "*Well, what does one do with a cherry?*" I ask. "*It is planted here.*" (He points to the location.) "*And what do you do when you would like to have flowers or grass in your yard?*" I ask. "*I don't know,*" he replies. "*Sure you do—what would your father do?*" "*You have to sow them.*" "*How does one sow? What do you need to sow?*" "*I don't know.*" "*But you have watched your father sow before.*" (The father keeps many jars filled with seeds around the house.) "*I don't know,*" he insists. "*Yes you do, you little rascal!*" "*Seeds.*" His mother was present during this conversation, which must have increased the "resistance" and encouraged his ignorance, because Valli once told me with no difficulty where he came from. When I asked him the same question in front of his mother, he smiled, buried his face in my lap and pretended not to know. He surely suspects that the origin of plants has something in common with the origin of humans and that this is something we should not discuss.[6]

Valli's father took a trip and his mother frets about it. "*Call me father and you will not miss him as much*," comforts the boy. The mother feels that the boy phrased this statement awkwardly and states, "*He was trying to say that I should call him by his father's name.*" This is highly likely because we have already noted that the boy competes with the father; he wants to be the older one for the mother. Nevertheless, one should be careful when trying to correct the words of the subject as a part of the analysis. Instead, one should further investigate the mistake (in this case, the slip of tongue) to find the reason grounded in the unconscious thoughts of the child.

Female lover and at the same time daughter, just like male lover and son: these connections are common in mythology as well as in a child's psyche. Eve was, after all, Adam's daughter and wife at the same time. The Egyptian myth in which the Queen of Heaven, Nuth, copulates with her son (the sun) and then gives birth to him is similarly peculiar. Since Valli claimed that his mother created her husband (as her son), we have to believe that he has the same ideas. On that same day, I ask the boy if he can tell me who created his mother. "*Father*," replies the boy. "*How come? You told me that your mother made your father. So, the mother made the father and the father made the mother?*" I ask. "*Yes.*" We should not let this apparent contradiction confuse us. The dream, like primitive people, does not know "either/or," and the same applies to the child (Freud).[7] Both theories have the same right to exist according to him and this is why he allows both of them to coexist; unconcerned, regardless of whether they contradict each other or not. It is imperative not to dismiss products of children's' "imagination" as nonsense.

The conscious desire to have a little girl just for himself is nothing new to Valli, he has been wanting to get a sweet little sister. He even asked his mother last year if she could buy him one. Around that time, he was invited over for lunch. That was when he "*picked out*" one of his little cousins, whom he kissed multiple times. One time, he gently hugged his mother and asked, "*Mom, do I have your hands?*" "*Yes.*" "*And what about my legs?*" "*Yes, my love.*" "*Am I completely yours?*" "*Of course.*" "*And also Dad's?*" "*Certainly.*" "*Am I Dad's son?*" "*You are my and your father's son.*" "*No, I am not your son. If I were a girl, I would be your daughter. I am Dad's son because I am a man and I look like Dad.*" The mother "produces" daughters, the father makes sons. This is also a well-known mythological and childish perception.

I then took the opportunity to find out about his ideas about death. I ask Valli if he has seen a dead body. He states that he once saw a dead person at a funeral. What happens to a person after he or she dies? After initial resistance, Valli replies, "*Blood.*" I ask a control question after some time passes and he replies, "*He is thrown into a hole in the ground.*" "*What does he do there?*" "*He swims in water.*" The end of life = the beginning. This too is an ancient mythological notion (see Rank, *The Myth of the Birth of a Hero* and *The Lohengrin Saga*).[8]

The next morning Valli tells us, "*I dreamed about a Hanswurst.*" "*Can you explain that to me?*" "*He shoves someone into water, into a pit. He has a hoof.*" "*Is it a human being?*" "*No, he lives in the woods and is made from a breast.*" "*From a breast? How come?*" "*From the breast. He comes out when someone is drinking tea, that's when he comes out of the mouth. He comes out of a tea urn.*" "*I thought you said he comes from the breast?*" "*Yes, from the breast.*" "*But now you said he comes out of the mouth?*" "*Yes, from the mouth, from the tea urn. He is made of flesh. He has horns on his head and pushes people down.*"[9] "*Have you seen one?*" "*Near Anna* (servant maid). *He has horns. I dreamed that horses were in front of the house,*" continues Valli, "*That's when Hanswurst showed up. The governor threw him into jail because he kept pushing people into the pit. He works for the governor.*" (The constable)

It is clear that Valli dreamed about a devil that kills people (he throws them into the pit—this is how Valli imagines death). At the same time, the devil is the developing child, who is about to come out of the breast, then the mouth, and then the tea urn. The next day, Valli's mother tells a farmhand that he should have children. He replies that it would be a sin to create sinners. Valli interrupts his mother, "*Mom, what should he do if a boy comes out of his mouth and what should his blind wife*[10] *do if a girl comes out of her mouth? She wouldn't even be able to see it.*" Hence, the dream he had the day before revealed additional facts about the boy's perceptions.

Stekel pointed out that soldiers (the constable) often represent death in dreams. And even Valli made "Hanswurst" a servant of the governor. The house in which Valli lives is adjacent to the governor's house, the servant, whom Valli sees on a regular basis, is the constable, and the constable owns a rifle that can be used to shoot or stab someone. Here we see the analogy between the horns and "*Hanswurst,*" which leads us to believe that he is condensing the two characters. The "*Hanswurst constable,*" who can stab people, creates new life just like Snow White (Sleeping Beauty), who created new life by pricking her finger. The boy does not show the slightest fear of his destructive fantasies. Today, he asked his mother how children are created and she promised to explain it to him in the near future. The mother, who has been observing the little one upon my recommendation, was surprised to find out that her child has such a large amount of sexual imagination, although she thought he was asexual. She confided in me that she is now starting to make sense of their conversations, which she simply dismissed in the past because she thought his stories were senseless products of his imagination—like most mothers. Yesterday, Valli told us that *every woman has a man*. Under no circumstances did he want to tell us why this is the case.

Final Conclusions

All three children intensively concern themselves with sexual problems. The first two children have something in common with regard to the development of their anxiety: the fear of being snatched and their flight to the parents (in the boy's case to his mother). Every child initially loves their parents; however, the little ones become unfaithful at a very young age. Valli pines for a little sister. My mother told me that my own brother fell in "love" when he was only two years old. He was in love with a little girl, whom he treated very gently, and he even helped her get seated at the table and once he gave her his favorite food, stewed fruit. I could name many other examples. Every attentive mother has observed something similar about their own child and it makes people chuckle because the "innocent" child acts as if it knew the secret of adults.

The subconscious of a child knows just that. Real objects can be replaced with imaginary objects. One wants to leave the parents' home to become a god,[11] a king or a queen. One is fascinated by religion (in fact, God and angels), the fairytale world in which heroes travel to faraway places, followed by a passion for travel adventures. Baron Winterstein once gave a lecture on the connection between wanderlust and sexuality at the Vienna Psychoanalytical Society. In his lecture, he explained that wanderlust portrays the act of leaving to look for a new love or to leave an old one behind. At this occasion, Freud told us about a tradition of primordial families whereby a father would expel his adult sons in order for them to find their own territories and women far away.

This tradition can often be observed in fairytales in which royal children frequently travel, according to Freud. A child who is going through its phylogenetic development and whose psyche finds plenty of resources in religion and fairytales, thinks about the desired new love by dreaming of a departure, travel, or flying away from his or her parents. Hence, young children's imaginary games revolve around bandits, witches, and survival on a deserted island. All of these fantasies are quite lustful. Then why do many children experience a time where lust turns into fear? Freud states that each and every neurotic fear is based on repressed desires. As a result, lust becomes anxiety. My case confirms this thesis. At the time I became scared of the kitten, I no longer knew the sexual meaning of it. I had forgotten about it because I "*repressed*" this fantasy into my unconscious. But Freud also said that not every repressed desire may necessarily cause anxiety.

Therefore, a causa movens needs to take place. In my case, it was a threat. My father did not tell me of what I would become afraid. But why did I become afraid of sexuality in particular? My case is certainly not unique and is well known, just like the fact that increased lust (e.g. in connection with some sort of conquest) becomes the lust before a sexual conquest. Every increased feeling will be "sexualized;" every increased love is "passion" (there is a reason why the term originated within a sexual context).[12] The difference between sexual and asexual is simply quantitative and maintaining this arbitrarily created category leads to the major misconception that children are not sexual and people want to believe that children's psychological life is different from that of adults. Sexuality itself can serve as a receptacle for opposite feelings such as lust and anxiety.

New life is created at the expense of old life. It seems to be priority that we seek life and avoid death; but a more thorough observation tells us differently: I am pointing out that it is the same content which impressed us once as the "beginning" and other times as the "end," just like my analyses show. It is *love* that makes us overlook the dangers of self-destruction, yet we seek it with joy. My childish love for God was still too weak, this is why my father's threat was able to cause my self-preservation instinct and fear of the end, which I had earlier perceived as the beginning. In the boy's case, I am not sure what the etiology of his anxiety was. However, the anxiety is also linked to notions of destruction and sexuality, and it is likely that it was also a scare or a threat that turned the fear of death into a fear of sexuality. In timid persons, particularly in young children, these destruction fantasies will prevail even in sexuality with corresponding emotions. These observations lead to the conclusion of pedagogical principals.

The Symbolic Meaning of Clocks[13]

Humans are highly interested and fascinated by the "tick tock" of a clock beginning in the first years and months of a child's life. The clock appears to be alive, because it moves and speaks on its own. Nothing is more amusing to a child than to wind up a clock and start it to life. Children enjoy playing with toys that are similar to living creatures, just think about a girl's desire to play with dolls that can say "Mama" or "Dada," that can move their arms and legs and open and close their eyes. Moreover, children are fascinated (and sometimes scared of) growling bears, meowing cats, mice on wheels, and so forth. Toys are constantly taken apart and recreated. I think it was Preyer who said that children quickly lose interest in toys that cannot be modified and recreated in many different ways. And we understand why: a toy should be capable of portraying as many children's desires as possible, just like a symbol in a dream which becomes more suitable if it is only vaguely predefined. A child wants to constantly create, regardless of whether it is a small house out of building blocks or a soldier cut out of paper. Even adults want to conquer nature and create new things; however, we are unable to create what we desire the most. The greatest miracle and most valuable creation is the creation of a creature in our own image: a human being.

A patient suffering from anxiety attacks believes that she will suffer a heart attack, her heart will be ripped out and she could be buried alive. Some of her attacks (a series of fantasies which she produces upon my request quickly and without taking too much time to think about it) go like this: "*Death, the grim reaper, cutting the thread of life. People often say the biological clock has run out of time, the heart stops beating, just like a clock stops ticking. When I was suffering from pericarditis I saw a clock in front of me; it seemed as if sand or water was leaking out of it. Grains of sand in the ocean. A human being is just like a grain of sand.*"

The clock represents the patient, her life, her sick heart, which she currently deals with. The leaking clock symbolizes the threat of dying. Imagining the beginning is impossible without imagining the end, and vice versa. Therefore, a patient referring to a death fantasy is also referring to a birth fantasy. "*A human being is just like a grain of sand* (in the ocean)," stated the patient. On the contrary, leaking sand is similar to human beings: humans emerge (from their mothers) like the grains of sand leak from the clock. Grains of sand = humans; in the ocean = amniotic fluid. The patient symbolizes herself, as mentioned before, as a leaking clock. It is noteworthy that the patient once compared giving birth to evisceration: the belly is opened up and one is eviscerated when the child is removed. And now she thinks of death and birth, which is like the evisceration of a clock.

Notes

1. As mentioned before, I verified my memories with my parents. I also consulted with my uncle and brother. In addition, I have a diary that I wrote. I was ten years old when I started writing in this diary. This is where I also found the God-uncle story and the subsequent dream from my early childhood.

2. Cf. Jung, the meaning of a father in the life of an individual.

3. In eastern mythology, there is a story about a creature that was half plant and half human. The creature was connected to the earth by an umbilical cord. When the umbilical cord was cut, the creature screamed and . . . died.

4. *Zentralblatt für Psychoanalyse*, II. volume, issue 5.

5. The death sentence is mitigated and then changed into sleep by a good witch. Hence, sleep and death are only marginally different in this case.

6. This suspicion might explain why Valli answers my question, "*Then why do you call him father?*" with "*Because he is an agronomist.*" Symbolizing human impregnation using images from the plant kingdom is one of the oldest types of symbolization in social psychology.

7. It is generally known that a child will reply "Mom and Dad," when asked which parent he or she likes best.

8. Papers on applied psychology.

9. Here again the concept of "either/or" is missing.

10. The woman does not see very well.

11. Jung states (see "Transformations and Symbols of Libido") that children should be taught religion because religion is especially suitable for the sublimation of love for their parents, based on its phylogenetic duration. In my case, it was also the love for my parents, or rather for my uncle, which was transferred to God (sublimed).

12. For example, the love for nature can be intensified by wanting to hug and kiss everything and by personifying objects, meaning that one tries to adopt a similar image. Basically, an individual only loves him or herself or the rest of the world insofar that the individual can identify himself or herself (projecting) with an object.

13. Some examples pertaining to the symbolic meaning of clocks have previously been described by Stekel and other researchers.

Appendix C

Sabina Spielrein in Image and on the Page

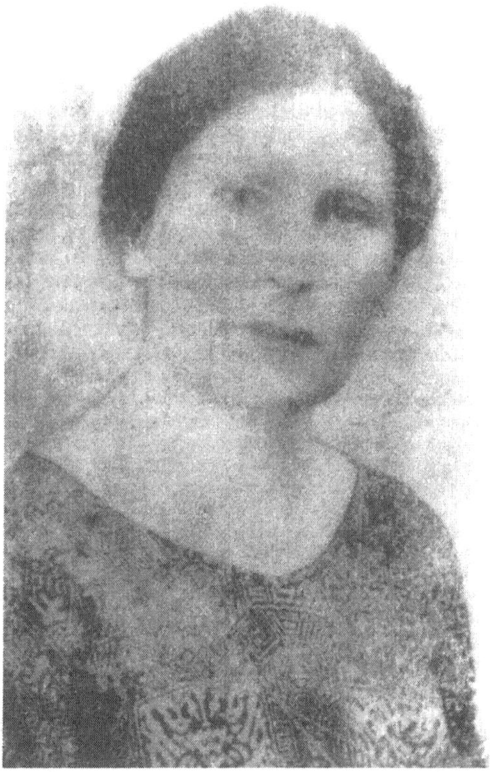

Figure 3. Sabina Spielrein, ca. 1925, Public Domain.

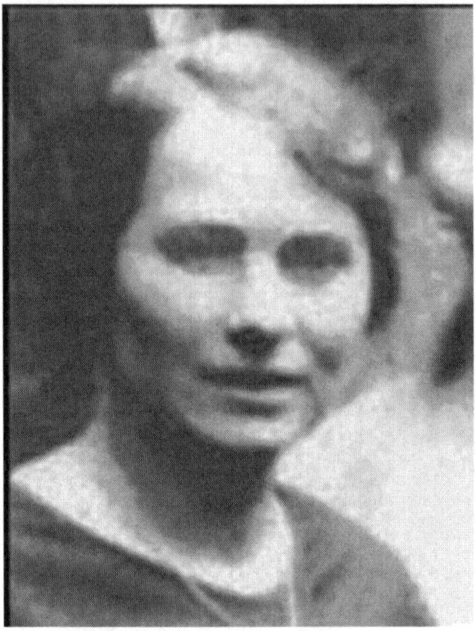

Figure 4. Sabina Spielrein, ca. 1909, Public Domain.

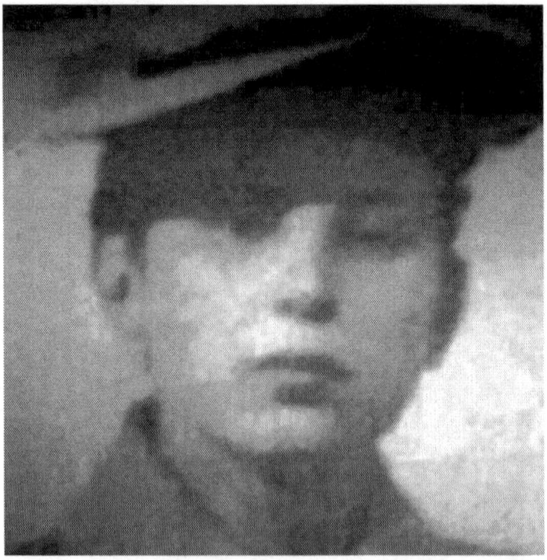

Figure 5. Sabina Spielrein, ca. 1898, Public Domain.

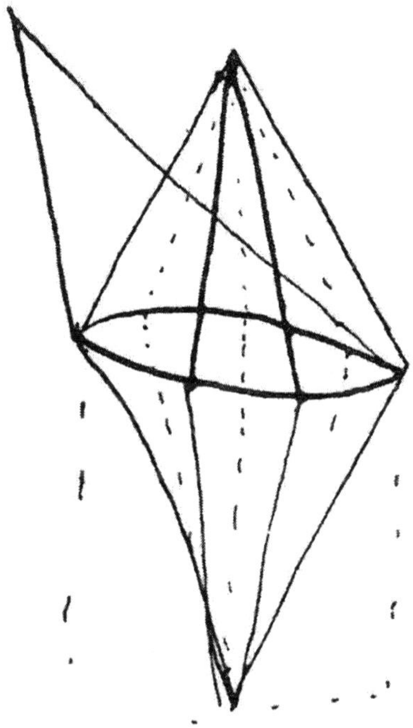

Figure 6. Sabina Spielrein's Diagram of the Unconscious, 1917, Public Domain (See *Tagebuch und Briefe*, Kore: Verlag, 2003).

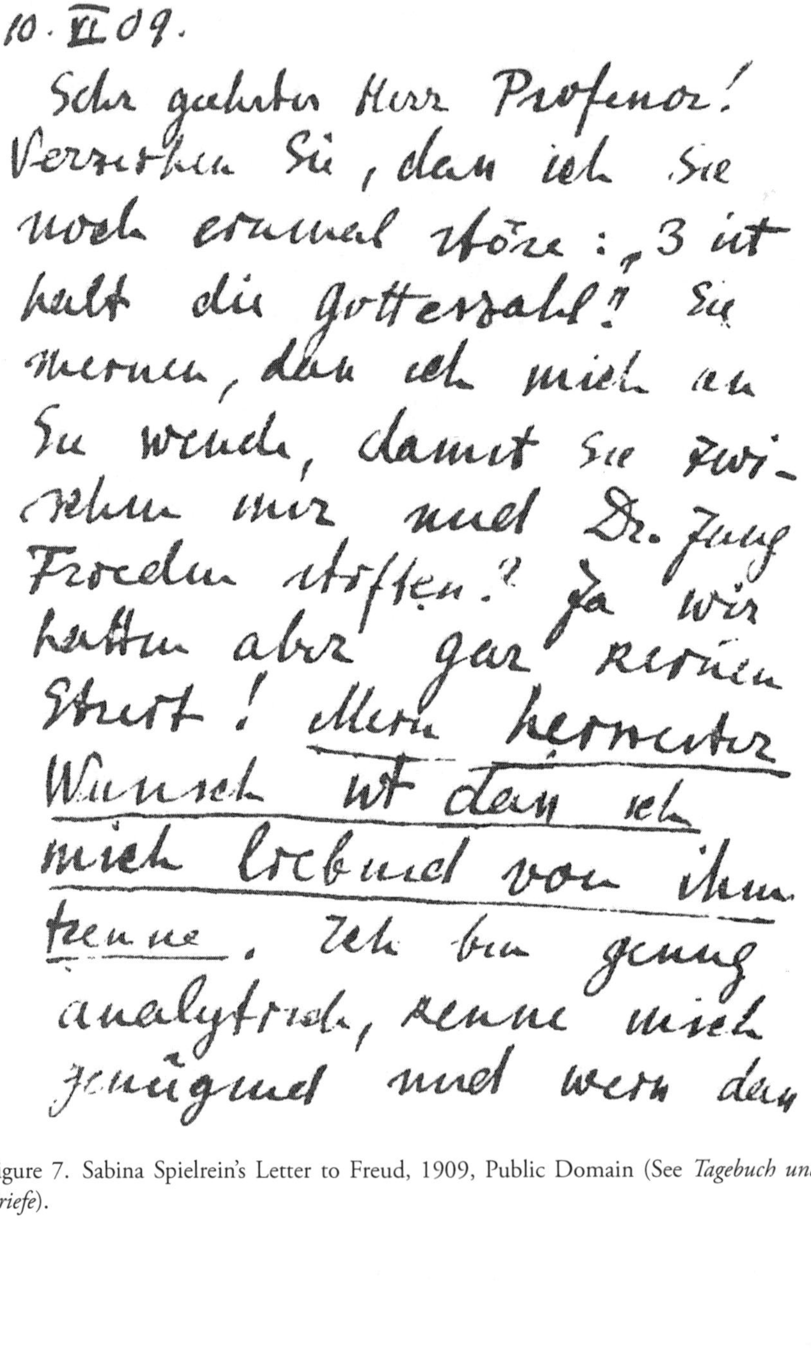

10. VI. 09.

Sehr geehrter Herr Professor!
Verzeihen Sie, dass ich Sie noch einmal störe: „3 ist halt die Götterzahl!" Sie meinen, dass ich mich an Sie wende, damit Sie zwischen mir und Dr. Jung Frieden stiften? Ja wir hatten aber gar keinen Streit! Mein heissester Wunsch ist dass ich mich liebend von ihm trenne. Ich bin genug analytisch, kenne mich genügend und wenn dass

Figure 7. Sabina Spielrein's Letter to Freud, 1909, Public Domain (See *Tagebuch und Briefe*).

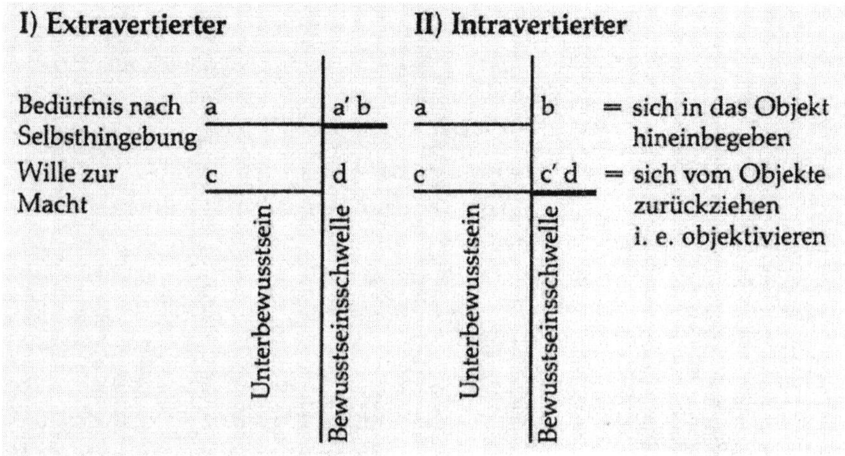

Figure 8. Sabina Spielrein's Diagram of Introvert and Extravert. This diagram appears originally in the Kore *Tagebuch* publication of Spielrein's unabridged diaries and correspondence (in German, p. 145) and is reproduced here.

Appendix D

Images of Myths Mentioned

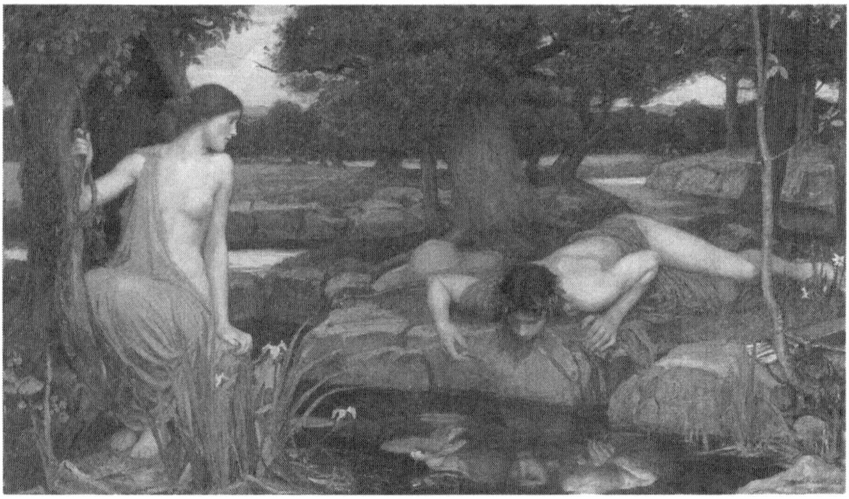

Figure 9. John William Waterhouse, *Echo and Narcissus*, 1903, Public Domain.

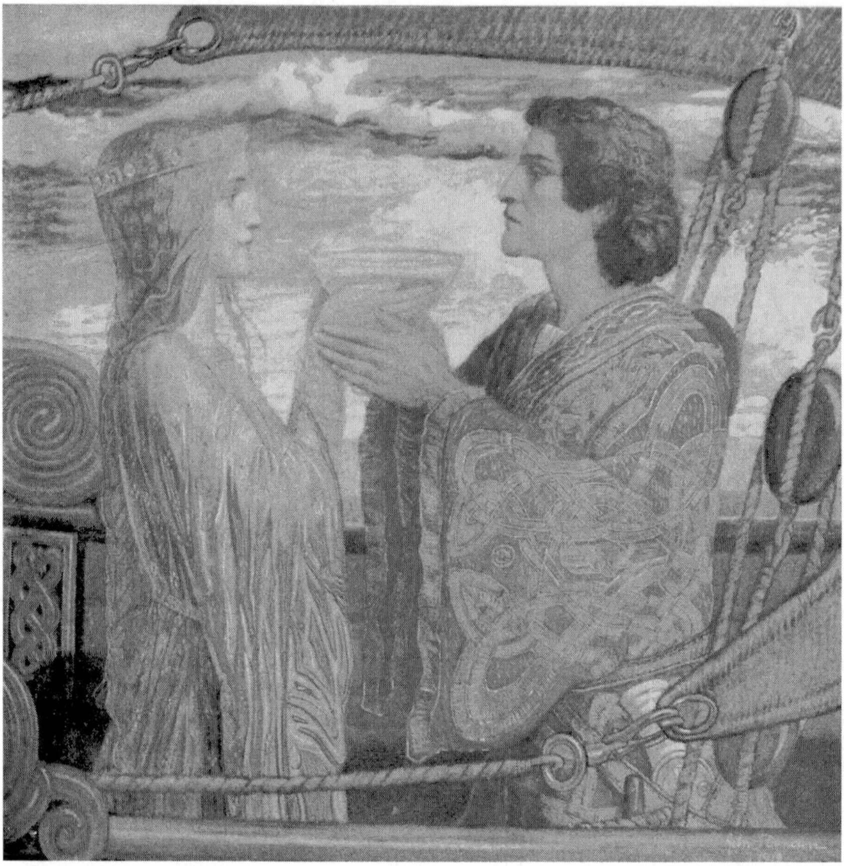

Figure 10. John Duncan, *Tristan and Isolde*, 1912, Public Domain.

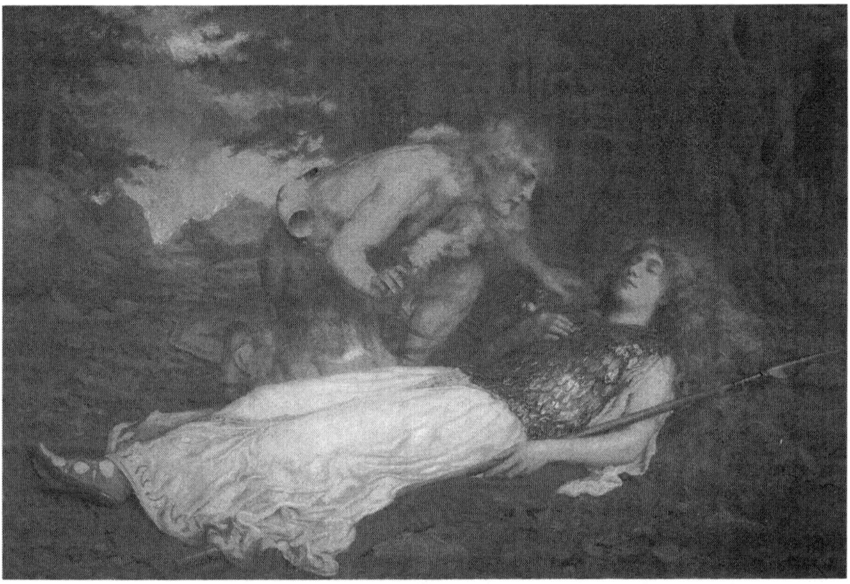

Figure 11. Charles Ernest Butler, *Siegfried and Brunnhilde*, 1909, Public Domain.

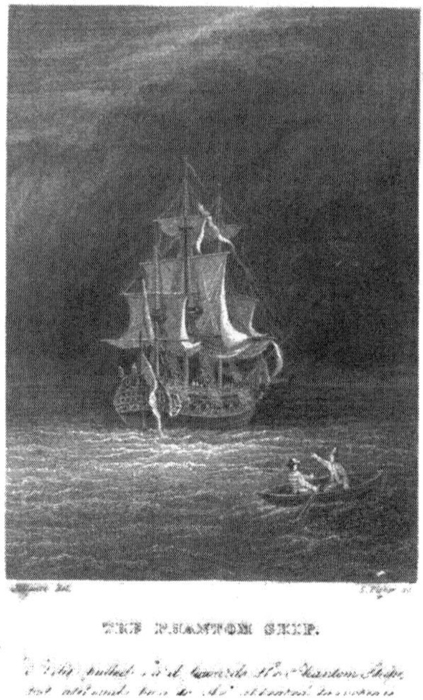

Figure 12. Frederick Marryat, *The Phantom Ship*, 1847, Public Domain.

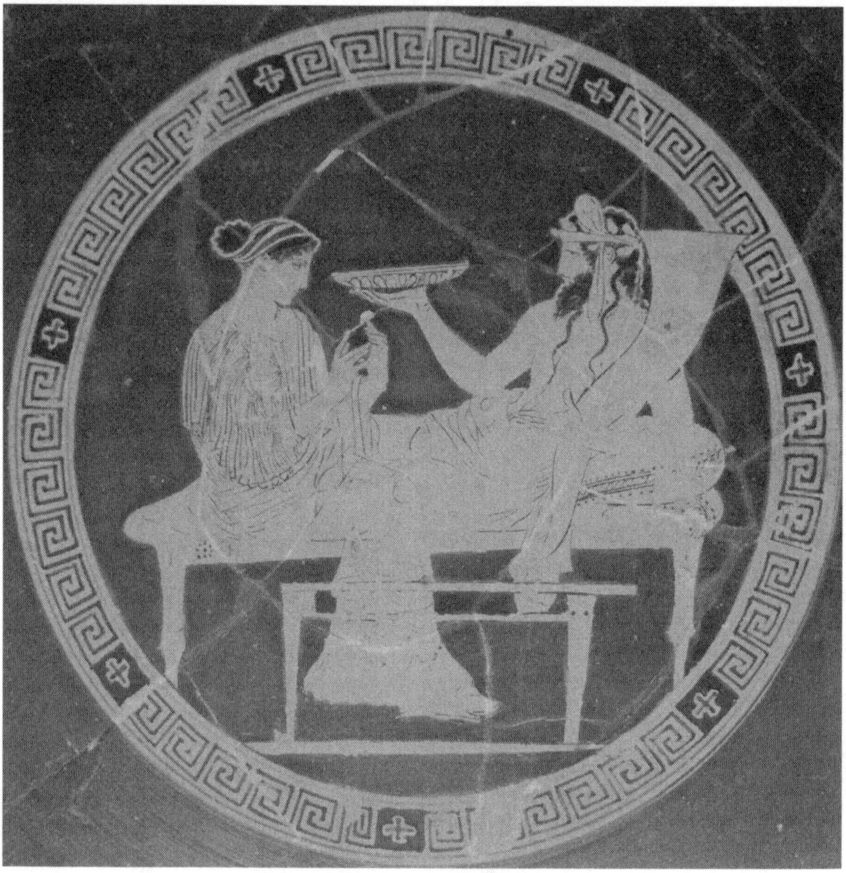

Figure 13. Persephone and Hades: tondo of an Attic red-figured kylix, ca. 440 BC. Public Domain, CreativeCommons.

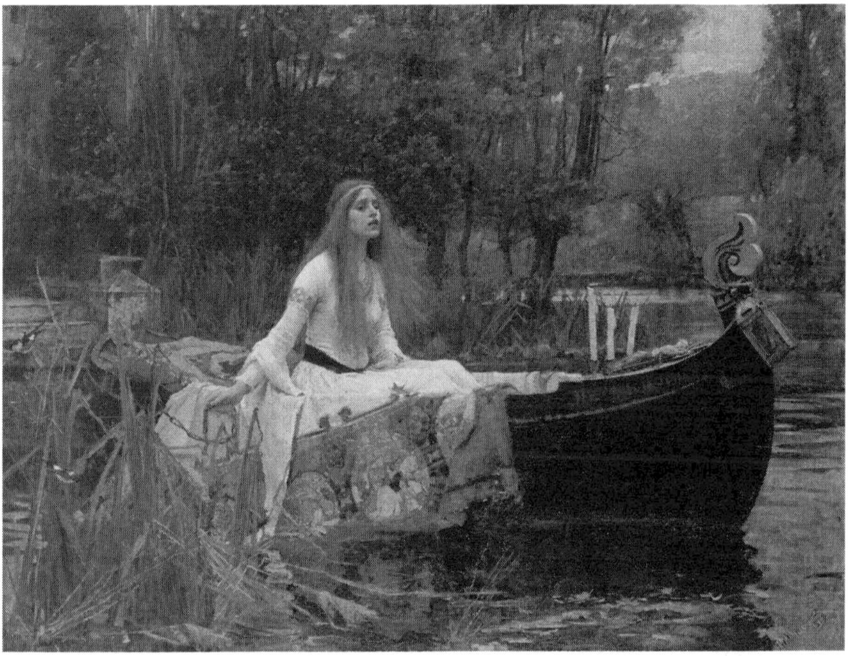

Figure 14. John William Waterhouse, *The Lady of Shalott*, 1888.

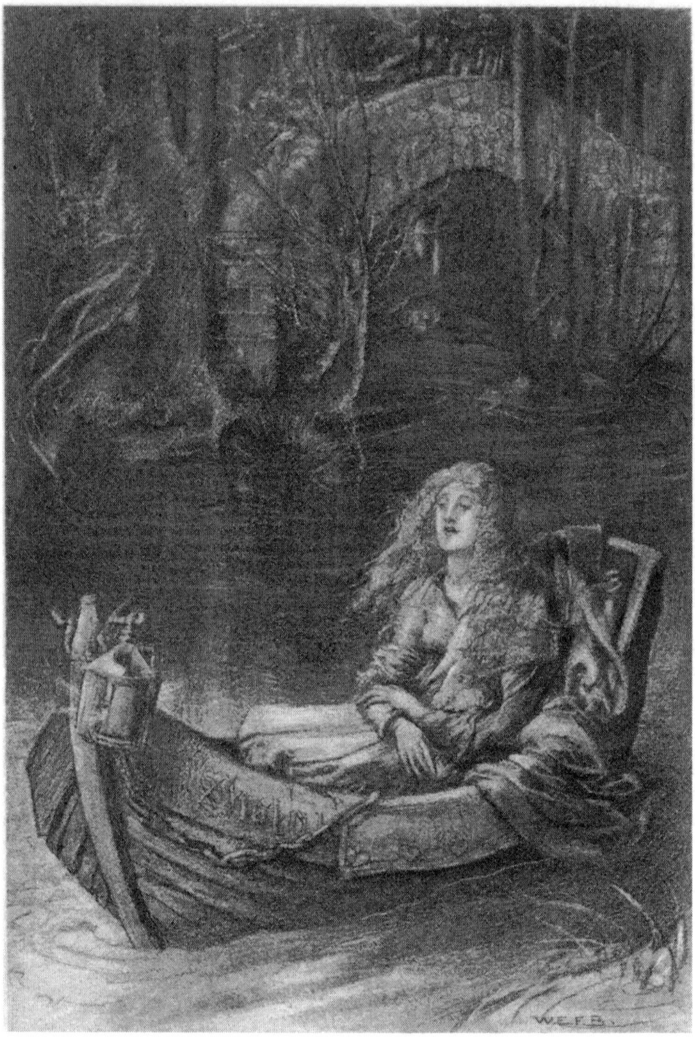

Figure 15. W. E. F. Britton, *The Lady of Shalott*, 1901, Public Domain.

Notes

Introduction

This book has been adapted from my 2015 dissertation at Pacifica Graduate Institute.

In addition to my own translations from the original German, I have had the assistance of translators (Annika Romero and Gabrielle Thompson) on new and updated English translations of Spielrein's diaries and letters.

1. Sabina Spielrein, *Tagebuch und Briefe*, ed. Traute Hensch (Kore: Psychosozial-Verlag, 1986/2002), 74.

2. Elaine Showalter, "Hysteria, Feminism, and Gender," in *Hysteria Beyond Freud*, ed. Sander Gilman, Helen King, Roy Porter, G. S. Rousseau, and Elaine Showalter (Berkeley: University of California Press, 1993), 335.

3. The original German article, "Beiträge zur Kenntnis der kindlichen Seele" (1912), has been translated with the assistance of Annika Romero; effort has been made to remain as faithful to the original publication as possible.

4. C. G. Jung and Marie-Louise von Franz, *Man and His Symbols* (New York: Dell, 1968), 16.

5. James Hillman, *Healing Fiction* (Spring 1994), 11.

6. Luce Irigaray, *This Sex Which Is Not One* (Ithaca: Cornell University Press, 1985), 213.

7. Rachel Hirshfeld, "New 'Babi Yar' Plaque Omits All Mention of Jewish Nazi Victims," *Israel National News Online* (August 14, 2012). Web.

8. "Russian Jews Win Rostov Holocaust Commemoration Fight," *Jewish Telegraphic Agency* (December 17, 2013). Web.

9. Elie Wiesel, *Night* (New York: Hill and Wang, 2006), xv.

10. René Major, "Love for Transference and Passion for Signifiers: Between Sabina S. and Anna G.," *Psychoanalytic Inquiry* 4, no. 2 (1984): 171–91.

11. Wiesel, xvii.

12. See William G. Doty, *Mythography: The Study of Myths and Rituals* (Birmingham: University of Alabama Press, 2000), 150.

13. Doty, 150.

14. By the intrinsically problematic term *Western,* I refer simply to the academic tradition stemming philosophically from Plato, circa 427–347 BC, as it permeated and influenced scholarship and scholars thereafter.

15. Bella Brodzki and Celeste Schenck, eds., *Life/Lines: Theorizing Women's Autobiography* (Ithaca: Cornell University Press, 1989), 287.

16. Marina Warner, *From the Beast to the Blonde: On Fairy Tales and Their Tellers* (New York: Farrar, Straus, and Giroux, 1996), 279, 239.

Chapter 1. Sabina Spielrein

1. For more bibliographic information, see Victor Ovcharenko, "Love, Psychoanalysis, and Destruction," *Journal of Analytical Psychology* 44, no. 3 (1999): 355–73. *PEP Archive*. Web.

2. Lisa Appignanesi and John Forrester, *Freud's Women: Family, Patients, Followers* (Other Press, 1992), 205.

3. Sabina Spielrein, "Contributions to the Knowledge of a Child's Soul" (1912/2013), my translation, 1; for original see Spielrein, "Beiträge zur Kenntnis der kindlichen Seele," *Zentralblatt für Psychoanalyse* 3 (1912): 57–72.

4. See Henry Zvi Lothane, "In Defense of Sabina Spielrein," *International Forum of Psychoanalysis* 5, no. 3 (1996): 203–17.

5. While the first occupation (1941) has been referenced as the site of her death—killed alongside other Jewish individuals in a synagogue—recent scholarship suggests her murder coincides with the brutal violence occurring during the second occupation in 1942.

6. See Viktor Frankl, *Man's Search for Meaning* (Boston: Beacon, 2006), "Preface."

7. Chapter 6 unpacks these epithets as related to sociohistorical gendered constructions.

8. John Kerr, *A Most Dangerous Method: The Story of Jung, Freud, and Sabina Spielrein* (New York: Vintage, 1994), 13.

9. Ibid.

10. Ibid., 15.

11. Johannes Cremerius, "Foreword to Carotenuto's *Tagebuch einer Heimlichen Symmetrie*," in *Sabina Spielrein: Forgotten Pioneer of Psychoanalysis*, ed. Coline Covington and Barbara Wharton. (New York: Routledge, 2003), 77.

12. See Covington and Wharton, eds., *Sabina Spielrein: Forgotten Pioneer of Psychoanalysis.*

13. See "Burghölzli Hospital Records of Sabina Spielrein," trans. Dorothee Steffens and Barbara Wharton, *Journal of Analytical Psychology* 46, no. 1 (2002): 28–29.

14. For example, see Victor Ovcharenko, "Love, Psychoanalysis, and Destruction," *Journal of Analytical Psychology* 44, no. 3 (1999): 355–73.

15. William Wordsworth, "Ode on Intimations of Immortality [1807]," in *Recollections from Early Childhood* (HardPress Publishing, 2012), 180–91.

16. Honoré de Balzac, *The Fatal Skin* (New York: Signet Classics, 1963), 14.
17. See Ovcharenko, "Love, Psychoanalysis," 356.
18. Balzac, 12.
19. See Carotenuto, ix and 187.
20. Ibid., ix.
21. *Tagebuch*, 85–86.
22. Carotenuto, 175.
23. Letter from Freud to Spielrein on June 20, 1913: see *Tagebuch* 117.
24. Carotenuto 187/158.
25. Ibid., 187.
26. Ibid., 158.
27. Ibid., 151.
28. See Major, "Love for Transference," 172, 190.
29. See "agent provocateur" in the *Oxford English Dictionary*.
30. See Major, "Love for Transference," 171.
31. Ibid., 172.
32. Ibid., 173; *Freud/Jung Letters*, 236.
33. See Lothane, "In Defense."
34. *Tagebuch*, 86.
35. See Bruno Bettelheim, "A Secret Asymmetry," in *Freud's Vienna & Other Essays* (New York: Vintage, 1989), 71.
36. *Tagebuch*, 87.
37. Bettelheim, 73.
38. See Major, "Love for Transference," 174.
39. Pamela White Hadas, "Jung and Easily Freudened': Sabina Spielrein's Analysis," in *Self Evidence: A Selection of Verse 1977–1997* (Evanston: Northwestern University Press, 1998). 177.
40. Major, "Love for Transference," 176.
41. James, *Healing Fiction*, 40.
42. Major, "Love for Transference," 176.
43. Ibid., 180.
44. Rosemary Balsam, "Women of the Wednesday Society: The Presentations of Drs. Hilferding, Spielrein, and Hug-Hellmuth," *American Imago* 60, no. 3 (2003): 304.
45. Ibid.
46. See Ernst Federn and Herman Nunberg, eds., *Minutes of the Vienna Psychoanalytic Society Volume IV: 1912–1918*, trans. M. Nunberg (New York: International Universities Press, 1975), 79.
47. Dan Agin, *An Evil Age: An Essay on Marriage and Sex in the Victorian Era* (Spectrum Focus, 2012); Kindle file, n.p.
48. Ibid.
49. William Acton, *The Functions and Disorders of the Reproductive Organs* (Lindsay and Blakiston, 1867), 102.
50. See Federn and Nunberg, *Minutes of the Vienna Psychoanalytic Society Volume I: 1906–1908*, trans. M. Nunberg (New York: International Universities Press, 1962), 199.

51. Ibid., 197.
52. Balsam, "Women of the Wednesday," 315.
53. Ibid., 320.
54. Ibid. 317.
55. Ibid.
56. See Carotenuto in 1982; Kerr in 1994.
57. Federn and Nunberg, *Minutes of the Vienna Psychoanalytic Society Volume III*, 329; Balsam, "Women of the Wednesday," 321.
58. Balsam, "Women of the Wednesday," 320.
59. Ibid., 316.
60. Mireille Cifali, "Sabina Spielrein, Woman Psychoanalyst: Another Picture," *Journal of Analytical Psychology* 46, no. 1 (2001): 135; for Spielrein's original words see Brinkmann and Bose, "Referat zur Psychoanalyse," 1986.
61. See Kerr, 496.
62. Balsam, "Women of the Wednesday," 317.
63. Balsam, "Women of the Wednesday," 316.
64. See Ovcharenko, "Love, Psychoanalysis," 360; Carotenuto, 158.
65. Sylvia Plath, "Edge," in *Ariel* (New York: HarperPerennial, 1961), 84.
66. See Carotenuto, 150.
67. Ovcharenko, "Love, Psychoanalysis," 359.
68. Alison Rose, *Jewish Women in Fin de Siècle Vienna* (Austin: University of Texas Press, 2008), 158.
69. Ibid.
70. See Brian Skea, "Sabina Spielrein: Out from the Shadow of Jung and Freud," *Journal of Analytical Psychology* 51, no. 4 (2006): 527–52. Web.
71. James Hillman, *The Myth of Analysis: Three Essays in Archetypal Psychology* (HarperPerennial, 1992), 118; additionally, see Skea, "Sabina Spielrein."
72. Spielrein, *On the Psychological Content of a Case of Schizophrenia* (Dementia Praecox), 1911; see Skea, 536, for translation.
73. Jung, *Man and His Symbols*, 32.
74. Ibid.
75. Skea, "Sabina Spielrein," 540.
76. Jung, *Symbols of Transformation*, *CW* 5 (Princeton: Princeton University Press, 1912/1953) 328n; see for numerous references to Spielrein's case study and "Destruction" article.
77. Skea, "Sabina Spielrein," 541.
78. Jane Ellen Harrison's *Prolegomena to the Study of Greek Religion* (1903) would be another striking example, written from the lens of anthropology, ritual studies, and classical studies.
79. See Lothane, "In Defense," 215.
80. Ovcharenko, "Love, Psychoanalysis," 363.
81. See *Tagebuch*, 79 [*Fortsetzung folgt*].
82. Ibid.
83. See Cifali, "Sabina Spielrein, Woman Psychoanalyst: Another Picture," 129.

84. *Tagebuch*, 64.

85. Cifali, "Another Picture," 131.

86. See Ovcharenko, "Love, Psychoanalysis," 365, for context.

87. *Tagebuch*, 49.

88. See Ovcharenko in 1999; Richebächer in 2003.

89. See Bernard Minder, *Sabina Spielrein as C. G. Jung's Patient at the Burghölzli* (1992 Thesis); see Ovcharenko, "Love, Psychoanalysis," 365.

90. Martin Miller, *Freud and the Bolsheviks: Psychoanalysis in Imperial Russia and the Soviet Union* (New Haven: Yale University Press, 1998), 45.

91. Ibid., 59.

92. Ibid., 60.

93. Ibid.

94. Alexander Etkind, *Eros of the Impossible: The History of Psychoanalysis in Russia* (WestView, 1997), 200.

95. Ibid., 211, 349.

96. See Martin Miller, "Freudian Theory Under Bolshevik Rule," *Slavic Review* (Winter 1985): 641; for further context see Etkind, 215.

97. See Etkind, 80, 165.

98. See Ovcharenko, "Love, Psychoanalysis," 366.

99. See Timothy Snyder, *Bloodlands: Europe Between Hitler and Stalin* (New York: Basic Books, 2012), 72.

100. Etkind, 272.

101. Ibid., 5, 350.

102. Ibid., 217.

103. See Hirshfeld, "Babi Yar."

104. Covington, "Introduction," in *Sabina Spielrein: Forgotten Pioneer of Psychoanalysis*, 13.

105. Ibid.

106. Ovcharenko, "Love, Psychoanalysis," 367.

107. Ibid., 368.

108. Ibid.

109. Covington, 13.

110. Ibid.

111. Skea, "Sabina Spielrein," 529.

112. Plath, *Ariel*, 84.

113. Christine Ruane, *The Empire's New Clothes: A History of the Russian Fashion Industry, 1700–1917* (New Haven: Yale University Press, 2009), 209–10.

114. Etkind, 176.

115. Ibid., 4.

116. Ibid., 61.

117. Ibid., 177.

118. See Sabina Spielrien, "Destruction as the Cause of Coming into Being" [1912], *Journal of Analytical Psychology* 39 (1994): 155–86.

119. See Etkind, 177.

120. Snyder, 230.

121. Tom Kirsch, "Two Pieces on the Movie: *A Dangerous Method*," *Jung Society of Washington* (11 March 2012); Web.

122. Skea, "Sabina Spielrein," 548.

123. Gottfried Heuer, " 'Soul Murder' and 'The Birth of Intersubjectivity' in David Cronenberg's *A Dangerous Method*," *Journal of Analytical Psychology* 57, no. 5 (2012); draft copy used here, from personal correspondence, 7.

124. Ibid.

125. *Tagebuch*, 45.

126. See Etkind, 177.

127. See chapter 3 for further discussion on abuse in therapy as related to "unconscious" desires.

128. See chapter 6 for a look at aspects of feminism, psychoanalysis, and oppression in revolutionary Russia solely in relation to Spielrein.

129. Theodore S. Hamerow, *Why We Watched: Europe, America, and the Holocaust* (New York: W. W. Norton, 2008), 394.

130. Ibid., 393.

131. Ilya Ehrenburg and Vasily Grossman, *The Black Book: The Ruthless Murder of Jews by German-Fascist Invaders Throughout the Temporarily-Occupied Regions of the Soviet Union and in the Death Camps of Poland During the War of 1941–1945* (Holocaust Library, 1980), 258.

132. Ibid., 261.

Chapter 2. Trauma, Transference, and Suppression

1. See Sigmund Freud and C. G. Jung, *The Freud/Jung Letters: The Correspondence Between Sigmund Freud and C. G. Jung*, ed. William McGuire, trans. Ralph Manheim and R. F. C. Hull (Princeton: Princeton University Press, 1974), 12–13.

2. Etkind, 125.

3. Marie-Louise Von Franz, *Alchemy: An Introduction to the Symbolism and the Psychology* (Inner City Books, 1980), 90.

4. C. G. Jung, "The Psychology of the Transference," trans. R. F. C. Hull, in *The Collected Works of C. G. Jung,* vol. 16 (Princeton: Princeton University Press, 1966), para 358; C. G. Jung, "Psychology and Alchemy," trans. R. F. C. Hull, in *The Collected Works of C. G. Jung,* vol. 12 (Princeton: Princeton University Press, 1953/1980), para 43.

5. Von Franz, *Alchemy*, 58.

6. See Carotenuto in 1982; Kerr in 1993; Covington and Wharton in 2003; Skea in 2003.

7. See Susan Sellers, ed., *The Hélène Cixous Reader* (Routledge, 1994), 3.

8. Gray Kochhar-Lindgren, *Narcissus Transformed: The Textual Subject in Psychoanalysis and Literature* (University Park: The Pennsylvania State University Press, 1993), 3.

9. Ibid., 17.

10. Laurence Coupe, *Myth* (New York: Routledge, 2009), 4.

11. Richard Palmer, *Hermeneutics* (Evanston: Northwestern University Press, 1969), 43.

12. Coupe, 15.

13. Palmer, 44.

14. Aristotle, *Poetics*, trans. S. H. Butcher (New York: Hill and Wang, 1961), 81.

15. Brodzki and Schenck, 281–82.

16. See *Center for the Study of Women in TV and Film*.

17. Wendy Doniger, *The Implied Spider: Politics and Theology in Myth* (New York: Columbia University Press, 2010), 87.

18. Ibid., 122.

19. See Simone de Beauvoir, *The Second Sex* ([1949] New York: Vintage, 2009), 13.

20. Ibid., 161.

21. Doniger, 122.

22. Hélène Cixous and Catherine Clément, *The Newly Born Woman*, trans. Betsy Wing (Minneapolis: University of Minnesota Press, 1986), ix.

23. George Stroup, "Between Echo and Narcissus: the Role of the Bible in Feminist Theology," *Interpretation* 42, no. 1 (1988): 20.

24. Ibid., 21; see Ruether, *Sexism and God-Talk: Toward a Feminist Theology* (Boston: Beacon, 1983), 22 for insight into the view that patriarchal traditions require feminist critique.

25. Elisabeth Schüssler Fiorenza, *But She Said: Feminist Practices of Biblical Interpretation* (Boston: Beacon Press, 1992), 57.

26. See Stroup, 26.

27. Doty, 206–207.

28. *The Metamorphoses of Ovid*, trans. Allen Mandelbaum (New York: Harcourt, 1995), 90.

29. Ibid.

30. Ibid., 91.

31. Christine Downing, *The Goddess: Mythological Images of the Feminine* (Authors Choice Press, 2007), 70–71.

32. Ibid., 83.

33. Thomas Bulfinch, *Bulfinch's Mythology. All Three Volumes: The Age of Fable, The Age of Chivalry, Legends of Charlemagne* (CreateSpace Publishing, 2010 [Kindle file]), 55.

34. Ibid.

35. Ibid.

36. Ibid.

37. *Metamorphoses*, trans. Stanley Lombardo and W. R. Johnson (Indianapolis: Hackett, 2010), 78.

38. *Metamorphoses*, trans. Mandelbaum, 78.

39. Susan Griffin, *Woman and Nature: The Roaring Inside Her* (Sierra Club Books, 2000), 3.

40. Ibid., 16.

41. Ibid., 21.

42. Mandelbaum, 93.

43. Bulfinch, 55.

44. *Metamorphoses*, trans. David Raeburn (New York: Penguin, 2004), 3.390–91.

45. Mandelbaum, 93.

46. Lombardo, 77.

47. Lya Chapman, *Revisioning Echo: The Mythical Figure of Echo and Her Importance to Clinical Depth Psychology.* Diss. (Pacifica Graduate Institute, Ann Arbor: ProQuest, 2010), 62.

48. Irigaray, *This Sex*, 30.

49. Raeburn, 3.61.

50. Judith Greenberg, "The Echo of Trauma and the Trauma of Echo," *American Imago* 55, no. 3 (1998).

51. See ibid.

52. Ibid.

53. Kochhar-Lindgren, 17.

54. Ibid., 124.

55. Jerrine Greer, *From Echo to Embodied Voice as Song of the Soul: Finding Voice as a Midlife Woman.* Diss. (Pacifica Graduate Institute, Ann Arbor: ProQuest, 1998), 19.

56. Hillman, *The Myth of Analysis*, 110.

57. Greer, 20.

58. Greenberg, "Echo of Trauma."

59. Chapman, 52.

60. Ibid., 63.

61. Cixous and Clément, vii.

62. Greenberg, "Echo of Trauma."

63. Dennis Slattery, "Narcissus, Echo and Irony's Resonance," in *Harvesting Darkness: Essays on Literature, Myth, Film, and Culture* (iUniverse, 2006), 1.

64. Slattery, "Echo," 39.

65. See "pathos" in the *Oxford English Dictionary.*

66. Spielrein, "Extracts," 159; Novelist Arthur Helps (1813–1875) once stated: "Strength is born in the deep silence of long suffering hearts;" Galatians 5:22: "The fruit of the Spirit is love, joy, peace, [and] longsuffering" (*King James Version*).

67. Maryanne Hannan, "A Psychoanalytic Interpretation of Ovid's Myth of Narcissus and Echo," *Psychoanalytic Review* 79, no. 4 (1992): 555–75.

68. Ibid., 563.

69. Ibid., 564.

70. Ibid., 565.

71. Ibid., 561, 572.

72. William Shullenberger, "Tragedy in Translation: The Lady Echo's Song," *English Literary Renaissance* 33, no. 3 (2003): 405; Lombardo, 3.454.

73. Shullenberger, 406.

74. See Dean Davis, "Echo in the Darkness," *Psychoanalytic Review* 92, no. 1 (2005), 141.

75. Phyllis Chesler, *Women and Madness* [1972], 2nd ed. (New York: Palgrave Macmillan, 2005), 100.

76. Hélène Cixous, "The Laugh of the Medusa," trans. Keith Cohen and Paula Cohen, *Signs* 1, no. 4 (1976): 878.

77. Patricia Berry, *Echo's Subtle Body: Contributions to an Archetypal Psychology* (Spring Publications, 2008), 114.

78. Ibid., 107.

79. Greenberg, "Echo of Trauma."

80. Ovid, "Narcissus. Echo," in *Metamorphoseon: Liber III*, ed. Hugo Magnus, *The Perseus Project* (Tufts University), 3.360.

81. See Greenberg, "Echo of Trauma"; See Longus, *Daphnis and Chlöe.*

82. Irigaray, *Marine Lover*, 5.

83. Michael Snediker, "In the Echo Chamber," *English Language Notes* 50, no. 1 (2012): 336–37.

84. Chapman, 53.

85. Stevie Smith, "Not Waving but Drowning," in *The Norton Anthology of English Literature*, ed. Stephen Greenblatt (New York: Norton, 2006), 2374.

86. Berry, 116.

87. Ibid., 111.

88. Paul Johnston, *Echo: An Aspect of the Archetypal Dependent Personality.* Diss. (Pacifica Graduate Institute, Ann Arbor: ProQuest, 1999), iii.

89. D. Davis, 138.

90. Ibid., 139.

91. Irigaray, *Marine Lover*, 4.

92. James Hillman, "From Mirror to Window: Curing Psychoanalysis of its Narcissism," [1989] *City & Soul*, Uniform Edition Volume 2 ([Kindle file, Loc xxx] Spring Publications, 2013), Loc 896.

93. Ibid., Loc 945.

94. Ibid., Loc 968.

95. See Skea, "Sabina Spielrein," 531–32.

96. Kerr, 33.

97. Ibid., 68.

98. Spielrein's subsequent shame regarding sexuality is discussed in detail in Covington and Wharton, *Sabina Spielrein: Forgotten Pioneer of Psychoanalysis*, 106.

99. See Kerr, 35.

100. See Covington and Wharton, 86.

101. See Kerr, 33; See Jung, "On Cryptomnesia" (1905), *C.W.* 1. 98.

102. See Covington and Wharton, 86.

103. Ibid., 88.

104. See Janet Sayers, "Transforming At-one-Ment: Spielrein, Jung, Bion," *Psychoanalysis and History* 6, no. 1 (2004): 37–56.

105. See Covington and Wharton, 85.

106. Sayers, "At-one-Ment," 38.

107. See Bernard Minder, "A Document. Jung to Freud 1905: A Report on Sabina Spielrein," in *Sabina Spielrein: Forgotten Pioneer of Psychoanalysis* (New York: Routledge, 2003 [135–140]), 139.

108. See Henry Zvi Lothane, "Tender Love and Transference: Unpublished Letters of C. G. Jung and Sabina Spielrein [1999] (with an addendum/discussion)," in *Sabina Spielrein: Forgotten Pioneer of Psychoanalysis* (New York: Routledge, 2003), 203.

109. See Lothane, "Tender Love," 203.

110. Carotenuto, 157.

111. René Major, "Love for Transference and Passion for Signifiers: Between Sabina S. and Anna G," *Psychoanalytic Inquiry* 4, no. 2 (1984): 171.

112. Ibid., 172.

113. Ibid., 175.

114. Ibid., 176.

115. Carotenuto, 214.

116. See Heuer, 9.

117. Beauvoir, 58.

118. Carotenuto, 171.

119. Ibid., 157.

120. Cremerius, 78.

121. *Tagebuch*, 63.

122. Peter Rutter, "Lot's Wife, Sabina Spielrein, and Anita Hill: A Jungian Meditation on Sexual Boundary Abuse and Recovery of Lost Voices," in *Breach of Trust: Sexual Exploitation by Health Care Professionals and Clergy*, ed. John Gonsiorek (London: Sage, 1992/1995), 77.

123. Ibid., 77.

Chapter 3. An Affair Misremembered

1. *Tagebuch*, 93.

2. See *The Freud/Jung Letters*, 93.

3. C. G. Jung, "The Letters of C. G. Jung to Sabina Spielrein," trans. Barbara Wharton, *Journal of Analytical Psychology* 46 (2001): 177.

4. Ibid., 194.

5. Hillman, *The Myth of Analysis*, 113.

6. See Lothane, "Tender Love," 204; also see Sayers, "Transforming At-one-Ment" for extended analysis.

7. See Lothane, "Tender Love," for further context to Spielrein's letters.

8. Ibid., 205.

9. Cremerius, 63.

10. See Jo Collins and John Jervis, eds., *Uncanny Modernity: Cultural Theories, Modern Anxieties* (New York: Palgrave Macmillan, 2008), 153.

11. See William McGuire, ed., *The Freud/Jung Letters: Abridged* (New York: Penguin, 1979), 46.

12. Griffin, 85.

13. See *Freud/Jung Letters*, 236.

14. Ibid.

15. Ibid., 210.

16. Ibid., 231.
17. Collins and Jervis, 153.
18. Carotenuto, 114–15.
19. *Tagebuch*, 97.
20. Carotenuto, 114.
21. *Tagebuch*, 103.
22. See Beauvoir, 9.
23. *Tagebuch*, 44.
24. Ibid., 85.
25. Ibid., 89.
26. Covington, 1.
27. See Lothane, "Tender Love," 206.
28. *Tagebuch*, 94.
29. See Madeleine Gobeil, "Simone de Beauvoir, The Art of Fiction No 35," *The Paris Review* 34 (1964).
30. See Lothane, "In Defense"; see Lothane's 2016 article on Spielrein, Jung, and the myth of Siegfried for his interpretation of the "scandal," the "love cure," and free association in an entirely different light: *International Forum of Psychoanalysis* 25, no. 1 (2016): 40–49.31. *Tagebuch*, 92.
32. *Tagebuch*, 95.
33. See Lothane, "In Defense;" see Ronald Hayman, *A Life of Jung* (New York: W. W. Norton, 1999), 106.
34. Bettelheim "A Secret Asymmetry," 75.
35. A slap in the face; see letter dated June 12, 1909, *Tagebuch*, 91.
36. Carotenuto, 120, see *Tagebuch*, 117–18.
37. *Tagebuch*, 84.
38. Ibid., 89.
39. Lothane, "Tender Love," 222.
40. Ibid.
41. Ibid.
42. *Tagebuch*, 102.
43. Erica Jong, "Autobiographical," in *Half-Lives* (New York: Holt, 1971), 71.
44. Balsam, "Women of the Wednesday," 319.
45. Hillman, *Myth of Analysis*, 111–12.
46. Marion Woodman, *The Pregnant Virgin* (Inner City Books, 1985), 48.
47. Carotenuto, 172.
48. Ibid., 171.
49. See Kerr, 170.
50. Carotenuto, 169.
51. Ibid., 177.
52. Jung to Freud, 10 October 1907. See *Freud/Jung Letters*, 93.
53. Kerr, 171.
54. Balsam, "Women of the Wednesday," 321.
55. Gary Schoener, "Historical Overview," in *Breach of Trust: Sexual Exploitation by Health Care Professionals and Clergy* (Sage, 1995), 95.

56. Carotenuto, 219.
57. See Schoener, 10.
58. Bettelheim, 79–80.
59. Heuer, "Soul Murder," 1.
60. Ibid., 16.
61. Ibid., 7.
62. Rutter, 79.
63. John Haule, *The Love Cure: Therapy Erotic and Sexual* (Spring Publications, 1996), 46, 164.
64. Ibid., 55.
65. See ibid., 146; see Chesler 194.
66. Haule, *Love Cure*, 146.
67. Ibid., 13.
68. Ibid., 167.
69. Ibid., 83.
70. Chesler, 206.
71. See *RAINN*, "Sexual Exploitation by Helping Professionals."
72. Lothane, "In Defense," 215.
73. Haule, *Love Cure*, 84.
74. Chesler, 199–200.
75. *Tagebuch*, 53; see Carotenuto, 20, for his translation.
76. See Chesler, 200.
77. Ibid., 203.

Chapter 4. Writing as a Way of Coming into Being

1. Doty, 19.
2. Brodzki and Schenck, 1.
3. Robert Ellwood, *The Politics of Myth: A Study of C. G. Jung, Mircea Eliade, and Joseph Campbell* (Albany State University of New York Press, 1999), 37.
4. Estelle C. Jelinek, *The Tradition of Women's Autobiography; From Antiquity to the Present* (Twayne, 1988), 13.
5. Shari Benstock, "Authorizing the Autobiographical," in *The Private Self: Theory and Practice of Women's Autobiographical Writings*, ed. Shari Benstock (Chapel Hill: University of North Carolina Press, 1988), 1.
6. Carolyn Heilbrun, "Non-Autobiographies of 'Privileged' Women: England and America," in *Life/Lines: Theorizing Women's Autobiography*, ed. Bella Brodzki and Celeste Schenck (Ithaca: Cornell University Press, 1989), 66.
7. See Benstock, 15, 16.
8. Brodzki and Schenck, 1.
9. Benstock, 2.
10. Ibid., 2–3.
11. Ibid., 4.
12. Ibid., 5

13. Ibid., 35.
14. Ibid., 5–6.
15. Ibid., 7, 14.
16. Katherine Goodman, "Elisabeth to Meta: Epistolary Autobiography and the Postulation of the Self," in *Life/Lines: Theorizing Women's Autobiography*, ed. Bella Brodzki and Celeste Schenck (Ithaca: Cornell University Press, 1989), 307.
17. Benstock, 35.
18. Susan Friedman, "Women's Autobiographical Selves," in *The Private Self: Theory and Practice of Women's Autobiographical Writings*, ed. Shari Benstock, ed., (Chapel Hill: University of North Carolina Press, 1988), 34.
19. Ibid., 35.
20. Ibid., 37.
21. Ibid., 38.
22. See chapters 6 and 7 where I continue to address these issues in light of gendered labels used against Spielrein.
23. Carotenuto, xvi.
24. Ibid., 149, 158, 145.
25. Woodman, 9.
26. Ibid.
27. *Tagebuch*, 35.
28. Ibid.
29. Hélène Cixous and Susan Sellers, *The Hélène Cixous Reader*, ed. Susan Sellers (New York: Routledge, 1994), 95.
30. Anaïs Nin, *The Diary of Anaïs Nin Volume One: 1931–1934*, ed. Gunther Stuhlmann (New York: Harvest, 1966), 47.
31. *Tagebuch*, 36 (September 1909).
32. Peter Nansen, *Love's Trilogy; Julie's Diary, Marie, God's Peace* [1908], trans. Julia Le Gallienne (John W. Luce, 2014), 3.
33. *Tagebuch*, 36–37.
34. Percy Bysshe Shelley, "Ode to the West Wind," in *The Complete Poetical Works of Percy Bysshe Shelley* (Thomas Y. Crowell, 1839), 24–25.
35. *Tagebuch*, 38.
36. Ibid., 40–41.
37. Nin, 42.
38. *Tagebuch*, 42.
39. Ibid., 43.
40. Ibid., 43–44.
41. Ibid., 45.
42. Ibid., 48.
43. Ibid., 50.
44. Ibid., 52.
45. Von Franz, *Alchemy*, 128.
46. Anthony Storr, ed, *The Essential Jung: Selected Writings* (Princeton; Princeton University Press, 1983), 21.
47. See Downing, *The Goddess*, 160.

48. Diane Di Prima, "La Loba," in *Loba* (New York: Penguin, 1998), 67–68.

49. Downing, *The Goddess*, 159, 163.

50. Ibid., 163.

51. Clarissa Pinkola Estés, *Women Who Run with the Wolves* (New York: Ballantine Books, 1992), 26.

52. Ibid., 10.

53. Ibid.

54. James Joyce, *Ulysses* (New York: Vintage, 1990 [1934]), 783.

55. Carotenuto, 188.

56. *Tagebuch*, 149–50 (December 20, 1917).

57. Carotenuto, 188.

58. Theodor Abt and Erik Hornung, *Knowledge for the Afterlife: The Egyptian Amduat—A Quest for Immortality* (Living Human Heritage, 2003), 25.

59. Ibid., 84.

60. Ibid., 92, 104.

61. R. T. Rundle Clark, *Myth and Symbol in Ancient Egypt* (London: Thames and Hudson, 1991), 140, 84.

62. Ibid., 256.

63. Von Franz, *Alchemy*, 73, 88.

64. Ibid., 98.

65. Jean Chevalier and Alain Gheerbrant, eds., *The Dictionary of Symbols*, 2nd ed. (New York: Penguin, 1996), 903–904.

66. Ibid., 904–905.

67. *Tagebuch*, 54 (October 18, 1910).

68. Ibid.

69. W. C. Sawyer, *Teutonic Legends in the Nibelungen Lied and The Nibelungen Ring* [1904] (University Press of the Pacific, 2003), 3.

70. Ibid., 278.

71. Freda Winworth, *The Epic of Sounds* [1897] (University of California Libraries Reprint, 2014), 73.

72. Ibid., 111.

73. Sawyer, 31.

74. Sawyer, 31.

75. Bulfinch, *Bulfinch's Mythology*.

76. *Tagebuch*, 56–57.

77. Simone de Beauvoir, *The Second Sex* [1949], trans. Constance Borde and Sheila Malovany-Chevallier (New York: Vintage, 2009), Kindle file, loc x.

78. *Tagebuch*, 58–59.

79. Julian of Norwich, *Revelations of Divine Love* (New York: Penguin, 1999), 4.

80. Teresa of Ávila, *Interior Castle*, trans. E. Allison Peers (New York: Dover Publications, 2007), Kindle file, loc 65.

81. *Tagebuch*, 70.

82. Ibid., 73.

83. *The Love Letters of a Portuguese Nun* [1669], trans. Guido Waldman (Harvill Press, 1996), 45.

84. Sylvia Plath, *The Unabridged Journals of Sylvia Plath, 1950–1962* (Garden City, Anchor Books, 2000), 512.

85. *Tagebuch*, 74–75 (Feburary, 1911).

86. H. D., *HERmione* (New York: New Directions, 1981), 4.

87. *Tagebuch*, 77.

88. Ibid., 76–77.

89. Ibid., 77.

90. Ibid., 78.

91. Ibid., 80 [*Nachts—"Freud"* . . .].

92. See above.

93. Adolf Guggenbühl-Craig, *From the Wrong Side: A Paradoxical Approach to Psychology*, trans. Gary V. Hartman (Spring Publications, 2007), 37.

Chapter 5. Sabina Speilrein in Academia

1. *Tagebuch*, 101 (fragment, 1909).
2. Ibid., 63.
3. See Carotenuto, 110.
4. See Spielrein, "Extracts," 167.
5. Ibid., 156.
6. Ibid., 157.
7. See ibid.
8. See ibid., 158.
9. Ibid.
10. Ibid.
11. Spielrein, "Extracts," 159.
12. Joseph Campbell, *Reflections on the Art of Living: A Joseph Campbell Companion*. (New York: HarperCollins, 1991), 53.
13. Spielrein, "Extracts," 159.
14. Ibid.
15. Ibid., 160.
16. Ibid., 161.
17. See ibid.
18. Immanuel Kant, *The Critique of Judgment* (Oxford: Oxford University Press, 1973), 83.
19. Ibid.
20. Spielrein, "Extracts," 159.
21. Ibid., 161.
22. Ibid.
23. Freda Winworth, *The Epic of Sounds* [1897] (University of California Libraries Reprint, 2014), 112–13.
24. See Spielrein, "Extracts," 161.
25. Llewellyn Vaughan-Lee, *Sufism: The Transformation of the Heart* (Sufi Center, 1995), 21.

26. Spielrein, "Extracts," 163.
27. Ibid., 162.
28. See ibid., 161–62 for her expanded anaylsis.
29. Sarette Anne Horwitz Zecharia, *Mysterium Coniunctionis: The Meeting Ground of the Masculine and the Feminine* (Diss.) (Pacifica Graduate Institute, Ann Arbor: ProQuest, 2000), 18.
30. Ibid., 156.
31. Spielrein, "Extracts," 161.
32. Martin Buber, *I and Thou* (Martino Publishing, 2010), 11.
33. Ibid., 6, 11.
34. Ibid., 34.
35. Spielrein, "Extracts," 162.
36. Christine Downing, *Preludes: Essays on the Ludic Imagination* (iUniverse, 2005), 4.
37. Spielrein, "Extracts," 164.
38. Ibid., 157.
39. Sayers, "At-one-Ment," 52.
40. Spielrein, "Extracts," 165.
41. Ibid., 164; emphasis added.
42. Jung acted as one of her dissertation advisors (with Bleuler) and used her text as a reference to his 1912 *Symbols of Transformation*, as previously noted.
43. See Spielrein's dissertation, *On the Psychological Content of a Case of Schizophrenia (Dementia Praecox)*. Originally in *Jarbuch Für Psychoanalytische und Psychopathologische Forschungen* Volume 3, 329–400. Refer also to *Sämtliche Schriften II*, ed. Traute Hensch (Kore, Verlag, 1987/2002), 87–90.
44. Spielrein, *Schriften II*, 91.
45. Ibid., 91.
46. Ernst Federn and Herman Nunberg, *Minutes of the Vienna Psychoanalytic Society Volume III: 1910–1911*, trans. M. Nunberg (New York: International Universities Press, 1974), 316.
47. See Adrian Carr and Cheryl A. Lapp, *Leadership is a Matter of Life and Death: The Psychodynamics of Eros and Thanatos Working in Organisations* (London: Palgrave Macmillan, 2006), 63.
48. Todd Dufresne, *Tales from the Freudian Crypt: The Death Drive in Text and Context* (Stanford: Stanford University Press, 2000), 22.
49. See Carr and Lapp, 63.
50. See Federn and Nunberg, *III*, 335.
51. Ibid., 332.
52. Ibid.
53. Ibid., 333.
54. Ibid., 330.
55. See ibid., 330–31.
56. Spielrein's article as printed in the *Jahrbuch*, an international psychology journal, was the first research paper submitted by a Russian contributor.

57. Spielrein, "Die Destruktion als Ursache des Werdens," ed. Eugen Bleuler and Sigmund Freud, *Jahrbuch Für Psychoanalytische* 4, no. 1 (1912): 466. *Internet Archive.*
58. Spielrein, "Destruction," 184.
59. Ibid., 155.
60. Ibid.
61. Ibid., 165.
62. Ibid., 156.
63. See ibid.
64. See ibid., 165; see W. Stekel, "Beiträge zur Traumdeutung," *Jahrbuch für Psychoanalytische und Psychopathologische Forschungen* 1 (1909): 458.
65. Spielrein, "Destruction," 165.
66. Ibid.
67. Julian of Norwich, *Revelations of Divine Love* (New York: Penguin, 1999), 6.
68. Ibid.
69. Ibid., 32.
70. The Portuguese Nun, *The Love Letters of a Portuguese Nun* [1669], trans. Guido Waldman (Harvill Press, 1996), 22.
71. Georges Bataille, *Erotism: Death and Sensuality* [1957], trans. Mary Dalwood, (San Francisco: City Lights Books, 1986), 11.
72. See Michael Freze, *They Bore the Wounds of Christ: The Mystery of the Sacred Stigmata* (Our Sunday Visitor Publishing, 1989), 232.
73. Ibid., 231.
74. Ibid., 232–34.
75. Caroline Walker Bynum, *Fragmentation and Redemption: Essays on Gender and the Human Body in Medieval Religion* (Zone Books, 1992), 66.
76. Spielrein, "Destruktion," 469.
77. Spielrein, "Destruction," 159.
78. Ibid., 163.
79. Spielrein, "Destruktion," 472.
80. Spielrein, "Destruction," 160.
81. Spielrein, "Destruktion," 471.
82. Spielrein, "Destruction," 162.
83. Ibid., 163.
84. Spielrein, "Destruktion," 491.
85. Spielrein, "Destruction," 163.
86. Ibid.
87. Spielrein, "Destruktion," 476.
88. Spielrein, "Destruction," 165.
89. Spielrein, "Destruktion," 471.
90. Hillman, *The Myth of Analysis*, 146–47.
91. Freud, *BPP*, Loc 732.
92. Hillman, *The Myth of Analysis*, 158, 141.
93. Spielrein, "Destruction," 166.
94. Ibid.

95. Ibid., 167.
96. Ibid., 169.
97. Hillman, *The Myth of Analysis*, 281.
98. Ibid., 280.
99. Spielrein, "Destruction," 169–70.
100. Ibid., 172.
101. Ibid.
102. Ibid., 173.
103. Ibid.
104. Spielrein, "Destruktion," 490.
105. Campbell, *Reflections*, 51–52.
106. Ginette Paris, *Heartbreak: Recovering From Lost Love and Mourning* (Mill City, 2011), 5.
107. Spielrein, "Destruction," 175.
108. Ibid., 179.
109. Ibid., 175.
110. Ibid.
111. Ibid., 179.
112. Ibid., 167.
113. Sayers, "At-One-Ment," 53.
114. Spielrein, "Destruction," 177.
115. Ibid., 178.
116. Joseph Campbell, *The Masks of God: Vol. 4, Creative Mythology* (Arkana, 1991), 176, 207.
117. Ibid., 186, 256.
118. Spielrein, "Extracts," 162.
119. Campbell, *Masks*, 195.
120. Ibid., 245.
121. Spielrein, "Destruction," 181.
122. Ibid., 182.
123. Ibid., 183.
124. Ibid.
125. Spielrein, "Destruktion," 502.
126. Ibid., 503.
127. Carly Knapp, *Eros and Thanatos: A Figuration of Death as an Imaginal Presence in Dialogue with Depth Psychology* (Diss.) (Pacifica Graduate Institute, Ann Arbor: ProQuest, 2005), 20.
128. Ibid., 20, 24.
129. Ibid., 34.
130. See Freud, *BPP*, Loc 732.
131. Ibid., Loc 589.
132. Ibid., Loc 603.
133. Ibid., Loc 606.
134. Ibid., Loc 676.
135. Ibid., Loc 732.

136. Ibid., Loc 695.
137. Ibid., Loc 732, 750.
138. Ibid., Loc 512.
139. See Carr and Lapp, 61, their translation of her article.
140. Freud, *BPP*, Loc 852.
141. Jessica Benjamin, *The Bonds of Love: Psychoanalysis, Feminism, and the Problem of Domination* (New York: Pantheon: 1988), 66.
142. Ibid., 74.
143. Mark Welman, "Thanatos and Existence: Towards a Jungian Phenomenology of the Death Instinct," in *Pathways into the Jungian World: Phenomenology and Analytical Psychology*, ed. Roger Brooke (New York: Routledge, 2000), 124.
144. Ibid., 125.
145. See Knapp, 62.
146. Ernest Becker, *The Denial of Death* (New York: Simon and Schuster, 1973), 99; Jean Laplanche, *Life and Death in Psychoanalysis* (Baltimore: The Johns Hopkins University Press, 1976), 106.
147. See Dufresne, 14.
148. Becker, 98.
149. Ibid., 99.
150. Welman, 125.
151. Ibid.
152. Jung, "Letters," 185.
153. Ibid.
154. Horace, *Ars Poetica*; see Tufts Digital Archive, *The Perseus Project.*
155. Knapp, 102.
156. See Balsam, "Women of the Wednesday," 321.
157. Spielrein, "Destruction," 158.
158. See Federn and Nunberg *III*, 332.
159. See Marija Gimbutas, *The Civilization of the Goddess*, and Cynthia Eller, *The Myth of Matriarchal Prehistory: Why an Invented Past Won't Give Women a Future*, for examples of arguments in support of and against (respectively) the historical validity of a matriarchal era.
160. Kerr, 502.
161. See ibid.; Dufresne 22.
162. Spielrein, "Destruktion," 489–90.
163. James Hillman, *Suicide and the Soul* (Spring Books, 1976), 80.
164. Skea, "Sabina Spielrein," 545.
165. See ibid.
166. See Balsam, "Women of the Wednesday," 323; see Federn and Nunberg *III*, 329.
167. Dufresne, 17.
168. Ibid., 21.
169. Ibid., 22.
170. Ibid.
171. Kerr, 502.

172. Dufresne, 22.

173. Ibid., 65, 72.

174. My translation; see Spielrein, *Schriften II*, 149.

175. See Balsam, "Women of the Wednesday," 320.

176. Ibid., 325.

177. Cifali, "Another Picture," 132.

178. See Doty, 194.

179. Ovcharenko, "Love, Psychoanalysis."

180. Ibid.

181. Henri Ellenberger, *The Discovery of the Unconscious: The History and Evolution of Dynamic Psychiatry* (New York: Basic Books, 1970), 515.

182. Ronald Britton, *Sex, Death, and the Superego: Experiences in Psychoanalysis* (Karnac Books, 2003), 2–3.

183. Ibid., 26.

184. Ibid., 38.

185. Ibid.

186. Ibid., 41.

187. My translation; see Paul Federn, "Sabina Spielrein: Die Destruktion als Ursache des Verdens," Review, *Zeitschrift* 1 (1913), 92.

188. Ibid., 89.

189. Ibid., 92.

190. Ibid., 90, 92.

191. Ibid., 92–93.

192. Otto Gross, *Selected Works 1901–1920* (Mindpiece, 2012), 262.

193. Ibid., 265.

194. See Ovcharenko, note 179, above.

195. Etkind, 52–53.

196. Carr and Lapp, 67.

197. John Launer, *Sex Versus Survival: The Story of Sabina Spielrein—Her Life, Her Ideas, Her Genius* (Lulu Self-Publishing, 2011), 41. New edition set to release 2016.

198. Spielrein, "Destruktion," 466–467.

199. Launer, 83.

200. Heuer, 10.

201. Etkind, 151.

202. Launer, 49.

203. Ibid., 101.

204. Patricia Hampl, *I Could Tell You Stories* (New York: W.W. Norton, 1999), 148.

205. Lynn Stuart Parramore, "Women, Sex, and Death—From Vampires to Psychoanalysis" (*Alternet*, 7 December 2011).

206. Ibid.; see Spielrein, "Destruction," 166.

207. Parramore, "Women, Sex, and Death."

208. See Federn and Nunberg *III*, 312.

209. Erin Collopy, "Blood Thirsty: Why Are Vampires Ruling Pop Culture?" *Texas Tech Today* (July 2, 2012) Web.

210. From the original French, "A propos du Sacrifice" in *Positif,* May 1986, 3–5. English translation taken from the booklet *The Sacrifice, An Artificial Eye Release* (1987) as reproduced on *Nostalghia.* Web.

211. Freud, *BPP*, Loc 814.

Chapter 6. Sabina Spielrein's Correspondence and Traps of the "Feminine"

1. Sidonie Smith, ed., *Women, Autobiography, Theory: A Reader* (Madison: University of Wisconsin Press, 1998), 176.

2. Sidonie Smith, ed., *A Poetics of Women's Autobiography: Marginality and the Fiction of Self-Representation* (Bloomington: Indiana University Press, 1987), 53.

3. See Joanna Russ, *How to Suppress Women's Writing* (Austin: University of Texas Press, 1983), 35.

4. See Mari Jo Buhle, *Feminism and its Discontents: A Century of Struggle with Psychoanalysis* (Cambridge: Harvard University Press, 1998), 329.

5. Jacques Lacan, *The Seminar, Book XX, Encore: On Feminine Sexuality, the Limits of Love and Knowledge* (New York: W. W. Norton, 1999), 73.

6. See Russ, 35.

7. Judith Butler, *Undoing Gender* (New York: Routledge, 2004), 198.

8. Ibid., 14.

9. Hélène Cixous and Susan Sellers, *The Hélène Cixous Reader* (New York: Routledge, 1994), 44.

10. Carotenuto, 42.

11. Spielrein, "Destruction as the Cause of Coming into Being, 161.

12. Jeanne Moll, "Prologue," in *Sabina Spielrein: Forgotten Pioneer of Psychoanalysis* (New York: Routledge, 2003), 15.

13. Spielrein, "Extracts," 159.

14. Carol P. Christ, Shawn Copeland, Mary Potter Engel et al., "Roundtable Discussion: Mysticism and Feminist Spirituality," *Journal of Feminist Studies in Religion* 24, no. 2 (2008): 167.

15. Spielrein, "Extracts," 164.

16. Ibid., 157.

17. Ibid., 158.

18. Ibid., 162.

19. Anthony Storr, ed., *The Essential Jung: Selected Writings* (Princeton: Princeton University Pree, 1983), 103; C. G. Jung, "Psychological Types" (1921), trans. R. F. C. Hull, in *The Collected Works of C. G. Jung* Vol. 6. Bollingen Series XX (Princeton: Princeton University Press, 1976), para 809.

20. Cifali, "Another Picture," 133.

21. Spielrein, "Extracts," 162.

22. Ibid., 164.

23. Ibid., 165.

24. Ibid., 167.
25. Ibid., 168.
26. Ibid., 169.
27. Aleksandr Pushkin, *Wondrous Moment: Selected Poetry of Alexandr Pushkin*, trans. Andrey Kneller (CreateSpace Publishing, 2008), Loc 401. Kindle file.
28. Spielrein, "Extracts," 167.
29. *Tagebuch*, 174; Carotenuto 85.
30. James Hillman, *The Myth of Analysis*, 108.
31. *Tagebuch*, 158.
32. See "Observations on Transference-Love" (1915).
33. Spielrein, "Extracts," 168, 170.
34. *Tagebuch*, 132–33.
35. Downing, *The Goddess*, 34, 49–50.
36. Claire Douglas, *Translate This Darkness: The Life of Christiana Morgan* (Princeton: Princeton University Press, 1997), 166.
37. Ibid.
38. Spielrein, "Extracts," 169.
39. This history is conflated with the construction of Boris (1598–1605) in Pushkin's play *Boris Godunov* (1831) and Modest Mussorgsky's opera of the same name (1873); Godunov reigned during the Time of Troubles, a dark period of famine and civil anarchy.
40. Spielrein, "Extracts," 169.
41. Ibid., 170.
42. Ibid.
43. Carotenuto, 122; Freud to Spielrein June 12, 1914.
44. Federn and Nunberg, *III*, 280.
45. *Tagebuch*, 106 (fragment, 1914).
46. See Kerr 227; see Rosemary Balsam, "Women of the Wednesday," 322.
47. Carotenuto, 124–25, August 2, 1919.
48. See Etkind, 61.
49. *Tagebuch*, 135, 137–38.
50. *Tagebuch*, 140.
51. Jung, "Letters,"188.
52. Ibid., 189.
53. *Tagebuch*, 143–45 (December 15, 1917).
54. Ibid., 148 (or, "side-awareness," *Seitenbewusstsein*).
55. Ibid., 145.
56. Ibid.
57. Sayers, "At-One-Ment," 49.
58. *Tagebuch*, 148.
59. Ibid., 149, 152.
60. Ibid., 148 (December 15, 1917).
61. Ibid., 152.
62. Ibid., 152, 153.

63. Jung, "Letters," 190.
64. *Tagebuch*, 161 (January 6, 1918).
65. Ibid.
66. Ibid., 169.
67. Jung, "Letters," 191–92.
68. Ibid.
69. *Tagebuch*, 174.
70. Ibid., 173.
71. Ibid., 176: December 20, 1917.
72. Ibid.
73. Ibid., 177.
74. Jung, "Letters," 192.
75. *Tagebuch* 178–79: 28 January, 1918, last letter.
76. Ibid., 180.
77. Kerr, 484.
78. Raymond de Saussure, the son of Ferdinand Saussure (1857–1913), the influential Swiss linguist and semiotician.
79. Carotenuto, 126 (June 12, 1922).
80. See Freud to Spielrein, June 12, 1922.
81. Carotenuto, 127 (February 9, 1923).
82. See *Freud/Jung Letters*, 469.
83. Cremerius, 77.
84. Cifali, "Another Picture," 130.
85. See Carotenuto 176, 178.
86. Hayman, 185.
87. Ibid.
88. André Haynal, *Psychoanalysis and the Sciences: Epistemology—History*, trans. Elizabeth Holder (Berkeley: University of California Press, 1993), 174.
89. Cremerius, 78.
90. *Tagebuch*, 64.
91. Sander Gilman, "The Image of the Hysteric," in *Hysteria Beyond Freud*, ed. Sander Gilman, Helen King, Roy Porter, G. S. Rousseau, and Elaine Showalter (Berkeley: University of California Press, 1993), 411.
92. Robert Ellwood, *The Politics of Myth: A Study of C. G. Jung, Mircea Eliade, and Joseph Campbell* (Albany: State University of New York Press, 1999), 25.
93. *Tagebuch*, 99.
94. See June 20, 1909, Spielrein to Freud.
95. See *Freud/Jung Letters*, 229.
96. Carotenuto, 121.
97. Beauvoir, Loc 168.
98. See *Tagebuch*, 49 ("*Eiene von den Vielen*").
99. Jung, "Letters," 192.
100. *Tagebuch*, 171–73.
101. C. G. Jung, "Answer to Job," trans. R. F. C. Hull, in *The Collected Works*

of C. G. Jung, vol. 11 (Princeton: Princeton University Press, 1973), para 718.

102. Adolf Guggenbühl-Craig, "Reflections on Jung and Anti-Semitism," in *Lingering Shadows: Jungians, Freudians, and Anti-Semitism*, ed. Aryeh Maidenbaum and Stephen Martin (Boston: Shambhala, 1991), 343.

103. Susan Griffin, *Woman and Nature: The Roaring Inside Her* (Sierra Club Books, 2000), 15.

104. Appignanesi and Forrester, 5, 164.

105. Ibid., 204–205.

106. A similar issue of objectification occurs in Maggy Anthony's *Jung's Circle of Women: The Valkyries* (1999).

107. Judith Herman, *Trauma and Recovery: The Aftermath of Violence—from Domestic Abuse to Political Terror* (New York: Basic Books, 1997), 14.

108. Carolyn Heilbrun, "Non-Autobiographies of 'Privileged' Women: England and America," in *Life/Lines: Theorizing Women's Autobiography*, ed. Bella Brodzki and Celeste Schenck (Ithaca: Cornell University Press, 1989), 73.

109. Linda Leonard in *Meeting the Madwoman* offers this definition: "The patriarchy . . . embodies the Western principles of linear rational thought, with its emphasis on order, abstractions, and judgment from above. Both women and men are influenced by patriarchal culture, although the patriarchy is experienced differently by men and women and women's experiences are different based on their race, class, and color" (16).

110. Showalter, 287.

111. Buhle, 3, 29.

112. Helen King, *The Disease of Virgins: Green Sickness, Chlorosis, and the Problems of Puberty* (New York: Routledge, 2004), 8.

113. Showalter, 305.

114. Mark Micale, "On the 'Disappearance' of Hysteria: A Study in the Clinical Deconstruction of a Diagnosis," *Isis* 84, no. 3 (1993): Web.

115. Jacqueline Simon Gunn and Brent Potter, "The Scarlet Label: Close Encounters with 'Borderline Personality Disorder,'" *Mad in America: Science, Psychiatry and Community* (Web, 2014).

116. Ibid.

117. R. D. Laing, *The Politics of Experience* (New York: Pantheon, 1967), 103.

118. Greg Mogenson, *The Dove in the Consulting Room: Hysteria and the Anima in Bollas and Jung* (Brunner-Routledge, 2003), 166.

119. Ibid., 168, 178.

120. Lyn Cowan, "Dismantling the Animus," *The Jung Page* (2003): 13.

121. Mogenson, 4.

122. William G. Doty, *Mythography: The Study of Myths and Rituals*, 2nd ed. (Birmingham: University of Alabama Press, 2000), 209.

123. James Hillman, *Alchemical Psychology*, Uniform Edition Volume 5 (Spring Publications, 2010), Kindle, Loc 6006.

124. Susan Rowland, *Jung: A Feminist Revision* (Polity, 2002), 76.

125. Von Franz, *Alchemy*, 156.

126. Janet Sayers, *Sexual Contradictions* (Tavistock, 1986), 101.

127. Jo Collins and John Jervis, eds., *Uncanny Modernity: Cultural Theories, Modern Anxieties* (London: Palgrave Macmillan, 2008), 146, 163.

128. *Tagebuch*, 94–95.

129. See Storr, 111; Jung, *CW* 9ii, para 27.

130. Jung's text is utilized within the context of its time and is not meant to offer a comprehensive review of Jung's thoughts on the feminine (or women) at large.

131. C. G. Jung, *Aspects of the Feminine*, trans. R. F. C. Hull, Bollingen Series XX (Princeton: Princeton University Press, 1982), 5.

132. Ibid., 10.

133. Ibid., 27.

134. Ibid., 29.

135. Ibid., 50.

136. Ibid., 58.

137. Cowan, 13.

138. Jung, *Aspects*, 59.

139. Ibid.

140. Sonu Shamdasani, "Memories, Dreams, Omissions," *Spring* 57 (1995): 115, 129, 133.

141. Gottfried Heuer, "Soul Murder' and 'The Birth of Intersubjectivity' in David Cronenberg's *A Dangerous Method*," *Journal of Analytical Psychology* 57, no. 5 (2012): 13.

142. Carotenuto, 166.

143. Spielrein, "Diaries 1906/07?" trans. Mireille Cifali, "Another Picture," 135.

144. Jung, "Letters," 175.

145. Claire Douglas, *The Woman in the Mirror: Analytical Psychology and the Feminine* (iUniverse, 2000), 86.

146. Douglas, *Mirror*, 210, 133.

147. Estella Lauter and Carol Schreier Rupprecht, *Feminist Archetypal Theory: Interdisciplinary Re-visions of Jungian Thought* (Knoxville: University of Tennessee Press, 1985), 60.

148. Ibid., 96.

149. Collins and Jervis, 157.

150. Kerr, 483.

151. Ibid., 487.

152. Karen Pechilis, "Devotional Subjectivity and the Fiction of Femaleness: Feminist Hermeneutics and the Articulation of Difference." *Journal of Feminist Studies in Religion* 30, no. 2 (2014): 114, 102.

Chapter 7. Sabina Spielrein

1. Etkind, 164.
2. Collins and Jervis, 162.
3. Benjamin, 87.

4. Ernst Federn and Herman Nunberg, *Minutes of the Vienna Psychoanalytic Society Volume IV: 1912–1918*, trans. M. Nunberg (New York: International Universities Press, Inc., 1975), 25.

5. Ibid., 55.

6. See Jane Ussher, "Health Check: Clash of the Orgasms, Clitoral vs. Vaginal," *The Conversation* (9 November 2014). Web.

7. Ibid.

8. On October 30, 1912, Lou Andreas-Salomé, a prominent figure in psychoanalysis on the topic of female eroticism, is mentioned as guest for the first time and Spielrein is not mentioned again; on October 8, 1913, noted scholar Hermine Hug-Hellmuth attends for the first time; see Federn and Nunberg, *IV*, 108 and 205.

9. Ibid., 78, 81.

10. Ibid., 80.

11. Ibid., 79.

12. Ibid.

13. Ibid.

14. Ibid., 81.

15. Ibid.

16. Susan Rowland, *Jung: A Feminist Revision* (Polity, 2002), 142.

17. See Balsam, "Women of the Wednesday," 327.

18. See Federn and Nunberg, *IV*, 85.

19. Ibid., 84–85.

20. Ibid., 85.

21. Balsam, "Women of the Wednesday," 323.

22. Chevalier and Gheerbrant, 845.

23. Ibid.

24. Audre Lorde, "Uses of the Erotic" (1978), in *Sister Outsider: Essays and Speeches* [1984] (The Crossing Press, 2007), 53.

25. See Hillman, *The Myth of Analysis*, 280; also discussed in chapter 5.

26. See Federn and Nunberg, *III*, 367.

27. Ibid., 40.

28. Carotenuto, 145.

29. Ibid., 137.

30. Spielrein, "Contributions to the Knowledge of a Child's Soul," my translation, 1 (in Appendix B); see Sabina Spielrein, "Beiträge zur Kenntnis der kindlichen Seele" (1912) via *Internet Archive*. Translated with the assistance of Annika Romero.

31. This is largely intrinsic to the Western women's liberation movement and based on the notion that the Goddess has been sublimated, oppressed, and repressed in patriarchal religion and culture, necessitating a "reclaiming" of these (female) figures and characteristics in modern society. For reference, a selection of early publications includes: Esther Harding's *Woman's Mysteries* (1971); Marija Gimbutas's *The Goddesses and Gods of Old Europe* (1974); Merlin Stone's *When God was a Woman* (1976); Christine Downing's *The Goddess* (1981); Jean Shinoda Bolen's *Goddesses in Everywoman* (1983); Ginette Paris's *Pagan Meditations* (1986); Starhawk's *The Spiral Dance* (1989); and Carol Christ's *Rebirth of the Goddess* (1997).

32. Downing, *Goddess*, 2, 7.
33. Spielrein, "Contributions," 5; my translation.
34. See Carotenuto, 139.
35. See Claire Douglas, *Mirror*, 96.
36. Ibid., 101.
37. Spielrein, "Contributions," 5; my translation.
38. *Literature Network Online*, public domain.
39. Spielrein, "Contributions," 6; my translation.
40. Ibid., 7.
41. Ibid., 8.
42. See Carotenuto, 138.
43. The pagination for this article is in accordance with my unpublished English translation of the work; the original, "Die Schwiegemutter," was first published in *Imago* Vol. 2 (1913): 589–92, and can be found in *Sämtliche Schriften II* (Kore, Verlag, 1987) and online via the *Internet Archive*. Translated with the assistance of Annika Romero.
44. Spielrein, "Mother-in-Law," 1–2.
45. Ibid., 2.
46. Ibid., 3.
47. Ibid.
48. Ibid., 4.
49. Nancy Chodorow, *Feminism and Psychoanalytic Theory* (New Haven: Yale University Press, 1991), 187.
50. Ibid., 194.
51. See my translation, Appendix B.
52. Etkind, 190.
53. Ibid., 198.
54. Appignanesi and Forrester, 223.
55. See Piaget, *The Language and Thought of the Child* (1926), where Spielrein is cited.
56. Etkind, 164.
57. See Carotenuto in 1982; see Skea, "Sabina Spielrein."
58. Sayers, "At-one-Ment," 52, her own translation of Spielrein 1920/1922.
59. Demaris Wehr, *Jung and Feminism: Liberating Archetypes* (Boston: Beacon Press, 1987), 118.
60. Barbara Wharton, "Part I: Comment on Spielrein's Paper 'The Origin of the Child's Words Papa and Mama,'" in *Sabina Spielrein: Forgotten Pioneer of Psychoanalysis* (New York: Routledge, 2003), 287.
61. Ibid., 287–88.
62. Sabina Spielrein, "Die Entstehung der kindlichen Worte Papa und Mama." *Imago* 8 (1922): 345–67. *Internet Archive*. Web. 346.
63. Ibid.
64. Sabina Spielrein, "The Origin of the Child's Words Papa and Mama: Some Observations on the Different Stages in Language Development," in *Sabina Spielrein: Forgotten Pioneer of Psychoanalysis*, trans. Barbara Wharton (New York: Routledge, 2003), 290.

65. Ibid.
66. Ibid., 291.
67. Ibid., 292.
68. Ibid., 293.
69. Ibid.
70. Ibid., 294.
71. Spielrein, "Die Entstehung," 353.
72. Spielrein, "Origin," 296.
73. Ibid.
74. Ibid., 297.
75. Ibid., 298.
76. Ibid.
77. Spielrein, "Die Entstehung," 365.
78. Dr. Hermine Hug-Hellmuth is considered one of the pioneers of child psychology, as already referenced briefly.
79. Spielrein, "Die Entsehung," 365.
80. Spielrein, "Origin," 303.
81. Ibid.
82. Spielrein, "Die Entstehung," 366–67.
83. Spielrein, "Origin," 303.
84. Federn and Nunburg, *III*, 303.
85. Rowland, 121; also see Sayers, "At one Ment" for another take on Spielrein's connection to Kristeva.
86. See Rowland, 121.
87. Barbara Alpern Engel, *Women in Russia, 1700–2000* (Cambridge: Cambridge University Press, 2004), 118.
88. M. Miller, 41.
89. Engel, 120.
90. Ibid., 112–13.
91. Alexandra Kollontai, "The New Woman," in *Selected Writings of Alexandra Kollontai*[1918], trans. Alix Holt (Allison and Busby, 1977).
92. Engel, 113.
93. Ibid., 195.
94. Ibid., 147.
95. For reference: *World War I: People, Politics, and Power* (1924).
96. Etkind, 131.
97. For reference: *Political Power in the U.S.S.R., 1917–1947: The Theory and Structure of Government in the Soviet State* (1948).
98. *Tagebuch*, 162–63 (January 6, 1918, Spielrein to Jung).
99. Etkind, 171.
100. Ibid., 173.
101. See ibid., 163; see James Rice, "Russian Stereotypes in the Freud-Jung Correspondence," *Slavic Review* 41, no. 1 (1982): 19–34.
102. See Spielrein, "L'Automobile—Symbole De La Puissance Mâle" and "Rêve et Vision Des Étoiles Filantes," both appearing in the *International Journal of Psychoanalysis* Vol. 4 (1923): 128–33.

103. M. Miller, 67–68.
104. Ibid., 61.
105. Ibid., 88.
106. Ibid., 69.
107. Ibid., 90.
108. According to Etkind, *Eros of the Impossible*, 172.
109. See Cremerius, 69.
110. Barbara Clements, *Bolshevik Women* (Cambridge: Cambridge University Press, 1997), 250.
111. Engel, 161.
112. Ann Taylor Allen, *Women in Twentieth-Century Europe* (London: Palgrave Macmillan, 2008), 20.
113. This resulted in more than one million casualties due to extreme starvation and violence; for reference: *Life and Death in Besieged Leningrad, 1941–44* (2005).
114. Taylor Allen, 71.
115. See Martin Gilbert, *The Holocaust: A History of the Jews of Europe During the Second World War* (New York: Holt, 1985), 387.
116. Ibid., 419.

Afterword

1. Federn and Nunberg, *III*, 280–81.
2. See Buhle, 55.
3. See Russ, 61.
4. Jean Baker Miller, *Toward a New Psychology of Women* (Boston: Beacon Press, 1986), 80.
5. Kerr, 479.
6. *Tagebuch*, 53–54.
7. Sabine Richebächer, "'In League with the Devil, and Yet You Fear Fire?' Sabina Spielrein and C. G. Jung: A Suppressed Scandal from the Early Days of Psychoanalysis," in *Sabina Spielrein: Forgotten Pioneer of Psychoanalysis*, trans. Covington and Wharton (New York: Routledge, 2003), 246–47.
8. Kirsch, "A Dangerous Method."
9. See Gert Sauer, "Sabina Spielrein and the Use of Symbols: Reflections of a Jungian Psychoanalyst," in *Barcelona '04: Edges of Experience: Memory and Emergence, Proceedings of the 16th International IAAP Congress for Analytical Psychology* DVD Supplement (Daimon Verlag, 2006).
10. See Sauer, "Symbols."
11. See Axel Hoffer, "Jung's Analysis of Sabina Spielrein and His Use of Freud's Free Association Method," *Journal of Analytical Psychology* 46 (2001), 123; Marcio Giovanetti, "S. Like Sabina. S. like Sabina, S. like Sergei: Brief Comments Regarding E. Márton's Film and G. Sauer's Paper," in *Barcelona '04.*
12. Greenberg, "Echo of Trauma."
13. See Lombardo, 3. 454.
14. Berry, 115.

15. Karl Kerényi, *Athene: Virgin and Mother in Greek Religion* (Spring Publications, 1998), 2.

16. See "Burghölzli Hospital Records of Sabina Spielrein," trans. Dorothee Steffens and Barbara Wharton, *Journal of Analytical Psychology* 46, no. 1 (2002): 28–29.

Bibliography

Abt, Theodor, and Erik Hornung. *Knowledge for the Afterlife: The Egyptian Amduat—A Quest for Immortality*. Living Human Heritage, 2003.

Agin, Dan. *An Evil Age: An Essay on Marriage and Sex in the Victorian Era*. Spectrum Focus, 2012. Kindle file.

Allain-Dupré, Brigitte. "Sabina Spielrein: A Bibliography." *Journal of Analytical Psychology* 49, no. 3 (2004): 421–33.

Allen, Ann Taylor. *Women in Twentieth-Century Europe*. Palgrave Macmillan, 2008.

Appignanesi, Lisa, and John Forrester. *Freud's Women: Family, Patients, Followers*. Other Press, 1992.

Aristotle. *Poetics*. Translated by S. H. Butcher. New York: Hill and Wang, 1961.

Balsam, Rosemary. "Women of the Wednesday Society: The Presentations of Drs. Hilferding, Spielrein, and Hug-Hellmuth." *American Imago* 60, no. 3 (2003): 303–42.

Bataille, Georges. *Erotism: Death and Sensuality*. Translated by Mary Dalwood. San Francisco: City Lights Books, 1986.

Becker, Ernest. *The Denial of Death*. New York: Simon and Schuster, 1973.

Benjamin, Jessica. *The Bonds of Love: Psychoanalysis, Feminism, and the Problem of Domination*. New York: Pantheon, 1988.

Benstock, Shari. "Authorizing the Autobiographical." In *The Private Self: Theory and Practice of Women's Autobiographical Writings*, edited by Shari Benstock, 1–34. Chapel Hill: University of North Carolina Press, 1988.

Berry, Patricia. *Echo's Subtle Body: Contributions to an Archetypal Psychology*. Dallas: Spring Publications, 2008.

———. "Rules of Thumb Towards an Archetypal Psychology Practice." In *Archetypal Psychologies: Reflections in Honor of James Hillman*, edited by Stan Marlan, 1–12. New York: Spring Publications, 2007.

Bettelheim, Bruno. "A Secret Asymmetry." In *Freud's Vienna & Other Essays*, 57–82. New York: Vintage, 1989

Britton, Ronald. *Sex, Death, and the Superego: Experiences in Psychoanalysis*. Karnac Books, 2003.

Brodzki, Bella, and Celeste Schenck. *Life/Lines: Theorizing Women's Autobiography*. Ithaca: Cornell University Press, 1989.

Brooke, Roger, editor. *Pathways into the Jungian World: Phenomenology and Analytical Psychology*. Routledge, 2000.

Brown, Norman O. *Life against Death*. 2nd ed. Hanover, NH: Wesleyan University Press, 1959.

Buber, Martin. *I and Thou*. Martino Publishing, 2010.

Buhle, Mari Jo. *Feminism and its Discontents: A Century of Struggle with Psychoanalysis*. Cambridge: Harvard University Press, 1998.

Bulfinch, Thomas. *Bulfinch's Mythology. All Three Volumes: The Age of Fable, The Age of Chivalry, Legends of Charlemagne*. CreateSpace Publishing, 2010.

"Burghölzli Hospital Records of Sabina Spielrein." Translated by Barbara Wharton. *Journal of Analytical Psychology* 46, no. 1 (2001): 15–42.

Butler, Judith. *Undoing Gender*. New York: Routledge, 2004.

Bynum, Caroline Walker. *Fragmentation and Redemption: Essays on Gender and the Human Body in Medieval Religion*. Zone Books, 1992.

Campbell, Joseph. *Reflections on the Art of Living: A Joseph Campbell Companion*. Edited by Diane Osbon. New York: HarperCollins, 1991.

———. *The Masks of God: Vol. 4, Creative Mythology*. Arkana, 1991.

Carotenuto, Aldo. *A Secret Symmetry: Sabina Spielrein between Jung and Freud. The Untold Story of the Woman Who Changed the Early History of Psychoanalysis*. Translated by Arno Pomerans, John Shepley, and Krishna Winston. New York: Pantheon Books, 1982.

Carr, Adrian, and Cheryl A. Lapp. *Leadership Is a Matter of Life and Death: The Psychodynamics of Eros and Thanatos Working in Organisations*. Palgrave Macmillan, 2006.

Carson, Anne. *Eros the Bittersweet*. Dalkey Archive Press, 1998.

Chapman, Lya. *Revisioning Echo: The Mythical Figure of Echo and Her Importance to Clinical Depth Psychology*. Diss. Pacifica Graduate Institute, 2010.

Chesler, Phyllis. *Women and Madness*. 2nd ed. Palgrave Macmillan, 2005.

Chevalier, Jean, and Alain Gheerbrant, eds. *The Dictionary of Symbols*. 2nd ed. Penguin, 1996.

Chodorow, Nancy. *Feminism and Psychoanalytic Theory*. New Haven: Yale University Press, 1991.

Christ, Carol P., Shawn Copeland, Mary Potter Engel et al. "Roundtable Discussion: Mysticism and Feminist Spirituality." *Journal of Feminist Studies in Religion* 24, no. 2 (2008): 143–87.

Cifali, Mireille. "Sabina Spielrein, Woman Psychoanalyst: Another Picture." *Journal of Analytical Psychology* 46 (2001).

Cixous, Hélène. "The Laugh of the Medusa." Translated by Keith Cohen and Paula Cohen. *Signs* 1, no. 4 (1976): 875–93.

———, and Catherine Clément. *The Newly Born Woman*. Translated by Betsy Wing. Minneapolis: University of Minnesota Press, 1986.

———, and Susan Sellers. *The Hélène Cixous Reader*. Edited by Susan Sellers. Routledge, 1994.

Claremont de Castillejo, Irene. *Knowing Woman: A Feminine Psychology*. Boston: Shambhala, 1997.

Clark, R. T. Rundle. *Myth and Symbol in Ancient Egypt*. New York: Thames and Hudson, 1991.
Clements, Barbara. *Bolshevik Women*. Cambridge: Cambridge University Press, 1997.
Clifton, Lucille. *The Collected Poems of Lucille Clifton: 1965–2010*. American Poets Continuum Series, Book 134, BOA Editions, 2012.
Collins, Jo, and John Jervis, eds. *Uncanny Modernity: Cultural Theories, Modern Anxieties*. Palgrave Macmillan, 2008.
Collopy, Erin. "Blood Thirsty: Why are Vampires Ruling Pop Culture?" *Texas Tech Today*, July 2, 2012.
Coupe, Laurence. *Myth*. Routledge, 2009.
Covington, Coline. "Introduction." In *Sabina Spielrein: Forgotten Pioneer of Psychoanalysis*, edited by Coline Covington and Barbara Wharton, 1–15. Routledge, 2003.
———, and Barbara Wharton, eds. *Sabina Spielrein: Forgotten Pioneer of Psychoanalysis*. Routledge, 2003. Original articles reproduced from special issue of *Journal of Analytical Psychology* 46, no. 1 (2001). A new edition of their title will be released in 2016.
Cowan, Lyn. "Dismantling the Animus." *The Jung Page*, November 22, 2003.
Cremerius, Johannes. "Foreword to Carotenuto's *Tagebuch einer Heimlichen Symmetrie*." In *Sabina Spielrein: Forgotten Pioneer of Psychoanalysis*, ed. Coline Covington and Barbara Wharton, 63–78. Routledge, 2003.
A Dangerous Method. Directed by David Cronenberg. Sony Pictures, 2011.
Davis, Dean. "Echo in the Darkness." *Psychoanalytic Review* 92, no. 1 (2005): 137–52.
De Balzac, Honoré. *The Fatal Skin*. New York: Signet Classics, 1963.
De Beauvoir, Simone. *The Second Sex*. Translated by Constance Borde and Sheila Malovany-Chevallier. New York: Vintage, 2009.
Di Prima, Diane. "La Loba." In *Loba*, 67–68. Penguin, 1998.
"Dia de los Muertos: Lovely Mexican Holiday Honors the Dead." *National Geographic Online*.
Doniger, Wendy. *The Implied Spider: Politics and Theology in Myth*. New York: Columbia University Press, 2010.
Doty, William G. *Mythography: The Study of Myths and Rituals*. 2nd ed. University of Alabama Press, 2000.
Douglas, Claire. *The Woman in the Mirror: Analytical Psychology and the Feminine*. iUniverse.com, 2000.
———. *Translate This Darkness: The Life of Christiana Morgan*. Princeton: Princeton University Press, 1997.
Downing, Christine. *Preludes: Essays on the Ludic Imagination*. iUniverse, 2005.
———. *The Goddess: Mythological Images of the Feminine*. Authors Choice Press, 2007.
Dufresne, Todd. *Tales from the Freudian Crypt: The Death Drive in Text and Context*. Stanford: Stanford University Press, 2000.
Ehrenburg, Ilya, and Vasily Grossman. *The Black Book: The Ruthless Murder of Jews by German-Fascist Invaders throughout the Temporarily-Occupied Regions of the Soviet Union and in the Death Camps of Poland during the War of 1941–1945*. Holocaust Library, 1980.

Eley, Geoff, and James Retallack, eds. *Wilhelminism and its Legacies: German Modernities, Imperialism, and the Meanings of Reform, 1890–1930*. Baghahn Books, 2008.

Ellenberger, Henri E. *The Discovery of the Unconscious: The History and Evolution of Dynamic Psychiatry*. New York: Basic Books, 1970.

Ellwood, Robert. *The Politics of Myth: A Study of C. G. Jung, Mircea Eliade, and Joseph Campbell.* Albany: State University of New York Press, 1999.

Engel, Barbara Alpern. *Women in Russia, 1700–2000.* Cambridge: Cambridge University Press, 2004.

Estés, Clarissa Pinkola. *Women Who Run with the Wolves.* New York: Ballantine Books, 1992.

Etkind, Alexander. *Eros of the Impossible: The History of Psychoanalysis in Russia*. WestView Press, 1997.

Federn, Ernst, and Herman Nunberg, eds. *Minutes of the Vienna Psychoanalytic Society Volume I: 1906–1908*. Translated by M. Nunberg. New York: International Universities Press, 1962.

———. *Minutes of the Vienna Psychoanalytic Society Volume II: 1908–1910*. Translated by M. Nunberg. New York: International Universities Press, 1968.

———. *Minutes of the Vienna Psychoanalytic Society Volume III: 1910–1911*. Translated by M. Nunberg. New York: International Universities Press, 1974.

———. *Minutes of the Vienna Psychoanalytic Society Volume IV: 1912–1918*. Translated by M. Nunberg. New York: International Universities Press, 1975.

Federn, Paul. "Sabina Spielrein: Die Destruktion als Ursache des Verdens." Review. *Zeitschrift*, vol. 1, 1913, 89–93; www.archive.org.

Fiorenza, Elisabeth Schüssler. *But She Said: Feminist Practices of Biblical Interpretation*. Boston: Beacon Press, 1992.

Freud, Sigmund. *Beyond the Pleasure Principle*. Acheron Press, 2012.

———. *Civilization and its Discontents*. New York: W. W. Norton, 2010.

———, and C. G. Jung. *The Freud/Jung Letters: The Correspondence between Sigmund Freud and C. G. Jung*. Edited by William McGuire. Translated by Ralph Manheim and R. F. C. Hull. Bollingen Series 64. Princeton: Princeton University Press, 1974.

Freze, Michael. *They Bore the Wounds of Christ: The Mystery of the Sacred Stigmata*. Our Sunday Visitor Publishing, 1989.

Friedman, Susan. "Women's Autobiographical Selves." In *The Private Self: Theory and Practice of Women's Autobiographical Writings*, edited by Shari Benstock, 34–63. Chapel Hill: University of North Carolina Press, 1988.

Gilbert, Martin. *The Holocaust: A History of the Jews of Europe during the Second World War.* New York: Holt, 1985.

Gilman, Sander. "The Image of the Hysteric." In *Hysteria beyond Freud*, edited by Sander Gilman, Helen King, Roy Porter, G. S. Rousseau, and Elaine Showalter, 345–453. Berkeley: University of California Press, 1993.

Giovanetti, Marcio. "S. Like Sabina. S. like Sabina, S. like Sergei: Brief Comments Regarding E. Márton's Film and G. Sauer's Paper." *Barcelona '04: Edges of Experience: Memory and Emergence, Proceedings of the 16th International IAAP Congress for Analytical Psychology*, edited by Lyn Cowan. Daimon Verlag, 2006.

Gobeil, Madeleine. "Simone de Beauvoir, The Art of Fiction No 35." *The Paris Review* 34 (1964); www.theparisreview.org/interviews/4444/the-art-of-fiction-no-35-simone-de-beauvoir.

Goethe, Johann Wolfgang. *Faust: Part One*. Translated by Philip Wayne. Penguin, 1949.

———. "The Erlking." *The Literature Network Online*, translated by Hyde Flippo; www.online-literature.com.

Gonsiorek, John, ed. *Breach of Trust: Sexual Exploitation by Health Care Professionals and Clergy*. Sage, 1995.

Goodman, Katherine. "Elisabeth to Meta: Epistolary Autobiography and the Postulation of the Self." In *Life/Lines: Theorizing Women's Autobiography*, edited by Bella Brodzki and Celeste Schenck, 306–20. Ithaca: Cornell University Press, 1989.

Graf-Nold, Angela. "The Zürich School of Psychiatry in Theory and Practice: Sabina Spielrein's Treatment at the Burghölzli Clinic in Zürich." In *Sabina Spielrein: Forgotten Pioneer of Psychoanalysis*, edited by Coline Covington and Barbara Wharton, 189–222. Routledge, 2003.

Greenberg, Judith. "The Echo of Trauma and the Trauma of Echo." *American Imago* 55, no. 3 (1998).

Greer, Jerrine. *From Echo to Embodied Voice as Song of the Soul: Finding Voice as a Midlife Woman*. Diss. Pacifica Graduate Institute, 1998.

Griffin, Susan. *Woman and Nature: The Roaring inside Her*. Sierra Club Books, 2000.

Gross, Otto. *Selected Works 1901–1920*. Mindpiece, 2012.

Guggenbühl-Craig, Adolf. "Reflections on Jung and Anti-Semitism." In *Lingering Shadows: Jungians, Freudians, and Anti-Semitism*, edited by Aryeh Maidenbaum and Stephen Martin, 341–49. Boston: Shambhala, 1991.

———. *From the Wrong Side: A Paradoxical Approach to Psychology*. Translated by Gary V. Hartman. Spring Publications, 2007.

Gunn, Jacqueline Simon, and Brent Potter. "The Scarlet Label: Close Encounters with 'Borderline Personality Disorder.'" *Mad in America: Science, Psychiatry, and Community*; www.madinamerica.com/2014/10/scarlet-label-close-encounters-borderline-personality-disorder/.

Gusdorf, George. "Conditions and Limits of Autobiography." In *Autobiography: Essays Theoretical and Critical*, edited by James Olney. Princeton: Princeton University Press, 1980.

H. D. *HERmione*. New York: New Directions, 1981.

Hadas, Pamela White. *Self-Evidence: A Selection of Verse 1977–1997*. Evanston: Northwestern University Press, 1998.

Hamerow, Theodore S. *Why We Watched: Europe, America, and the Holocaust*. New York: W. W. Norton, 2008.

Hampl, Patricia. *I Could Tell You Stories*. New York: W. W. Norton, 1999.

Hannan, Maryanne. "A Psychoanalytic Interpretation of Ovid's Myth of Narcissus and Echo." *Psychoanalytic Review* 79, no. 4 (1992): 555–75.

Haule, John R. *Divine Madness: Archetypes of Romantic Love*. Fisher King Press, 2010.

———. *The Love Cure: Therapy Erotic and Sexual*. Woodstock: Spring Publications, 1996.

Hayman, Ronald. *A Life of Jung*. New York: W. W. Norton, 1999.

Haynal, André. *Psychoanalysis and the Sciences: Epistemology—History*. Translated by Elizabeth Holder. Berkeley: University of California Press, 1993.

Heilbrun, Carolyn. "Non-Autobiographies of 'Privileged' Women: England and America." In *Life/Lines: Theorizing Women's Autobiography*, edited by Bella Brodzki and Celeste Schenck, 62–77. Ithaca: Cornell University Press, 1989.

Heller, Laurence, and Aline LaPierre. *Healing Developmental Trauma: How Early Trauma Affects Self-Regulation, Self-Image, and the Capacity for Relationship*. North Atlantic Books, 2012.

Herman, Judith. *Trauma and Recovery: The Aftermath of Violence—from Domestic Abuse to Political Terror*. New York: Basic Books, 1997.

Heuer, Gottfried. " 'Soul Murder' and 'The Birth of Intersubjectivity' in David Cronenberg's *A Dangerous Method*." *Journal of Analytical Psychology* 57, no. 5 (2012): 667–78.

Hillman, James. *Alchemical Psychology*. Uniform Edition Volume 5. Putnam, CT: Spring Publications, 2010.

———. *Anima: An Anatomy of a Personified Notion*. Putnam, CT: Spring Publications, 1985.

———. "From Mirror to Window: Curing Psychoanalysis of its Narcissism." *City & Soul*. Uniform Edition Volume 2. Putnam, CT: Spring Publications, 2013.

———. *Healing Fiction*. Woodstock: Spring Publications, 1994.

———. *Suicide and the Soul*. Revised edition, Austin: Spring Books, 1976.

———. *The Myth of Analysis: Three Essays in Archetypal Psychology*. New York: HarperPerennial, 1992.

Hirshfeld, Rachel. "New 'Babi Yar' Plaque Omits All Mention of Jewish Nazi Victims." *Israel National News Online*; www.israelnationalnews.com/News/News.aspx/158891.

Hoffer, Axel. "Jung's Analysis of Sabina Spielrein and His Use of Freud's Free Association Method." *Journal of Analytical Psychology* 46, no. 1 (2001): 117–28.

Hollander, John. *The Figure of Echo: A Mode of Allusion in Milton and After*. Berkeley: University of California Press, 1984.

Irigaray, Luce. *Marine Lover of Friedrich Nietzsche*. New York: Columbia University Press, 1993.

———. *Speculum of the Other Woman*. Ithaca: Cornell University Press, 1985.

———. *This Sex Which Is Not One*. Ithaca: Cornell University Press, 1985.

Jelinek, Estelle C. *The Tradition of Women's Autobiography; From Antiquity to the Present*. Twayne Publishers, 1988.

Johnston, Paul. *Echo: An Aspect of the Archetypal Dependent Personality*. Diss. Pacifica Graduate Institute, 1999.

Joyce, James. *Ulysses*. New York: Vintage, 1990.

Jong, Erica. "Autobiographical." In *Half-Lives*. New York: Holt, 1971.

Julian of Norwich. *Revelations of Divine Love*. Penguin, 1999.

Jung, C. G. "Answer to Job." In *The Collected Works of C. G. Jung*, translated by R. F. C. Hull, vol. 11. Princeton: Princeton University Press, 1973.

———. "Aspects of the Feminine." In *The Collected Works of C. G. Jung*, translated by R. F. C. Hull, vols. 6, 7, 9i, 9ii, 10, 17. Bollingen Series XX. Princeton: Princeton University Press, 1982.

———. "The Letters of C. G. Jung to Sabina Spielrein," translated by Barbara Wharton. *Journal of Analytical Psychology* 46, no. 1 (2001): 173–99.

———. "Psychological Types." In *The Collected Works of C. G. Jung*, translated by R. F. C. Hull, vol. 6. Bollingen Series XX. Princeton: Princeton University Press, 1976.

———. *Psychology and Alchemy*. In *The Collected Works of C. G. Jung*, translated by R. F. C. Hull, vol. 12. Princeton: Princeton University Press, 1980.

———. *Symbols of Transformation*. In *The Collected Works of C. G. Jung*, translated by R. F. C. Hull, vol. 5. Princeton: Princeton University Press, 1953.

———. "The Psychology of the Transference." In *The Collected Works of C. G. Jung*, translated by R. F. C. Hull, vol. 16. Princeton: Princeton University Press, 1966.

———, and Marie-Louise von Franz. *Man and His Symbols*. New York: Dell, 1968.

Kant, Immanuel. *The Critique of Judgment*. Translated by J. C. Meredith. Oxford University Press, 1973.

Kenny, Anthony. *A New History of Western Philosophy*. Oxford University Press, 2010.

Kent, Kathleen. *The Heretic's Daughter: A Novel*. Boston: Back Bay Books, 2009.

Kerr, John. *A Most Dangerous Method: The Story of Jung, Freud, and Sabina Spielrein*. New York: Vintage, 1994.

King, Helen. *The Disease of Virgins: Green Sickness, Chlorosis, and the Problems of Puberty*. Routledge, 2004.

Kirsch, Thomas. "Two Pieces on the Movie: *A Dangerous Method*." *Jung Society of Washington*, March 11, 2012.

Knapp, Carly. *Eros and Thanatos: A Figuration of Death as an Imaginal Presence in Dialogue with Depth Psychology*. Diss. Pacifica Graduate Institute, 2005.

Kochhar-Lindgren, Gray. *Narcissus Transformed: The Textual Subject in Psychoanalysis and Literature*. State College: The Pennsylvania State University Press, 1993.

Kollontai, Alexandra. "The New Woman." In *Selected Writings of Alexandra Kollontai*, translated by Alix Holt. Allison and Busby, 1977.

Lacan, Jacques. *The Seminar, Book XX, Encore: On Feminine Sexuality, the Limits of Love and Knowledge*. Edited by Jacques-Alain Miller. Translated by Bruce Fink. New York: W.W. Norton, 1999.

Laing, R. D. *The Politics of Experience*. New York: Pantheon, 1967.

Laplanche, J. M. *Life and Death in Psychoanalysis*. Baltimore: The Johns Hopkins University Press, 1976.

Launer, John. *Sex Versus Survival: The Story of Sabina Spielrein—Her Life, Her Ideas, Her Genius*. Lulu Self-Publishing, 2011.

Lauter, Estella, and Carol Schreier Rupprecht. *Feminist Archetypal Theory: Interdisciplinary Revisions of Jungian Thought*. Knoxville: University of Tennessee Press, 1985.

Lauretis, Teresa de. *Alice Doesn't: Feminism, Semiotics, Cinema*. Bloomington: Indiana University Press, 1984.

Leonard, Linda. *Meeting the Madwoman: Empowering the Feminine Spirit*. New York: Bantam, 1994.

Lévi-Strauss, Claude. *Myth and Meaning: Cracking the Code of Culture*. 2nd ed. New York: Schocken, 1995.

———. *Structural Anthropology*. New York: Basic Books, 1974.

Lewis, C. S. *Till We Have Faces: A Myth Retold*. New York: Harcourt, 1956.

Liddell, Henry George, and Robert Scott. "Thanatos." *Perseus Digital Library at Tufts University*; www.perseus.tufts.edu.

Lorde, Audre. "Uses of the Erotic." In *Sister Outsider: Essays and Speeches*. The Crossing Press, 2007.

Lothane, Henry Zvi. "In Defense of Sabina Spielrein." *International Forum of Psychoanalysis* 5, no. 3 (1996).

———. "Tender Love and Transference: Unpublished Letters of C. G. Jung and Sabina Spielrein (with an addendum/discussion)." In *Sabina Spielrein: Forgotten Pioneer of Psychoanalysis*, edited by Coline Covington and Barbara Wharton, 89–122. Routledge, 2003.

Major, René. "Love for Transference and Passion for Signifiers: Between Sabina S. and Anna G." *Psychoanalytic Inquiry* 4, no. 2 (1984): 171–91.

———. "The Voice behind the Mirror." *International Review of Psycho-Analysis* 7 (1980): 459–69.

Micale, Mark S. "On the 'Disappearance' of Hysteria: A Study in the Clinical Deconstruction of a Diagnosis." *Isis* 84, no. 3 (1993): 496–526.

Miller, Jean Baker. *Toward a New Psychology of Women*. 2nd ed. Boston: Beacon Press, 1986.

Miller, Martin. *Freud and the Bolsheviks: Psychoanalysis in Imperial Russia and the Soviet Union*. New Haven: Yale University Press, 1998.

Miller, Nancy. "Writing Fictions: Women's Autobiography in France." In *Life/Lines: Theorizing Women's Autobiography*, edited by Bella Brodzki and Celeste Schenck, 62–77. Ithaca: Cornell University Press, 1989.

Minder, Bernard. "A Document. Jung to Freud 1905: A Report on Sabina Spielrein." In *Sabina Spielrein: Forgotten Pioneer of Psychoanalysis*, edited by Coline Covington and Barbara Wharton, 135–40. Routledge, 2003.

———. "Sabina Spielrein. Jung's Patient at the Burghölzli." In *Sabina Spielrein: Forgotten Pioneer of Psychoanalysis*, edited by Coline Covington and Barbara Wharton, 109–34. Routledge, 2003.

Mogenson, Greg. *The Dove in the Consulting Room: Hysteria and the Anima in Bollas and Jung*. Brunner-Routledge, 2003.

Moll, Jeanne. "Prologue." In *Sabina Spielrein: Forgotten Pioneer of Psychoanalysis*, edited by Coline Covington and Barbara Wharton, 15–16. Routledge, 2003.

My Name Was Sabina Spielrein. Dir. Elisabeth Márton. Haslund Film (Denmark), 2002.

Nansen, Peter. *Love's Trilogy; Julie's Diary, Marie, God's Peace*. Translated by Julia Le Gallienne. John W. Luce, 2014.

Nin, Anaïs. *The Diary of Anaïs Nin Volume One: 1931–1934*. Edited by Gunther Stuhlmann. Harvest, 1966.

Ovcharenko, Victor. "Love, Psychoanalysis, and Destruction." *Journal of Analytical Psychology* 44, no. 3 (1999): 355–73.

Ovid. "Narcissus. Echo." *Metamorphoseon: Liber III*. Edited by Hugo Magnus, *The Perseus Project at Tufts University*; www.perseus.tufts.edu.

———. *Metamorphoses*. Translated by Stanley Lombardo and W. R. Johnson. Indianapolis: Hackett, 2010.

———. *Metamorphoses*. Translated by David Raeburn. Penguin, 2004.

———. *Ovid's Metamorphoses: The Arthur Golding Translation of 1567*. Edited by John Nims. Paul Dry Books, 2000.

———. *The Metamorphoses of Ovid*. Translated by Allen Mandelbaum. New York: Harcourt, 1995.

Palmer, Richard. *Hermeneutics*. Evanston: Northwestern University Press, 1969.

Paris, Ginette. *Heartbreak: Recovering From Lost Love and Mourning*. Mill City, 2011.

Parramore, Lynn Stuart. "Women, Sex, and Death—From Vampires to Psychoanalysis." *Alternet*, December 7, 2011.

Pechilis, Karen. "Devotional Subjectivity and the Fiction of Femaleness: Feminist Hermeneutics and the Articulation of Difference." *Journal of Feminist Studies in Religion* 30, no. 2 (2014): 99–114.

Pindar. *The Olympian and Pythian Odes*. Edited by Diane Arnson Svarlien. *Perseus Digital Library at Tufts University*; www.perseus.tufts.edu.

Plath, Sylvia. *Ariel*. New York: HarperPerennial, 1961.

———. *The Unabridged Journals of Sylvia Plath, 1950–1962*. New York: Anchor Books, 2000.

Prendimi L'Anima. Dir. Roberto Faenza. Perf. Iain Glen and Emilia Fox, 2002.

Pushkin, Aleksandr. *Wondrous Moment: Selected Poetry of Alexandr Pushkin*. Translated by Andrey Kneller. CreateSpace Publishing, 2008.

Rank, Otto. *The Myth of the Birth of the Hero*. CreateSpace Publishing, 2013.

Richebächer, Sabine. " 'In League with the Devil, and Yet You Fear Fire?' Sabina Spielrein and C. G. Jung: A Suppressed Scandal from the Early Days of Psychoanalysis." In *Sabina Spielrein: Forgotten Pioneer of Psychoanalysis*, edited by Coline Covington and Barbara Wharton, 223–46. Routledge, 2003.

Rose, Alison. *Jewish Women in Fin de Siècle Vienna*. Austin: University of Texas Press, 2008.

Rowland, Susan. *Jung: A Feminist Revision*. Polity, 2002.

Ruane, Christine. *The Empire's New Clothes: A History of the Russian Fashion Industry, 1700–1917*. New Haven: Yale University Press, 2009.

Rūmī, Jalāl al-Dīn. *Rumi: The Book of Love: Poems of Ecstasy and Longing*. New York: Harper, 2003.

———. "The Guest House." In *The Essential Rumi*, translated by Coleman Barks. Castle Books, 1997.

———. Line of poem quoted in Ruffell, Annabel. "Life Changing Events." *Journey for Earth*, April 2013; www.annabelruffell.wordpress.com/category/life-changing-events/.

Russ, Joanna. *How to Suppress Women's Writing*. Austin: University of Texas Press, 1983.

"Russian Jews Win Rostov Holocaust Commemoration Fight." *Jewish Telegraphic Agency*, December 17, 2013; http://www.jewishpress.com/news/breaking-news/russian-jews-win-rostov-holocaust-commemoration-fight/2013/12/18/.

Rutter, Peter. "Lot's Wife, Sabina Spielrein, and Anita Hill: A Jungian Meditation on Sexual Boundary Abuse and Recovery of Lost Voices." In *Breach of Trust: Sexual Exploitation by Health Care Professionals and Clergy*, edited by John Gonsiorek, 75–81. Sage, 1995.

Sauer, Gert. "Sabina Spielrein and the Use of Symbols: Reflections of a Jungian Psychoanalyst." *Barcelona '04: Edges of Experience: Memory and Emergence, Proceedings of the 16th International IAAP Congress for Analytical Psychology*, edited by Lyn Cowan. Daimon Verlag, 2006.

Sawyer, W. C. *Teutonic Legends in the Nibelungen Lied and The Nibelungen Ring*. University Press of the Pacific, 2003.

Sayers, Janet. *Sexual Contradictions*. Tavistock, 1986.

———. "Transforming At-one-Ment: Spielrein, Jung, Bion." *Psychoanalysis and History* 6, no. 1 (2004): 37–56.

Schapiro, Rich. "Woody Allen's Daughter Dylan Farrow Details How He Sexually Abused Her in Open Letter." *New York Daily News Online*, February 1, 2014.

Schenck, Celeste. "All of a Piece: Women's Poetry and Autobiography." In *Life/Lines: Theorizing Women's Autobiography*, edited by Bella Brodzki and Celeste Schenck, 281–306. Ithaca: Cornell University Press, 1989.

Schoener, Gary. "Historical Overview." In *Breach of Trust: Sexual Exploitation by Health Care Professionals and Clergy*, edited by John Gonsiorek, 3–18. Sage, 1995.

"Sexual Exploitation by Helping Professionals." *RAINN*. January 14, 2014; www.rainn.org.

Shamdasani, Sonu. "Memories, Dreams, Omissions." *Spring* 57 (1995): 115–37.

Shelley, Percy Bysshe. "Ode to the West Wind." In *The Complete Poetical Works of Percy Bysshe Shelley*, 24–25. Thomas Y. Crowell Company, 1839.

Shepherd, Reginald. "Mythology in Poetry." *Reginald Shepherd's Blog*, April 17, 2007; www.reginaldshepherd.blogspot.com/2007/08/mythology-in-poetry.html.

Showalter, Elaine. "Hysteria, Feminism, and Gender." In *Hysteria beyond Freud*, edited by Sander Gilman and Elaine Showalter et al., 286–344. Berkeley: University of California Press, 1993.

Shullenberger, William. "Tragedy in Translation: The Lady Echo's Song." *English Literary Renaissance* 33, no. 3 (2003).

Skea, Brian. "Sabina Spielrein: Out from the Shadow of Jung and Freud." *Journal of Analytical Psychology* 51, no. 4 (2006): 527–52.

Slattery, Dennis Patrick. *Creases in Culture: Essays toward a Poetics of Depth*. Fisher King Press, 2014.

———. "Mytho-Poiesis: The Shared Ground of Psyche's Dreaming and Poetic Impulse." *Quadrant: Journal of the C. G. Jung Foundation for Analytical Psychology* 41, no. 1 (2011): 70–85.

———. "Narcissus, Echo and Irony's Resonance." In *Harvesting Darkness: Essays on Literature, Myth, Film, and Culture*. iUniverse, 2006.

Smith, Sidonie. *A Poetics of Women's Autobiography: Marginality and the Fiction of Self-Representation*. Bloomington: Indiana University Press, 1987.

Smith, Sidonie, and Julia Watson, eds. *Women, Autobiography, Theory: A Reader*. Madison: University of Wisconsin Press, 1998.

Smith, Stevie. "Not Waving but Drowning." In *The Norton Anthology of English Literature*, edited by Stephen Greenblatt. New York: Norton, 2006.

Snediker, Michael. "In the Echo Chamber." *English Language Notes* 50, no. 1 (2012): 33–38.

Snyder, Timothy. *Bloodlands: Europe between Hitler and Stalin*. New York: Basic Books, 2012.

Spacks, Patricia Meyer. "Female Rhetorics." In *Women, Autobiography, Theory: A Reader*, edited by Sidonie Smith and Julia Watson, 176. Madison: University of Wisconsin Press, 1998.

Spielrein, Sabina. "Contributions to the Knowledge of a Child's Soul." Translated by Annika Romero and Angela Sells, 2013. Original: "Beiträge zur Kenntnis der kindlichen Seele." *Zentralblatt für Psychoanalyse* 3 (1912): 57–72; www.archive.org. Also refer to *Sämtliche Schriften II*. Freiburg, Germany: Kore, Verlag Traute Hensch, 1987/2002.

———. "Destruction as the Cause of Coming into Being." *Journal of Analytical Psychology* 39 (1994): 155–86.

———. "Die Destruktion als Ursache des Werdens." Edited by Eugen Bleuler and Sigmund Freud. *Jahrbuch Für Psychoanalytische* 4, no. 1) (1912): 465–503; www.archive.org.

———. "Die Entstehung der kindlichen Worte Papa und Mama." ("The Origin of the Child's Words Papa and Mama.") *Imago* 8 (1922): 345–67; www.archive.org.

———. "Mother-in-Law." Translated by Annika Romero and Angela Sells from "Die Schwiegermutter"; www.archive.org.

———. *On the Psychological Content of a Case of Schizophrenia (Dementia praecox)*. Translated by Annika Romero and Angela Sells, 2013. Original: "Über den psychologischen Inhalt eines Falles von Schizophrenie." Edited by Eugen Bleuler and Sigmund Freud. *Jarbuch Für Psychoanalytische und Psychopathologische Forschungen* 3, no. 1 (1911): 329–400; www.archive.org. Also refer to *Sämtliche Schriften II*. Kore: Verlag Traute Hensch, 1987/2002.

———. "The Origin of the Child's Words Papa and Mama. Some Observations on the Different Stages in Language Development." In *Sabina Spielrein: Forgotten Pioneer of Psychoanalysis*, edited by Coline Covington and Barbara Wharton, Routledge, 283–306. 2003.

———. *Tagebuch und Briefe*. Edited by Traute Hensch. Kore: Psychosozial-Verlag, 1986/2003.

———. "Unedited Extracts from a Diary (1906/7?)." Translated by Jeanne Moll (French) and Barbara Wharton (English). *Journal of Analytical Psychology* 46, no. 1 (2001): 155–71. Also refer to *Sabina Spielrein: Forgotten Pioneer of Psychoanalysis*, edited by Coline Covington and Barbara Wharton, 15–33. Routledge, 2003.

Stekel, Wilhelm. *Sadism, Masochism: The Psychopathology of Sexual Cruelty*. Translated by Domino Falls. Solar Books, 2010.

Storr, Anthony, ed. *The Essential Jung: Selected Writings*. Princeton: Princeton University Press, 1983.

Stroup, George. "Between Echo and Narcissus: the Role of the Bible in Feminist Theology." *Interpretation* 42, no. 1 (1988): 19–32.

Tagebuch Einer Heimlichen Symmetrie: Sabina Spielrein Swischen Jung und Freud. Kore: Verlag Traute Hensch, 1986.

Tarkovsky, Andrei. "A propos du Sacrifice." *Positif*, May 1986, 3–5. English translation taken from the booklet *The Sacrifice, An Artificial Eye Release* (1987) as reproduced on *Nostalghia*; www.nostalghia.com.

Teresa of Ávila. *Interior Castle*. Translated by E. Allison Peers. New York: Dover Publications, 2007.

The Love Letters of a Portuguese Nun [1669]. Translated by Guido Waldman. Harvill Press, 1996.

Ussher, Jane. "Health Check: Clash of the Orgasms, Clitoral vs. Vaginal." *The Conversation*, 9 November; www. theconversation.com/health-check-clash-of-the-orgasms-clitoral-vs-vaginal-32732.

Von Franz, Marie-Louise. *Alchemy: An Introduction to the Symbolism and the Psychology*. Inner City Books, 1980.

———. *Projection and Re-collection in Jungian Psychology*. Open Court Publishing, 1985.

Wagner, Richard. "Siegfried." *Richard Wagner Libretti*, Richard Wagner Libretti Online; www.rwagner.net.

Warner, Marina. *From the Beast to the Blonde: On Fairy Tales and Their Tellers*. New York: Farrar, Straus, and Giroux, 1996.

Wehr, Demaris. *Jung and Feminism: Liberating Archetypes*. Boston: Beacon Press, 1987.

Weil, Simone. *Simone Weil: An Anthology*. Edited by Siân Miles. New York: Grove Press, 1986.

Welman, Mark. "Thanatos and Existence: Towards a Jungian Phenomenology of the Death Instinct." In *Pathways into the Jungian World: Phenomenology and Analytical Psychology*, edited by Roger Brooke, 123–41. Routledge, 2000.

Wharton, Barbara. "Part I: Comment on Spielrein's Paper 'The Origin of the Child's Words Papa and Mama.'" In *Sabina Spielrein: Forgotten Pioneer of Psychoanalysis*, edited by Coline Covington and Barbara Wharton, 281–83. Routledge, 2003.

Wiesel, Elie. *Night*. 2nd ed. Translated by Marion Wiesel. New York: Hill and Wang, 2006.

Winworth, Freda. *The Epic of Sounds* [1897]. University of California Libraries Reprint, 2014.

Woodman, Marion. *The Pregnant Virgin: A Process of Psychological Transformation*. Inner City Books, 1985.

———. *The Ravaged Bridegroom: Masculinity in Women*. Inner City Books, 1990.

Wordsworth, William. "Ode on Intimations of Immortality." In *Recollections from Early Childhood*. HardPress, 2012.

Zecharia, Sarette Anne Horwitz. *Mysterium Coniunctionis: The Meeting Ground of the Masculine and the Feminine*. Diss. Pacifica Graduate Institute, 2000.

Copyright Acknowledgments

Anna Akhmatova, "But not for anything would we exchange this splendid," and an excerpt from "All this you alone can guess . . ." from *Complete Poems of Anna Akhmatova*, translated by Judith Hemschemeyer, edited and introduced by Roberta Reeder. Copyright © 1989, 1992, 1997 by Judith Hemschemeyer. Reprinted with the permission of The Permissions Company, Inc., on behalf of Zephyr Press; www.zephyrpress.org.

"Burghölzli Hospital Records of Sabina Spielrein." Trans. Dorothee Steffens and Barbara Wharton. *Journal of Analytical Psychology*. Reprinted with permission by John Wiley and Sons. Copyright © 2002. All rights reserved. Permission conveyed through Copyright Clearance Center, Inc.

"Destruction as the Cause of Coming into Being." Translated by Barbara Wharton. *Journal of Analytical Psychology*. Reprinted with permission by John Wiley and Sons. Copyright © 2006. All rights reserved. Permission conveyed through Copyright Clearance Center, Inc.

"i am accused of tending to the past," from *The Collected Poems of Lucille Clifton*. Copyright © 1987 by Lucille Clifton. Reprinted with permission of The Permissions Company, Inc., on behalf of BOA Editions Ltd.; www.boaeditions.org.

"Jung and Easily Freudened': Sabina Spielrein's Analysis." Pamela White Hadas. Copyright © 1998 by Northwestern University Press. Published 1998. All rights reserved.

"Lot's Wife, Sabina Spielrein, and Anita Hill: A Jungian Meditation on Sexual Boundary Abuse and Recovery of Lost Voices." Peter Rutter. *Breach of Trust: Sexual Exploitation by Health Care Professionals and Clergy*, edited by John Ray

Gonsiorek. Sage Publications. Copyright © 1995. All rights reserved. Permission conveyed through Copyright Clearance Center, Inc.

"Love, Psychoanalysis, and Destruction." Victor Ovcharenko. *Journal of Analytical Psychology*. Reprinted with permission by John Wiley and Sons. Copyright © 1999. All rights reserved. Permission conveyed through Copyright Clearance Center, Inc.

"Sabina Spielrein: Out from the Shadow of Jung and Freud." Brian Skea. *Journal of Analytical Psychology*. Reprinted with permission by John Wiley and Sons. Copyright © 2006. All rights reserved. Permission conveyed through Copyright Clearance Center, Inc.

Sabina Spielrein: Echoes and Reflections on Female Suppression. Diss. Pacifica Graduate Institute. Ann Arbor, MI: ProQuest, 4 June 2015. Copyright © Angela Sells.

Spielrein's words: English translations of Aldo Carotenuto remain with Random House. Copyright © 1982, excerpts not to exceed "fair use"; Christian T. Flierl, Editor/Foreign Rights for Kore, Verlag Germany. Copyright © 2002; German originals in public domain.

The Freud/Jung Letters reprinted by permission of Princeton University Press. Copyright © 1974. All rights reserved. Permission conveyed through Copyright Clearance Center, Inc.

Excerpts from "The Letters of C.G. Jung to Sabina Spielrein," *The Journal of Analytical Psychology*. Copyright © 2002. Permission granted by John Wiley and Sons.

"The Letters of CG Jung to Sabina Spielrein." English translation, *Journal of Analytical Psychology*. Reprinted with permission by John Wiley and Sons. Copyright © 2002. All rights reserved. Permission conveyed through Copyright Clearance Center, Inc.

Excerpts from *The Metamorphoses of Ovid: A New Verse Translation*, translated by Allen Mandelbaum. English translation copyright © 1993 by Allen Mandelbaum. Reprinted by permission of Houghton Mifflin Harcourt Publishing Company. All rights reserved.

Excerpt(s) from A SECRET SYMMETRY by Aldo Carotenuto, translated by Random House, Inc., translation and foreword copyright © 1982 by Random

Index